INTRODUCING INTERCULTURAL COMMUNICATION

Sara Miller McCune founded SAGE Publishing in 1965 to support the dissemination of usable knowledge and educate a global community. SAGE publishes more than 1000 journals and over 800 new books each year, spanning a wide range of subject areas. Our growing selection of library products includes archives, data, case studies and video. SAGE remains majority owned by our founder and after her lifetime will become owned by a charitable trust that secures the company's continued independence.

Los Angeles | London | New Delhi | Singapore | Washington DC | Melbourne

THIRD
EDITION

SHUANG LIU, ZALA VOLČIČ & CINDY GALLOIS

INTRODUCING INTERCULTURAL COMMUNICATION

• GLOBAL CULTURES AND CONTEXTS •

Los Angeles | London | New Delhi
Singapore | Washington DC | Melbourne

Los Angeles | London | New Delhi
Singapore | Washington DC | Melbourne

SAGE Publications Ltd
1 Oliver's Yard
55 City Road
London EC1Y 1SP

SAGE Publications Inc.
2455 Teller Road
Thousand Oaks, California 91320

SAGE Publications India Pvt Ltd
B 1/I 1 Mohan Cooperative Industrial Area
Mathura Road
New Delhi 110 044

SAGE Publications Asia-Pacific Pte Ltd
3 Church Street
#10-04 Samsung Hub
Singapore 049483

Editor: Michael Ainsley
Assistant editor: John Nightingale
Senior assistant editor, digital: Chloe Statham
Production editor: Imogen Roome
Copyeditor: Sarah Bury
Proofreader: Leigh C. Smithson
Indexer: Adam Pozner
Marketing manager: Lucia Sweet
Cover design: Lisa Harper-Wells
Typeset by: C&M Digitals (P) Ltd, Chennai, India
Printed in the UK

Library of Congress Control Number: 2018943073

British Library Cataloguing in Publication data

A catalogue record for this book is available from the British Library

ISBN 978-1-5264-3169-1
ISBN 978-1-5264-3170-7 (pbk)

At SAGE we take sustainability seriously. Most of our products are printed in the UK using responsibly sourced papers and boards. When we print overseas we ensure sustainable papers are used as measured by the PREPS grading system. We undertake an annual audit to monitor our sustainability.

CONTENTS

PREFACE

This third edition of *Introducing Intercultural Communication: Global Cultures and Contexts* consolidates its reputation as an introduction to intercultural communication from the global perspective. This global perspective made the previous editions stand out among other competitors in the market. The realization that the second edition was so well received by scholars, colleagues, instructors, and, more importantly, students across the world in the past three years has left us with a sense of achievement. We interpret this success to mean that a book with a global perspective has resonated with an international audience. We sincerely appreciate the positive feedback we have received from instructors across the world, who describe the second edition as a book that not only helps students to apply theory to the real world, but also fosters critical thinking. The clarity and scope of the second edition were highly praised, as was the diversity of content. Instructors who adopted the second edition recognized the learning features as both pedagogically helpful and visually appealing, making complex materials more accessible yet retaining the book's academic rigour to take students further in the intercultural communication field. In this third edition of the book, we embrace the opportunity to refine and improve on the content and features that have proven successful in the second edition, while also updating and expanding the book to keep abreast of current theories and research in the field.

This new edition continues our commitment to presenting intercultural communication theories and applications through a global prism and in a lively, interesting, relevant and accessible writing style. At the same time, it maintains the high standard of intellectual depth and rigour in scholarly discussions about theories and applications. New content has been added to the book in relation to theories, concepts, applications and case studies, which take students into some new territory, empower them in active learning and encourage critical thinking. We have updated the content of each chapter to reflect the state-of-the-art knowledge and current research in the field. We have replaced 11 out of 13 case studies from the second edition, and updated the remaining two case studies with new material. Further, more examples from a diverse set of cultures have been added to broaden the coverage of cultures even more. These include Scandinavia, Kosovo, North Africa, the Netherlands, Sweden, Russia, Saudi Arabia, Finland and the United States. Theoretical debates throughout the book give students opportunities to exercise their potential, and possibly to target postgraduate students. This new edition has a stronger emphasis on the application of knowledge and skills. Hands-on exercises, entitled 'Do it!', have been added to each chapter to encourage students to apply what they have learned to real-life situations. In response to the reviews, we have also streamlined the presentation of various topics and expanded the coverage of theories. At every point in the new edition we have tried to put ourselves in the student's place, drawing upon the learning experiences of hundreds of culturally diverse students whom we have been privileged to teach.

NEW TO THE THIRD EDITION

- *Updated content.* Various new sections and content have been added throughout the book to fill in the gaps identified in the reviews and to reflect current developments in the field. New and updated content includes refugees in Europe, discursive construction of culture and identity, the transactional model of communication, digital communication and digital media, fake news, nation branding, culture jamming, and technology diffusion theories. These are just some examples.
- *Combined Theory Corner and Theory in Practice.* The Theory Corner section in the third edition combines Theory Corner with Theory in Practice from the second edition to achieve a clearer layout by reducing the number of boxed texts. The questions at the end of the Theory in Practice from the second edition have been moved to the Online resources for instructors.
- *Application exercises within text – named 'Do it!'.* Three hands-on exercises have been added to each chapter as 'experiential tasks'. This new feature puts more emphasis on the application of knowledge and encourages students to experiment with what they have learned in class in real-life situations.
- *New case studies.* All reviewers and our own students embraced and endorsed the case studies. To build on the success of this feature, we have replaced 11 case studies from the second edition with completely new cases, and we have updated the other two case studies with new materials. These case studies cover a range of topics and cultures, ranging from refugees in Europe, food culture in China, culture jamming, to freedom of expression and hate speech, Barbie dolls, Turkish soap operas, fake news and the Building Brand Australia programme *Australia Unlimited*.
- *Links to SAGE video sources.* A URL link to a video relevant to the content of each chapter is provided at the end of each chapter. The video, drawn from the SAGE video library, usually features experts in the specific field talking about the subject area (e.g., nonverbal communication). It complements and consolidates the chapter content.

RETAINED FROM THE SECOND EDITION

- *Join the Debate.* The Join the Debate feature in the second edition was endorsed by instructors and students alike. These sections pose challenging questions and highlight current debates in the intercultural communication field. This feature enables students to explore the field further and encourages them to engage in scholarly discussion about issues surrounding intercultural communication research and practice.
- *Annotated further readings.* Annotated further readings at the end of each chapter consolidate and complement students' learning. In this new edition, the five further readings in each chapter are updated. In addition, a list of further readings is provided in the Online resources for instructors.
- *Chapter summaries.* The summary of each chapter highlights the key points covered. In response to the reviews, the chapter summaries in this new edition are updated in accordance with the updated content of each chapter, but retain the format of bullet points, as in the second edition, to make them more concise and easier to follow.
- *Pictures.* The illustrative pictures were praised by reviewers and students as original and interesting. We retained this feature, but we have replaced many of the pictures in the third edition in order to align with the revised text and enhance their illustrative power.
- *Glossary.* The glossary, containing definitions of all the key terms used in the text, is retained to give users a quick index of the key concepts covered and their definitions. We have retained this feature but updated the glossary to incorporate new content from this third edition.
- *Online resources for instructors and students.* In this edition, we have updated all the exercises and activities, as well as the multiple-choice questions, to align with the new content. The original sections have been retained with updated content: lecture notes, power points, further readings, exercises and activities, and multiple-choice questions. Additional multiple-choice questions have been added for student access as well.

REMOVED FROM THIS EDITION

- *Theory in Practice.* This feature is combined with Theory Corner in the third edition. In other words, the Theory Corner in this edition contains both theory and theory in practice. The further readings and questions in the Theory in Practice boxes in the second edition have been moved to the Online resources.
- *Critical thinking questions within the text.* Critical thinking questions in the second edition have been replaced by hands-on experiential tasks in this third edition, to enable students to apply their knowledge in practice. This new feature is named 'Do it!'.

ACKNOWLEDGEMENTS

We would like to thank all those who have helped us as we progressed through the journey to complete this third edition. We thank the reviewers for their insightful comments on the second edition, and we appreciate their valuable suggestions for improvement. A special note of thanks goes to the many instructors who have adopted the second edition over the past two years, as well as scholars who have provided their feedback through various channels, including the website of SAGE Publications. Their positive comments on the second edition are especially gratifying, and their suggestions for improvement have helped us to rethink and reshape this new edition. We have all had the privilege of teaching and doing research in intercultural communication, and these experiences have framed our outlook on this fascinating field.

We are indebted to our colleagues, friends and students, both at The University of Queensland and at other institutions around the world where we have studied, worked or spent periods of research leave. All of them have contributed to this book in various ways, including providing feedback on our intercultural communication classes, sharing their ideas with us, and lending us references and photos from their collections. In particular, we are grateful to Professor Carley Dodd from Abilene Christian University, who granted us permission to include his model of culture, and to Alison Rae for granting us permission to use the photos she took while travelling around the world collecting stories as a reporter. We express our sincere gratitude to colleagues who have shared their exercises with us to help the development of the online resources for instructors and students. Special thanks go to everyone who has given us support, time and encouragement.

We express sincere appreciation to the Commissioning Editor at SAGE Publications, Michael Ainsley. Without his encouragement and support, this third edition would not have come to fruition. We are grateful to Mila Steele at SAGE Publications, who was the senior Commissioning Editor for the first and second editions of this book. If it had not been for the confidence and support she gave us, the previous two editions of this book would not have come into being, either. Special thanks also go to the assistant editor, John Nightingale, others on the editorial staff, and the anonymous reviewers who reviewed sample chapters of the manuscript. Their insightful suggestions have greatly contributed to an improved book.

We would like to thank everyone from SAGE Publications whose work has transformed the manuscript into its present form.

Finally, we are deeply indebted to our families for their support, love, encouragement and patience throughout the writing of this book.

ONLINE RESOURCES

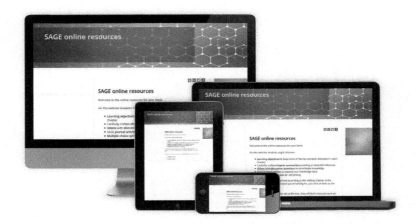

Introducing Intercultural Communication is supported by a wealth of online resources for both students and instructors to support learning, studying and teaching. They are available at http://study.sagepub.com/liu3e

For students

- **Further reading** suggestions to guide you deeper into the literature. These include books, journal articles and web sources. For those articles published in SAGE Journals there are links providing free access.
- **Multiple choice questions** to help you test your knowledge on key topics.
- **Videos** tied to each chapter in which experts in the field discuss key ideas, trends, themes and debates covered in the text.

For instructors

- **Discussion questions** and **activities** to help structure seminars and group work.
- **Instructor notes** to aid the integration of each chapter's learning objectives with classroom sessions.
- **PowerPoint slides** to help structure lectures in line with the book.
- **Multiple choice questions and answers** to help inspire ideas for assessments.

INTRODUCTION: COMMUNICATING IN A CULTURALLY DIVERSE SOCIETY

Since ancient times, borders (visible and invisible) have always existed between countries, states, cities, regions, villages, and even houses. Geographic and artificial boundaries – rivers, oceans, mountains, walls, fences and signs – all separate country from country, region from region, and people from people. However, culture has never been confined to these geographic or artificial borders. For example, as early as the fifteenth century, *Aesop's Fables* was translated from Greek, the language in which the fables were originally written, into English, thus making them accessible to entirely new cultural, national and geographical audiences. Today, the fables, available in many languages across the world, have permeated many cultures as myths and legends, providing entertainment and moral truisms for children and adults alike. Regardless of where we live, the colour of our skin or what language we speak, it is likely we have at some time encountered many of the morals or adages of *Aesop's Fables* – for instance, 'Slow and steady wins the race' from the tale of the tortoise and the hare. While we might not know whether those stories were in fact written by Aesop, exactly when they were written or how many languages they have been translated into, the tales still teach us universal virtues like honesty, perseverance, modesty and mutual respect. Other cultural and material products are also spread beyond borders, including tools, technology, clothing, food, furniture, electric appliances, music, customs and rituals. Thanks to ever-advancing digital communication technology and devices, we find our lives intertwined with people we have never met, places we have never visited, and events we have never participated in. Indeed, we have become neighbours of the interconnected global community.

This does not mean that the whole world has been subsumed into one culture. Contact between cultures may accentuate differences as well as similarities, because culture is both inclusive and exclusive: it unites members within the cultural group, as well as marks the boundary for non-members. *Culture* defines a group of people, binds them to one another and gives them a sense of shared identity. The word 'culture' is derived from the Latin root 'colere', meaning 'to cultivate'. Our language, customs, expectations, behaviours, habits – our thinking, doing and being – have and continue to be formed over a long period of cultivation within the specific physical environments and social contexts in which we were born, with which we grew up, and in which we presently live. During the process of learning and adapting to the environment, different groups of people have learned distinctive ways to organize their world (Dodd, 1998). A group's unique ways of doing and thinking become their beliefs, values, worldviews, norms, rituals, customs, and their communication patterns – ultimately, their cultural traditions.

Culture is the means by which a society expresses its structure and function, its views of the universe, and what it regards as the proper ways to live and to treat other people. Cultural traditions go through a process of development and are passed on from generation to generation. Central to this entire process of cultural change and maintenance is human *communication*. The word 'communication' is derived from the Latin root 'communicare', which means 'to make common', as in sharing thoughts, hopes and knowledge. In ancient times, our ancestors shared information largely on a face-to-face basis. The successive historical breakthroughs of print, telephone, broadcasting, television and the internet have progressively expanded the domain of communication beyond the immediate cultural and geographic borders. The frequency and necessity of global interaction in business, politics, education, medical practice and travel, to mention just a few, requires us to communicate competently with people whose cultures are different from our own. However, the ability to communicate effectively and efficiently in our increasingly diverse society does not come naturally; it must be learned.

ORIGIN OF THE STUDY OF INTERCULTURAL COMMUNICATION

The origin of the study of intercultural communication can be traced to the Chicago School, known for pioneering empirical investigations based on the theories of German sociologist Georg Simmel (1858–1918; Rogers and Steinfatt, 1999). Simmel studied at the University of Berlin, and taught there and at the University of Strassburg in the late nineteenth and early twentieth centuries. Simmel analysed concepts related to his own life. He was the son of Jewish parents, and the anti-Semitism he experienced in Germany undoubtedly influenced his development of the concept of 'der Fremde', or stranger, the intellectual descendants of which are key concepts in the fields of both sociology and intercultural communication today. The stranger (Simmel, 1950) is a member of a system, but not strongly attached to it or accepted by the other members of the system. Simmel's insights into the role of the stranger are part of his general concern with the relationships between individuals. His examination of reciprocal interactions at the individual level within a larger social context inspired much of the research at the Chicago School (Rogers, 1999), and from there, subsequent research in the field of intercultural communication. The notion of communicating with someone who is different from us – an intercultural 'stranger' – lies at the heart of *intercultural communication*.

The key scholar in translating and applying Simmel's concept of the stranger was Robert E. Park, a former newspaper reporter who also earned his PhD degree in Germany. In 1900 Park took Simmel's course in sociology at the University of Berlin, and in 1915 began teaching sociology at the University of Chicago. Inspired by Simmel's notion of the stranger, Park developed the concept of social distance, which he defined as the degree to which an individual perceives a lack of intimacy with individuals different in ethnicity, race, religion, occupation or other variables (Park, 1924). Park's student Emory S. Bogardus later developed a scale that measured the social distance people perceive between themselves and members of another group. For example, in the scale respondents are asked such questions as 'Would you marry someone who is Chinese?' and 'Would you have Chinese people as regular friends or as speaking acquaintances?' (Bogardus, 1933). The Bogardus Social Distance scale quantified the perceived intimacy or distance of an individual's relationships with others in various social groups.

As social distance is largely culturally prescribed, intercultural communication is invariably affected. For instance, Australians often use first names with someone they have just met, and in a university setting it is common for students to address the lecturers by their first name. This can be very puzzling to Korean students, who are more formal in their social relationships, using first names only with very close friends, who are usually of the same age or social status as themselves. For example, an American Korean who has taught in the United States for over 30 years still feels some discomfort when students address her by her first name. When asked why she did not explain her preference to her students, she answered that she would only do it indirectly, a preferred Asian communication style. If a student addressed her by first name, instead of calling her 'Professor', she would respond in an unenthusiastic, subdued manner, in the hope that her student would gradually learn the 'appropriate' way to address her as a professor.

Simmel's concept of the stranger and subsequent derivative concepts all deal with individual relationships, both with others and with the larger society. The concept of the stranger implies that some individuals do not have a high degree of cohesion with the larger system of which they are part. Park also conceptualized the 'marginal man', an individual who lives in two different worlds and is a stranger in both. Park studied the children of European immigrant parents in the United States, who typically rejected the European culture and language of their parents, but did not consider themselves to be true North Americans either. Their freedom from the norms of both systems led to a relatively high crime rate. To Park, the marginal person is a cultural hybrid, an individual on the margin of two cultures that never completely fuse. Park's concept was later extended to 'the sojourner', an individual who visits another culture for a period of time, but who retains his or her original culture.

The experience of sojourning or visiting often gives individuals a unique perspective for viewing both the host and home cultures. The sojourner later became a favourite topic of study for intercultural communication scholars, leading to concepts such as the U-curve of adjustment model, culture shock and reverse culture shock.

Although the concepts of stranger, social distance and marginality are among those at the heart of intercultural communication, this field did not really emerge until after the Second World War. At that time, the United States had emerged as a leading world power. With the advent of the United Nations, a number of new programmes, such as the World Health Organization, the United Nations' assistance programmes and the World Bank, were initiated to provide assistance to developing nations. However well intended, not all development programmes were successful, largely because they failed to comprehend the multifaceted and interrelated nature of culture. In Thailand, for example, where obtaining clean water was identified as the highest-priority problem, most of the hand-pump wells drilled in hundreds of villages by American development workers were broken within six months (Niehoff, 1964). An investigation into the problem showed that no local person was responsible for the maintenance of the pumps. When a well was dug on Buddhist temple grounds, the monks would look after the pump; other wells were neglected. The well-drilling project had not considered the important role that Buddhist monasteries played in Thai culture, and the vital contribution they could make to the success of the project. It was clear that cultural issues had to be taken into account, along with the economic, political and technical dimensions.

American diplomats also experienced cultural frustrations. They were often poorly trained and lacking in cultural awareness and intercultural communication insight. They usually lived and worked in a small circle of English-speaking individuals, seldom venturing outside the capital city of their posting. In 1946, the US Congress passed an Act to provide training to American diplomats and technical assistance workers in the Foreign Service Institute (FSI). Edward T. Hall, a leading anthropologist and teacher at the FSI, and his anthropological and linguistics colleagues initially taught the participants the language and anthropological concepts of the nation to which they were assigned. The language programme was successful, but participants reported to Hall that they needed to communicate across cultures and thus wanted to understand intercultural differences, rather than simply gaining an understanding of the single culture in which they were to work. In response to these requests, Hall and his colleagues created a new approach that he called 'intercultural communication'. The publication of his famous book, *The Silent Language* (1959), signals the birth of intercultural communication study.

As teaching and research in intercultural communication as an independent disciplinary area developed, the meaning of 'culture' in intercultural communication broadened from national culture to subcultures: cultures defined by ethnicity, socioeconomic status, age, gender, sexual orientations or even lifestyle. A key figure in broadening this field was William B. Gudykunst, a professor of communication at California State University. In a textbook co-authored with Young Yun Kim from the University of Oklahoma, *Communicating with Strangers: An Approach to Intercultural Communication* (Gudykunst and Kim, 1984), Gudykunst broadened the meaning of intercultural communication, arguing that cultural differences could involve national or organizational culture or the culture of the deaf. This broader definition of the field is reflected in most intercultural communication textbooks today.

ORGANIZATION OF THIS NEW EDITION

This third edition of *Introducing Intercultural Communication* consists of 13 chapters, which continue to reflect our commitment to present intercultural communication knowledge and skills, and the application of knowledge and skills through global perspectives. We aim to enable you to:

- be equipped with knowledge and skills about communication between people from diverse backgrounds;
- critically reflect upon the influence of your own culture on how you view yourself and culturally different others;
- compare the communication behaviour, verbal and nonverbal, of different cultural groups, and interpret their behaviour through culture;
- apply knowledge and skills to resolve practical problems and cultural conflicts in various contexts;
- demonstrate respect, autonomy, expert judgement, adaptability and responsibility as an effective and ethical communicator across diverse contexts.

Chapters 1 to 6 introduce theories and skills that address critical questions at the intersection of communication and culture. As the world becomes more globalized because communication technology keeps us connected, it is more important than ever before for us to explore what it means to be a citizen of the global community. Chapter 1 identifies the challenges that we face in a diverse society. Chapter 2 identifies the components and characteristics of culture, and explores the discursive construction of culture and identity. An in-depth analysis of the relationship between culture and communication is presented in Chapter 3, along with a critical examination of models of communication. Chapter 4 discusses culture's influence on people's perceptions of themselves and others, and how perception influences communication. Chapter 5 analyses cultural value orientations and the fundamental universal problems they address. Chapter 6 explores identities and subgroups, including how group membership influences communication and how identities can be shaped through communication.

Chapters 7 to 13 focus on the application of knowledge and skills in intercultural communication. While Chapter 7 focuses on the application of verbal communication skills, Chapter 8 concentrates on nonverbal communication skills. Both chapters discuss how culture permeates performing and interpreting communication. Chapter 9 addresses issues surrounding immigration. Special attention is paid to migration as part of a transnational revolution that is reshaping the world. The question of to what extent ethnic minorities should maintain their cultural practices without creating a threat to the national culture is also explored. Chapter 10 discusses the development of relationships with cultural others, and Chapter 11 focuses on resolving conflicts between groups, regions and nations. Special attention is paid to the historical reasons for conflicts, such as historical antagonism between ethnic groups (e.g., Arabs and Jews, Serbs and Albanian Kosovars). We present the approaches of different cultures to address the legacies of widespread or systematic human rights abuses, as cultural groups move from a period of violent conflict or oppression towards peace, democracy, the rule of law and respect for individual and collective rights. In Chapter 12 we discuss the role of the media in cultural change and explore how media construct and shape social reality around us. Finally, Chapter 13 brings readers back to the issues raised in Chapter 1 regarding the challenges of living in a culturally diverse society. It explores the dialectics of the homogenization and fragmentation of cultures, presents arguments about understanding the global through the local context, and discusses how local cultures challenge, negotiate and adjust to globalization.

This textbook does not simply raise questions and provide answers. We aim to equip you with the capacity to explore the field of intercultural communication, apply knowledge and skills to resolve practical problems, to engage in scholarly debates in the field, and to empower you to ask further critical questions. Your journey to become a competent intercultural communicator starts here!

Whether the borders that divide us are picket fences or national boundaries, we are all neighbors in a global community.

Jimmy Carter, 39th US President, 1924–

1

CHALLENGES OF LIVING IN A GLOBAL COMMUNITY

LEARNING OBJECTIVES

At the end of this chapter, you should be able to:

- Identify different contributors to cultural diversity in our global community.

- Recognize issues surrounding cultural diversity and multiculturalism.

- Appreciate intercultural communication as an integral part of life in a global community.

INTRODUCTION

Our early ancestors lived in small villages; most of them rarely ventured far from their own communities. They lived and died close to where they were born, and much of their information sharing was done through face-to-face communication with people who were much like themselves. Over the years, modern transport facilities, cross-border trade, international education, human migration and communication technologies have brought strangers from different parts of the world into contact, either face to face or through mediated platforms such as the internet. Canadian media culture analyst Marshall McLuhan (1964) coined the term *global village* to describe a world in which communication technology, such as television, radio and news services, brings news and information to the most remote parts of the world. Today, McLuhan's vision of a global village is no longer an abstract idea, but the very place we live in. We can exchange ideas as easily and quickly with people across the world as our ancestors did within the confines of their village. We encounter people from different cultures in business, at school, in public places, in neighbourhoods and in cyberspace. We may wear clothes made in China, purchase seafood from Thailand, dine out with friends in an Italian restaurant, work at a computer made in the United States or drive a car manufactured in Japan – the list goes on. Each encounter with new food, clothing, languages, products, services or practices teaches us new things. Indeed, more than ever before, we realize that our lives are often intertwined with people, places, practices and events outside our 'village' culture.

This chapter explores various contributors to cultural diversity, identifies the challenges of living in a culturally diverse society, and highlights intercultural communication as an integral part of life in a global community. We first discuss the contributors to cultural diversity in our global community, where people are constantly moving across geographic borders. Next, the chapter identifies the challenges that increased cultural diversity and multiculturalism bring to citizens of the global community, asking the questions of how we can live harmoniously as citizens of this global community and in what ways communication technologies make us connected or disconnected. Given that intercultural encounters bring opportunities for understanding between peoples as well as possibilities of misunderstanding, the final section of the chapter discusses the necessity of equipping ourselves with knowledge and skills in intercultural communication, thereby highlighting the importance of building our capacity to apply knowledge and skills of intercultural communication in the global community.

CONTRIBUTORS TO CULTURAL DIVERSITY

Living in a culturally diverse society today is no longer a choice, but a compelling reality, thanks to *globalization*, which refers to the process of increasing interconnectedness between societies and people at the economic, political and cultural levels. However, connections between cultures are as old as humankind. The Silk Road, for example, began during the Han Dynasty (206 BC to 220 AD) and lasted until the fifteenth century. It was an ancient network of trade routes that connected the East with the West, stretching from Central Asia, South Asia and the coast of Arabian Peninsula to the Mediterranean Sea. In addition to traders, the routes were travelled by explorers, missionaries, philosophers, warriors and foreign emissaries, spreading products, philosophy, religion, ideas and innovation in all directions and among people from different cultures. Similarly, the Ottoman Empire (Ottoman Turkey) was an empire founded at the end of the thirteenth century in north-western Anatolia by the Oghuz Turkish tribal leader Osman. After the fourteenth century the Ottomans crossed into Europe, and the empire was transformed into a transcontinental one. During the sixteenth and seventeenth centuries, it was a multinational, multilingual empire controlling much of south-eastern Europe, parts of Central Europe, Western Asia, the Caucasus, North Africa and the Horn of Africa. Those examples showed that the connection between cultures and the mass migration of people have a long history; the advent of communication technologies has just accelerated the process (McDaniel and Samovar, 2015). As leading intercultural communication researcher Young Yun Kim put it, 'We are all migrants now' (2015: 430), living simultaneously within a particular culture and between different cultures.

THEORY CORNER

THE GLOBAL VILLAGE

The notion of the global village and the process of globalization poses many questions. The metaphor of a global village has caught the imagination of many people, including political leaders and intellectuals. Globalization is defined as the widening, deepening and speeding up of worldwide interconnectedness in all aspects of contemporary social life (Goonasekera, 2001). In particular, this interconnectivity breaks down the boundary between East and West. Goonasekera further argues that 'paradoxically, we find that while technology has given the world the means of getting closer together into a global village, this very same technology has also given rise to unprecedented fears of domination by the technologically powerful nations' (2001: 278). Some Asian leaders even fear that globalization might result in cultural liquidation, particularly among smaller nations.

(Continued)

Nevertheless, globalization has accelerated the mobility of goods and people on a global scale. Correspondingly, it has challenged the traditional static and universal definition of place. In tourist destinations, for example, the construction of places for tourists' consumption involves the strategic mobilization of resources on a global–local continuum. Gao (2012) studied a tourist site – West Street, in Yangshuo County in China – to illustrate how tourists and foreign business people can transform a former residential neighbourhood into a 'global village'. The place, which was once home to local villagers, is now known for its craft shops, calligraphy and painting shops, cafés, bars and Chinese *Kung Fu* houses, all of them targeting foreign tourists. Gao argues that globalization is not simply Westernization, but a social construct of language and culture at the local level. While some scholars view increasing interconnectedness brought about by globalization as a threat to cultural uniqueness, other scholars argue that globalization may accentuate the distinctive characteristics of local cultures.

REFERENCES

Gao, Shuang (2012) 'Commodification of place, consumption of identity: The sociolinguistic construction of a "global village" in rural China', *Journal of Sociolinguistics*, 16(3): 336–357.

Goonasekera, Anura (2001) 'Transnational communication: Establishing effective linkages between North and South', in N. Chitty (ed.), *Mapping Globalization: International Media and a Crisis of Identity*. Penang, Malaysia: Southbank. pp. 270–281.

Advances in communication technology and transport systems

Communication technology is a key contributor to cultural diversity. With emails, social media, satellites and smartphones, we can contact people anywhere and anytime. If we want a more personal exchange, Skype or video desktop technology can bring a person at the other end of the globe onto the computer screen right in front of us. Words like 'blogs' (an abridgment of the term web log) and 'podcasting' (an amalgam of ipod and broadcasting) have appeared in our dictionaries since the beginning of the twenty-first century. Facebook, Twitter and Instagram are now global phenomena, allowing people to post their profiles and pictures online, and to communicate with other users across the world. The choices of media to connect with other people anywhere and anytime are multiplying.

Advanced communication technologies also affect how people form relationships with others. In past centuries, social relationships were typically circumscribed by how far one could walk (Martin and Nakayama, 2001). With each technological advance – the train, motor vehicle, telephone and the internet – social relationships have been transformed and expanded manyfold. There are millions of global users of the internet every day. In 2012, the Internet Society conducted a survey of more than 10,000 people in 20 countries and found that 90 per cent of the participants indicated that they used social media and 60 per cent of them accessed social media daily (Internet Society, 2012). Users spend time online building personal relationships, including friendship networks and romantic relationships. The internet has led to new ways of socializing that especially seem to attract young people. Research shows that in

PHOTO 1.1   We continue to be connected during our work or leisure time.
Copyright © Jaka Polutnik. Used with permission.

Western European countries most people know someone who has met a romantic partner on the internet. As Sveningsson (2007) writes, one of Sweden's most popular online meeting places is a web community called Lunarstorm (www.lunarstorm.se), which is visited weekly by 85 per cent and daily by 29 per cent of all Swedes aged 15–20 years old. Most young Swedes have become members of Lunarstorm. The media have even called it Sweden's largest online youth recreation centre. The idea of internet-based romantic relationships is gaining popularity as the mobility of society increases. However, other studies with college students found that undergraduates reported Facebook as a threat to their romantic relationships (Gershon, 2010). Thus, fears about new technology often come alongside their benefits.

DO IT!

Interview one person who was successful in an online romantic relationship and one person who had an unsuccessful experience with an online romantic relationship. Ask them in what ways they think online communication can shape the structure and development of romantic relationships. Identify three contributors to success and three barriers. Write one paragraph summarizing your findings and present it to your class.

Information and communication technologies also transform the potential reach and influence of economic and business transactions from a local to a global level. Global transformation refers to the worldwide economic and technological changes that influence how people relate to one another (Cooper, Calloway-Thomas and Simonds, 2007). For example, people in nearly every part of the world can buy Nike shoes or iPhones! Cross-cultural business transactions today are as common as trade between two persons in the same village was centuries ago. The clothes we wear, the food we purchase from the local supermarket, the cars we drive, the electric appliances we use at home and the movies we watch may all be from different countries. Our local market is as culturally diverse as the global market. Cultural diversity brings many opportunities, particularly in the economic realm, and helps to make our society the cosmopolitan, dynamic and exciting place it is today. However, one of the biggest economic and social challenges facing citizens of the global community is how to unlock the barriers to the acceptance of cultural diversity.

International migration and global business

The most significant contributor to the culturally diverse society today is the ever-increasing flow of people through international migration. According to the *International Migration Report 2015* (United Nations, 2016), large movements of migrants continue worldwide, often from low- and middle-income countries to high-income countries. The United Nations Department of Economic and Social Affairs' *2017 Revision of the World Population Prospects* (2017) shows that there was an average net inflow of 3.2 million migrants per year to high-income countries between 2010 and 2015. Of the 244 million international migrants globally in 2015, 104 million (43 per cent) were born in Asia. Europe was the birthplace of the second largest number (62 million or 25 per cent), followed by Latin America and the Caribbean (37 million or 15 per cent) and Africa (34 million or 14 per cent). The majority of the migrants (67 per cent) lived in 20 countries, with the United States hosting the largest number of international migrants (47 million), equal to about a one-fifth (19 per cent) of the world's total. Germany and the Russian Federation hosted the second and third largest numbers of migrants (12 million each), followed by Saudi Arabia (10 million). The report observes that the Syrian refugee crisis has had a major impact on levels and patterns of international migration in recent years, affecting several countries. The estimated net outflow from the Syrian Arab Republic was 4.2 million persons in 2010–15. Most of these refugees went to Syria's neighbouring countries, leading to a substantial increase in the net inflow of migrants, especially to Turkey, Lebanon and Jordan. Interestingly, Europe and Asia, while being the largest regions of origin of international migrants, are also the top destination regions of international migrants. (See Table 1.1, which outlines the top six destination regions for migrants in 2015.)

TABLE 1.1   International migrants by major area of destination (2015)

Area of destination	Number of migrants (millions)	% of total population
Europe	76.1	10.3
Asia	75.1	1.7
North America	54.5	15.2
Africa	20.6	1.7
Latin America and Caribbean	9.2	1.5
Oceania	8.1	20.6

Source: Adapted from United Nations Department of Economic and Social Affairs, Population Division (2016) *International Migration Report 2015: Highlights* (ST/ESA/SER.A/375). New York: United Nations. pp. 6, 17.

International migration increases diversity in the composition of populations in destination countries, and contributes to social and economic development both in the countries of origin and in the countries of destination. A steadily increasing proportion of migrant populations is made up of international students, particularly in developed English-speaking countries such as the United States, Australia, Canada and the UK. To date, the United States has been the world's largest receiving country for international students, receiving over 1 million international students, according to the *Open Doors 2017 Data* by the Institute of International Education (IIE, 2017). Asia remains the largest source region, accounting for 66.1 per cent of the total US international enrolments, followed by the Middle East and North Africa (10.4 per cent) and Europe (8.8 per cent). According to the IIE report, international students contributed approximately $36 billion to the US economy during the 2015–16 academic year. A similar trend was found in Oceanic countries such as Australia, where international education remains the third largest export, behind iron ore and coal. Figures from the Department of Education and Training (2017) of the Australian government show that over half a million international students were studying in Australia as of 2016, generating a record AU$20.3 billion (approximately U$16 billion) in export income for Australia in 2015–16, and China and India are the largest source countries.

Of more permanent residential status than international students are those people who migrate to the host country to make a living. In Australia, for example, immigration has always been a central part of nation building. Since the end of the Second World War, more than 7 million migrants have relocated to Australia. In the immediate post-war period, however, only 10 per cent of Australia's population was born overseas (Marden and Mercer, 1998);

PHOTO 1.2   Eat Street in Brisbane, showcasing food and cuisine from different cultures.

Copyright © Shuang Liu. Used with permission.

the percentage has risen steadily since then. The proportion of people from Asian countries is also on the increase. Between 2000 and 2005, the number of the East Asians in Australia rose by 17 per cent (from approximately 850,000 to 1 million). In comparison, the total Australian population grew only by approximately 5 per cent (from 19.4 million to 20.3 million) during the same period (Australian Bureau of Statistics, 2005). Today, nearly 25 per cent of the 24 million Australian population were born overseas (including all three authors of this book), and approximately 300 languages are spoken in the country.

Migrants move to their host countries for a variety of reasons, including access to a better living environment or to give their children a good education in an English-speaking country. Other people intend to explore business opportunities that are unavailable in their home country, while some migrate to seek refuge or political protection. Regardless of the reasons for migration, migrants worldwide dream of the freedom to be their own boss, to have autonomy in their choice of work and to achieve prosperity in the host country. Small businesses, such as take-away shops, convenience stores, trading companies or immigration consultancy companies, are considered by many migrants as ways to realize their dreams of freedom and financial security. As a result, walking along a street in Sydney, Auckland, San Francisco or London one would not have difficulty finding an Indian restaurant, a Chinese take-away shop, a Vietnamese green grocery store, an Italian deli, a Japanese sushi bar – the list goes on.

In response to economic transformations, businesses are continually expanding into world markets as part of a wider process of globalization. Billions of dollars in goods and services are exchanged each year in international businesses. Similarly, multinational corporations are increasingly moving their operations overseas to take advantage of lower labour costs, a trend that has far-reaching implications. There is a global trend for multinational corporations to shift businesses from developed economies in the West to emerging markets in the East. In 2000, 95 per cent of the largest international companies had their headquarters in developed countries, but it is estimated that by 2025 nearly half of companies with revenues of $1 billion or above will be based in emerging markets such as Asia (Dobbs, Manyika and Woetzel, 2015). Having a multicultural workforce allows organizations to make use of scarce resources and thus increase their competitive advantage. As a result of such economic and cultural shifts, people with diverse cultural backgrounds are working side by side in many countries, creating a culturally diverse workplace. Ethnic diversity within workplaces is continually changing the organizational composition of most parts of the world. For example, during the middle of the twentieth century, the discovery of oil reserves in Saudi Arabia led to rapid industrialization and a great demand for skilled labour not present in the country. Subsequently, Saudi Arabia's population of foreign workers increased significantly over the next few decades, with a particularly significant increase of 38 per cent between 1975 and 2000. This population grew dramatically again in 2004, when there were approximately 12.5 million foreign workers in the country, making up 65 per cent of the entire labour force (Looney, 2004). Similar trends were found in Europe, where the number of migrants joining the European workforce from Africa, Asia and the Middle East increases each year. The UK is the most popular target European country among foreign workers, according to *The Telegraph* (26 June 2017), although there is a fear that Brexit might cause non-British workers in the UK to consider leaving in the near future.

Cross-border movements of workers have vastly increased both the amount and the importance of intercultural communication in workplaces. Communication problems can be exacerbated when people interact with those whose communication behaviours are guided by a different set of beliefs and values (Guirdham and Guirdham, 2017). Not just face-to-face communication, but also mediated modes of communication affect and are affected by cultural differences between communicators. In the 1990s, less than 3 per cent of the world's population had a mobile phone; now two-thirds of the world's population have one, and one-third of all people worldwide are able to communicate on the internet (Dobbs et al., 2015). The internet revolution, particularly since around 1990, means that a very high proportion of work-related communication takes place via email, instant messaging, Skype, video conferencing, mobile phone and social media. For example, work-related activities such as selection interviewing, service encounters, decision-making meetings and business negotiations are routinely conducted through mediated, rather than face-to-face, communication. The pervasive reliance on the internet for work communication, along with the increasingly diverse ethnic composition of the workforce, makes businesses realize the importance of intercultural understanding in workplaces where people from different ethnic backgrounds work side by side.

THEORY CORNER

CULTURAL HOME

The concept of 'cultural home' refers to an individual's sense of belonging to an ethnic, racial or geographic community with shared traditions and practices (Vivero and Jenkins, 1999). A cultural home provides its members with emotional attachments to a cultural group as well as a sense of identity and belonging because its members share a common history and culture, and even similar physical features. Cultural home is often used together with the term 'ethnic enclave', which is described as an area where relatively large numbers of people from the same ethnic or racial background live in their host country. Although a cultural home may be geographically defined, such as an area densely populated by migrants from the same cultural heritage, a stable location is not always an essential defining feature of a cultural home. For example, Gypsies are nomadic people; they move geographically all the time, but their cultural home travels with them. They own no territory, but each community sustains a cultural identity through its language, strong traditions, rituals, dress, social structure and way of communication. All of these characteristics distinguish them from other cultural groups. Thus, the boundaries of cultural home can be symbolic.

Globalization and the increasing cross-border movements of people raise the question of whether or not we need a cultural home in a multicultural society. The answer to this question is yes, but as Bennett (1993: 110) writes, this cultural home is 'in the middle of many cultures'. Cultural home forms the basis for the development of identity and nurtures a feeling of belonging, although the belief in a single cultural identity that is itself based on a nation, culture, religion and way of life is changing. As the famous American poet Robert Frost (1874–1963) describes it: 'Home is the place where, when you have to go there, they have to take you in'. Just as our geographical home is located in our local community, so too is our cultural home located within the global community. Yet citizens of this global community identify themselves not with the global community as a whole, but oftentimes with various ethnic or subcultural groups that are the constituent parts of the global community.

REFERENCES

Bennett, Janet M. (1993) 'Cultural marginality: Identity issues in intercultural training', in R. M. Paige (ed.), *Education for the Intercultural Experience*. Yarmouth, ME: Intercultural Press. pp. 109–135.

Vivero, Veronica N. and Jenkins, Sharon R. (1999) 'Existential hazards of the multicultural individual: Defining and understanding cultural homelessness', *Cultural Diversity and Ethnic Minority Psychology*, 5: 6–26.

DO IT!

Skilled migrants are accepted into the receiving country to fill in skill shortages. However, international research has found that many of them are under-employed or unemployed in the country of settlement. Search on the government website or from census data in your country for information on the number of skilled immigrants in your home country. Identify the three top source countries of skilled immigrants in your country, and search for data on the top three job categories immigrants work in. Design a programme for a training workshop (of about three hours in duration) to train one key skill (e.g., English language) that you think skilled migrants need in the job market in your country.

CHALLENGES FROM CULTURAL DIVERSITY AND MULTICULTURALISM

All over the world, nations are trying to come to terms with the growing diversity of their populations. When migrants, refugees, asylum seekers, expatriates, international students or transnational business people move from one country to another, they bring their heritage culture to the new country. Central to the debate surrounding the benefits and threats of cultural diversity is the question of whether the preservation of ethnic cultures creates a threat to the uniqueness and dominance of the mainstream culture. Behind the overt, visible symbols of cultural diversity is a complex and often implicit concept of multiculturalism. At a descriptive level, *multiculturalism* can be used to characterize a society with diverse cultures. As an attitude, it can refer to a society's tolerance towards diversity and acceptance of equal societal participation. In attempting to maximize the benefits of cultural diversity, there has been an accompanying awareness of some potential threats to the uniqueness of the mainstream culture. Immigrants have long been forming associations or diaspora communities to maintain their ethnic and cultural heritage and promote the survival of their languages within a host country's mainstream institutions. On the other hand, host nationals have expressed concerns over the threat that different ethnic cultures may pose to their mainstream cultural values, the political and economic power structure and the distribution of employment opportunities. Some countries are addressing these concerns by trying to control diversity through tighter entry requirements. Other countries are developing government policies concerning the rights of immigrants to preserve their home culture within the host country.

In Germany, immigrants are considered 'Ausländer' (foreigners) and their naturalization is only possible if they agree to renounce their original citizenship and demonstrate loyalty to their 'adoptive' country (these laws were slightly relaxed when the Social Democrats gained power in the 1990s). Even so, there is raging controversy regarding the amendment of the citizenship laws and the implications for German national identity (Blank, Schmidt and Westle, 2001). France has built its nation-state, since the nineteenth century, on the premise that all regional and cultural differences should be eliminated. French citizens have to show loyalty to a powerful, centralized, secular nation-state, and adhere to national political values. Linguistic as well as cultural diversity within France has always been seen as a sign of regression and a hindrance to achieving national unity; interestingly, English (and the use of English words in French speech) has increasing prominence in France, in spite of attempts to maintain the purity of the French language. This restriction of citizenship opportunities is also evident elsewhere. In Australia during the nineteenth century there were no restrictions on anyone entering what was then a set of colonies, provided that they were not convicts serving out their time. Consequently, free settlers moved in from Great Britain, Germany, America, Scandinavia and Asia. Similarly, the slogan of the post-Second World War immigration programme was *Populate or Perish*! However, since 2007, a citizenship test has been in place to check migrants' knowledge of the English language and comprehension of Australian moral principles and history, as well as national and Aboriginal symbols. The test is available in English only, and a migrant applicant for citizenship must pass the test before an application for citizenship can be lodged. The maintenance of nationalism and protecting the mainstream culture have been key challenges facing host nationals in immigrant-receiving countries.

With the opening up of national borders within the European Union, European nations have been granting social rights, although no real political rights, to migrants (Soysal, 1994). This change has increased the perception of competition on the part of the native population. For example, there is a large North African presence in Europe. Reaching 3.5 million today, North Africans began arriving in Europe as early as the 1940s to help rebuild fledgling European economies severely weakened by the war. This migration accelerated in the 1950s and 1960s to meet the high demand for low-skilled workers in factories and mines and to compensate for slow demographic growth in Western Europe. For many years, North African immigrants were considered temporary residents (guest workers) and had no share in the social, political and cultural life of the host societies. It was only after the 1974 policies of family reunion that immigrants, their families, traditions and religions became visible in everyday life. France, for example, is home to the largest number of North African immigrants (because of its long colonial involvement in Algeria, Morocco and Tunisia), followed by Holland, Belgium, Spain, Italy and Germany. Different citizenship and immigration laws, as well as the socio-political climate of each host country, determine to a large extent how North Africans have engaged with the host culture. While acknowledging the benefits that can be obtained from an ethnically and culturally diverse workforce, studies consistently indicate problems that are often experienced by multi-ethnic workers, such as conflicts in expectations, lack of communication competence, differences in preferred communication styles, and attitude problems such as mistrust. Thus, understanding the cultural tensions created by cultural diversity is a challenge we face in the global community.

Cultural diversity and multiculturalism require us to reconsider our cultural identity. Cantle (2014) examined multiculturalism in a global society and its impact on identities from a European perspective, with its focus on race and socioeconomic analysis. He argues that while multiculturalism is right to continue to focus on inequalities, it has failed to adapt to super-diversity and the multifaceted aspects of difference and otherness, including those based on disability, age and gender. Further, Cantle believes that while multiculturalism has become rooted in differences between cultural groups within a nation, an intercultural approach is now necessary to support the changing concepts and patterns of national identity, for example the multiple identities for those whose ethnic and national identities are not the same. The key issues about diversity, citizenship, multiculturalism and national identity are directly related to intercultural communication. The fundamental question yet to be answered, as Cantle points out, is how we can increase the possibilities for peace, tolerance and social cohesion by building relationships across many divides in a multicultural society.

Increasing mobility and technology make our 'village' more global and diverse. However, this does not mean that the physical and psychological borders between countries and people are removed. Brown (2011) observes that ever since the fall of the Berlin Wall there has been a paradoxical increase in wall-building, in order to separate people. It is not simply that there is a resurgence in the construction of physical walls, such as the Israeli West Bank barrier, the US–Mexico border fence, or similar barriers on the edges of the European Union or the borders of India and Saudi Arabia, or the non-physical boundaries in maritime countries like Australia. There is also an increase in attempts at enclosure, as if nations can wrap themselves safely behind walls. Think of the town of Michalovce in Slovakia, where residents built a cement barrier to separate themselves from the town's majority Roma population. This wall has nothing to do with sovereignty or security, but with aversion and xenophobia. Thus, while communication technology and modern transport systems have facilitated contact between peoples, they may have also accentuated an awareness of differences between peoples and psychological borders. Breaking down the cultural and psychological walls is a challenge we face today, living in a global society.

DO IT!

Choose two immigrant families in your country – one family that shares the same native language with you and another family that speaks a different native language (this is because language strongly influences cultural distance). Ask members of each family about the extent to which they believe immigrants should maintain their ethnic and cultural traditions and practices without being considered as posing a threat to the unity of the mainstream host culture. Compare similarities and differences in the views from the two families.

NECESSITY AND BENEFITS OF INTERCULTURAL COMMUNICATION

As citizens of the global community, we face the task of promoting intercultural understanding, so as to reap the benefits of cultural diversity and reduce intercultural tensions between cultural groups. Intercultural scholars such as Anthony J. Marsella (2017), who is known internationally for his work on peace, development and social responsibility, use the word 'fractionation' to describe the divisive separation of people, societies and nations. Brexit, Trumpism, Putinism, and scores of similar populist movements across the world, lead to intense nativist–alien competitions for power. Widespread fears, anger and rage are endemic in populist movements, and globalization is blamed as the cause for tensions and problems. Governments, corporations and military power sources in many places seek homogenization, because uniformity will assist them to control the population. The issue of respect, tolerance and social and cultural space for a diverse population is much more than just a matter of recognizing and celebrating cultural diversity. Recognition is an essential first step, but unless it is translated

PHOTO 1.3   US–Mexican border at Friendship Park in San Diego, CA.

Copyright © Shuang Liu. Used with permission.

into practice in everyday lives, there will not be understanding. The key to building the necessary understanding between cultural groups is effective intercultural communication.

THEORY CORNER

PERSPECTIVES ON GLOBALIZATION

Held and McGrew (2007) identified three perspectives on globalization. *Globalists* view globalization as an inevitable development which cannot be resisted or significantly influenced by human intervention, particularly through traditional political institutions, such as nation-states. *Traditionalists* argue that the significance of globalization as a new phase has been exaggerated. They believe that most economic and social activity is regional, rather than global, and they still see a significant role for nation-states. *Transformationalists* contend that globalization represents a significant shift, but they question the inevitability of its impacts. They argue that there is still significant scope for national, local and other agencies.

Globalists and sceptics represent two basic positions in the field of global media studies, and there is an ongoing conflict between them. Globalists emphasize the possibility of transnational media systems and communication technology to create a global public sphere, whereas sceptics stress the persistent national features of the news media, and the continuing stability of the nation-state paradigm. In her study on the emergence of a transnational (European) identity in national news reporting on global climate change, Olausson (2013) analysed climate reporting in Indian, Swedish and US newspapers. The findings showed that some domestic discourses created explicit interconnections between the national or the local and the global, for example by situating Earth Hour in a small city in Sweden within the global framework of the event. Other discourses worked in a counter-domestic manner; that is, they lacked nationalizing elements around the issue of climate change. Scholars conclude that the local and global perspectives are not necessarily mutually exclusive; rather, the seemingly opposing positions reinforce and reconstruct one another. In other words, they constitute two sides of the same coin.

REFERENCES

Held, David and McGrew, Anthony (eds.) (2007) *Globalization Theory: Approaches and Controversies*. Cambridge: Polity Press.

Olausson, Ulrika (2013) 'Theorizing global media as global discourse', *International Journal of Communication*, 7: 1281–1297.

Building intercultural understanding

Understanding is the first step towards acceptance. The biggest benefit of accepting cultural differences is that cultural diversity enriches each of us. Throughout history, people around the world have accumulated a rich stock of cultural traditions and customs, but we are often not aware of the cultural rules governing our own behaviour until we encounter behaviours different from our own. Local laws and customs vary from country to country; if you are unaware of them and act according to your own customs when in the new country, you may very well end up in prison! For example, it is illegal in Egypt to take photographs of bridges and canals (including the Suez Canal), as well as military personnel, buildings and equipment. In India, trespassing on and photography of airports, military establishments and dams is illegal, with penalties ranging from 3 to 14 years imprisonment. Similarly, maiming or killing a cow in India is an offence that can result in a punishment of up to 5 years imprisonment. In Thailand, lengthy prison terms of up to 15 years can be imposed for insulting the monarchy; this includes destroying bank notes bearing the king's image. And Honolulu has become the first major US city to ban pedestrians from looking at mobile phones, texting or using digital devices while crossing the road. The Bill, also known as the Distracted Walking Law, aims to reduce injuries and deaths from 'distracted walking'.

If some of these local laws do not make much sense to you, you may find some local customs even stranger. Behaviours that are considered perfectly appropriate and acceptable in one culture may appear harsh or offensive in another. For example, in Saudi Arabia women are legally required to wear the abaya, a long black coat that conceals their body shape, in all public places, while men must avoid wearing shorts, or short-sleeved or unbuttoned shirts. Public displays of affection, including kissing and holding hands, are considered offensive. Hotels may refuse accommodation to couples who are unable to provide proof of marriage, because it is illegal for unmarried couples to live together. In Thailand, simple actions such as showing the soles of your feet or touching the top of a person's head are likely to cause grave offence. Even unknowingly breaching local customs may either get you into trouble or make you unwelcome!

The key to appreciating cultural differences is to acquire intercultural knowledge and develop intercultural skills. Intercultural knowledge opens doors to the treasure house of human experience. It reveals myriad ways of experiencing, sensing, feeling and knowing. It helps us to start questioning our own stance on issues that we may have once taken for granted. It widens our vision to include an alternative perspective of valuing and relating. By understanding the beliefs, values and worldviews that influence alternative communication approaches, we can understand the logic that motivates the actions or behaviours of others who are culturally different from ourselves. Culturally sensitive communication can increase relational closeness and deepen cultural self-awareness (Ting-Toomey and Chung, 2005).

The more that people from different cultures get to know each other, the more they can appreciate the differences and perceive the deep commonalities among them. The key to building a stock of intercultural knowledge, therefore, is to engage in intercultural communication. Intercultural communication can help us to build our knowledge of other peoples and their cultures, as well as enhancing and consolidating our knowledge about our own culture. The result is invariably greater intercultural understanding.

Promoting intercultural cooperation in the workplace

Managing diversity in the workplace is an essential competence that managers need to have in the twenty-first century (Guirdham and Guirdham, 2017). When money and jobs cross borders, there are challenges and opportunities facing individuals of different backgrounds who live and work together. People of different ethnic backgrounds bring their cultural baggage to the workplace. In a multinational organization, for instance, Malay employees may heavily emphasize the values of family togetherness, harmony in relationships and respect for seniority, whereas North American employees may value individuality and personal achievement more highly. A workgroup consisting of members from different cultural backgrounds is more likely to experience difficulties in communication or to experience miscommunication, conflict and turnover if group members are not interculturally competent. For example, the relative importance that managers place on task versus relationship orientations may vary across cultures. A comparison of the management styles of Nordic, Latin-European and Hungarian managers revealed that Latin-European managers showed the strongest task orientation, supporting an authoritarian decision-making style, whereas Nordic managers showed the highest levels of relationship orientations, indicating greater communication and reliance on their subordinates in decision-making (Lindell and Arvonen, 1996). Ethnic diversity in the workplace creates challenges for management in today's businesses, but the constructive management of diversity issues has the potential to bolster employee morale, create an inclusive climate in organizations and spark creative innovation.

Communicating in unfamiliar cultures does not simply mean finding a translator to facilitate discussions in a foreign language (Beamer and Varner, 2008). Communication is about unarticulated meanings and the thinking behind the words, not just the words *per se*. To understand the significance of a message from someone, you need to understand that person's perception and the most important values in that person's view of the world. You need to know what to expect when someone engages in a particular behaviour. *Guanxi*, for example, is a special type of Chinese relationship which contains trust, favour, dependence and adaptation. It constitutes a highly differentiated and intricate system of formal and informal social subsets, which are governed by the unwritten law of reciprocity. The Chinese people view human relationships as being long-term, and consequently place great emphasis on cultivating a good relationship with their business partners prior to any business transaction. While economic factors are important to the Chinese, those factors alone cannot sustain the motivation to maintain long-term business relations. In fact, non-economic factors such as acceptance, face-giving, complementary social reciprocity and trust may play a bigger role in influencing decision making. The emphasis on developing *guanxi* is reflected in business negotiations with Chinese partners, which tend to be much lengthier than those with a Westerner. As culture profoundly influences how people think, communicate and behave, it also affects the kinds of deals they make and the way they make them. A good understanding of cultural differences is a key factor in promoting mutually productive and successful international business exchanges.

Facilitating cross-cultural adjustment

Cross-cultural adjustment has to be understood as a manifestation of broader social trends that are not confined to the experience of immigrants, but rather as extending to many other kinds of associations and networks, as well as into cultural life at large. Globalization is a process by which geographic borders as boundaries between nations and states are eroding. There are new contours of transnational spaces and societies, and new systems of identity. Advances in technology and transport systems now provide people with greater freedom to travel beyond national borders, as well as with more choices for belonging. Ultimately, interconnectedness between people and the erosion of geographic borders make our 'village' more global, but our world smaller. The arrival of immigrants brings various changes to the host cultural environment. Intercultural encounters provide opportunities for understanding between people, as well as the potential for misunderstanding.

Cross-cultural adjustment is not a process that is unique to immigrants; host nationals also have to experience cultural adjustments when their society is joined by culturally different others. The tension between immigrants and host nationals often centres on the extent to which immigrants can maintain their heritage culture in the host country. Research conducted on immigrants' cultural adaptation strategies indicates that they identify integrating into the host culture and, at the same time, maintaining their ethnic cultural heritage as their preferred acculturation strategy (Liu, 2015). A key question is whether or not the host society provides immigrants with an environment in which they feel welcome to integrate. In countries receiving many immigrants, ethnically different populations can be perceived as threats to collective identity and to the standard of living of the natives. For host nationals, multiculturalism can be interpreted as a threat to their cultural dominance. For migrant groups, however, multiculturalism offers the possibility of maintaining their own culture and still integrating into the host society. Thus, policies of multiculturalism that highlight the importance of recognizing cultural diversity within a common framework, as well as equal opportunities, can lead to inter-ethnic distinctions and threaten social cohesion.

The extent to which host nationals allow members of immigrant groups to maintain their own culture and partake in relationships with the dominant cultural group plays an important role in the construction of a truly multicultural society. Promoting inter-ethnic understanding facilitates cultural adaptation by both migrants and host nationals; the key to inter-ethnic understanding is intercultural communication. Interacting with immigrants is often difficult for host nationals because of differences in language and cultural values, and this adds anxiety to intercultural interactions. To reduce anxiety of this nature, we must equip ourselves with knowledge about other cultures. Intercultural knowledge reduces anxiety and uncertainty, making the communication process smoother and more successful. Intercultural knowledge and intercultural communication skills, however, do not come naturally; they have to be acquired through conscious learning.

SUMMARY

- Advances in communication technologies, modern transport systems, the global economy, international business, mass migration and international education are major contributors to cultural diversity in our society.
- While geographic borders that used to separate people from people and country from country are receding, there are still many issues arising from cultural diversity and multiculturalism, such as protecting the uniqueness of the mainstream culture.
- Culture governs our behaviour; however, our way of doing things is usually neither the only way nor the only right way. Different cultural customs and practices need to be interpreted in their own contexts.
- In order to harness the benefits of cultural diversity in our society, it is necessary to develop sound knowledge and skills in intercultural communication.
- Intercultural communication equips us with the necessary knowledge and skills to interact with culturally different people effectively and appropriately.

JOIN THE DEBATE

Communication technologies, such as the mobile phone and the internet, have become an inseparable part of our daily lives. These were celebrated at the time of their invention as being able to overcome geographical boundaries and time constraints, hence bringing people across the world together. But has this happened? The digital divide, or the gap between those who have access to

DOES COMMUNICATION TECHNOLOGY BRING US CLOSER OR SEPARATE US FURTHER?

communication technologies and those who do not, continues to grow. While this concept is generally applied to developing versus developed countries, it is also of concern within the same country across different regions or communities, and even between generations. With so much of our communication now being dependent on mobile phones and internet-enabled computers or tablets, older people, those in regional or remote areas, or people of lower socioeconomic status may be at a significant disadvantage. On the other hand, those of us who have easy access to the all-powerful modern communication gadget – the mobile phone – become very reliant on it: we take mobile phones to restaurants, meetings, the dinner table at home, the bedroom and even the bathroom; we text contacts on the train, at the airport and in shops, sometimes instead of talking to people. Even when we set aside some time to catch up with friends face to face, we might be 'phubbing' (snubbing someone in a social setting by looking at our mobile phone instead of talking to them). Does communication technology bring us closer together, or set us more apart?

CASE STUDY

TURKISH SOAP OPERAS IN THE ARAB WORLD

Global media products coming from the West and their influence on Arab audiences has long been constituted as one of the most crucial debates around cultural imperialism in the Arab context. Over the past few years, the media landscape in the Middle East has undergone profound changes that can be attributed to the spread of digital technologies, the growing integration between old and new media, and the rise in popularity of (Turkish) television soap operas. Although there are many regional media production centres, whether established ones as in Egypt or Turkey or emergent ones as in Lebanon, media in the Middle East are characterized by large-scale Saudi ownership. It was Saudi businessmen who began acquiring pan-Arab media in the 1970s and who now control many media, such as Al-Hayat and Asharq-Al-Awsat (Kraidy, 2015). However, by far the most popular television genre in the region is that of the Turkish TV series. It is estimated that approximately 70 different Turkish TV series have been broadcast to audiences in at least 50 different countries. Dramas, in particular soap operas, have been one of the most popular forms of television programmes in Turkey for the last few decades, and these serials have now been exported with great success to the Middle East and around the world (Yanardagoglu and Karam, 2013).

Turks and Arabs have a shared history spanning more than half a century, incorporating a common culture, heritage and religion, but not a shared language. It is only since the early 2000s that Turkish dramas have developed from being local programmes to being internationally exported products that compete successfully with US programmes in terms of viewership figures. Turkish television programmes have also expanded into countries over and beyond their own linguistic regions, for example Bulgaria, Bosnia, Egypt and Syria to mention just a few. As such, they are seen as a key part in spreading culture. Since the early 2000s, Turkish television in particular has developed from a modest local presence to a transnational explosion across the Middle East. Arab channels started broadcasting Turkish content, and viewership figures across the Arab world rose, especially when the Saudi-owned and Dubai-based MBC (Middle East Broadcasting Center) satellite network started broadcasting the television soap opera *Noor* (Gümüş) in 2008. *Nour* attracted an unprecedented 85 million viewers over the age of 15 years (Yanardagoglu and Karam, 2013). The characters are known by different names in different countries. For example, Gümüş, the female protagonist for whom the soap opera is named, is known in Arabic as Noor, in Persian as Nur, and in Bulgarian as Perla. Names are often changed in dubbed shows to sound natural in the language into which they are translated. However, this name change also serves to remove these characters from their Turkish context and de-nationalize them, or even re-nationalize them according to the viewers' liking.

The Turkish soap operas are viewed with some suspicion and caution in the Middle East, particularly by political and religious leaders who fear (Turkish) cultural imperialism. The popularity of Turkish soap operas in the Arab world caused some concerns among political and religious leaders because of the culture that is spread along with the media products. While women from all across the Arab world watch, negotiate and identify with Turkish soap opera programmes broadcast on satellite television, governments and religious leaders in the Middle East region condemn these programmes as immoral, because they deal with topics such as love, sex, marriage, family, money, violence, social class, organized crime, corruption, domestic violence and divorce. Series are often eschewed as being not only a misrepresentation of Arab culture, but also a threat to 'authentic' Arab culture. While many viewers see these shows as deeply authentic, critics continue to regard the shows as dangerous because they represent an immoral and inaccurate Muslim society (Kraidy, 2015). The argument is that, by depicting people drinking alcohol after Ramadan, engaging in open relationships and having sex before marriage, Turkish television soap operas create a falsified version of the Muslim lifestyle which, it is feared, could corrupt the public's morality (Kraidy, 2015).

The Turkish series *Fatmagül* follows the experience of a woman who is raped, but is eventually able to stand up for herself against societal stigmas and take legal action against her assaulters. The show sparked an intense reaction among many women who were victims of sexual assault but had previously felt unable to speak up about their experiences. Fans began to write in, and many were even shown in the final episode of the series as extras, making up a throng of women cheering for *Fatmagül* as she enters the courtroom to testify against her rapists.

Kismet, a documentary made by Greek filmmaker Nina Maria Pschalidou (2013), explored the transnational perspectives of Turkish soap operas. Pschalidou included in the documentary women from Greece, Lebanon, Bulgaria, Saudi Arabia, Egypt and Syria, who make up some of the many groups of passionate Turkish soap fans. Although these documentary series were distinguished as uniquely Turkish in a number of ways and non-Turkish women who view them often separate themselves culturally from various elements of Turkish modernity, each non-Turkish female viewer can find a way to bring the story close to herself. For many viewers, identification deepens beyond this instilled cultural familiarity, often on a more personal level.

Kismet follows an Egyptian woman who was so inspired by the show *Fatmagül* that she gained enough courage to leave an abusive marriage of 13 years. 'She showed me that a woman can gain her rights', the Cairo woman says of Fatmagül. 'I watched her go to court and win. Why can't I do the same?' (cited in *Kismet*, 2013). Seeing the bravery and success of a woman on screen, the viewer was able to translate that bravery into her own life and bring the narrative arc of *Fatmagül* into reality, embodying fictitious courage and making it tangible. The fact that the narrative is fictional becomes irrelevant, as does the nationality of Fatmagül. The main catalyst to action, the main thing on which the viewer focuses, is the simple narrative in which the viewer is able to identify and embody her personal experiences and potential future.

Fatmagül speaks to survivors of sexual assault across national and cultural boundaries. As such, Turkish soap operas are a powerful space where we can start to understand the global impact of the media (Kraidy, 2015). The boom of Turkish television and the spread of its media products coincides with a rise in Turkey's political power. Opinion polls in 2009 of seven Arab countries reveal telling percentages: 78 per cent of respondents indicated that they had watched

Turkish television, 80 per cent welcomed Turkey's mediatory role in regional politics, and 66 per cent believed that Turkey could be a 'model' for other countries in the Middle East (Kraidy, 2015). Turkey's rise in media influence certainly has earned it political favour. As a by-product, Turkish tourism greatly increased in this same time period, particularly among Arab tourists.

REFERENCES FOR CASE STUDY

Kismet: How Soap Operas Changed the World. Directed by Nina Maria Pschalidou (2013).

Kraidy, Marwan M. (2015) 'The politics of revolutionary celebrity in the contemporary Arab world', *Public Culture*, 27(1): 161–183.

Yanardagoglu, Eylem and Karam, Imad N. (2012) 'The fever that hit Arab satellite television: Audience perceptions of Turkish TV series', *Identities: Global Studies in Culture and Power*, 1(5): 561–579.

QUESTIONS FOR DISCUSSION

1. Do you think that soap operas, like Turkish soap operas, have the potential power to educate viewers on sensitive topics such as domestic violence?

2. Have you ever watched any television genres (such as soap operas and/or talk shows) and identified strongly with the characters? Why?

3. Do you think the popularity of Turkish TV series will become a powerful medium for the spread and dominance of Turkish culture in the Arab world?

4. Are there any TV soap operas in your country that had a great impact on viewers and led to discussions on issues of public concerns? If so, give an example.

5. Do you think that global media will marginalize local media products or do you think globalization will provide a space for local media products to grow? Why?

FURTHER READINGS

Baylis, John, Smith, Steve and Owens, Patricia (2011) *The Globalization of World Politics: An Introduction to International Relations* (5th edn). Oxford: Oxford University Press.

This book provides a coherent, accessible and engaging introduction to the globalization of world politics from a unique non-US perspective. Its fifth edition has been fully revised and updated in light of recent developments in world politics. New chapters on post-colonialism and post-structuralism give the most comprehensive introduction to international relations available. This text is ideal for students who are approaching the subject for the first time.

Castells, Manuel (2008) 'The new public sphere: Global civil society, communication networks, and global governance', *ANNALS of the American Academy of Political and Social Science*, 616: 78–93.

This article discusses the relationships between government and civil society and their interaction in the public sphere. The public sphere as the space of debate on public affairs has shifted from the national to the global as a result of globalization, and it is increasingly constructed around global communication networks. The author demonstrates how the global public sphere builds shared cultural meaning, which is the essence of communication.

Movius, Lauren (2010) 'Cultural globalisation and challenges to traditional communication theories', *PLATFORM: Journal of Media and Communication*, 2(1): 6–18.

This article examines the challenges that the current developments of globalization present to traditional ways of thinking about communication and media. A brief history of the concept of globalization is provided, followed by theoretical approaches to globalization that are critical to communication scholars, such as the cultural imperialism theory. In addition, the article discusses how audiences negotiate meanings differently in specific cultural contexts.

Oxley, Laura and Morris, Paul (2013) 'Global citizenship: A typology for distinguishing its multiple conceptions', *British Journal of Educational Studies*, 61(3): 301–325.

This article constructs a typology to identify and distinguish the diverse conceptions of global citizenship. The typology incorporates political, moral, economic, cultural, social, critical, environmental and spiritual conceptions. The article illustrates how the typology can be used to evaluate the critical features of curriculum planning to promote global citizenship in Britain.

Tervonen, Miika and Enache, Anca (2017) 'Coping with everyday bordering: Roma migrants and gatekeepers in Helsinki', *Ethnic and Racial Studies*, 40(7): 1114–1131.

This article examines intra-European borders through the case of Eastern European Roma in Helsinki. State authorities at various levels have responded to the loss of direct control over legitimate yet unwanted migrants by mobilizing municipal workers and local police forces as everyday gatekeepers. The article explores how migrants strive to improve their disadvantaged position through transnational, family-based livelihood strategies.

This video features an interview with Professor Cees Hamelink, who discusses the impact of global communication on our society. It will help you to achieve the learning objective of recognizing intercultural communication as an integral part of life in a global community. Watch the video to see how Professor Hamelink describes intercultural communication and misconceptions of communication.

SAGE VIDEO SOURCES

This video is available at http://study.sagepub.com/liu3e

Culture is the name for what people are interested in, their thoughts, their models, the books they read and the speeches they hear, their table-talk, gossip, controversies, historical sense and scientific training, the value they appreciate, the quality of life they admire. All communities have a culture. It is the climate of their civilization.

Walter Lippmann, American journalist and sociologist, 1889–1974

2

CULTURE AND PEOPLE

LEARNING OBJECTIVES

At the end of this chapter, you should be able to:

- Identify different components and characteristics of culture.

- Define and analyse different types of subcultures.

- Explain discursive construction of culture and identity.

- Evaluate different approaches to studying culture.

INTRODUCTION

The word 'culture' originated from the Latin word 'cultura', which means 'to till' (as in till the soil or land). In its original meaning, therefore, culture is a process related to the tending of something, such as crops or animals. The word shares its etymology with modern English words such as agriculture, cultivate and colony. Eventually, the term was extended to incorporate ideas related to the human mind and a state of being 'cultivated'. Basically, culture consists of a group or community's traditions, customs, norms, beliefs, values and thought patterns, passed down from generation to generation. This includes food, music, language, dress codes, artefacts, family, organization, politics, stories, the production and distribution of goods, and so on. As Edward T. Hall (1966: x) states, culture is 'those deep, common, unstated experiences which members of a given culture share, communicate without knowing, and which form the backdrop against which all other events are judged'. Being a member of a cultural group implies that you have been nurtured by its core values and understand what constitutes 'desirable' and 'undesirable' behaviours in that particular system (Ting-Toomey and Chung, 2005). While different people might have different norms for judging behaviours, common to all people is that we see our world through culturally tinted lenses, and we rarely take them off.

This chapter explores the relationship between culture and people. As culture permeates the entire way of life of a group of people, it can be defined at macro and micro levels. At the micro level, culture can be defined by race, gender, ethnicity, religion, sexual orientations, religion, political affiliation, physical ability and so forth. Hence, there are subcultures within culture. Either at the macro or micro level, culture fosters a sense of shared identity and solidarity among its members. The chapter first identifies the components and characteristics of culture, and then analyses the different types of subcultures. In analysing the relationship between culture and people, the chapter discusses the discursive construction of culture and identity. We also introduce emic and etic approaches to studying culture. Throughout the chapter, we emphasize that culture is not innate; it is learned through communication. Therefore, culture and communication are intertwined.

COMPONENTS AND CHARACTERISTICS OF CULTURE

For decades, scholars across the academic spectrum have grappled with and attempted to define culture. Almost 200 definitions can be located, each attempting to delineate the boundaries and inclusions of the concept by drawing upon such synonymous ideas as community, minorities, social groups, social class, nationalities, geographic units, societies and so forth. For example, the Italian philosopher Antonio Gramsci (2000) conceptualized culture as the creative meaning-making process by which people make sense of their social world. It represents their active relation to the wider social and material world. American anthropologist Clifford Geertz (1973) defines culture as a web that people themselves have spun. As a web, culture both confines members to their social realty and facilitates their functioning in this reality. Raymond Williams (1989), a British cultural studies scholar, argues that culture is the product of individuals' whole committed personal and social experience; it is the product of a whole people and offers individual meanings. Everett M. Rogers and Thomas M. Steinfatt (1999: 79) define culture as 'the total way of life of a people, composed of their learned and shared behaviour patterns, values, norms, and material objects'. While Gramsci, Geertz, Williams, and Rogers and Steinfatt represent only a small number of the scholars who have attempted to define culture, they serve to illustrate the multifaceted nature of culture.

Although definitions of culture vary across different fields, scholars agree that culture is pervasive in human life and governs people's behaviours. Building on this consensus about culture, this chapter defines *culture* as the particular way of life of a group of people and the meaning-making process by which people make sense of their social world. Culture comprises the deposit of knowledge, experience, beliefs, values, traditions, religion, notions of time, roles, spatial relations, worldviews, material objects and geographic territory. This definition emphasizes the pervasive nature of culture; it also confirms that culture is a process as well as a product of communication because culture is developed, manifested, shared and maintained through communication. As Carley Dodd (1998: 37) argues, 'Culture is like the luggage we carry', and when we open each pocket of our cultural suitcase, we explore an interrelated set of group identities, beliefs, values, activities, rules and customs, institutions and communication patterns arising from our daily needs and rituals.

DO IT!

Talk to five people to find out about their specific morning rituals. Write down their responses. How does their morning start? Do they drink tea, coffee or milk when they wake up? Do they read a print newspaper, or do they read news online, or do they listen to news on the radio? Or do they avoid media completely in the morning? After carefully going over their responses, write one paragraph summarizing the patterns of behaviour related to their morning rituals and see whether you can relate them to culture.

Components of culture

Intercultural communication scholars have categorized the components of culture by levels to help us better understand the influence of culture on different aspects of our life.

This chapter adopts the model by Dodd (1998), which groups cultural components into three levels, as shown in the model in Figure 2.1: the inner core, the intermediate layer and the outer layer of culture.

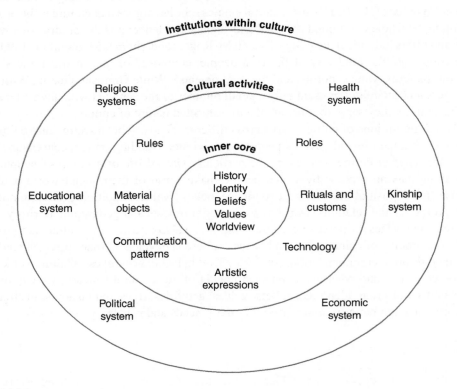

FIGURE 2.1   A model of culture

Source: Adapted from Dodd, Carley H. (1998) *Dynamics of Intercultural Communication* (5th edn). Boston, MA: McGraw-Hill. p. 38. Used with permission.

The inner core of culture

The inner core of culture consists of history, identity, beliefs and values, and the worldviews of a cultural group (Dodd, 1998). Every culture has a history that is the repository of cultural heritage and development. Totems, archives, architecture, ancient languages and paintings are just some of the ways in which a culture records and expresses its heritage and tradition. The power of heritage demonstrates the continuity of a culture from generation to generation, binding its members together and providing a sense of *identity*. Identity (or, more appropriately, identities) gives us a location in the world and reflects the link between us and the society. For example, pre-colonial Maori society in what today is New Zealand was communal and tribal based. Within Maori society, identity was determined by the satisfactory fulfilment of social obligations towards biological kin through *whanau* (extended family based on shared genealogy), *hapu* (sub-tribes comprising several *whanau*) and *iwi* (tribes comprising *hapu*) (Houkamaua, 2010). In this regard, *whanau* obligations were central to self-identity.

Each culture has a window through which its members perceive reality and other people. *Beliefs* are an individual's representations of reality viewed through that cultural window. Some beliefs are seen as very likely to be true; others are seen as less probable. For example, Aboriginal cultural beliefs are based on spiritual beliefs, where there are direct links between land, language, dreaming and people. Aboriginal and Torres Strait Islander people in Australia traditionally have a strong physical and spiritual bond with the Australian landscape through 'the Dreaming', which is believed to represent their origin and early existence. Another example of a belief from Slovenian culture is that people hang horseshoes over their doors to bring positive spirits and good luck. A further example is worshipping in Wong Tai Sin

Temple, a well-known shrine in Hong Kong. The temple is famed for the many prayers answered: 'What you request is what you get.' On the Chinese New Year's Eve, thousands of worshippers wait outside the temple before midnight and rush in to the main altar to offer Wong Tai Sin their glowing incense sticks when the new year comes. As the tradition goes, the earlier they offer the incense, the better luck they will have that year.

Culture also has concepts of ultimate significance and of long-term importance, known as *values*, that go beyond statements of truth. Values tell the cultural group members how to judge good or bad, right or wrong. Values enshrine what is worth fighting for, what is

PHOTO 2.1   Wong Tai Sin Temple, a well-known shrine and major tourist attraction in Hong Kong.

Copyright © Shuang Liu. Used with permission.

worth sacrificing, what should be protected and what should be given up. Cultural values involve judgements, and so values differ across cultures. For example, US American culture teaches people the values of independence, privacy and competition. Malay culture teaches people the values of harmony, reciprocity, non-competitiveness, loyalty to superiors and thrift. Hierarchy is valued in Korean culture, while equality is treasured in Switzerland. Our core understanding of good and evil, right and wrong, true and false, is taught in a cultural context.

A culture's belief about nature and the working of the universe is called a *worldview*. Understanding the worldview of a culture can help predict its members' thoughts and behavioural patterns. For example, according to the Judaeo-Christian understanding of human nature, the first humans were created in the image of God. *Genesis* declares that God said 'Let us make [humans] in our image, in our likeness and let them rule over the fish of the sea and the birds of the air, over the livestock, over all earth, and over all the creatures that move along the ground'. In Japanese Shinto (an ancient Japanese religion), the gods, called *kami* (deities) take the form of wind, rain, mountains, trees, rivers and fertility. Nature is sacred; to be in contact with nature is to be close to the gods, hence natural objects are worshipped as sacred spirits. Believers of Shinto also respect animals as messengers of the gods. From these examples we can see that a worldview is a belief system about the nature of the universe, its perceived effects on human behaviour, and humans' place in the universe (Dodd, 1998).

THEORY CORNER

DIGITAL CULTURE

Culture as a powerful force affects human behaviour and the ways we experience the world. At the same time, culture is shaped by the dominant economic and political system of the society (Bourdieu, 1977). The rapid spread of digital culture in most parts of the world has been attributed to many global social, political and economic changes. Digital culture stands for the changes brought about by contemporary digital, networked and personalized media in our society and it signifies the transformation from print- and broadcast-centred media to networked media which rely on digital communication technologies. Hence, digital culture represents the contemporary phase of communication technologies. The emergence of digital culture is associated with more user participation and a more personalized and visually rich media environment. Young people born in and after 1990 are commonly regarded as the digital generation; and the term 'digital culture' has come to refer to the multiple ways in which young people engage with digital media and technologies in their daily lives.

Research on digital culture investigates the roles that the internet, new media and digital technologies play in contemporary society, including the everyday life of ordinary people. Not only in developed countries or urban regions, even in developing countries and in rural areas, youth digital culture is emerging. Pathak-Shelat and DeShano (2013) studied the case of a small town of Gujarat in India, where class, caste, gender, geographical location, beliefs, values, schools and infrastructure are only some of the elements that influence the digital culture of the youth. India has the largest youth population in the world, with approximately 600 million people under the age of 25. The strong cultural divides in India heavily influence the life experiences of young people. Pathak-Shelat and DeShano (2013) examined how location and dominant discourses intersect with digital technologies and reconfigure aspects of youths' daily lives, such as study, leisure and friendship, how youths negotiate their interactions with digital media as one aspect of their real life, and how these negotiations influence cultural practices within social environments. In this study, youths were found to treat new media and technologies as one component of their lives and social experiences.

REFERENCES

Bourdieu, Pierre (1977) *Outline of a Theory and Practice*. Cambridge: Cambridge University Press.

Pathak-Shelat, Manisha and DeShano, Cathy (2013) 'Digital youth cultures in small town and rural Gujarat', *New Media and Society*, 1(2): 1–19.

The intermediate layer of culture

The intermediate layer of culture consists of activities as manifestations of culture. According to Dodd (1998), cultural activities can be expressed in many ways: as technology, material objects, roles, rules, rituals, customs, communication patterns and artistic expressions. The rituals and customs people observe and the festivals people celebrate reflect culture. For example, the celebration of King's Day (Koningsdag, King's or Queen's day) in the Netherlands on 30 April every year reinforces the belief that the Dutch King or Queen is an embodiment of hope and unity in times of war, adversity and natural disaster. In a different arena, the power of football (soccer) in many countries, starting in Europe and South America and symbolizing a core value of pride in the nation, is astonishing. One only needs to look at the TV viewing parties and celebrations around the Football World Cup to understand that.

Artworks are cultural products. In many paintings by Western artists, humans tend to be portrayed as the focal point, whereas in paintings produced by Eastern artists (such as those of the Chinese), natural scenes or animals are more likely to be the centre of the painting. This reflects the importance and power of nature in the Chinese culture versus the power of human agency and action in Western European and American culture. In addition to artwork, technology is a very salient feature of a culture, and is reflected in its transportation, communication, food, clothing, shelter and tools. What people wear, how they eat and prepare food, the kinds of tools they use for work – all these reflect the culture of a particular group. As Everett Rogers (1995) states, technology has form (what it is or how it looks), function (what it does and how it works) and meaning (what it represents).

What we do in a cultural context forms relationships with others; these relationships generate a dynamic of roles and expectations. The behavioural norms associated with these roles and expectations are governed by culture. As well as roles, rules, norms, customs and rituals, each culture expects particular communication patterns. Communication behaviours such as gestures, loudness, directness and turn-taking are all expected to conform to a culture's expectations. In this, the contrasts between cultures are striking. For example, Ghanaian culture dictates that people address elderly men as 'grandfather'. In Australia, Indigenous people call elders 'uncle' or 'auntie' to show respect. In Japan, indirectness in conversation is valued as it functions to preserve harmony between the speakers, whereas in Germany directly 'speaking your mind' is preferred in interpersonal communication. In Iran, people often belittle their own achievements in public in order to appear humble, which is valued in Iranian culture. Intercultural misunderstandings often occur because we do not share the cultural rules governing the communication behaviour of others.

Nonverbal communication behaviour such as posture and gestures and concepts of time and space are

PHOTO 2.2   A colourful array of spices in the Deira Spice Souq in Dubai.

Copyright © Alison Rae. Used with permission.

also influenced by culture. In Western countries, people view time with great precision, and punctuality is a cultural expectation. People make an appointment or reservation to see a doctor, go to a hairdresser or dine in a restaurant. Being late is regarded as bad manners. For example, the Dutch and Germans are very punctual, and being even five minutes late for an appointment is considered inappropriate – if anything, people arrive a minute or two early as a sign of respect. In Africa, Malaysia and Latin America, however, people are deliberately a little late in order not to disturb their hosts' other activities. Meetings may not start until everyone arrives. A doctor may schedule all patients for the 8:00am appointment, and it is the patients' responsibility to negotiate among themselves whose turn it is to see the doctor. There are core cultural values in both these time orientations, and people with one orientation tend to think those with the other are lazy and disrespectful or over-punctual and obsessive. Both culture and communication, therefore, are a way of living and a whole social process. The intermediate level of culture reflects our definitions of social and cultural rules, and our communication patterns.

DO IT!

Watch an old movie from your grandmother's time. Identify the roles of the main male characters portrayed in the movie. Watch a movie from the last few years with a similar theme (e.g., romantic love or war) and identify the roles of the main male characters in this movie. Compare the roles in the two movies. Have the roles of men changed over time? If so, in what ways? What does this tell us about cultural change?

The outer layer of culture

The outer layer of culture involves the institutions of a culture (Dodd, 1998). Institutions constitute the formalized systems, including religion, the economy, politics, family, healthcare and education. These systems are the products of culture. Religion refers to any system of thought that provides answers to the big questions of life, death and life beyond death. Religion supplies maps for individuals on their journeys towards belief and faith. For example, the 'Abrahamic' faiths (Judaism, Islam and Christianity) are called monotheistic religions, meaning that each believes in only one God. Hindus tend to be both monotheistic and polytheistic. Buddhism, on the other hand, offers the possibility for personal self-realization, and the Buddha is considered a teacher, not a God. Aboriginal people in Australia have a spirituality that puts value on integrated communities, based on beliefs about connections between people and the environment, including the land and animals. In modern societies, religion is sometimes used to explain events in life, including death, accidents, illness and even natural disasters. In this sense, religion and culture are intertwined. Knowledge of religious practice can help one to understand a particular culture, and to avoid cultural mistakes and prejudice.

In addition to religious systems, the economic system of a society reflects its culture. In some remote villages, people still use barter trade for business transactions, whereas in more developed regions, people are more likely to use cash or credit cards to make a purchase. With the advent of communication technologies, digital currency or electronic money is replacing credit/debit cards and cash in physical form, such as banknotes and coins. Like traditional money, digital currency may be used to purchase goods and services, although there might be some restrictions depending on the country. For example, in 2011, Google wallet was released in the US to make it easy to carry credit/debit cards on one's mobile phone. The Danish Chamber of Commerce supports the move to a cashless economy. Nearly one-third of the Danish population uses MobilePay, a smart phone application for transferring money.

At the outer layer, cultural influences are reflected in family structure. Take family size, for example. In Western countries, the nuclear family (a unit referring to the father, mother and children) is the major family structure. In other cultures, the extended family, which includes the nuclear family along with grandparents, uncles and aunts, cousins and so on, is valued and more likely to be the norm. This structure can affect the number of children in a family in any generation. Moreover, political, health and educational systems are also elements of culture, and they vary across cultures. For example, some countries have a one-party system (e.g., communist regimes), whereas others have two or more parties (e.g., democratic regimes) governing the country. In some cultures, religion and politics are separate, whereas in other cultures they are interrelated – the religious leader may also be a political figure. For example, the Roman Catholic Pope, as the leader of his church, has full legal, executive and judicial power in its seat, the Vatican City. On the one hand, religion offers the possibility of peace and unites people. On the other, religion can play a divisive role when different ethnic groups or nations struggle over resources. In addition, people's beliefs about health and medicine are shaped by culture. Some societies rely on Western medicine to cure illness; others have more faith in traditional herbal medicine; and still others believe that praying is a way to relieve pain and illness. Furthermore, a society's educational system also reflects its culture. In Malaysia, Singapore or Hong Kong, memorization or rote learning is the preferred pedagogy, whereas in Anglo-Saxon cultures, the skills of critical and creative thinking and problem solving are more valued in the classroom. The outer layer of cultural systems includes numerous aspects of a culture's ultimate survival in ways that are accepted and often sanctioned by law. They are fundamental to the economic, legal, social and spiritual nature of a culture (Dodd, 1998).

Characteristics of culture

Culture is holistic. To this point, we have isolated the components of culture, for ease of description and explanation. In reality, culture functions as an integrated and complex whole. While the various parts of culture are interrelated, the whole is more than simply the sum of these interconnected parts (McDaniel and Samovar, 2015). As Hall (1977: 13–14) said, 'You touch a culture in one place and everything else is affected'. For example, during the Hindu Annaprasanam, a festive event to celebrate the first birthday of a child, the baby is given a mixture of rice, sugar and milk, which is generally his or her first solid food after a year on a liquid diet. All aspects of the event must be interpreted as a whole – none makes sense on its own. Another example of culture as a whole is the ritual of drinking tea. The custom of tea drinking can symbolize culture, from which different values and cultural orientations can be learned. One very specific example is the Japanese tea ritual. Chadō, or the 'Way of Tea', is a key part of Japanese culture. The tea ritual is a detailed procedure, which takes years to learn and which can take up to four hours to perform. The aim of the tea ceremony is to achieve inner peace and harmony, which are valued in Japanese culture. It also aims to open the mind in preparation for meditation. Thus, the tea ritual must be interpreted as an integral part of the whole Japanese cultural system.

Culture is learned. The Dutch psychologist and sociologist Geert Hofstede (1991: 32) writes that every person 'carries within him or herself patterns of thinking, feeling, and potential acting which were learned throughout his or her lifetime'. We learn cultural rules as we grow up from sources like family, friends, teachers, proverbs, adages and folk-tales. We learn our cultural rules and norms through communication, at both the conscious and unconscious levels. A Chinese mother might tell her daughter that once married, she should follow her mother-in-law's ways of doing things around the house, and in doing so the daughter learns about the expected roles of a married woman. This is cultural learning at a conscious level. Identifying cultural learning at the unconscious level is more difficult, but just as significant nevertheless. While we may be unable to specify a particular experience that taught us about our view of ageing, for example, the attitudes we have developed are still the product of our cultural learning. As an example, the French convention of addressing older relatives with the formal pronoun for 'you' – 'vous', whereas younger relatives are called by the more informal and intimate 'tu', reinforces the value of respect for older people that is central to this culture, even with the changes of modern life. Culture is pervasive; it is like the water that fish swim in and the air we breathe (Beamer and Varner, 2008). Often we are not able to see their effects on our lives until we encounter different cultural rules or practices.

Culture is dynamic. Culture is subject to change over time. When different cultures are in contact, cultural change may occur. For example, think of how Russian culture has been changing over the past few years – many aspects of its culture have noticeably changed since the collapse of communism in 1991. A new cultural and political order, economic recovery, growth, and increasing openness to Western ideas have led many to see present-day Russia as more 'individualistic' and 'Western'. As our cultural environment changes, so does our view of cultural practices. The waltz was considered as savage during the 1700s. During the 1800s, the tango was viewed as a primitive dance that was too sexual to be socially acceptable. In fact, it was banned in Argentina. Today, the tango is very popular all over the world, even in places far from its origins, such as Finland. Similarly, in the United States, rock and roll was decried by many people as being too sexual in the 1950s and the 1960s, which caused considerable intergenerational conflict. Nowadays, the waltz, the tango and the music and dance associated with rock and roll are accepted as part of our social life. However, we also need to be aware that different elements of culture or different layers of culture may not change at the same speed or at the same time. While technology, transport systems, material objects and architecture are becoming increasingly similar across different cultures, our beliefs, values and worldviews – the inner core of culture – can prove more resistant to change. An American may wear the traditional costume of an Indian woman, but their beliefs, values or worldviews may still differ considerably. We could build a city in Africa similar in appearance to London, but it would still not be London.

Culture is ethnocentric. The term ethnocentrism refers to the belief that one's own culture is superior to other cultures (see Chapter 4). Anthropologists generally agree that ethnocentrism is found in every culture (McDaniel and Samovar, 2015). Ethnocentrism builds fences between cultures and thus creates barriers for intercultural communication. How we view a culture invariably affects how we interact with people from that culture. When Captain James Cook arrived in Hawaii in 1778, he described the native culture as being savage, animal-like and heathen, comparing (unfavourably) the practices of the Hawaiian people to the European culture of which he was a part. Today, we know that no culture is superior to any other, but simply that some cultural practices might appear strange or inappropriate to members of other cultures. Australians think it is cruel that Koreans eat dog meat; Koreans feel it is heartless that Australians and other Anglo-Saxons send their elderly parents to nursing homes. Similarly, people in Sweden think Anglo-Saxons are cruel for spanking their children, but many Anglo-Saxons think that corporal punishment is central to bringing up a child properly. Of course, we do not have to accept or practise what is acceptable in other cultures. What is important is recognizing and respecting the differences. Culture is what is distinctive about the way of life of a people, community, nation or social group. This implies that no culture is inherently superior to any other.

THEORY CORNER

EMIC AND ETIC APPROACHES

There are two main approaches to studying culture: emic and etic. They were first described by Kenneth Pike (1967) and the terms originally came from the field of linguistics. The *emic approach* views each culture as a unique entity that can only be examined by constructs developed from inside the culture. In other words, this approach focuses on identifying culture-specific aspects of concepts and behaviour that cannot be compared across all cultures. Emic knowledge and interpretations are those existing within a culture, that are shaped by local customs, values, meanings and beliefs, and are best described by a 'native' or an 'insider' of a culture. The cultural anthropologists' endeavour to understand culture form 'the native's point of view' is the main foundation of emic approach.

In contrast, the *etic approach* assumes that culture can be examined with predetermined categories that can be applied to all cultures in the search for cultural universals. Etic researchers attempt to identify universal aspects of human behaviour and seek to find universal processes that can be utilized across cultures. In other words, this approach assumes that all cultures can be compared in terms of generalizable phenomena, and that researchers should seek to segregate common components of culture and test hypotheses. A synthesis of etic and emic approaches can be found in Lung-Tan Lu's (2012) paper. Lu found that found that one of the most difficult aspects of doing business in a foreign country is to understand the similarities and differences in cultural values. Cross-cultural studies using an etic approach with quantitative methods have led researchers to compare similar elements (etic) of national cultures around the world. However, critics argue that it is time to explore the relationship between different parts of culture (emic) and international business activities because people living in a country are not homogeneous. While etic categories may be useful for comparative analysis, they need corroboration from fieldwork and must allow for new elements collected through an emic approach.

(Continued)

Hence, etic and emic approaches are complementary, and researchers should combine both approaches in studying culture.

REFERENCES

Lu, Lung-Tan (2012) 'Etic or emic? Measuring culture in international business research', *International Business Research*, 5(5): 109–115.

Pike, Kenneth L. (1967) *Language in Relation to Unified Theory of the Structure of Human Behavior*. The Hague, The Netherlands: Mouton.

DO IT!

Some cultures (or aspects of culture) transcend national and ethnic boundaries. One example in contemporary society is consumer culture, or the value put on buying and using products and services. One way to explore the concept of consumer culture is to find out when and why people make purchases of goods and services. Ask your family members what they shop for and why, and what they like to consume. You may also ask whether they always need what they buy. Relate their answers to etic and emic approaches. Think about what aspects of consumer culture each approach allows you to see. Write a paragraph summarizing your views.

CULTURES WITHIN CULTURE

Within any dominant culture, there are cultures within culture, which are referred to as *subcultures* or co-cultures (this chapter uses the term 'subculture'). Subcultures can be categorized using a number of indicators, including gender, ethnicity, religion, profession, social class, organization and geographic region. We focus on four types of subcultures, defined as ethnicity, social class, organization and geographic region. Subcultures, like cultures, give their members identity, and members of a subcultural group can mark their identity through rituals, language and other behaviour.

Ethnic culture

Ethnicity is frequently the basis of a subculture that people use to categorize immigrants. Ethnic groups are identifiable groups of people who have a common heritage and cultural tradition passed on through generations. Examples include Chinese Australians, Mexican Americans, Vietnamese Italians, and Greek New Zealanders. Some people use the terms 'racial group' and 'ethnic group' interchangeably; others differentiate the two terms by specifying that racial groups emphasize the genetically transmitted traits of physical appearance (Dodd, 1998). It is important to note that racial group boundaries are very fluid and blurred, and very few people today (if any) belong to only one racial group. Therefore, many people resist the use of the term 'race' altogether, preferring a term like 'ethnic or cultural group'.

PHOTO 2.3   Slovene Hall in Fontana, near Los Angeles, offers Slovene music, dance and food to its visitors.

Copyright © Zala Volčič. Used with permission.

Ethnic groups in the host country are often referred to as minority groups, even though they may be the numerical majority, such as blacks in South Africa. An example of the complexity of belonging to ethnic groups comes from Latin America. There is a notion of 'Latina/o' (or Latinx), which is a pan-ethnic identity label used by scholars and some grassroots activists to describe people from a variety of ethnic and linguistic backgrounds but who are of Mexican, Latin American and Spanish Caribbean descent and living in the United States. 'Chicana/o' is a political grassroots identity label used to describe people of Mexican descent and is most widely used in California. Analogous groups and identities exist in most countries today, but people's preferences vary by culture. The term 'minority' is sometimes associated with disadvantage and lower social status. The Sami people in Scandinavia, for example, have long been an economically and socially disadvantaged indigenous minority in the relatively (but not completely) homogeneous cultures of Sweden, Norway and Finland. Communication between people from an ethnic minority and those from the ethnic majority can be problematic, due to language and cultural barriers as well as negative stereotypes (see Chapter 4).

Social class culture

Socioeconomic status (SES) can be the basis for a subculture. SES can be derived from a person's income, education, occupation, residential area and family background. For example, your income is strongly associated with where you are most likely to reside, the type of occupation you have and the position you hold, the brand of clothes you wear, the kind of people you tend to associate with, whom you marry or which school your children attend. The Indian caste system is an example of a hierarchically ordered social class ranking. Class ranking predicts attitudes and communication between different castes within the larger Indian culture. Similarly, previous research in Western countries has found differences between middle-class and working-class parents in regard to the values placed on raising their children (Zhou, 2014). Liu (2015) argues that working-class parents' emphasis on obedience can transfer to their children as obedience to authority, acceptance of what other people think and hesitancy in expressing desires to authority figures outside the home. Research also shows that due to the social stereotypes favouring whites in the West, it is common for blacks to be perceived as being lower class and even less intelligent, despite their actual middle-class status (Hendrix, 2017).

Organizational culture

Subcultures also include organizational cultures. Each organization has its ways of doing things and its ways of communicating, which together constitute its organizational culture (Pacanowsky and O'Donnell-Trujillo, 1983). Employees hold beliefs, values and assumptions to organize their behaviour and interpret their experience. Through communication, these beliefs and values develop into organizationally based understanding and shared interpretations of organizational reality. These expectations and meanings form the framework of organizational culture. The IBM Corporation, for example, has a distinctive organizational culture in which male employees are expected to wear dark blue suits, white shirts and conservative neckties. The dress code reflects unity and conformity to IBM's management style. On the other hand, innovativeness is an espoused value of the 3M Corporation. Employees who put forward suggestions become heroes for demonstrating the spirit of innovation. In Japanese companies, employee loyalty is highly valued, whereas opportunities for career advancement may be seen as being more important in Western organizations. In some organizations, subordinates can address people in management by their first name; in other organizations, employees of lower rank must address senior-level managers by their last name and their title. Even subsidiaries of the same company operating in different countries may report value differences. Members of each organization share knowledge about appropriate behaviours and use this knowledge to guide their activities at work. Organizational cultures give members a sense of identity.

Organizational culture can be a strong determinant of attitudes to organizational and cultural change (see Chapter 6 for Hofstede's cultural dimensions). For example, employees in a large hospital in Australia undergoing job change and physical relocation were classified by organizational level, from the CEO to the cleaning and grounds staff (Rooney et al., 2010). Their attitudes to the change were strongly influenced by their level, with those at the higher levels being more positive about the change, which modernized the hospital organization, and less concerned about the physical move. It emerged that for lower level workers, the location of the hospital and the actual buildings were central to their identity, as their families had been employed in this place for several generations.

Regional culture

Geographic region is also a basis for categorizing people into different cultural groups. Regional differences often imply differences in social attitudes, lifestyle, food preferences and communication. People from rural areas are different from people in urban areas. The Dutch, in addition to the regions within the Netherlands but outside Holland (such as Friesland) that have their own languages and cultures, distinguish between two major cultural urban/rural subdivisions in their nation. The most important distinction is between the Randstad (Rim City) and non-Randstad cultures. Randstad culture is distinctively urban, located in the provinces of North Holland, South Holland and Utrecht. The non-Randstad culture follows the historical divide between the predominantly Protestant north and the Catholic south. Interpersonal relationships may seem tighter in rural communities than in urban regions, partly due to apartment living and busy lifestyles in urban environments.

Language or regional dialects are also markers of regional cultures. For example, the Swedish language has been standardized for more than a century, but regional variations in pronunciation between urban areas and rural ones persist. Similarly, the Japanese language spoken in Okinawa, for example, differs from the Japanese spoken in Tokyo, and the Mandarin spoken in Beijing is different from the Mandarin spoken in Shanghai. Likewise, the American English spoken in Virginia is different from that spoken in Ohio (much less the English spoken in London, Sydney or Singapore).

DISCURSIVE CONSTRUCTION OF CULTURE AND IDENTITY

Members of a particular cultural group have collective representations of the defining characteristics of their culture. As they interact with each other to establish consensual meanings of their shared experiences, they come to agree on what is important to their culture. Such collective agreements become shared knowledge, developed through the negotiation of meaning at both the individual and collective levels. While cultural differences cannot be reduced to differences in cognitive content (Markus and Kitayama, 1991), they are ingrained in an individual's sense of being. Therefore, any deviance from a social or cultural norm in the group can lead to a stigmatized identity.

Identity is a product of social construction. In *The Presentation of Self in Everyday Life* (1969), Erving Goffman proposes that identity is a theatrical performance that conveys the self to others in the best possible light, in conformity to cultural and societal norms. However, critics argue that Goffman's dramaturgical perspective over-extends the notion of acting or performing and gives an undue concern to impression management, which might cast doubt on any notion of a true self (Elliott, 2001). Despite the criticisms, Goffman's influential model of self-presentation offers insights into the discursive construction of identity (identity construction through talk and discourse) and the social presentation of self.

One important method of self-presentation is through identification with a cultural group. Cultural identity implies that a person shares a worldview, value system, and attitudes and beliefs with their cultural group. In this sense, cultural identity both locates a person in a cultural group and distinguishes the person from others who are in other groups. When an individual calls himself or herself a Chinese, an African, a Buddhist, a woman or Blake Smith, that person is presenting parts of their self-image that are recognizable to others. For example, the Chinese view the self as a relational concept that is embedded in the social presence of others. The ultimate goal of life is to realize the self through developing harmonious social relationships with others (Chen, 2017).

Identity representation is shaped by social interaction (Hecht et al., 2005). From the social constructionist's perspective, people use linguistic and other cultural resources in the ongoing construction and reconstruction of personal and group identity. Smith (2007) argues that constructing an ethnic identity provides immigrants with a sense of belonging and continuity with their home culture. Although there has been very little consensus among scholars regarding a universally accepted definition of 'identity' due to its complex and multifaceted nature, common to all conceptions of identity is that it is socially constructed through communication and is a pivotal point connecting individuals with the society.

THEORY CORNER

ETHNOGRAPHY

Ethnography refers to a specific research methodology that has been employed to study different cultures and subcultures. According to Grbich (2007: 40), this approach has 'strong links with the anthropological tradition of observation of culture *in situ*'. Ethnographic research aims to describe the whole culture. This will usually involve participation for several years in the setting, learning the language and collecting data. Many ethnographers today spend a shorter time in the field but use a number of data collection techniques to speed up the process of data collection. These include focus groups, face-to-face interviewing, participant observation and document analysis. Data gathered from ethnographic studies often cast light on our understanding of the life and culture of particular communities.

In her book on restaurants, Gatta (2002) combines interviews and several months of participant observation in a variety of restaurant spaces, from fast food to expensive restaurants. Her goal is to look at the strategies used by servers to negotiate their emotions when confronted with rude and demanding customers, as well as their dealings with managers and co-workers. Thus, Gatta believes that restaurants provide a stage to explore how workers attempt to maintain, lose and regain emotional balance amid these potentially disturbing situations. She carefully observed and listened to mostly waitresses and their stories. She claims that there are different strategies used by servers, which can be inward-directed or outward-directed, active or passive. They range from spitting in a customer's food (relatively rare) to withdrawing friendly service, stealing food or alcohol from their restaurants, re-engaging in routines that allow one to forget a particular incident, or engaging in various stress-management techniques outside work, such as excessive drinking and yoga (some techniques are more effective than others). From her ethnography research in restaurants, Gatta provides a sense of the daily culture of servers, their coping strategies, and the ways that they create a sense of community in response to the challenges posed by the job.

REFERENCES

Gatta, Mary L. (2002) *Juggling Food and Feelings*. Lanham, MD: Lexington Books.

Grbich, Carol (2007) *Qualitative Data Analysis: An Introduction*. London: Sage.

SUMMARY

- It is difficult to have a concrete definition of culture because the characteristics that we use to denote cultural differences are not universally applicable.
- Culture is defined as the particular way of life of a group of people. Culture is developed, manifested, shared and maintained through communication.
- Subcultures can be defined by ethnicity, social class, organization and geographic region. Subcultures share similar characteristics of the larger culture.
- Culture and identity are discursively constructed and socially defined. Identification with a cultural group gives us a sense of identity.
- Both emic and etic approaches help us in studying cultures from within and from outside a system. We can achieve greater knowledge and awareness of the issues of cultural expression, creativity and art through interdisciplinary thinking about culture.

JOIN THE DEBATE

ARE WE WHAT WE EAT?

It is often said 'We are what we eat'. Food, cooking and eating habits constitute an integral part of every culture. The consumption of food is more than a purely biological activity; it is always imbued with meaning. Food choices, eating habits and cooking are expressions of culture and cultural identity. Food is also an important part of religion, separating one creed from another by means of dietary taboos. The techniques utilized to prepare food and the ways of consuming it have an important influence on social and familial relationships. Fast-food like KFC, for example, does not encourage people to spend the whole evening with friends or family members over a meal at home or in a restaurant, which is a favourite social activity for continental Europeans. Thus, people who eat different foods, or eat the same foods in different ways, are often thought to be different. However, along with globalization, multinational food companies like Starbucks and Pizza Hut have been expanding their presence around the world. Do you think this change is a good or a bad thing? With the increasing variety of cuisines from different cultures readily available, and with our gradual acquisition of culturally diverse foods, will we gradually assimilate different cultures, cultural values and cultural identity? Or will our food just become more Westernized? What will be the impact on our original cultures? Will we become increasingly similar as we eat more similar foods in similar ways?

Food and cuisine constitute an important part of Chinese culture. Dining goes far beyond meeting the biological needs to satisfy hunger; food and eating, including what to eat, how to eat and when to eat (or not to eat), can be inextricably linked with culture. There are many Chinese idioms that are associated with the act of eating. For example, someone who is popular at work is called 'eat open'; on the other hand, those who are unpopular among colleagues are described as 'eat closed'. If you visit someone who happens to be not at home or are denied entrance, it is called 'eat closed door'. 'Eat loss' is used to describe someone who is in a disadvantaged position, whereas 'eat sweetness' describes someone who gains benefits from an event or situation. Those who undergo hardships are referred to as people who 'eat bitterness' – the list goes on. Food reflects customs, social norms, festivals, status, religion, beliefs and rituals; above all, it is a common language that bonds the Chinese people together. The Chinese saying that 'To the people, food is heaven' (*min yi shi wei tian*) dates back thousands of years. For the Chinese people, food is viewed as heavenly; eating communicates their desire for harmony between human beings and nature, harmony between heaven and earth, and harmony in social relationships.

The history of Chinese cuisine is marked by both variety and change. Preferences for seasoning and cooking techniques vary across provinces because of the geographical features of the region, the climate and social customs. Moreover, due to imperial influence and trading, ingredients and cooking methods from other cultures have been integrated into Chinese cuisines over time. The 'Silk Road' is the conventional term for the routes through Central Asia that linked the Iranian plateau with western China. Along this trade route passed exotic foods that expanded Chinese cuisines, although only some of them preserved their foreign names. All of them became locally grown and consumed over the course of history. For example, it is thought that sesame, peas, onions, coriander and cucumber were all introduced into China from the West as early as the Han Dynasty (206 BC–220 AD), although the accuracy of this could be challenged. In addition, rice is a staple food across regions. Chinese food is mostly eaten with chopsticks, which are also believed to have been introduced in the Han Dynasty, along with the wok, a characteristic Chinese cooking utensil.

Chinese cuisines are conventionally categorized into eight groups based on geography, cooking techniques and taste (see Table 2.1).

CASE STUDY

FOOD CULTURE IN CHINA

TABLE 2.1   Summary of eight Chinese cuisines

Cuisine	Geographic region	Characteristic taste
Cantonese cuisine (粤菜)	Guangdong Province and Hong Kong	Mild flavour, lightly seasoned, and a little sweet (e.g., dry-fried beef and noodles)
Sichuan cuisine (粤菜)	Sichuan Province	Spicy, often mouth-numbing, with lots of chili (e.g., chili fish-flavoured beef shreds)
Jiangsu cuisine (粤菜)	Jiangsu Province	Fresh, moderately salty and sweet (e.g., sweet and sour Mandarin fish).
Zhejiang cuisine (浙菜)	Zhejiang Province	Similar to Jiangsu cuisine (e.g., West Lake fish in vinegar gravy)
Fujian/Min cuisine (闽菜)	Fujian Province	Light spicy, with a mild sweet and sour taste (e.g., Buddha jumping wall – sea food and poultry casserole)
Hunan cuisine (湘菜)	Hunan Province	Quite spicy, even hotter than Sichuan food (e.g., steamed fish head with diced spicy red peppers)
Anhui cuisine (徽菜)	Anhui Province	A delicate lightness in taste, with herbs adding aroma and medicinal effects (e.g., ham and whippy bamboo stew)
Shandong cuisine (鲁菜)	Shandong Province and northern part of China	Salty and crispy, with less heavily applied chili than in Sichuan cuisine (e.g., diced pork cooked in a pot)

Food in China has many symbolic meanings. When a baby is born, the parents distribute eggs dyed in a red colour to relatives, friends and neighbours to celebrate. Eggs symbolize the continuity of life, and eating eggs implies Chinese people's desire to pass family names from generation to generation. Dumplings are served on Chinese lunar New Year's Eve (which often falls between the end of January and early February) to symbolize family reunions and togetherness. Although abundant dishes are served at the New Year's Eve dinner, what people actually eat is secondary to the significance of being together with the family. Oranges mean good luck, and they are used as decorations at the New Year. On Lantern Festival Day (the fifteenth day of the lunar new year), glutinous rice balls are eaten to indicate that all family members stick together. When celebrating birthdays in China, often noodles and boiled eggs are served. Noodles symbolize longevity and eggs, and on this occasion represent one's smooth life. On wedding days, people tend to spread the couple's bed with dates (which in Chinese is pronounced in the same way as the word for 'early') and peanuts (pronounced in the same way as the word for 'birth'), in the hope that the couple can have children soon. At the time of their wedding and moving into a new house, the couple may eat noodles with gravy, which symbolizes a flavoured life (Zhang and Ma, 2016). There are also food taboos. For example, people do not like to share pears, because dividing a pear means separation.

Food in China has social functions as it establishes and maintains relationships between people. In Western cultures, it is common for individuals sitting at the same table to order separate food; in China, a group dining together usually shares the food. When Chinese people gather together in a restaurant, people sit at a round table, which symbolizes unity, courtesy and an atmosphere of sharing. Dishes are placed in the middle of the table. People pour drinks into each other's glass, asking each other to eat more, reflecting mutual care and respect. The food *per se* is less important than the social significance of sharing. Dining together is a medium for making new friends or maintaining established relationships. In Hong Kong, a common parting expression is 'we will dine together when we have time'. People talk about business and exchange information over morning or afternoon tea (Ma, 2015).

In Chinese food culture, certain etiquettes are observed while eating. Family members usually wait to eat until the whole family is seated. The elders and the young are the first served, although habits vary in different regions. In some parts of China, for example, the whole family eat together; in others, men and women may eat separately. When taking food from the dishes, the rule is that you should take food first from the plates in front of you, rather than from those in front of others. It is also considered bad manners to use chopsticks to burrow through the food. When finding your favorite dish, you should not gobble it up as quickly as possible or put the plate in front of yourself. You should consider others at the table. If there is not much left on a plate and you want to finish it, you should usually ask if anyone at the table wants more from that plate – if not, then you may finish it.

In terms of presenting food, fish or meat can be served with bones in Chinese dishes. When removing bones or other inedible parts of the food from your mouth, you should use chopsticks or a hand to take them and put them on a side plate in front of you. The Chinese eat with chopsticks; spoons are often used for soup or sometimes for dessert. There are some conventions governing the use of chopsticks. For example, you should not put chopsticks vertically into your food when you are not using them, especially not into rice. Such a gesture will make Chinese people think of funerals, because at funerals sticks of incense are stuck into a rice pot at the ancestor altar. Knives are traditionally seen as breakers of harmony, so they are normally not provided at the table.

REFERENCES FOR CASE STUDY

Ma, Guansheng (2015) 'Food, eating behaviour, and culture in Chinese society', *Journal of Ethnic Foods*, 2: 195–199.

Zhang, Na and Ma, Guansheng (2016) 'Noodles, traditionally and today', *Journal of Ethnic Foods*, 3: 209–212.

QUESTIONS FOR DISCUSSION

1. Have you tasted any of the eight Chinese cuisines listed in Table 2.1? If yes, which cuisine is your favourite? If not, which one would be your favourite and why?

2. Think of a traditional food in your culture that is eaten on a particular occasion, such as a birthday or a wedding. What kind of food is it? What symbolic meaning does it convey?

3. In your culture, do people normally eat with chopsticks, forks and knives, or hands? Why do you think they do this?

4. Are there any food taboos in your culture, for example certain foods that should not be served at weddings?

5. Can you give an example from your country to show how food is related to your culture?

FURTHER READINGS

Aoki, Kayoko (2012) 'Name and ethnic identity: Experiences of Korean women in Japan', *Journal of Asian and African Studies*, 47(4): 377–391.

This paper explores the experiences of Zainichi Korean women and examines how using Japanese or Korean names has impacted their identity. Koreans living in Japan, so-called Zainichi Koreans, were historically forced to use Japanese names during the annexation (1910–45) and have been using them until today. While most Zainichi Koreans use Japanese names in public, some use Korean names all the time or only when they associate with fellow Zainichi Koreans. Zainichi Korean women have been marginalized not only by the dominant group, the ethnic Japanese, but also by their own group.

García-Gómez, Antonio (2017) 'Teen girls and sexual agency: Exploring the intrapersonal and intergroup dimensions of sexting', *Media, Culture, and Society,* **39(3): 391–407.**

The electronic swapping of sexually provocative images and texts, commonly known as sexting, seems to have become part and parcel of adolescents' social lives. Questions remain about the way(s) young women navigate sexual relationships and construct their gendered identity discursively by endorsing or challenging social and behavioural norms of sexual agency. This article reports on a study where guided discussions involving 36 young women were conducted. The main of aim of this study was to gain insight into the characteristics of sexualized adolescent cyber-culture by analysing their discourses about sexting, its effects on their lives and its implications.

Hochschild, Arlie R. (2016) *Strangers in Their Own Land*. **New York: New Press.**

The book explains the worldview of the supporters of the Tea Party movement in Louisiana, in the United States. Hochschild claims that both conservative and liberals have 'deep stories' about who they are and what their values are. Deep stories are the stories we tell ourselves to capture our hopes, pride, disappointments, fears and anxieties. Their deep story, she argues, focus on the American Dream: the idea that if you work hard and play by the rules you can have a better life. But what happens when that dream does not come true – or when people see 'line cutters' getting ahead while their own lives do not seem to be going anywhere?

Ossman, Susan (2013) *Moving Matters: Paths of Serial Cultural Migration*. **Stanford, CA: Stanford University Press.**

This book is a rich portrait of a culture of serial migrants: people who have lived in several countries, calling each one at some point 'home'. Serial migrants must negotiate a world of territorial borders and legal restrictions and they create their own culture. They often become masters of settlement as they turn each country into a life chapter. Ossman follows this diverse and growing population not only to understand how they produce certain cultures, but also to illuminate an ongoing tension between global fluidity and the power of nation-states.

Ruelle, Olivier and Peverelli, Peter (2017) 'The discursive construction of identity through interaction on social media in a Chinese NGO', *Chinese Journal of Communication,* **10(1): 12–37.**

This article adopts the social constructionist theory approach to investigate the discursive construction of social identity in a Chinese NGO through analysing online discussions on WeChat, which is China's fastest-growing social networking site. Data were collected from ongoing interactions in a group on WeChat over a period of eight months. The findings revealed the way in which key members of a Chinese NGO are engaged in a process of group identity construction.

SAGE VIDEO SOURCES

In this video, Dr Nick Bentley speaks about characteristics of subcultures. This video will help you to achieve the learning objective of analyzing different types of subcultures. Watch it to learn how Dr Bentley defines and describes subcultures.

This video is available at http://study.sagepub.com/liu3e

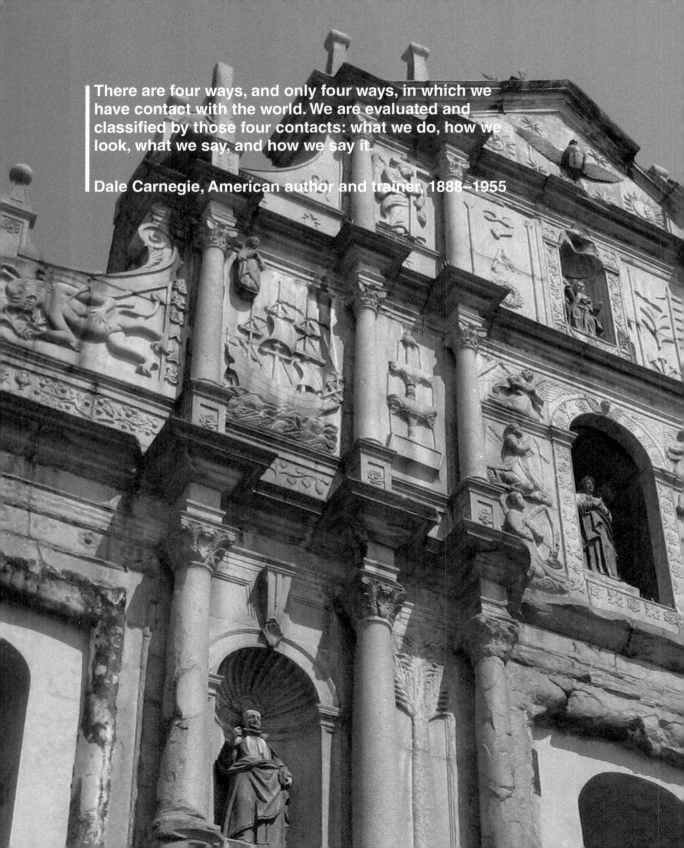

There are four ways, and only four ways, in which we have contact with the world. We are evaluated and classified by those four contacts: what we do, how we look, what we say, and how we say it.

Dale Carnegie, American author and trainer, 1888–1955

3

COMMUNICATION AND CULTURE

LEARNING OBJECTIVES

At the end of this chapter, you should be able to:

- Understand the multifaceted nature of communication.
- Identify components and characteristics of communication.
- Evaluate widely known models of communication.
- Recognize the influence of culture on communication.

INTRODUCTION

As the opening quote by Carnegie indicates, we make our contact with the world through 'what we do, how we look, what we say and how we say it'. Each of these communicates a message to the people around us. *Communication* – our ability to share who we are and what we know with others – is the basis of all human contact. The English word 'communication' is derived from the Latin root *communicare*, meaning 'to make common', as in sharing thoughts, hopes and knowledge. For example, greeting one another is a basic communication act practised in every culture. We may do this by saying 'hello', or by using touch, eye contact, kissing, or a gesture to exchange greetings. These communication behaviours reflect the functions and characteristics of communication; that is, we use a shared code to exchange meaning. Communication requires that all parties understand a common 'language', be it in words, symbols or gestures. Auditory means of exchanging meaning include speaking, singing and tone of voice; on the other hand, physical means such as body language, sign language, touch, eye contact, pictures or writing can communicate meaning equally effectively, depending on the context. Whether we live in a large city like New York, a small Peruvian village like Los Molinos, a remote region like Christmas Island or a metropolitan city like Paris, we all communicate via different media.

This chapter focuses on the relationship between communication and culture. It first illustrates the multifaceted nature of the concept of communication and then examines its components and characteristics. Following this, we critically analyse and evaluate widely used models of communication, broadly grouped into two categories: linear and interactive. Finally, the chapter discusses the influence of culture on communication, drawing on examples from various cultures. Throughout the chapter, we draw your attention to the need to communicate effectively and appropriately with people from different cultures. As our contact with people from other cultures expands, intercultural communication skills become an integral part of our life. This is because although all of us share our ideas and feelings with others, how we share them with others varies from culture to culture.

THE MULTIFACETED NATURE OF COMMUNICATION

Human communication is as old as human history. Cave paintings in prehistoric Europe, for example the famous rock paintings at Lascaux in France, chart the beginning of human communication. At Lascaux the paintings were hidden from outsiders and appear to have been a means of communication within the group. In Australia, however, paintings and pteroglyphs (scratching on rock to make pictures) by Indigenous people can be found more easily on rocks and in caves, illustrating an ancient means of communication both within and across groups. The paintings in the caves and on the rocks of Uluru – a red sandstone monolith in central Australia – reveal that this place has been the focus for religious, cultural, territorial and economic relations among the Aboriginal people of the Western Desert for thousands of years. Many other means of conveying messages have been used throughout history, via members of our own species and other animals. For example, pigeons were used by European armies to carry military messages during the First World War (Greelis, 2007), while warriors in ancient China used burning fire and smoke to warn fellow soldiers in different military camps of danger. Human beings have long been used as message couriers. In ancient times, human messengers were probably the most reliable and efficient means of sending official information and communiqués, even though it meant weeks or months of long, often dangerous travelling time.

Advances in information technology have brought tremendous changes to communication media and to the role of communicators. From print, telephone, radio, telegraph, television, satellites to the internet, email, Facebook, Twitter, texting and instagram, the twenty-first century has witnessed a proliferation of media, devices and platforms, which have expanded human communication beyond the confines of time, space, geographic region, culture and nation-states (Flew, 2014). Everyone is a node on the 'wired' communication network. However, the same communication media that bring us closer together may also separate us from each other by accentuating differences. Advances in communication technologies require us to rethink conventional definitions of communication.

Finding a single definition of communication is a difficult task. Dance (1970), who reviewed some 95 definitions of communication published in the 1950s and 1960s, argues that the definitions differed in so many ways that communication might better be theorized as a 'family' of related concepts, rather than as a unitary concept. This reflects the multifaceted nature of communication. Consider the simple act of greeting a friend. From the secretion of chemicals in the brain

PHOTO 3.1   The ruins of St Paul's from the seventeenth century is one of Macau's best-known landmarks. It is a UNESCO World Heritage Site.

Copyright © Shuang Liu. Used with permission.

to the moving of one's lips to produce sound, thousands of components are in operation. To overcome problems created by the complexity of the concept of communication, scholars concentrate on the aspects of communication that are most germane to their interests (McDaniel and Samovar, 2015). For example, neurologists look at what the brain and nervous system do during communication; psychologists examine issues related to perception; linguists inspect people's use of language; philosophers are more interested in whether communication is essential to thought; anthropologists focus on the question of whether communication is universal; in the electronic world, scientists focus on the transfer of data and information from one location to another. Communication researchers are more interested in how people share meaning through common codes such as language, gesture, picture, or other codes. Each of these disciplines carves out but one piece within the territory of human communication. As each field of study explores its own area of communication, it is very important to be aware that no single definition can include all aspects of communication. Given that our interest lies in communication between culturally different people, we focus on those elements that influence sharing understanding and meaning between different cultures. Thus, communication is defined in this chapter as the process by which people use shared verbal or nonverbal codes, systems and mediums to exchange information in a particular cultural context. This is a broad definition of communication. We know a communicator's success in one context might not be transferable to another scenario. Therefore, we now turn to identifying the components and characteristics of communication.

TABLE 3.1   Levels of communication

Level of communication	Characteristics
Intrapersonal communication	The process of understanding and sharing meaning within the self.
Interpersonal communication	The process of understanding and sharing meaning between at least two people when relatively mutual opportunities for speaking and listening exist.
Group communication	Purposeful communication in limited-sized groups in which decision making or problem solving occurs.
Organizational communication	Communication in large cooperative networks including virtually all aspects of both interpersonal and group communication.
Mass communication	The process of understanding and sharing meaning with a broad audience through mediated channels. Mass media like radio, television and newspapers are specifically conceived and designed to reach a large audience.

COMPONENTS AND CHARACERISTICS OF COMMUNICATION

Although definitions of communication vary across disciplines, scholars agree that embedded in all definitions of communication are people, message, channel and context. Based on this consensus, scholars identify eight basic components of human communication, which usually operate simultaneously. They are source, message, channel, receiver, encoding, decoding, noise and feedback. All these components exist in the specific context that permeates communication processes (Guirdham and Guirdham, 2017).

Components of communication

Source. A source is the origin of information; it is someone who needs and wants to exchange information with others. The need may be conscious, such as asking someone for directions (seeking information), expressing feelings about a wedding attended (sharing experience), or assigning tasks to an employee (giving instructions). The need to communicate may also be non-conscious, for example frowning when tasting food one does not like or when disagreeing with someone's opinion. Conscious or non-conscious communication is the sharing of thoughts and feelings, with varying degrees of intention by the source, and it affects the feelings and behaviour of another person or group of people.

Message. A message is the verbal and/or nonverbal form of ideas, thoughts or feelings that one person intends to communicate to another person or group in a specific context. A message is composed of *verbal codes* such as language (and some gestures) and/or *nonverbal codes*, including facial expressions, body movements, tone of voice, use of space, time orientation and so forth. Each culture has its own way of expressing meaning. In India and Bulgaria, 'wiggling' the head from side to side indicates 'Yes', whereas a Dutch person would shake her head to express the same idea.

Channel. Messages must have a means by which they move from one person to another. This route is known as the channel (or channels, as much communication involves several channels at once). The channel can be sound, sight, words, telephone, the internet, mobile cellular phone and so on. The degree to which a communicator chooses one channel over another is often determined by his or her culture. In the United States, words are highly valued, while in some Mediterranean cultures, touch is a major communication channel. In Finland and Japan, silence is as significant a carrier of messages as words and sound.

Receiver. The receiver is the intended target of the message. The target person or group normally shares the same code as the source. Of course, in most interpersonal communication participants are both sources and receivers; this is the case even for mass communication nowadays with interactive media platforms. Unlike programmed computers, human beings do not respond uniformly to all messages, nor do they always compose the same message in exactly the same way. Individual differences characterized by race, sex, age, education, culture, values and attitudes, for example, can all affect how people both send and receive messages.

Encoding. Encoding is the process by which the source uses shared codes to convert concepts, thoughts and feelings into a message (McDaniel and Samovar, 2015). In encoding we select and arrange verbal and nonverbal symbols according to rules that are known and shared by the group. Although symbolic representation is universal, the particular codes selected, and how they are shared, are culturally based. For example, a member of one culture might see a close friend and decide to smile, encoding her message of greeting according to the 'rules' of her language community. A member of another culture might instead place her hands in front of the chest and bow to her friend, encoding the message of greeting according to a different set of cultural rules.

Decoding. Decoding is the process by which the receiver, as the target of the message, converts the coded message into meaning. Decoding permits the receiver to attach meaning to the source's message. Like encoding, the interpretation of the message is influenced by culture. The same coded message may be decoded differently by different people. For example, Italians may regard animated conversation and loud laughing in public as a sign of happiness, whereas a Thai woman might believe that such an outward display of emotions should be reserved for the privacy of one's home.

Noise. Noise refers to all factors that interfere with information transfer and the receipt of the message. Noise can be physical (distracting sounds or sights), psychological (nervousness) and semantic (different interpretations of a concept). For example, in Germany, individualism is a positive concept; it means people are independent, assertive and goal-oriented. In South Korea, however, individualism is more likely to be associated with selfishness and a lack of concern for the group – a negative feature in a culture that traditionally values a group orientation. Therefore, a message sent about this concept from a German person to a Korean may not be well received because of the culturally influenced semantic noise that affects the encoding and decoding of the message. When source and receiver have (even subtly) different interpretations of the same concept, the effect of communication will inevitably be affected.

Feedback. Feedback refers to the response of the receiver after receiving the message. It is information generated by the receiver and made available to the source, allowing the source to judge the communication while it is taking place. Feedback can function to adjust the attitudes and behaviours of both source and receiver and is yet another component that is modified by culture. For example, while members of US American culture would feel comfortable saying 'I don't agree with what you said' as a means of feedback in a conversation, members of Chinese culture would communicate the same thought by taking a deep breath.

Characteristics of communication

Communication is a dynamic process. Although a specific communication act (e.g., speaking) has definite beginning and ending points, the overall process of communication does not. Meanings are dynamic, continually changing as a function of earlier usage and interpretation. The encoding and decoding of messages is influenced by prior interactions between communicators, and feedback influences the subsequent exchange of messages. The dynamic nature of communication is also reflected in that once a word or action is deployed, it cannot be retracted. We probably all know the saying by the ancient Greek philosopher Heraclitus, 'You cannot step into the same river twice'. People cannot experience exactly the same thing twice with exactly the same feeling. As an example, you may see the same movie twice, but have different feelings each time. You cannot repeat exactly the same experience of seeing the movie for the first time. Similarly, we cannot take back what we said and did. Once you have said and done something, it is irretrievable – many people have found this out the hard way when using email, Facebook and Twitter, but it applies to all modes of communication. If you have hurt a friend's feelings, you can apologize, but you cannot unsay what you said or undo what you did.

Communication is interactive. Communication is interactive because it requires the active participation of at least two persons. To communicate, one has to address another person or persons. Of course, you can communicate with yourself (intrapersonal communication), but you are still interacting with another imagined self. You must act as if you are two people. Human communication is shaped by the anticipated response. During this interactive process, communicators may modify the content or form of their conversation. Their thoughts and feelings may also be adjusted during the interaction process. For example, a late arrival to a meeting might be interpreted by the other attendees as bad manners, and they might react with frowns. However, if they learned that the person's reason for being late was stopping to help someone injured in a car accident, their reactions would most likely change from negative to positive.

Communication is symbolic. A symbol is an arbitrarily selected and learned stimulus that represents something else. Symbols can be verbal or nonverbal, such as a sound, a mark on paper, a statue, Braille, a movement or a painting. They are the vehicles by which the thoughts and ideas of one person can be communicated to another. Human beings are able to generate, receive, store and manipulate symbols (McDaniel and Samovar, 2015). Words are not actual objects or ideas, but we use these symbols to create meaning. Meaning resides in people. Imagine how difficult communication could become if two people from different cultures come together with different symbol systems. Not only are languages different, but the same gesture can have different meanings. Patting a child on the head in Australia usually indicates affection; however, in Thai culture, it may be considered offensive, as it is thought to damage the spirit of the child, which resides in the head.

DO IT!

Make a list of five symbols that are related to the history, tradition or customs of your country or culture (e.g., the sign of the orange communicates Chinese people's wish for good luck in the New Year). Ask a classmate or a friend from a different cultural background from you to do the same. Share your symbols with your classmate or friend and discuss what symbols can tell you about a culture and people. Write a one-page summary of the cultural meanings of the symbols you have identified.

Communication is contextual. We interact with others not in isolation but in a specific setting. Communication always occurs in a context, and the nature of communication depends largely on this context (Littlejohn, 1996). A context stands for the cultural, physical, relational and perceptual environment in which communication occurs (Neuliep, 2017). A context is also historical, and cultures that are past-oriented may emphasize this facet of context. Dress, language, topic selection and the like are all adapted to contexts. For example, attending a graduation ceremony without wearing a shirt or using profanity in the classroom are likely to be frowned upon, whereas in other contexts these behaviours might be more acceptable. Context influences what we communicate and how we communicate – once again, these rules are culture-bound. Take the example of the classroom. In Mexico, children are encouraged to move around the classroom and to interact verbally and physically with their classmates; in Singapore, students are expected to remain in their seats during class, and not to talk to one another unless the teacher gives permission. The same behaviour is interpreted differently depending on the context in which it occurs.

THEORY CORNER

COORDINATED MANAGEMENT OF MEANING THEORY

Coordinated management of meaning (CMM) theory began as an interpretative theory focusing on interpersonal communication, but it has now become a practical theory to improve patterns of communication (Pearce, 2005). The term 'coordination' highlights the fact that whatever we do always intermeshes with the interpretations and actions of other people. CMM theorists identified three goals of the theory: (1) to understand who we are, what it means to live a life, and how that is related to particular instances of communication; (2) to render cultures comparable while acknowledging their incommensurability; and (3) to generate an illuminating critique of cultural practices. Given that we have to engage in interactions with people who are not like us, the challenge is to find ways of acting together in order to create a social world where cultural tensions are reduced and at the same time people from different cultural groups can find comfort and stability in their cultural traditions.

CMM theorists believe that communication is, at the same time, idiosyncratic and social, and that it is necessary to describe the cultural context if we are going to understand communication within and/or across cultures. It is also necessary to understand individuals' interpretations of their communication. Orbe and Camara (2010) examined how everyday discrimination is perceived by a diverse set of individuals. They collected 957 stories of discrimination as part of a larger study on uncertainty in oppressive forms of communication. Specifically, they focused on how a large, diverse group of individuals defined their experiences with discrimination – based on race, gender, age, sexual orientation and abilities – in similar and different ways. Using the CMM theoretical framework, their analysis revealed that individuals interpret everyday discrimination through the content of the message and how it is said.

REFERENCES

Orbe, Mark P. and Camara, Sakile K. (2010) 'Defining discrimination across cultural groups: Exploring the [un-]coordinated management of meaning', *International Journal of Intercultural Relations*, 34(1): 283–293.

Pearce, Barnett W. (2005) 'The coordinated management of meaning (CMM)', in W. B. Gudykunst (ed.), *Theorizing about Intercultural Communication*. Thousand Oaks, CA: Sage. pp. 35–54.

MODELS OF COMMUNICATION

Communication models are representations of communication processes and characteristics; they illustrate the main components of communication and their relationships to each other. We introduce two categories of communication models: linear and interactive. Models are simplified versions of theories. If theories need modification, so too do models. The key to the usefulness of a communication model is the degree to which it conforms to the underlying determinants of communicative behaviour (Mortensen, 1972).

The linear model

Early scholars conceptualized communication as transmitting information, concepts, understanding and thought, as if along a pipeline. The most influential *linear model* is

Claude Shannon and Warren Weaver's mathematical model of communication, presented in their book *The Mathematical Theory of Communication* (1949). Shannon developed the basic model of communication while conducting cryptographic research at Bell Laboratories during the Second World War. The original model was designed to mirror the functioning of radio and telephone technologies, consisting of three primary components: sender, channel and receiver. The sender was the part of a telephone a person speaks into, the channel was the telephone, and the receiver was the part of the telephone through which one could hear the person on the other end of the line. As an engineer for the Bell Telephone Company, Shannon's goal was to formulate a model to guide the most efficient way of transmitting electrical signals from one location to another (Shannon and Weaver, 1949). They also recognized that there may be background interference with the process of information transmission, referred to as *noise*. When the field of communication studies first emerged in the 1950s and 1960s, Shannon and Weaver's basic communication model was adapted to describe the process of human communication. The linear model was subsequently elaborated by non-mathematical scholars. David Berlo (1960) expanded it to create his Sender–Message–Channel–Receiver (SMCR) model of communication. The SMCR model proposes that effective communication requires the sender and the receiver to be on the same level of communication. For example, if the sender is a good speaker, then the receiver should have equally good listening skills.

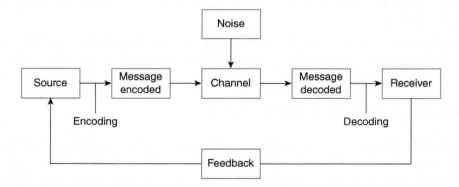

FIGURE 3.1   The linear model of communication

Source: Adapted from Shannon, Claude and Weaver, Warren (1949) *The Mathematical Theory of Communication*. Urbana, IL: University of Illinois Press. p. 5.

The linear model is often known today as the *transmission model*, which conceptualizes messages as 'containers' of meaning, and communication as a process of sending and receiving information. Although viewing communication as a linear process, the transmission model makes us aware of the ever-present danger of misunderstanding in communication. The transmission model was subsequently applied to study media effects. A typical example of this endeavour was reflected in Harold Lasswell's (1948) 5W model: 'Who', 'says What', 'in Which channel', 'to Whom', and 'with What effect'. Lasswell's primary interest was in the mass media and propaganda, and the 5W model embraced the 'administrative research' dominant among the pioneers of communication at the time (Gitlin, 1978). Although the 5W model was intended to direct people to media effects research, it was also useful when applied to other forms of communication, such as persuasion. The mathematical theory of information principles, upon which the transmission model is based, is sometimes regarded by communication scholars as evidence of their field's scientific status (Craig, 1999).

However, the linear model has encountered criticisms since the 1980s and 1990s, because it does not account for the complexity of communication. Some critics argue that the transmission model is flawed because this model constructs communication as a literal transmission of information from one location to another. In actual communication processes, the message is not like an object in a parcel which the receiver opens (Fiske, 1982). By limiting content to transmission, the linear model reduces communication to a merely technical process (Shepherd, 1993), whereas meaning is actually constituted symbolically during the communication process (Deetz, 1994). Moreover, communication is not a one-way process; oftentimes, it involves interaction. The critics suggest that the linear model should at least be supplemented, if not entirely replaced, by a model that conceptualizes communication as a constitutive process that produces and reproduces shared meaning (Pearce, 2005).

Wilbur Schramm (1954) was one of the first to challenge the mathematical model of communication. He conceived of decoding and encoding as activities maintained simultaneously by sender and receiver; he also made provision for a two-way interchange of messages. In actual communication, speaking and listening are not separate activities, nor do they occur one at a time. The sender channels a message to the receiver and the receiver then becomes the sender and channels a message to the original sender. This model has added feedback, indicating that communication is not a one-way but a two-way process. Even mass communication is a two-way process. For example, media organizations examine audience ratings to gauge the impact of their programmes. In this sense, both the audience and the media organization are senders and receivers. A strength of Schramm's model is that it provides the additional notion of the experience of the interactants. The model also includes context and postulates that a message may be different in meaning, depending on the specific context. Even so, Schramm's model, while less linear, still accounts only for bilateral communication between two parties. Complex, multiple levels of communication across several sources are beyond the scope of this model.

THEORY CORNER

CONCEPTUALIZING 'WHOM' IN DIGITAL MEDIA

In the linear model of communication, the 'whom' (the target of communication messages) receives the output of communication, and as a result may change opinions or behaviour. The advent of digital media, however, allowed 'whom' to enter the sphere of media content producers, who thus become 'influencers' themselves. For digital and social media, 'whom' may differ greatly from communication offline. The norms governing communication in a digital setting are different from those in face-to-face interactions, and also different from the traditional mass communication spectrum of print, television and radio. The intersection between interpersonal and mass communication necessitates a reconceptualization of audience in digital media. This is the beginning of an ongoing theoretical journey to enhance our knowledge about how audiences create media and media create audiences.

Think of interactive storytelling in video games, where the narrative and its evolution can be influenced and co-produced by the users themselves. Video game players become actors and directors at the same time. They choose who they are and how they will act in the digital world. Many video games stress exploration, unpredictability and branching narrative possibilities, and show how audiences/players help to create digital content itself. Digital technology has not only challenged traditional definitions of interpersonal and mass communication; it has also changed the ways in which we develop relationships with others. This can be illustrated in virtual social worlds, where inhabitants live a virtual life analogous to their life in the real world. In virtual social worlds, 'residents' appear in the form of avatars and interact in an apparent three-dimensional virtual environment that more and more closely resembles real-life settings (Kaplan and Haenlein, 2009). Arguably, the most prominent example of virtual social worlds is the *Second Life* application, founded and managed by the San Francisco-based company Linden Research, Inc. Residents of *Second Life* can do simple things that are possible in real life, such as speaking to other avatars, taking a walk and enjoying the virtual sunshine. *Second Life* also allows users to create content (e.g., to design virtual clothing or furniture items) and sell this content to others in exchange for Linden Dollars, a virtual currency traded against the US dollar on the *Second Life* website.

REFERENCE

Kaplan, Andreas and Haenlein, Michael (2009) 'The fairyland of *Second Life*: About social words and how to use them', *Business Horizons*, 52(6): 563–572.

The interactive model

Further development on Schramm's view of two-way communication processes is reflected in Dean Barnlund's (1970) *transactional model*, which was developed as an elaboration of the linear model of communication. Similar to Schramm's view, the basic premise of the transactional model is that individuals are simultaneously engaging in the sending and receiving of messages. The transactional model posits communication as the process of continuous change and transformation, where people, their environments and the medium used are changing at multiple levels. Thus, it assumes that communicators are independent as well as interdependent (Barnlund, 1970). Embedded in Barnlund's transactional model is the constructionist approach, which relates communication to an individual or a group of people in social, cultural and relational contexts. The constructionist approach describes communication as a process in which communicators generate social realities within social, relational and cultural contexts; contexts, in turn, shape communication. It is this emphasis on context and people that forms the basis for the *interactive model of communication*.

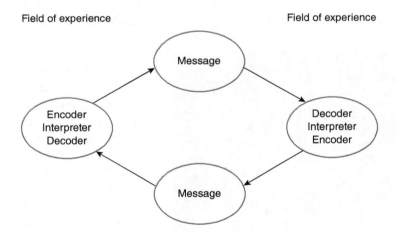

FIGURE 3.2 Schramm's interactive model of communication

Source: Adapted from Schramm, Wilbur (1971) 'The nature of communication between humans', in W. Schramm and D. F. Roberts (eds.), *The Process and Effects of Mass Communication*. Urbana, IL: University of Illinois Press. p. 24.

Everett Rogers and Thomas Steinfatt (1999) put forward a more elaborate interactive model, based on their understanding of communication as a process through which participants create and share meaning in order to reach mutual understanding. One of the major changes that intercultural communication scholars made to the linear model was to emphasize the subjectivity of communication. When the source and receiver are individuals instead of machines, their perceptions, paradigms and past experiences inevitably filter the encoding and decoding process. This subjectivity is one reason why the receiver seldom decodes a message into exactly the same meaning that the source has in mind. Furthermore, the participants exert mutual control over the process, rather than serving as either active sources or passive receivers. This principle of communication applies as much to intercultural communication as it does to other types of human communication. Advocates of the interactive model in the field of intercultural communication propose that communication systems operate within the confines of cultural rules and expectations: a message may have different meanings associated with it, depending on the culture in which it is sent or received.

In this chapter, we adopt the interactive model proposed by Rogers and Steinfatt (1999) to explain intercultural communication phenomena. This model replaces the terms 'sender' and 'receiver' with 'communicator'; in addition, it incorporates communicators' perceptions into the model. This model represents communication as a process of creating and sharing meaning in order to reach mutual understanding. The process itself is influenced by communicators' perceptions of the context and of each other. The model also theorizes each communication action as building upon the previous experience of the communicators and as having consequences for future communication. Rogers and Steinfatt's model reflects the dynamic nature of the communication process as well as the potential influence of perceived cultural differences on the communication process. Indeed, James Carey (1977) called the interactive model a 'ritual' model. He claimed that a ritual model of communication is about sharing, participating, drawing people together and building a community through communication processes.

PHOTO 3.2   The Hollywood Walk of Fame in Los Angeles is a public monument to achievements in the entertainment industry.

THEORY CORNER

COMMUNICATION ACCOMMODATION THEORY

Communication accommodation theory (CAT) was developed in the context of intercultural communication in the 1970s (see Giles, 2016). The theory is based on three assumptions: (1) communication is embedded in a socio-historical context; (2) communication is about both exchange of meaning and negotiation of personal and social identities; and (3) communicators achieve their goals by accommodating (or not) through language, paralanguage, discourse and nonverbal behaviours, including dress and appearance. Key concepts of this theory are *ingroups* and *outgroups* (communicators create group boundaries to include or exclude others), accommodation (communicators adjust their communicative behaviour because of a desire for social integration, approval, identification or communication effectiveness), and non-accommodation (communicators maintain social distance from others by accentuating differences).

CAT has been applied to the media, family relations, doctor–patient communication, job interviews, police–citizen encounters, the courts, music and dance performance, and even messages left on telephone answering machines and online communication. Lexical convergence has been documented as a primary means of accommodation, partly represented by the use of politeness terms to influence perceptions of rapport and to build trust. An interesting area is the application of this theory to investigate temporal convergence, such as in instant messaging conversations. For example, Riordan, Markman and Stewart (2012) conducted a study to examine temporal convergence in instant messaging conversations between friends in social and task-related interactions. Findings from their study revealed a general tendency towards convergence on both length and duration. Not only temporal cues, but also the extent to which communicators adapt to each other's use of these cues, influence the outcomes of communication. CAT adds a level to our understanding of effective communication by taking account of cultural and social identities as well as skills. Training programmes are now being developed to apply these skills in interpersonal, mass media and social media communication.

REFERENCES

Giles, Howard (ed.) (2016) *Communication Accommodation Theory: Negotiating Personal Relationships and Social Identities across Contexts*. Cambridge: Cambridge University Press.

Riordan, Monica A., Markman, Kris M. and Stewart, Craig O. (2012) 'Communication accommodation in instant messaging: An examination of temporal convergence', *Journal of Language and Social Psychology*, 32(1): 84–95.

DO IT!

Talk to five friends or classmates, asking them to tell you what their indicators of successful communication are, who they believe is at fault when communication goes wrong, and if it makes sense to say that two parties in conflict are communicating successfully if they decode each other's messages correctly, even though they continue to disagree. Collate their answers and write a one-page summary of your findings.

INFLUENCE OF CULTURE ON COMMUNICATION

Culture is learned and shared through communication. Culture and communication, therefore, mutually influence one another, producing different behavioural patterns in different contexts. Culture influences how we adapt and learn, our perception of reality, our language patterns, habits, customs, expectations, norms and roles – in other words, it shapes what we do, how we look, what we say and how we say it. Communication and culture are inseparable. One implication of this insight, as Dodd (1998) noted, is that culture generates symbols, rituals, customs and formats. In most Western cultures, the symbols for success include an individual's acquisition of degrees, promotions, certificates, money, material objects and technology. In other cultures, such as Chinese culture, the achievements of the primary group are more important than those of individuals. Cultural misunderstandings occur when we fail to interpret communication behaviours in a specific cultural context.

Here is an example. As a cultural practice of showing modesty, a Chinese technician in a Sino-German joint venture factory expresses some doubt over how to fix a machine breakdown when interacting with his German manager. The technician's hesitation is intentional and meant to 'give face' to the German manager, by showing that the technician does not know much more than the manager (who is supposed to be more knowledgeable). However, this hesitation might be misinterpreted by his German manager as a lack of confidence or ability, rather than an expression of modesty. Many cultural imprints are subtle and elusive, if not beyond conscious recognition. Nonetheless, we tend to become more aware of the cultural rules governing our behaviour when we interact with culturally different others. Communication involves sharing – what is shared and understood in the communication process is meaning. Difficulties may arise when we try to share meaning with people whose communication behaviours are governed by cultural rules different from our own.

The intricate link between culture and communication can be illustrated in a number of ways. In the first place, culture teaches us significant rules, rituals and procedures, such as our orientation towards time, perceived power relations, how to dress, when and what to eat, and how to work. The overall process of learning these things is called *socialization*, which refers to the process by which we develop a sense of proper and improper behaviour and communication within the confines of those cultural rules (Samovar and McDaniel, 2015). Think of one of the many thousands of rules that your culture or your family may have taught you. As a young child, when you went to dinner at a friend's house your mother probably told you that before you leave you should thank the hostess and say the food was very nice and you enjoyed it very much. In this way, you consciously learned a rule of politeness. Politeness, however, may involve very different rules in different cultures. In the more traditional homes of Slovenia (the former Yugoslavia), guests are greeted with bread and salt to show that they are part of the family (in the past, this was also a practice in Great Britain and Ireland, but it no longer is). When meeting people in Denmark, introductions are often made on a first-name basis with a handshake. It is important not to speak in a loud voice – Danish culture views this as being disrespectful. In Russia, when you are invited to a meal, you can expect the hosts to offer you a lot of food, and they will expect you to finish it all – it is through food that their generosity and respect for you as a guest is expressed. What is polite or rude falls under the rubric of rules, rituals and procedures taught by our culture.

These rules are very important: they are the means by which we determine inclusion and self-worth, and they help to define boundaries between 'us' and 'them'.

More than simply determining and teaching the 'rules', culture cultivates and reinforces beliefs and values. Our core understanding of the world is taught in a cultural context. Consequently, we develop culturally reinforced approaches to thoughts and beliefs about the world. These beliefs and values are reflected in our communication behaviour. For example, Australian culture teaches people the values of a 'fair go': independence, privacy, competition, mateship and directness. 'Fair enough' – a common Australian expression – reveals the value placed

PHOTO 3.3   Day of the Dead (Día de Muertos) is a holiday celebrated throughout Mexico to remember the dead.

on equality in this cultural context. In reflecting these values, Australian communication styles tend to be more direct. It is common for two people to confront each other to 'sort things out' when there is interpersonal conflict. In an Asian context such as India, however, a third party might be brought in to act as an intermediary to resolve the conflict. This communication style avoids direct confrontation and loss of face, and reflects the values of harmony, non-competitiveness and loyalty to superiors in Asian culture. Both the Asian and Australian approaches are valid within their cultural context, and they serve to highlight the impact of cultural beliefs and values on communication behaviour.

Furthermore, culture teaches us how to develop relationships with others. Every communication event establishes a certain relationship. Initiating and maintaining relationships with others is one of the most necessary and challenging functions of human survival. From our relationships with others we receive feedback that we use to evaluate ourselves. The relationships formed in a cultural context generate a dynamic of roles and expectations. Where to stand, how far to stand from each other, when to talk to others, when to visit, when to call/not to call people at home, and the level of formality in language are highly influenced by the nature of the relationship between the communicators. According to Yum (1988), East Asian cultures tend to foster a long-term interpersonal relationship characterized by complementary social reciprocity. In this type of relationship, people always feel indebted to others. For example, the Chinese saying 'to return a drop of kindness with a fountain of kindness' indicates how important it is for one to return the favour in a social interaction. On the other hand, North American culture does not treat commitments or obligations as such important elements in interpersonal relationship development as do East Asian cultures. Instead, they might consider extra generosity in a relationship as a potential threat to freedom or autonomy, and tend to prefer reciprocity – returning another's generosity at the same level. Hence, for example, it is common for Westerners to split the bill when having dinner together with friends.

Our verbal and nonverbal behaviours reflect our cultural imprints. Each culture expects a particular communication style. Features such as loudness, pitch, tempo, turn-taking and gestures characterize communication behaviours and vary considerably across cultures. If you buy clothes from a marketplace stall in Hong Kong, you have to be prepared to engage in intensive bargaining, loud and hard. Hence, the stereotypical perception is that Asians are good at haggling over price. In America, it would seem unusual to see two male friends kiss in public, while in Peruvian culture this behaviour would be perceived as commonplace. In Norway, the traditional national costume is called Bunad. It dates back to the early 1800s and has lots of embroidery and jewellery on it. It is part of Norway's culture to wear the Bunad as national dress for folk dancing, at official celebrations and weddings, and especially on 17 May, which is Constitution Day in Norway. Wearing it means communicating your cultural identity to the world. But it is also important to understand the diversity of Bunad dress: it comes in different styles for different regions of Norway. Communication shows us that we are alike and we are different. We are similar in that each of us experiences the same feelings – anger, joy, sadness, anxiety. However, our unique cultural experiences and habits keep us apart. Misunderstanding occurs because we do not understand each other's cultural rules governing communication behaviour.

DO IT!

A person's name often has a specific meaning. Names are perceived to have consequences for an individual and because they often signal family or group memberships. Even in cultures where the literal meanings of names are not seen as having protective powers, names may be chosen with great care. Talk to a friend or classmate from a culture different from your own. Find out from each other how names are usually chosen in each person's culture, and give an example to show the cultural meaning associated with some names. Write a one-page summary of these names, their meanings, and what they say about each culture.

SUMMARY

- Human communication is multifaceted in nature and finding a single definition of communication is difficult, if not impossible.
- Scholars tend to agree on some basic components of communication and its characteristics, and there is consensus that communication occurs in a particular context.
- Models of communication provide a useful blueprint to see how the communication process works, but they are usually not complex enough to capture communication as it is experienced.
- Scholarly debates surround the definition of communication; digital media challenge the boundary between interpersonal and mass communication.
- Our cultural upbringing provides an inventory consisting of values, sets of expectations and norms which influence our communication behaviour.

JOIN THE DEBATE

In 1990, the *Western Journal of Speech Communication* published Michael Motley's article calling for a re-examination of Watzlawick, Bavelas and Jackson's (1967) axiom that 'one cannot *not* communicate'. The main theme of Motley's article was that, on the one hand, this axiom may be taken to suggest that all

CAN WE *NOT* COMMUNICATE?

behaviour is communicative behaviour. On the other hand, several generally accepted postulates of communication, such as that it is interactive, encoded and symbolic, clearly suggest that not all behaviour is communicative. The debate centres on whether communication depends more upon the *receiver*'s interpretation of behaviour or on the *sender*'s intentions and orientation to it. This is an important debate. Certainly much communication is intentional – we use verbal or nonverbal codes often as an attempt to modify the behaviour of other people. Thus, communication is not a random or unconscious activity, but rather a consciously planned action. People may thus be very surprised that their messages are misunderstood by members of another culture. However, other scholars propose that the concept of intentionality does not account for all the circumstances where messages are assigned meaning, such as yawning at a meeting. What is your view on whether communication is intentional or unintentional? What are your reasons for taking the position you do?

CASE STUDY

COMMUNICATING BEAUTY THROUGH BARBIE DOLLS

Every culture has a way of communicating beauty standards. The rise of Western beauty standards around the world can be observed through the successful global sales of Mattel's Barbie doll, an icon of American fashion and beauty. Three Barbie dolls are sold every second around the world, and roughly 1 billion Barbie dolls are sold each year. Barbie has a way of dictating and establishing cultural norms globally. A toy Barbie powerfully represents a tall figure with long slim legs, a thin waist, sizeable buttocks and large breasts. The computer magnification of Barbie places her at 5' 10" in height and 110 lbs in weight, whereas the average size of American women is 5' 4" in height and 145 lbs in weight (Chinyere, 2007). That is why Barbie is a problematic icon for women, as has been argued by Mary Rogers in her book *Barbie Culture* (1999).

Barbie has been around for almost six decades. The doll was created in 1959 for the Mattel Industry by Ruth Handler. Inspired by a German doll, Lilli (a 'pin-up' for German men after the Second World War, derived from a comic), Handler designed the doll and named it after her daughter, Barbara (Rogers, 1999). The result is a tall blonde beauty. Playing with Barbie dolls communicates femininity. It gives little girls opportunities to costume and decorate her, to style her hair, and to position her in different settings, such as a school or a shopping mall. Although there is no research to show how much time girls in different cultures spend on playing with dolls, it is estimated that they spend about two hours a day during their pre-school years (Karniol, Stuemler-Cohen and Lahav-Gur, 2012).

Barbie is not only a lot of fun for children, but also helps to socialize girls into particular female-stereotyped behaviours, such as caring for children.

Barbie dolls communicate fashion and style. When they were first introduced in 1959, they were regarded as teenage fashion models (Rogers, 1999). Historically, dolls were first documented during the Renaissance, when they were used as diplomatic gifts to help women become familiar with foreign dress styles and promote fashion trends. Dolls were introduced as play toys in France in the late nineteenth century (Karniol et al., 2012). Fashion dolls differ from other types of dolls in having more adult characteristics. Before Barbie, girls played at being mothers to dolls that were generally portrayed as babies or young children, Barbie, which was more of a teenager or adult doll, transferred girls to the make-believe world of Barbie and her friends, as well as her social, occupational and consumer lifestyles. Barbies became flight attendants, went on dates and had many parties. Many authors point out that the number of Barbie dolls that girls possess is on the rise. It is estimated that an average girl owns seven Barbies (Karniol et al., 2012). Thus, Barbie has become more than just a toy. She has become an icon of female beauty and fashion. Even for girls who may not identify with her, the odds are that they will 'know' Barbie.

Criticism of the limitations of Barbie as a blonde white (Western) woman led to the expansion of her world to include non-blondes and racial minorities, such as 'Christie' (black), introduced in 1966, and 'Teresa' (Hispanic), introduced in 1988. There are also Indian, Japanese and Chinese Barbie dolls, and Barbies of other nationalities. In this way, Barbie has brought Western cultures to other environments and made them more local. For example, the Chinese standards of beauty have been heavily influenced by Western beauty images, with the influx of Western movies, pop culture, and the fashion and beauty industry, ever since China re-opened its doors to the outside world. The prevailing Western images of beauty in China can be easily found in films, television programmes, fashion magazines, advertisements, and dolls. Wen (2013) shows how China's market is so lucrative that Mattel, the world's premier toy company and the producer of Barbie, opened its first Barbie flagship store in Shanghai in 2009. Richard Dickson, a senior vice president in charge of the Barbie brand, said that Shanghai was chosen as the site for its flagship store because of its large population and vast market potential (Wen, 2013).

However, in other cultural contexts, for example in some Islamic countries like Saudi Arabia, sales of Barbie dolls are prohibited because she promotes the 'wrong values'. The Saudi religious police (the Committee for the Propagation of Virtue and Prevention of Vice) denounced the doll as a blasphemous object, a threat to Islamic teachings. As Dunn and Dunn (2016) write, the Institute for the Intellectual Development of Children and Young Adults in Iran in 2002 produced Sara, and her brother Dara, to replace Barbie and Ken (Barbie's boyfriend). 'Sara and Dara wear modest clothing to display traditional Islamic values. I think Barbie is more harmful than an American missile', explains the Iranian toy seller Masoumeh Rahimi, stressing that the danger of Barbie is that the doll is a threat to Iranian culture (Dunn and Dunn, 2016: 276). In Iran, the Fatima doll was created as an authentic Islamic doll and is designed to fight 'the enemy's cultural invasion' (Dunn and Dunn, 2016). Similarly, in Indonesia Sukmawati Suryaman described the process of creating the Salma Islamic doll for the Indonesian market. She was inspired by watching her niece play with a Barbie and was concerned that her niece would lose connections to Indonesian culture. Suryaman explained: 'I was thinking I wish we have these dolls in traditional garb that fit our tradition. As we all know, children are easily influenced and often imitate their toys' (Dunn and Dunn, 2016: 277).

REFERENCES FOR CASE STUDY

Chinyere, Okafor G. (2007) 'Global encounters: Barbie in Nigerian Agbogho-mmuo mask context', *Journal of African Cultural Studies*, 19(1): 37–54.

Dunn, Rima and Dunn, Adam (2016) 'Bad dolls/reappropriating badness: Performing the feminine with reference to Arab Muslim dolls and Tiqqun's young-girl', *Journal of Middle East Women's Studies*, 12(2): 275–283.

Karniol, Rachel, Stuemler-Cohen, Tamara and Lahav-Gur, Yael (2012) 'Who likes Bratz? The impact of girls' age and gender role orientation on preferences for Barbie versus Bratz', *Psychology and Marketing*, 29(11): 897–906.

Rogers, Mary (1999) *Barbie Culture*. London: Sage.

Wen, Hua (2013) *Buying Beauty: Cosmetic Surgery in China*. Hong Kong: Hong Kong University Press.

QUESTIONS FOR DISCUSSION

1. Do you think fashion dolls communicate beauty standards for a culture? Do you think the influence is on girls only or both boys and girls? Why?

2. Many women strive for the so-called modern, slim and tall appearance that is inspired by Western cultures. Do you think such trends may ultimately suppress traditional, local identities of female beauty?

3. Mattel's former Barbie general manager and senior vice president Richard Dickson once claimed that 'People grew up with Barbie'. Do you have any memories of Barbie? What are they, and what do you think they mean?

4. Do you think that Barbie can stand as an icon of whiteness and femininity, regardless of cultural context?

5. What dolls do young girls in your culture play with? What kind of beauty ideals do these dolls communicate to the society?

FURTHER READINGS

Baraldi, Claudio (2006) 'New forms of intercultural communication in a globalized world', _International Communication Gazette_, 68(1): 53–69.

This article reviews the changing functions of intercultural communication from the seventeenth century to the twentieth century, especially the last decade of that century, when a transcultural form of communication based on dialogue was proposed as a basis for cross-cultural adaptation, multicultural identities and a construction of a hybrid multicultural society. This article discusses difficulties in intercultural communication and argues for the need of a new form of intercultural dialogue, dealing with differences and conflicts.

Bovillain, Nancy (2014) _Language, Culture and Communication: The Meaning of Messages_ (7th edn). Upper Saddle River, NJ: Pearson/Prentice-Hall.

This book presents a discussion of the multifaceted meanings and uses of language. It emphasizes the ways that language encapsulates speakers' meanings and intentions, using data from cultures and languages throughout the world in order to document both the similarities and differences in human language. The book is a useful source of reference, particularly for students who are entering the field of intercultural communication from the field of language or linguistics.

Craig, Robert T. (1999) 'Communication theory as a field', _Communication Theory_, 9(2): 119–161.

This essay reconstructs communication theory as a dialogical-dialectical field according to two principles: the constitutive model of communication as a meta-model, and theory as meta-discursive practice. The essay argues that all communication theories are mutually relevant and that each communication theory derives from certain beliefs about communication while challenging other beliefs. The complementarities and tensions among traditions generate a theoretical meta-discourse that intersects with and potentially informs the ongoing practical meta-discourse in society.

Eadie, William F. and Goret, Robin (2013) 'Theories and models of communication: Foundations and heritage', in P. Cobley and P. J. Schulz (eds.), *Theories and Models of Communication*. Berlin/Boston, MA: Walter de Gruyter. pp. 17–36.

This chapter provides a comprehensive chart of the historical influences on the theories and models that shaped the communication discipline. It illustrates the importance of US and European scholars from not only the beginnings of the communication discipline, but also including those who were pre-eminent in other academic disciplines, such as sociology, psychology, political science and journalism. The chapter also examines emerging scholarship from Asia that focuses on understanding cultural differences through communication theories.

Fuchs, Christian (2017) *Social Media: A Critical Introduction* (2nd edn). London: Sage.

This book provides a critical discussion on the complexities and contradictions of social media and the Information Society. With social media changing how we use and understand everything from communication and the news to transport, more than ever it is essential to ask questions about the business and politics of social media. This second edition takes readers into the politics and economy of social media in China and puts forward powerful arguments for how to achieve a social media that serves the purposes of a just and fair world.

SAGE VIDEO SOURCES

In this video Professor Charlton Mcilwain discusses how culture affects communication. It will help you to achieve the learning objective of understanding the influence of culture on communication. Watch the video to learn about how different perspectives on time, power, stereotypes and more influence communication.

This video is available at http://study.sagepub.com/liu3e

The eye sees only what the mind is prepared to comprehend.

Robertson Davies, Canadian novelist, 1913–1995

4

PERCEPTION AND CATEGORIZATION

LEARNING OBJECTIVES

At the end of this chapter, you should be able to:

- Define perception and identify three stages of the perception process.

- Explain social categorization and its impact on communication.

- Analyse the influence of culture on perception.

- Identify the impact of ethnocentrism, stereotypes, prejudice and racism on intercultural communication.

INTRODUCTION

We receive information about the world around us through our sense of sight, sound, smell, taste and touch. These stimuli are selected, organized and interpreted, and from them we create a meaningful picture of our world. Much like a computer, the human mind processes information in a sequence of stages akin to data entry, storage and retrieval, with each stage involving a specific operation on incoming information. The first stage of information processing is *perception*, which refers to how we see or sense things around us. Human perception is an active process in which we use our sensory organs to selectively identify the existence of stimuli and then subject them to evaluation and interpretation. The information we manage every day can be external or internal. While knowledge, past experiences and feelings make up our internal world of information, people, events and objects are sources of external information. Successful information processing depends on the merging of external and internal information. To use the computer metaphor again, how people enter, store and retrieve information is a combination of what they are experiencing (external) with what they know and feel (internal). The images of our world, based on our merging of internal and external stimuli, become filters to guide further information processing. Since the way we behave is influenced by how we perceive the world around us, perception is the very basis of how we communicate with others.

This chapter concentrates on the human perception process and the relationship between perception and culture. We first describe three stages of the perception process: selection, categorization and interpretation. Next, the chapter explains the social categorization of people and its impact on how categorization influences our intergroup and intercultural communication. We discuss the influence of culture on perception, using various examples to illustrate how human perception is related to beliefs, values, worldviews and attitudes. Violating the expectations of culturally governed behavioural rules potentially impairs further communication. Finally, the chapter explains the formation of ethnocentrism, stereotypes, prejudice, racism and their impact on intercultural communication. The chapter emphasizes that although information processing is a universal phenomenon, it is nevertheless influenced by culture. It follows, therefore, that if culturally different people vary in their interpretation of reality, communication problems may occur.

STAGES OF THE PERCEPTION PROCESS

Human information processing involves three stages, each of which can be influenced by culture. Culture provides us with a perceptual frame of reference through which information is selected, categorized and interpreted.

The selection stage

The first stage in the process is selection, in which information is received via the senses and attended to and interpreted by the brain. Selection plays a major part in the larger process of converting environmental stimuli into meaningful experience. There is an enormous array of stimuli in everyday life, but we are limited in the number of stimuli we can meaningfully process. This is where the selection process helps us to discern those stimuli that are immediately or potentially useful to us. For example, if you intend to rent an apartment, you are more likely to pay more attention to the real estate section in a newspaper than those who are without such a need.

Scholars argue that human beings do not consciously 'see' an object unless they pay direct, focused attention to that object, engaging in what is known as selective perception. Selective perception involves three steps: selective exposure, selective attention and selective retention (Klopf, 1995). We selectively expose ourselves to certain kinds of information from our environment, pay attention to the elements of this information that are immediately relevant to us, and selectively retain for later recall the information that is likely to be used in the future. For example, if your budget for the rent is $2,000 per month, as you read the 'For rent' section of an online newspaper you will disregard accommodation above your budget and remember only those within your budget. Another example is the so-called DREAMers in the United States. The term DREAMer has been used to describe young undocumented immigrants who were brought to the United States as children and have lived and gone to school there. They pay special attention to different bills in Congress that might grant them legal status, and allow them to stay in the United States. These examples show that not only is perception a selective process, but we also share the three perceptual tendencies of closure, familiarity and expectations (Goss, 1995).

Closure refers to humans' tendency to see things as complete wholes instead of incomplete configurations. Based on a tiny amount of data, people often make inferences about an incomplete sentence, figure, thought or idea. Figure 4.1 illustrates this point – while the triangle and circle are presented as partial forms, most people tend to see a full triangle and a full circle.

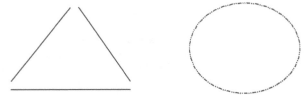

FIGURE 4.1   Incomplete triangle and circle

Familiarity refers to people using their existing knowledge to identify what they see. We are more inclined to recognize the familiar than the unfamiliar aspects of things. When presented with Figure 4.2, it is likely that people will see two overlapping squares rather than three irregular shapes, the reason being that we are more familiar with the former, and tend to look for the familiar rather than the unusual.

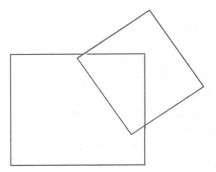

FIGURE 4.2   Three irregular shapes or two squares

Expectation can be illustrated in the old adage that we see what we want to see and hear what we want to hear. Perception involves expectations; the more frequently we see something, the more inclined we are to form a 'fixed' image of that thing in our mind which informs our future expectations of it. For example, we expect older people to have white hair and workers in childcare centres to be female. Over time, these 'fixed' images become habits and make it difficult for us to see the same thing differently. This is demonstrated in Figure 4.3. The saying is well known, so you might not immediately detect the duplication of the word 'one', but instead read it according to your expectation of what it should be.

FIGURE 4.3   Ungrammatical sentence

The notions of closure, familiarity and expectation show that perception is both a product and process. As a process, it is a way of forming images in the head based on recognizable objects, thoughts, ideas and categories of people. As a product, perception stores those images in the memory to be retrieved and utilized when we need them.

The categorization stage

Humans are surrounded by such an enormous amount of information in the environment that it is impossible to process it all at once. It is therefore necessary to employ some mental economy strategies (Neuliep, 2017). *Categorization* is one such strategy, defined as the process of ordering the environment by grouping persons, objects and events on the basis of similar features or characteristics (Tajfel, 1978). Categories are useful because they help the human brain to reduce uncertainty and increase the accuracy of predictions. Categories assist us in making attributions about the behaviour of others and help us to recall information. For example, we may categorize books by subjects such as literature, education, history, law, health and so forth. We may categorize people based on skin colour, race, sex, language, occupation, political affiliation, geographic location or desirable/undesirable qualities. Once people are categorized, other associated collective traits are also attributed to them. The fact that membership categories are associated with specific features and activities provides people with a powerful resource for making sense of their social world, allowing them to make discursive connections to people in the membership categories (Tajfel, 1978).

THEORY CORNER

ATTRIBUTION THEORY

Attribution theory was initially developed by Fritz Heider in 1958 and has been modified since that time by Edward Jones, Keith Davis and Harold Kelley, all of whom are social psychologists. According to Heider (1958), a person seeking to understand why another person acted in a certain way may attribute causes to the behaviour in question. A person can make internal or external attributions. Internal attribution refers to the inference that a person is behaving in a certain way because of something about that person, such as attitude, beliefs or personality. External attribution

(Continued)

ascribes situational causes to a person's behaviour. Attributions, whether internal or external, are significantly driven by emotional and motivational factors. While we commonly attribute our own success and others' failures to internal factors, we tend to attribute our own failures and other people's success to external ones.

Attribution theory has been applied in a wide range of areas, including psychology, management, criminal law, marketing, education, decision making and ethics. For example, Park and colleagues (2013) studied the deadly shooting incident on the Virginia Tech University campus in April 2007, in which the perpetrator, a Korean American, killed 32 people and injured 17. The researchers compared non-Korean Americans, Korean Americans, Koreans in the United States, and Koreans in Korea in terms of their attributions and emotions concerning the shooting incident. Participants were asked to rate the extent to which they attributed the cause of the incident to the American society or the perpetrator, their emotions (e.g., sad or upset), and how they categorized the perpetrator (e.g., American or Korean). Findings showed that people residing in the United States had more negative emotions than Koreans in Korea. Americans who viewed the perpetrator as a Korean were more likely to hold the perpetrator responsible, while Koreans who viewed him as an American were more likely to attribute the cause to American society. This study showed that not only attribution of the cause but also emotions regarding the incident can differ depending on individuals' self-categorization (as American or Korean).

REFERENCES

Heider, Fritz (1958) *The Psychology of Interpersonal Relations*. New York: Wiley.

Park, Hee S., Yun, Doshik, Choi, Hye J., Lee, Hye E., Lee, Dong W. and Ahn, Jiyoung (2013) 'Social identity, attribution, and emotion: Comparisons of Americans, Korean Americans, and Koreans', *International Journal of Psychology*, 48(5): 922–934.

The interpretation stage

Interpretation is the attachment of meaning to data obtained through the sensory organs. It is synonymous with decoding in communication. People filter information physiologically (e.g., hearing, eyesight, touch), sociologically (e.g., demographics, group membership) and psychologically (e.g., attitudes, beliefs and dispositions), according to Goss (1995). When interpreting, we tend to rely on familiar contexts and compare new stimuli with them in order to look for clues. The more ambiguous the stimuli, the more room there is for differing interpretations. Consequently, the same situation can be interpreted differently by different people. Figure 4.4 provides a set of optical illusions. Different people may interpret them differently depending on their past experiences and their familiarity with the context in which each image is situated. While the physical mechanism of perception is much the same in all people, assigning meaning is not.

FIGURE 4.4   Optical illusions

Perception is a learned process and therefore subject to cultural influences (Samovar et al., 2013). For example, an American mother may interpret assertiveness in her children's speech as positive, whereas a Korean mother who observes the same behaviour in her children might regard it as disrespectful and lacking in discipline. Similarly, the Dutch regard an outspoken person as credible, while the Japanese tend to consider constant talking as a sign of shallowness. In the Netherlands, people tend to respond positively to a direct approach to resolving an interpersonal conflict, yet this same behaviour is frowned upon in most Asian cultures. The issue of interpretation becomes more complex when we factor in further variables such as age, gender, social status, and relationship between communicators. Misinterpretation of the information that has been perceived has the potential to impede intercultural interactions. The influence of culture on perception and intercultural communication, therefore, cannot be overstated.

SOCIAL CATEGORIZATION AND INTERCULTURAL COMMUNICATION

People categorize for a variety of reasons – to reduce uncertainty, maintain self-esteem and draw distinctions between ingroups (the groups they belong to) and outgroups (the groups they do not belong to). Individuals construct social categories, such as sports clubs, liberals and Jews, and use their beliefs, attitudes, feelings and behaviours as prototypes to differentiate their own group from other groups that are salient in the situation. On the positive side, categorization helps to give incoming information structure and reduces uncertainty in our environment. However, in categorizing people, we can overlook individual elements and overgeneralize based on group membership.

Social categorization and intergroup communication

Research on intergroup relations indicates that once established, categories have a filtering effect on perceptions, so that the mere categorization of persons into groups is sufficient to foster bias (Tajfel, 1978). This leads us to the perception that we (the ingroup) are who we are because they (the outgroup) are *not* what we are. Hogg and Abrams (1988) argue that individuals are more inclined to align themselves with the norms of their group when they experience a sense of uncertainty. Think of what it means to be 'white', and how 'whiteness' works as an invisible marker. Indigenous critical theorist Aileen Moreton-Robinson (2015: 13) describes 'whiteness' as 'the white possessive', and she gives a sense of how national space is experienced by those at whose expense it exists. According to Moreton-Robinson, white possession is hypervisible. Indigenous people experience it on the streets of Otago or Sydney, in the tourist shops in Vancouver, or in a restaurant in New York. She feels that these cities signify with every building and every street that the land is now possessed by other – as signs of white possession are embedded everywhere in the landscape.

Social identity theory posits that a product of social categorization is social identity formation (Hogg and Abrams, 1988). Individuals form identities based on membership of social groups, based on gender, political affiliation, profession and so forth. Through this process, society is internalized by individuals on the basis of social categories. Social identities connect individuals to society through group memberships which influence their beliefs, attitudes and behaviour in their relationships with members of other social groups. It is important to remember that social identities, and indeed our group memberships, are not fixed. As our memberships or the social context changes, we need to reconstruct or renegotiate our social identities. Indian feminist scholar Chandra Talpade Mohanty vividly illustrated this point by drawing upon her own experience (Mohanty, 2003: 190):

> Growing up in India, I was Indian; teaching in high school in Nigeria, I was a foreigner (still Indian), albeit a familiar one. As a graduate student in Illinois, I was first a 'Third World' foreign student, and then a person of color. Doing research in London, I was black. As a professor at an American university, I am an Asian woman – although South Asian racial profiles fit uneasily into the 'Asian' category – and, because I choose to identify myself as such, an antiracist feminist of color. In North America I was also a 'resident alien' with an Indian passport – I am now a US citizen whose racialization has shifted dramatically (and negatively) since the attacks on the World Trade Center and the Pentagon on September 11, 2001.

Characteristics of ingroups and outgroups

Ingroups are called membership groups; in contrast, outgroups are often referred to as non-membership groups. Membership groups can be involuntary (like age, race or sex), or they can be voluntary (like political affiliation, religion or occupation). Ingroups represent a special class of membership group that is characterized by internal cohesiveness among members. An ingroup's norms, aspirations and values shape the behaviour of its members. When the ingroup is salient, members are concerned about each other's welfare and are willing to cooperate without demanding equitable returns. Ingroups are characterized by some shared experiences (sometimes via the mass media) and an anticipated shared future, so that they create a sense of intimacy, solidarity and trust.

Like membership groups, non-membership groups can be voluntary or involuntary. An outgroup is a non-membership that is salient to the ingroup. An outgroup is seen as distinct from the ingroup or sometimes standing in the way of the accomplishment of the ingroup's goals (Jandt, 2016). Outgroups comprise people whose welfare we are not concerned about, and groups with whom we require at least an equitable return in order to cooperate.

Attributions made about ingroup and outgroup members are typically biased in favour of the ingroup. Ingroup bias occurs on the dimensions on which we compare ingroups and outgroups (e.g., intelligence, language proficiency), even though any real difference may be on another dimension altogether (e.g., national origin). We tend to see outgroups as homogeneous, and to see more variability in ingroups. People have a tendency to create categories that maximize the advantages of the ingroup. People also tend to label members of competing outgroups with undesirable attributes, while labelling ingroups with desirable qualities.

Different cultures ascribe different meanings to ingroup and outgroup relationships. In cultures where individuality is valued, such as those of the United States and Australia, people are considered as independent, and fewer and less sharp distinctions are made between ingroups and outgroups. In more group-oriented cultures, such as Greece and Nigeria, individuals are considered as interdependent and are hence very close to their ingroups. As survival of both the individual and society is more dependent on the group, sharper distinctions are made between ingroups and outgroups. Distinctions between salient ingroups and outgroups lead to a sense of belonging, security and trust. We often treat strangers or outsiders with suspicion and control them carefully while deciding whether or not we can trust them. We tend to be more tolerant of the behaviour of ingroup members than that of outsiders, creating a distinction between what is known as '*inside* morals' and '*outside* morals'. The reach of morals is called the scope of justice. As Coleman (2000: 118) describes, 'Individuals or groups within our moral boundaries are seen as deserving of the same fair, moral treatment as we deserve. Individuals or groups outside these boundaries are seen as undeserving of this same treatment'.

The tendency to maximize the advantages of the ingroup has implications for initial intercultural interactions. When meeting someone from another culture for the first time, there may be salient features that can lead us to categorize their entire culture. For example, a British tourist first boarding

PHOTO 4.1   A chief from the Baragam community in Papua New Guinea is dressed in his traditional attire.

Copyright © Alison Rae. Used with permission.

an MTR (subway) in Hong Kong and hearing a local person chatting loudly on a mobile phone might categorize the entire Hong Kong population as discourteous and inconsiderate of others. This tendency to see members of outgroups as 'all alike', without recognizing the individual differences that we appreciate in ingroup members, is called the *outgroup homogeneity effect* (Mullen and Hu, 1989). On the other hand, categorization can also lead us to minimize differences between members of the ingroup on valued characteristics, but to maximize differences between the ingroup and outgroup on these things. However, bias of this nature may be reduced by decreasing distance between ingroups and outgroups. According to Tajfel (1978), when we perceive an outgroup as similar to our group on a valued characteristic, we are more likely to think positively about that group and to engage members in interaction. Perceived similarity reduces uncertainty about intergroup interaction.

DO IT!

Think about a time when you were treated as an outgroup member. What was done by others that made you feel like an outgroup member? How did you react to being excluded? How has this changed your subsequent communication with people from that group? Write a one-page reflective essay and share it with the class to learn about the impact of social categorization on intergroup and intercultural communication.

THEORY CORNER

IMPLICIT PERSONALITY THEORY

Implicit personality theory describes assumed relationships among personality traits (Schneider, 1973). The theory suggests that we organize our individual perceptions into clusters. When we identify an individual trait in someone, we assume the person also possesses other traits in the cluster. For example, people were found to cluster 'intelligent', 'quiet' and 'friendly' together so that, if we view someone as friendly, we also attribute to them the characteristics of quietness and intelligence. Various researchers have found that people tend to exaggerate the extent of relationships among personality traits. People all face the task of forming impressions of others

(Continued)

based on incomplete information. In making such inferences, we often rely on implicit personality theories, that is, beliefs about how personality traits tend to be associated within people. The tendency to presume that someone who has one good trait is likely to have other good traits is called the *halo effect*. Once we have formed a first impression of someone, we tend to look for cues that are consistent and supportive of this impression and ignore those that are inconsistent.

Critcher and Dunning (2009) conducted five studies with undergraduate students at Cornell University to examine how people construct their implicit personality theories when forming judgements of other people. Participants were asked to rate themselves and their roommates on a number of personality traits (e.g., aggressive, dominant, passive). They were also asked to estimate the percentage of people in the general population who possessed each trait as well as the conditional probabilities that people would possess a particular trait if they showed evidence of possessing another trait. The study found that people use the way traits are configured in the self to form beliefs about how traits are related in other people. Critcher and Dunning used the term 'egocentric pattern projection' to describe such a tendency. They claimed that if two traits go together in the self, then they are assumed to go together in other people. Their studies concluded that one important source of a person's implicit personality theories is the self. People's knowledge of themselves can have a profound influence on their beliefs about other people.

REFERENCES

Critcher, Clayton R. and Dunning, David (2009) 'Egocentric pattern projection: How implicit personality theories recapitulate the geography of the self', *Journal of Personality and Social Psychology*, 97(1): 1–16.

Schneider, David J. (1973) 'Implicit personality theory: A review', *Psychological Bulletin*, 79(5): 294–309.

THE INFLUENCE OF CULTURE ON PERCEPTION

The influence of culture on human perception has long been studied by social scientists. As Marshall Singer (1987: 9) notes, 'We experience everything in the world not as it is – but only as the world comes to us through our sensory receptors'. The way we respond to the external world is primarily the result of how our cultural filters influence what we see, hear, smell, feel and taste. Consistent findings from studies in this area suggest that people's ability to select incoming information, categorize and interpret it differs across cultures because our culture has given us the criteria to apply in order to perceive the world around us.

Perception and intercultural communication

Culture influences all three stages of the perception process: selection, categorization and interpretation. For example, research has found cultural differences in how people select information to use to categorize objects. Nisbett and Miyamoto (2005) showed that people from Western cultures focus on salient objects and rules when categorizing the environment. By contrast, people in East Asian cultures focus more on relationships and similarities among objects when organizing the environment. For example, a study in which both Chinese and American children were presented with pictures of three objects (e.g., man, woman and baby) and then asked to pick two objects of the three that went together showed that Chinese children tended to group their two objects on the basis of relational-contextual information (e.g., grouping the woman and the baby together because the mother takes care of the baby). American children, on the other hand, tended to group objects based on shared properties or categories (e.g., grouping a man and woman together because they are both adults).

As well as objects, we also interpret meanings of events, based on our past experience (Cooper et al., 2007). All events occur in a social context that has specific meaning to the group of people involved. For example, the onset of the New Year is celebrated across cultures, but in very different ways. Unlike the Western New Year (based on the Roman calendar), the Chinese New Year is based on the lunar calendar and usually falls between the end of January and the beginning of February. The celebration lasts 15 days. Celebrations begin on the

PHOTO 4.2   Red envelopes with lucky money are customarily given to children by parents or grandparents on the eve of the Chinese New Year to wish them a smooth and happy new year.

eve of the New Year. Specific traditional dishes are served at dinner to signify wishes or blessings for the coming year: fish for prosperity, chicken representing good luck, and 'jiaozi' (Chinese dumpling) signifying family reunion. People also put up good luck papers outside their front door and feed the Kitchen God sweets before he ascends to heaven to report to the Jade Emperor on the family's activities during the previous year. (This is a bit similar to the European custom of leaving sweets for St Nicholas at Christmas.) It is also common to see parents or grandparents give children 'lucky money' in bright red envelopes, signifying wishes for a smooth and happy New Year.

Culture also affects what information people emphasize when interpreting behaviour. Listening more and talking less is viewed as showing respect in Japanese culture; in Australia, the same behaviour may be viewed as signifying a lack of confidence. People also try to explain an observed behaviour by attributing it to either personal or situational causes. Whenever we explain someone's behaviour in terms of personality, motivation or personal preferences, we are using personal attributes. When we explain someone's behaviour in terms of unusual circumstances, social pressure or physical forces beyond their control, we are using situational attributes. When we make attributions of people's behaviours on the basis of either personality or situational factors, we are prone to biases. In particular, we engage in a self-serving bias – we tend to attribute positive behaviour by ingroup members to internal factors and their negative behaviour to situational variables. In contrast, we tend to attribute positive behaviour by outgroup members to situational variables and negative behaviour to personality variables. For example, a student's failure to pass an exam could be attributed to a lack of intelligence on the part of the student (internal factor) or too much social/family pressure as a cause of under-performance (external factor).

These differences in interpretations also manifest themselves culturally and can result in misunderstandings. The Chinese are reluctant to say 'no' in business negotiations, especially to foreign business partners, because this may upset harmony. When asked a question to which the answer is 'no', they might instead reply 'maybe'. Difficulties of this nature have arisen in negotiations between an Australian university and a Chinese government agency over the establishment of an institute to be affiliated with the university. Part of the problem in reaching an agreement is the frustration that the Australian representatives feel with either getting no answer or 'maybe' in response to significant or difficult questions. A Westerner is more likely to assume that a response of 'maybe' suggests possibility, whereas to a Chinese 'maybe' is an indirect way of saying 'no'. To improve the accuracy of our attributions so as to be more effective in intercultural communication, we can use techniques such as perception checking, active listening and feedback. These techniques can help us to ensure that our interpretation of another's words or actions is what was intended.

Ethnocentrism, stereotypes, prejudice and racism

Culture plays a key role in influencing what information we select from available external stimuli, how we categorize the incoming information, and the meanings we assign to the information. As a result, our cultural socialization can foster ethnocentrism. Higher levels of ethnocentrism can lead to stereotypes, prejudice and even racism – all are barriers to successful intercultural communication.

Ethnocentrism is the tendency for people to see their own culture (or ingroup) as the point of reference, while seeing other cultures (or outgroups) as insignificant or inferior (Neuliep, 2017). Gudykunst (2004) points out that one's cultural orientation acts as a filter for processing incoming and outgoing verbal and nonverbal messages. To this extent, all intercultural communication events are inescapably charged with some degree of ethnocentrism. At its most benign, ethnocentrism has the capacity to foster ingroup survival, solidarity, conformity, loyalty and cooperation. Many researchers recognize ethnocentrism as a ubiquitous phenomenon. As Charon (2007: 156) states:

> Groups develop differences from one another, so do formal organizations, communities and societies. Without interaction with outsiders, differences become difficult to understand and difficult not to judge. What is real to us becomes comfortable; what is comfortable becomes right. What we do not understand becomes less than right to us.

Ethnocentrism is a continuum; our position on this continuum determines the distance we create when we communicate with people from other cultures or groups. At the high end of the continuum, there is a larger distance between ingroups and outgroups, along with insensitivity to the other group's feelings and perspective. At the other end of the scale, low ethnocentrism reflects a desire to reduce communicative distance between ourselves and others and the use of inclusive language. Highly ethnocentric people tend to engage in self-centred dialogue in which they use their own cultural standards to judge the experience of communicating with others. Ethnocentrism at this level may lead to stereotypes, prejudice or discrimination and thus prohibits effective intercultural communication by impairing or preventing understanding. In contrast to ethnocentrism, *cultural relativism* is the degree to which an individual judges another culture by its context (Chen and Starosta, 2005). Taken in isolation, a single element of a culture may seem strange to a non-member, but generally makes sense when considered in light of the other elements of that culture. For example, eating food with fingers is more acceptable in India than in Anglo-Saxon culture. When one considers this single cultural element within a broader context – that is, the Indian belief that God gives people hands so that they may give and eat food – then this Indian behaviour makes sense to Anglo-Saxons. It follows, therefore, that to understand another culture we need to communicate with its people and broaden our understanding of its practices and beliefs, thus enhancing our sense of cultural relativism.

Stereotypes are preconceived beliefs about the characteristics of certain groups based on physical attributes or social status. Stereotypes are overgeneralizations and thus may be wrongly generalized to some members of the group (Hilton and von Hippel, 1996). A stereotype can be a conventional and preconceived opinion or image based on the belief that there are attitudes, appearances or behaviours shared by all members of a certain group. They can emerge from an illusory correlation or false association between two variables. For example, Eastern European countries see Western Europeans as heartless, efficiency-driven and soulless. In Slovenia, a popular saying illustrates their assumptions about the West: 'In heaven, the police are British, the cooks are French, the engineers are German, the administrators are Swiss and the lovers are Italian.' However, 'In hell, the police are German, the cooks are British, the engineers are Italian, the administrators are French and the lovers are Swiss.' This popular saying also reveals our commonly-held stereotypes: Britons are perceived as logical and systematic, French people are seen as having a delicious cuisine, Germans are often portrayed as efficient and hardworking, the Swiss are seen as being well organized and the Italians are believed to be warm and emotional. Stereotypes are forms of social consensus rather than individual judgements; while we do not construct them ourselves, in using them we contribute to the consensus that perpetuates them.

Stereotypes often form the basis of prejudice and are usually employed to explain real or imagined differences, such as those due to race, gender, religion, ethnicity, social class, occupation or sexual orientation. Stereotypes can have an impact on both the holder and the subject. For example, non-English speakers are disadvantaged in English-language social and academic settings because of their accent, and their accent is often believed to signify their incapacity to perform as well as the majority group (Woodrow, 2006). Consequently, ethnic minorities may experience anxiety and performance decrement and

PHOTO 4.3   Muslim women, wearing traditional abayas, shop in downtown Dubai.

Copyright © Alison Rae. Used with permission.

withdraw from communication with people of the host culture (Lesko and Corpus, 2006). Should the person perform poorly in a stereotypical domain (e.g., academic performance), the performance can then be concluded as typical, reinforcing the negative stereotype attached to the particular group. Interestingly, Clark and Kashima (2007) have demonstrated the important role played by narratives in encouraging us to maintain our stereotypes about other groups – we tell and remember stories that emphasize stereotype-consistent traits and behaviour.

THEORY CORNER

SELF-FULFILLING PROPHECY

A *self-fulfilling prophecy* is a statement that causes itself to become true by directly or indirectly altering actions. In Robert Merton's book *Social Theory and Social Structure* (1968) he states that a self-fulfilling prophecy is a false definition of the situation, evoking a new behaviour which makes the original false conception 'come true'. In other words, a false prophecy may sufficiently influence people's behaviours so that their reactions ultimately fulfil it. A self-fulfilling prophecy can be applied to a self-concept. When people are given a label that supposedly describes them, they behave according to the label. Calling someone 'lazy' can increase the chances that the person will act that way. If an Asian student believes that 'Asians are good at mathematics', she might have less trouble with her statistics course than those who have declared a deficiency in maths, simply because she is self-confident about the subject.

Wandke, Sengpiel and Sönksen (2012) applied the self-fulfilling prophecy to understand its impact on influencing older people's use of communication technologies. Although there is consensus that communication technologies have great potential to improve and enrich the life of older people, computer designers, engineers, programmers, and even older people themselves are convinced that 'You can't teach an old dog new tricks'. Some of the widespread myths are that older people are simply not interested in using computers because they consider it unnecessary for their personal lives, they lack the knowledge and language required to describe computer functions, and they are not cognitively able to learn new technologies. While there might be an element of truth in those myths, they are overgeneralized, resulting in some older people avoiding computer

(Continued)

usage. As myths have a tendency to be self-fulfilling and self-reinforcing, this study argues that we should encourage older people to use communication technologies and take responsibility to design user-friendly programs for all age groups.

REFERENCES

Merton, Robert K. (1968) *Social Theory and Social Structure*. New York: Free Press.

Wandke, Hartmut, Sengpiel, Michael and Sönksen, Malte (2012) 'Myths about older people's use of information and communication technology', *Gerontology*, 58: 564–570.

DO IT!

Interview three classmates from cultural backgrounds different from your own. Ask them these questions about gender stereotypes: What are some traits that women might associate with less masculine-looking men in your culture? What are some traits that men might associate with less feminine-looking women in your culture? Then compare their answers to your own answers to those two questions. Write a one-page summary comparing culturally informed gender stereotypes and reflect on whether these gender stereotypes reflect a universal mechanism or cultural influences. Present your summary to the class.

Prejudice is a negative attitude towards individuals resulting from stereotypes (Cooper et al., 2007). Prejudice constitutes generalized evaluations about a person, object or action that are the result of individual experience, interpersonal communication or media influence. Prejudiced people distort evidence to fit their prejudice or simply ignore evidence that is inconsistent with their viewpoint (Allport, 1954). Brislin (1981) suggests that prejudice serves several functions, the first of which is utilitarian: our prejudices may be rewarded economically or socially. For example, prejudice against immigrant groups might put people from the mainstream culture in a more favourable position when competing in the job market. The second function is ego-defensive: prejudice allows us to avoid admitting certain things about ourselves. For example, if you are unsuccessful in some pursuit, you can blame those who were successful and, in doing so, avoid examining the reasons for your own failure and protect your self-esteem. Prejudice also has a value-expressive function: it allows people to highlight the aspects of life they value, such as affiliation with a particular social group. Prejudice also performs a knowledge function: it allows us to organize and structure our world in ways that make sense to us and are relatively convenient. Thus, it is a learned tendency to respond to a given group of people in a certain way. When we are prejudiced against a group, this can manifest in biased actions, such as discrimination.

Brislin (1981) further categorizes prejudice according to the intensity of action or response: verbal abuse, physical avoidance, discrimination, physical attack and massacre. The first of these five forms of prejudice, verbal abuse, is often accompanied by labelling. For example, verbal abuse motivated by racial prejudice includes a host of racist labels, such as 'Chink', 'Pom' or 'Kaffir'. The second form of prejudice, physical avoidance, occurs when a group of people are disliked and shunned because of their religious beliefs, language systems and customs. Prejudice of this nature might lead someone to avoid making friends, going out or working with certain people on the basis of their perceived differences. *Discrimination*, the third form of prejudice, refers to the denial of opportunities to outgroup members. Discrimination exists in employment, housing, political rights, educational opportunities and elsewhere. It is usually based on gender, social class, religion, skin colour or other physical characteristics. The 'White Australia' policy, an immigration guideline that was not repealed until the 1980s, was an example of this form of prejudice. It legitimized discrimination towards potential immigrants who were not of a 'desirable' ethnic background – initially anyone who was not of Western European origin. As the degree of discrimination intensifies, physical punishment of the targeted group becomes likely. The worst form of prejudice is massacre. The burning of women as witches in the American colonies, Hitler's attempted genocide of the Jewish people in Germany and, more recently, the conflict and ethnic cleansing in Bosnia and Rwanda are examples of this extreme form of prejudice.

Racism refers to the belief that some racial groups are superior and that other racial groups are necessarily inferior. It is grounded in a belief in the supremacy of some races over others and that this superiority is biologically based. It therefore devalues and renders certain racial or ethnic groups inferior based on biological features. As such, racist people believe that race differences cannot be influenced by culture or education, and that biological superiority translates into cultural, intellectual, moral and social superiority. Racism is usually the product of ignorance, fear and hatred. It is a worldwide phenomenon, and often reflects and is perpetuated by deeply rooted historical, social, cultural and power inequalities in society. The misconceptions it engenders are often founded on the fear of difference, including differences in customs, values, religion, physical appearance, and ways of living and viewing the world. Racism, stereotyping, prejudice and discrimination are often linked. When a racial group is labelled as inferior, stereotypes about it tend to be negative. Because of this, people become prejudiced against the racial group and discriminate against it. Racist attitudes may be manifested in a number of ways, including expressions of racial prejudice, stereotypical assumptions about other cultures, as well as more extreme forms of prejudice, such as xenophobia. Racism circulates in most communities of the world, in different contexts and forms and with different intensities. Stuart Hall (2014) differentiates two kinds of racism: (1) overt racism, which involves the explicit expression of racist attitudes – overt racists are easy to spot, because they actively argue on behalf of such racist attitudes; and (2) inferential racism, which is subtler and involves such things as the unthinking acceptance of racial stereotypes (e.g., all blacks are good athletes). Racist behaviour can include ridicule, abuse, property damage, harassment and physical assault. Its underlying beliefs are reinforced by prevailing social attitudes towards people who are seen as different. In many countries, racism is inextricably linked to a colonial and/or immigrant history. In Australia, the Indigenous inhabitants were dispossessed of their land and were discriminated against by European settlers. Over time, the migration of peoples from all parts of the world led to an increased cultural and linguistic diversity of the Australian population, but there has nevertheless been prejudice and discrimination against people of non-English-speaking backgrounds or non-European appearance over much of Australia's history. South Africa, New Zealand and some Asian countries have similar histories of colonization and dispossession of Indigenous groups; in some countries, this has led to a backlash by Indigenous groups and subsequent discrimination against long-established immigrant groups. In the United States, on the other hand, racism grew in large part from the history of importing slaves from Africa. In most cases, racism is associated with a chauvinist view of who the 'real' members of the culture are. Racism leads to conflicts and difficulties in intercultural communication.

DO IT!

Locate two fashion magazines. Construct a table that summarizes the types of clothes advertised and the characteristics of the model promoting each type of clothes (e.g., white, tall, thin, Asian, black). What impressions do the faces create and what cues drive your impressions of these faces? Write a paragraph answering these questions and whether you think our judgement of faces is universal or culture-specific. Share your paragraph with a classmate of a different cultural background and see whether there are similarities and differences in your views.

SUMMARY

- Perception is the process of organizing incoming stimuli from the surrounding environment into recognizable categories. The first step is assigning meaning.
- The outcome of interpretation and the process of assigning meaning is not the same for all people. Interpretation is a learned process and is thus subject to psychological, physiological and cultural influences.
- While the propensity to categorize and stereotype is common to all humans, it is our cultural socialization that influences the way in which this process is undertaken.
- To overcome the barriers to intercultural communication created by ethnocentrism, stereotypes, prejudice and racism, we need to practise cultural relativism and keep an open mind when interacting with people from different cultures.

JOIN THE DEBATE

WHY DOES APPEARANCE MATTER?

We form first impressions from facial appearance despite knowing that we should not 'judge a book by its cover'. The impact of face is shown in our impression of people as well as in our behaviour towards them, such as whom we help, whom we trust, whom we hire or whom we ask for a date. Facial appearance can even be used to predict criminal justice decisions. Scholars researching social perceptions hold that people's facial qualities are so useful in guiding adaptive behaviour that even a trace of those qualities can elicit a response. For example, a cute baby face elicits protective responses, whereas an angry face invites defensive responses. Although our perception of face may be accurate on many occasions, at other times certain facial information can produce biased perceptions through overgeneralization. However, the errors produced by these overgeneralizations are presumed to be less maladaptive than those that might result from failing to respond appropriately. Generalizing across faces is just one instance of the broader cognitive mechanism of categorization that is essential for adaptive behaviour. Therefore, scholars of social perception argue that the world would be quite overwhelming if we had no expectations about our social and non-social environment because we failed to generalize from known cases to similar unknown ones. Do you agree with this view? Do you think facial appearance matters? What cues drive our impressions of faces?

The veil for Muslim women comes in all sizes, shapes and colours, and there are different types of veil, the most common of which being the *hijab*. Hijab in Arabic means 'cover'. There are various forms of hijab with different names. The most common type of hijab is a scarf that covers only the hair and chest. This is the most common religious dress for Muslim women in non-Muslim-dominant countries. The other common form of hijab is called *shayla*, which is a long, rectangular scarf that is wrapped loosely around the head and tucked or pinned at the shoulders. It covers the head but often leaves the face clear. Another variant of hijab is a black garment that covers the body and face to expose only the eyes. This type of hijab is referred to as *niqab*. The *burqa*, which is often worn by women in Muslim countries, covers the entire face and body, leaving a small mesh screen through which the woman can see.

Muslim women choose to wear the hijab or other coverings for a variety of reasons. Some women wear the hijab because they believe that God has instructed women to wear it as a means of fulfilling His commandment for modesty. For these women, wearing the hijab is a personal choice that is made after puberty and is intended to reflect one's personal devotion to God. In many cases, the wearing of a headscarf is often accompanied by the wearing of loose-fitting, non-revealing clothing. While some Muslim women do not perceive the hijab to be obligatory to their faith, other Muslim women wear the hijab as a means of visibly expressing their Muslim identity (Hoodfar, 1991). In some Western countries, such as the United States, particularly since 9/11, the hijab is perceived to be synonymous with Islam and, by extension, terrorism. This association has resulted in prejudice against Muslim women, or Islamophobia.

The conservative practice of 'wearing the veil' appears to have originated in Persia 1,000 years ago (Wagner, Sen, Permanadeli and Howarth, 2012). Veiling is mandatory for Muslim women in Saudi Arabia, where women wear the burqa. While most Muslim women wear the hijab for religious reasons, there are other Muslim women who choose to wear the hijab as an expression of their cultural identity as a response to perceived discrimination. By wearing the hijab, those Muslim women challenge the prejudice of Western feminist discourses that present hijab-wearing women as oppressed as well as to be feared and pitied (Wagner et al., 2012). However, not all Muslim women choose to wear the hijab. Some Muslim women believe that the values espoused by the wearing of the headscarf, such as Muslim identity and modesty, can be achieved in other ways. Moreover, the headscarf in contemporary Western society brings more attention to Muslim women and is thus contradictory to its original purpose. Instead, they choose to focus on their internal and spiritual relationship with God. In many Western countries, many Muslim women agree that it is a woman's choice whether or not she wears the hijab.

Nevertheless, the veil on Muslim women's heads is not simply a piece of cloth; it has been the subject of heated debates across the world. For Muslim women, their account of veiling stretches from religiously inspired arguments through to reasons of convenience, modesty, fashion, and a way of affirming their cultural identity. On the other hand, those who are in favour of banning the burqa and hijab in public places, based their arguments on the grounds of security. Internationally, there are plenty of precedents for banning the burqa. France imposed a total ban on wearing full-face veils in public in 2011; in the same year, Belgium outlawed any clothing that obscures people's faces in public, with a penalty of seven days in jail. Women in the Netherlands cannot cover their faces in schools, hospitals or on public transport. Switzerland enforced a ban on the full-face veil in 2016. It means that women wearing a burqa or niqab in public could face fines of about €10,000.

Given the current debates on the controversial issue of Muslim women covering their heads, Wagner and colleagues (2012) undertook a study to compare Muslim women's understandings of the use of the veil in different socio-political contexts. They interviewed 30 middle-class Muslim women from Jakarta, Indonesia (a country with a Muslim majority), and 20 respondents from Mumbai, India (a country with a Muslim minority). The respondents were asked questions about the symbolic value of the veil and their reasons for wearing or not wearing it. The findings showed that for women in a majority-Muslim context (Indonesia), they wear the veil for convenience, fashion and modesty. There was little reference to religion as their reason for veiling. The veil is not a contested issue and therefore is not questioned. In contrast, the social and political experience for minority Muslim women in India is quite different. The responses of Muslim-minority women range from religiously inspired arguments through to opposition against stereotypes and discrimination. For them, the veil is part of an identity construction that is triggered by stereotype and prejudice on the one hand, and by the need to affirm their cultural and religious identity on the other hand. Some Indian Muslim respondents felt that when non-Muslims see a hijab, they immediately infer backward and illiterate women underneath the veil.

REFERENCES FOR CASE STUDY

Hoodfar, Homa (1991) 'The veil in their minds and on our heads: The persistence of colonial images of Muslim women', *Resources for Feminist Research*, 22(2–3): 5–18.

Wagner, Wolfgang, Sen, Ragini, Permanadeli, Risa and Howarth, Caroline S. (2012) 'The veil and Muslim women's identity: Cultural pressures and resistance to stereotyping', *Culture & Psychology*, 18: 521–541.

QUESTIONS FOR DISCUSSION

1. How far have we come since the 1990s with respect to understanding and accepting veiling and the various ways in which it is used?

2. Do you think the matter of Westerners trying to ban the veil is an issue of racism or sexism? What implications does it have for intercultural relations between Muslim and non-Muslim groups?

3. What are the major sources of the negative stereotypes about Islam and Muslim women? What roles do mass media play in creating and reinforcing stereotypes?

4. Muslim women are often perceived as a homogeneous group – of one culture. Can you use implicit consistency theory to explain this phenomenon?

5. What kind of strategies would you suggest to overcome prejudice and stereotypes against Muslim women?

FURTHER READINGS

Freeman, Jonathan B., Ma, Yina, Han, Shihui and Ambady, Nalini (2013) 'Influences of culture and visual context on real-time social categorization', *Journal of Experimental Social Psychology*, 49: 206–210.

This article reported a study on the extent to which Chinese and Americans relied on visual context in social categorization. American and Chinese participants were presented with faces varying along a White–Asian morph continuum in American, neutral or Chinese contexts. The results showed that context systematically influences social categorization, sometimes altering categorization responses and at other times only temporarily altering the process. Further, the timing of contextual influences differs by culture.

Jain, Parul and Slater, Michael D. (2013) 'Provider portrayals and patient–provider communication in drama and reality medical entertainment television shows', *Journal of Health Communication*, 18(6): 703–722.

This study analysed the content of 101 episodes (85 hours) of portrayals of physicians in medical dramas broadcast during the 2006–07 viewing season. Findings indicated that women are under-represented as physicians in reality shows, although they are no longer under-represented as physicians in dramas. However, they are not as actively portrayed in patient-care interactions as are male physicians in medical dramas. Asians and international medical graduates are under-represented relative to their proportion in the US physician population.

Ng, Audrey S. and Tong, Eddie M. W. (2013) 'The relation between implicit theories of personality and forgiveness', *Personal Relationships*, **20: 479–494.**
This article reported a study on the effect of implicit theories of personality on interpersonal forgiveness and the mediating factor underlying such effects. The findings from two experiments show that incremental personality theorists are less forgiving than entity personality theorists. These phenomena hold true regardless of whether forgiveness is measured by self-report or assessed as responses to angry words.

Peng, Kaiping and Knowles, Eric (2003) 'Culture, ethnicity and the attribution of physical causality', *Personality and Social Psychology Bulletin*, **29: 1272–1284.**
This paper reported two studies that investigated the impact of culturally instilled folk theories on the perception of physical events. Study 1 found that Americans and Chinese with no formal physics education emphasize different causes in their explanations for eight physical events, with Americans attributing them more to dispositional factors (e.g., weight) and less to contextual factors (e.g., a medium) than did the Chinese. Study 2 found that Asian-primed participants endorsed dispositional explanations to a lesser degree and contextual explanations to a greater degree than did American-primed participants.

Peucker, Mario and Ceylan, Rauf (2017) 'Muslim community organizations: Sites of active citizenship or self-segregation?', *Ethnic and Racial Studies*, **40(14): 2405–2425.**
The article examines the potential of Muslim community organizations to mobilize their members into performing their citizenship through civic and political participation. It synthesized research on the citizenship-enhancing effects of mosque involvement and conducted 30 in-depth interviews with socially active Muslims in Australia and Germany. The findings provide evidence that many

Muslim community organizations, rather than promoting social segregation, act as an accessible entry point for Muslims' civic participation, facilitate cross-community engagement and provide gateways to political involvement.

SAGE VIDEO SOURCES

This video shows two versions of a conversation between Liz and Ben, which demonstrates the importance of perceptual checking in interpersonal communication. It will help you to achieve the learning objective of understanding perception, categorization and communication. Watch the video to see how Liz and Ben can communicate more effectively with perception checking.

This video is available at http://study.sagepub.com/liu3e

If we are to achieve a richer culture, rich in contrasting values, we must recognize the whole gamut of human potentialities, and so weave a less arbitrary social fabric, one in which each diverse human gift will find a fitting place.

Margaret Mead, American cultural anthropologist, 1901–1978

5

VALUE ORIENTATIONS AND BEHAVIOUR

LEARNING OBJECTIVES

At the end of this chapter, you should be able to:

- Identify Hofstede's five dimensions of culture.
- Compare Kluckhohn and Strodbeck's value orientations.
- Explain Schwartz's cultural taxonomies.
- Apply ethical principles in intercultural communication.

INTRODUCTION

Culture provides the overall framework for humans to organize their thoughts, emotions and behaviours in relation to their environment. At the core of culture are *values*, defined as an explicit or implicit conception, distinctive of an individual or characteristic of a group, which influence the selection of behaviours. Values are communicated both explicitly and implicitly through symbolic behaviours. Most of our verbal and nonverbal behaviours reflect the values we have learned through the socialization process and they have become internalized in our mind. For example, the Japanese proverb 'A single arrow is easily broken, but not ten in a bundle' illustrates the value of collectivity. Values influence the way we communicate with others. The Koreans often avoid saying 'no' when someone makes a request that probably will not be fulfilled. Instead, such a request would elicit a response such as 'we need to think it over' or 'it is a bit difficult', in order to preserve harmony. In contrast, to 'speak your mind' is preferred by US Americans, who value direct communication. Finns, on the other hand, hold an attitude of only speaking if one has something to say, and not to simply fill a void – long periods of silence between people sitting at the same table are not uncommon (Carbaugh, Berry and Nurmikari-Berry, 2006). These examples demonstrate that values and communication are closely related.

This chapter focuses on the relationship between value orientations and behaviours, including communication behaviours. The chapter first describes the five widely known cultural dimensions developed by Hofstede and his associates, based on their studies on cultural values in organizations. These five cultural dimensions have been applied to study the influence of culture not only in organizations but also in other contexts. We then discuss the value orientations developed by Kluckhohn and Strodtbeck, which address fundamental questions that all societies deal with, such as human beings' relations with nature, human nature, social relationships, and orientations to activity and time. Next, we explain Schwartz's cultural taxonomy, drawing on examples from various cultures to illustrate its application. This chapter concludes with a discussion of the ethical principles governing intercultural communication. Throughout the chapter, we highlight that our values provide criteria for us to evaluate our own behaviours and those of others, and therefore value orientations influence how we communicate with others.

HOFSTEDE'S CULTURAL DIMENSIONS

Hofstede (1980) compared work-related attitudes in IBM across more than 53 different cultures and identified four consistent cultural dimensions that influenced the behaviours of 160,000 managers and employees. He suggested that these cultural dimensions have a significant impact on behaviour in all cultures. They are individualism–collectivism, masculinity–femininity, power distance and uncertainty avoidance. Later, a fifth dimension of long-term orientation (also known as Confucian work dynamism) was added to the model by Hofstede and Bond (1988). Since the publication of Hofstede's book *Culture's Consequences: International Differences in Work-Related Values* in 1980, these cultural dimensions have been applied in various disciplines, including intercultural training, cross-cultural psychology, management and leadership, cultural anthropology, organizational psychology, sociology and communication.

Hofstede's work is not without criticisms, though. For example, McSweeney (2002) commented that nations may not be the best units for studying cultures, that a study of the subsidiaries of one company (IBM) cannot provide information about entire national cultures, and that surveys are not suitable ways of measuring culture. It is important to note that Hofstede's work measured cultural dimensions at a national rather than individual level, and therefore those dimensions characterize the dominant culture of a particular society. Within the larger culture of any country, various subcultural groups do co-exist, and you can find variations across different groups along each value continuum. Nevertheless, over the past decades, researchers from different disciplines have tested and added more validations to the IBM scores and contributed to the overall picture originally developed by Hofstede (e.g., House et al., 2004).

Individualism–collectivism

The *individualism–collectivism* dimension describes the relationship between the individual and the groups to which he/she belongs. In individualistic cultures, emphasis is placed on individuals' goals over group goals (Guirdham and Guirdham, 2017). People in an individualistic culture tend to stress the importance of the self and personal achievements. Social behaviour is guided by personal goals, perhaps at the expense of other types of goal. Individuals are encouraged to pursue and develop their abilities and aptitudes. In contrast, collectivistic cultures emphasize values that serve and preserve the ingroup by subordinating personal goals to this end. The collective is more important than the individual, and people are expected to be interdependent and show conformity to ingroup norms. As seen in large-scale research programmes like GLOBE (House et al., 2004), Confucian Asia (China, Hong Kong, Japan, Singapore, South Korea and Taiwan) is characterized by a societal collectivism based on networks, trust, and loyalty to ingroups such as organizations or families. Research has demonstrated that people in collectivistic cultures are more concerned with social acceptance and others' opinions than are people in individualistic cultures (Hui and Triandis, 1986). This is because collectivists are more likely to comply with the wishes of the ingroup than individualists. In Hofstede's (1980) study, countries such as Australia, the United States,

Great Britain, Canada, the Netherlands, New Zealand, Italy, Belgium and Denmark are ranked high on individualism, whereas Columbia, Venezuela, Pakistan, Peru, Taiwan, Thailand, Singapore, Chile and Hong Kong are ranked towards the lower end of the continuum.

A culture's orientation towards individualism or collectivism has important behavioural consequences for its members. However, cultures are never completely individualist or collectivist, but can be conceived as being positioned somewhere along a continuum between high individualism and high collectivism. It is also important to note that individualism or collectivism at the cultural level does not mean that every individual in the culture conforms to the culture's position on this dimension. In intercultural communication, we need to be aware that an individual's orientation to cultural values influences interaction.

Masculinity–femininity

The *masculinity–femininity* dimension describes how a culture's dominant values are assertive or nurturing. In masculine cultures, people strive for maximal distinction between how men and women are expected to think and behave. Cultures that place high value on masculine traits stress assertiveness, goals, competition and material success. Cultures labelled as feminine are those that permit more overlapping of social roles for the sexes and place high value on feminine traits such as quality of life, interpersonal relationships, care, compassion and concern for the weak. For example, in some cultures it is acceptable for the wife to go out to work while the husband stays at home minding the children and taking care of domestic chores. In cultures with more masculine values, however, such a practice would probably be frowned upon. Japanese women are traditionally taught to be obedient and to make household skills and domesticity the centre of their life. The Japanese wife is expected to be an able homemaker and mother. However, these traditions are changing, with women increasingly joining the workforce and becoming

PHOTO 5.1   A-Ma Temple, a temple to the Chinese sea-goddess Mazu, which was built in 1488, is one of the oldest religious temples in Macau.

Copyright © Shuang Liu. Used with permission.

professionals. Sweden, Norway, the Netherlands, Denmark, Finland, Chile, Portugal and Thailand represent more feminine cultures. For example, in Norway the softer aspects of culture are valued and encouraged, such as consensus and sympathy for the underdog. Trying to be better than others is neither socially nor materially rewarded. According to Hofstede's (1980) study, Japan is at the top of the list of masculine cultures. Australia, Venezuela, Switzerland, Mexico, Ireland, Great Britain and Germany also belong to this category.

DO IT!

A manager of an Australian firm importing toys from China found that members of the purchase department routinely obtained supplies through their network instead of following the company procedure of obtaining three quotes for larger amounts by tender. When she raised her concerns, her colleagues' reply was that they could always get a better deal through their contacts. Search the internet for another example of cultural effects on how networks operate at work. Explain the effects by applying the individualism–collectivism dimension.

Power distance

Power distance refers to the extent to which a culture tolerates inequality in power distribution. In cultures with a larger power distance, inequalities among people are both expected and desired. Less powerful people are expected to depend on more powerful people. Children are expected to be obedient towards parents, instead of being treated more or less as equals, and people are expected to display respect for those with higher status. For example, in Thailand, where a status hierarchy is observed, people are expected to display respect for monks by greeting and taking leave of monks with ritualistic greetings, removing hats in the presence of a monk, seating monks at a higher level and using a vocabulary that shows respect. Cultures with a smaller power distance emphasize equality among people, stressing that there should be interdependence between people at different power levels. In New Zealand, characterized as a low power distance culture, it is common for subordinates to address managers by their first name; in Hong Kong, which is high in power distance, people of lower rank in the workplace usually address those of higher rank with titles to preserve hierarchical relationships.

Power distance also refers to the extent to which power, prestige and wealth are distributed within a culture. Cultures with high power distance have power and influence concentrated in the hands of a few rather than distributed throughout the population. These cultures may communicate in a way that reinforces hierarchies in interpersonal relationships. High power distance cultures tend to orient to authoritarianism, which dictates a hierarchical structure of social relationships. In such cultures, the differences between age and status are maximized.

The Philippines, Mexico, Venezuela, India, Singapore, Brazil, Hong Kong, France and Columbia represent high power distance cultures (Hofstede, 1980). On the other hand, low power distance cultures are characterized by 'horizontal' social relationships. People in these cultures tend to minimize differences of age, sex, status and roles. Social interactions are more direct and less formal. Countries such as Australia, Israel, Denmark, New Zealand, Ireland, Sweden, Norway, Finland and Switzerland score low in power distance.

THEORY CORNER

MICHEL FOUCAULT'S THEORY OF POWER

Michel Foucault (2006), a French philosopher, argued that communication rarely takes place between pure 'equals', even though most of our models of understanding communication make this assumption. In every culture there is a social hierarchy that privileges some groups over others. These groups hold more power, be it economic, political or cultural, and they determine, to a great extent, the communication system. Therefore, social hierarchies are always present, however subtle, in communication interactions. Foucault's work reveals an interest in questions of where power is 'located' in a culture; who has and who does not have it; how power is distributed; how those in power obtain and keep power; and to what/whose ends power is used. He believed that power is dynamic, flowing through individuals in various contexts and relationships. Importantly, people who are the subjects of power often find ways to resist this power, but this does not mean such resistance is easy. Power is also institutional in that human institutions embody and sustain power relations. This is true of cultural institutions such as marriage, legal/political institutions and physical institutions such as prisons, schools or hospitals. Certain institutional roles (e.g., teacher or police officer) can offer occupants accompanying institutional power.

Foucault's theories around power and knowledge have been very influential in a range of disciplines, including development, philosophy, business and social work. Over the past few years, new policy frameworks have influenced the structure and terrain of the 'caring' professions in England, including social work. The introduction of quasi-markets has led to the division of service departments. Quasi-markets refer to institutional structures designed to gain free-market efficiency without compromising the equity benefits of traditional public administration. A study by Powell and Khan (2012: 136) shows that quasi-markets have led to 'the role of social workers [being] shaped by increasing managerialist demands for information, particularly in response to audit and risk assessment'. They argue that this kind of practice reinforces power relationships in organizations.

REFERENCES

Foucault, Michel (2006) *History of Madness*. New York: Routledge.

Powell, Jason L. and Khan, Hafiz T. A. (2012) 'Foucault, social theory and social work', *Sociologie Romaneasca*, 10(1): 131–147.

Uncertainty avoidance

The *uncertainty avoidance* dimension reflects a culture's tolerance of ambiguity and acceptance of risk. Some cultures have a high need for information and certainty, whereas other cultures seem to be more comfortable dealing with diversity and ambiguity. In high uncertainty avoidance cultures, people are active and security seeking; cultures weak in uncertainty avoidance are contemplative, less aggressive, unemotional, relaxed, accepting of personal risks and relatively tolerant. According to Hofstede's (2001) scale, Greece, Portugal, Belgium, Japan, Peru, France, Chile, Spain and Argentina are high in uncertainty avoidance, whereas Denmark, Sweden, Norway, Finland, Ireland, Great Britain, the Netherlands, the Philippines and the United States tend to be at the lower end of the scale. These latter cultures are oriented to cope with the stress and anxiety caused by ambiguous situations. They take more initiative, show greater flexibility and feel more relaxed in interactions. People from high uncertainty avoidance cultures tend to avoid risk taking, whereas those from low uncertainty avoidance cultures are more comfortable with risk and are able to cope with the stress and anxiety that it causes.

High uncertainty avoidance tends to be found in collectivistic cultures. The combined influence of uncertainty avoidance and collectivism can be found in research on consumer decisions to purchase products online, which involves risk taking. For example, Zheng (2017) examined how culture makes a difference in the perceived risk of buying on the internet in individualistic and collectivistic cultures. The findings from surveys completed by online consumers in China and in France revealed that online retailer reputation is more valued in collectivist cultures (China) and helps to reduce the perceived risk, whereas privacy and security protection are more valued in individualist cultures (France) and help to reduce perceived risk. On the other hand, Weber and Hsee (1998) contend that people from collectivistic cultures may be more willing to take risks because in a collectivistic society family and other ingroup members are expected to help a person bear the possible adverse consequences of risky choices. Nevertheless, the consensus is that people from cultures with different levels of uncertainty avoidance respond differently to risk situations.

Long-term and short-term orientation

This dimension was added in response to criticisms of Hofstede's work for its Western bias in data collection. This fifth dimension was identified based on the Chinese Value Survey (CVS), which was developed from values suggested by Chinese scholars (Hofstede, 2001). Hofstede originally called this dimension *Confucian work dynamism* because the survey items seemed to be related to the teachings of Confucius. Minkov and Hofstede (2012) later drew upon the World Values Survey (WVS) data to extend the study from the original 23 countries to 38 countries. Based on their analysis, they found high scores among some Eastern European nations on long-term orientation. Hofstede and his colleagues then considered it no longer appropriate to link this dimension with Confucianism. Thus, they now consider the long-term and short-term orientation dimension to be another universal dimension of national culture.

The long-term versus short-term orientation is concerned with values in social relations. Long-term orientation was identified in an international study with Chinese employees and managers (Hofstede and Bond, 1988). People with *long-term orientation* tend to be dedicated, motivated, responsible and educated individuals with a sense of commitment and organizational identity and loyalty. Countries and regions high in long-term orientation are Hong Kong, Singapore, Taiwan, South Korea and Japan – the five economic dragons. Long-term orientation encourages thrift, savings, perseverance towards results, ordering relationships by status and a willingness to subordinate oneself for a purpose. Other studies have found that long-term orientation encouraged Chinese consumers to place a greater emphasis on the quality of products when making purchasing decisions. For example, quality and utilitarian values were found to be strong predictors of Chinese consumers' intention to purchase Canadian pork sausages (Zhou and Hui, 2003). *Short-term orientation*, which characterizes Western cultures, is consistent with spending to keep up with social pressure, less saving for the future, and a preference for quick results (Hofstede, 2001).

THEORY CORNER

BUSINESS CULTURE

Business culture constitutes norms governing business practices and the ways business people talk about what they do in conducting businesses. A country's national culture influences and, to some extent, determines the business culture of that country, for example how their businesses are organized, how business people interact with each other, how business relationships are established and how problems are resolved. While some cultural problems might exist prior to commencing business collaborations, most problems tend to emerge and intensify after a period of contact, cooperation and interaction, particularly during the day-to-day business routine (Hofstede and Hofstede, 2005). In today's multinational organizations, business partners use English as the lingua franca for communication, wear similar clothes and work side by side in a similar environment. Often, when problems occur people tend to attribute the causes to readily perceivable factors such as distribution in the network, personality characteristics, financial systems and so forth, instead of identifying the cultural roots of the problems.

Here is an illustration of German business culture. German businesses have a fairly strict division among its staff into blue-collar and white-collar employees, and also between white-collar clerical positions and management posts (Hofstede and Hofstede, 2005). Therefore, German corporations are seen as bureaucratic organizations in which personal relations play a minor role because the focus is on the tasks at hand. Like US Americans, Germans are very task-oriented. According to Hinner (2015), German managers consider the expertise of individuals to be very important because it is assumed that such expertise leads to the best possible results. Consequently, it is not surprising to see Germans argue and try to convince others with facts and data because the more facts and data one presents, the more convincing one will be. Germans tend to strictly separate business relationships from private relationships. Friendship with colleagues in a business context is considered to be nice, but is not essential for a successful interaction in a business context in Germany. The use of title is another expression of uncertainty avoidance and also of larger power distance. If someone has a title, then that person will be addressed by that title. Titles identify a person's qualifications, competence and rank within a corporate and social hierarchy at a glance. Germans are very punctual in business appointments and most Germans would expect an apology if one is more than one minute late. When Germans make appointments, they do not reconfirm them – even if the appointment is made half a year in advance. This reinforces reliability and avoids uncertainty. One usually only contacts the other party if one needs to cancel or postpone the appointed meeting.

REFERENCES

Hinner, Michael B. (2015) 'Comparing and contrasting German and American business cultures', in L. A. Samovar, R. E. Porter, E. R. McDaniel and C. S. Roy (eds.), *Intercultural Communication: A Reader* (14th edn). Boston, MA: Cengage Learning. pp. 273–287.

Hofstede, Geert and Hofstede, Gert J. (2005) *Cultures and Organizations: Software of the Mind*. New York: McGraw-Hill.

KLUCKHOHN AND STRODTBECK'S VALUE ORIENTATIONS

Kluckhohn and Strodtbeck (1961) argue that all human cultures are confronted with universal problems that emerge from relationships with others, and with time, activities and nature. Value orientations are the means that a society uses to solve these universal problems. The concept entails four assumptions. First, all human societies face the same problems. Second, they use different means to solve them. Third, the means to address universal problems are limited. And fourth, value orientations are behaviourally observable through empirical studies. *Value orientation theory* suggests that cultures develop unique positions on five value orientations: (1) the relationship of people with nature (people should be subordinate to–in harmony with–dominant over nature), (2) activity (a state of being–inner development–industriousness), (3) time (past–present–future), (4) human nature (people are good–mixed–evil), and (5) social relations (individualistic–collective–hierarchical). Each orientation represents a way of addressing a universal problem.

Man–nature orientation

The *man–nature orientation* address the question: What is the relationship of humans to nature? A society's conception of the relationship of humans to nature is determined by the worldview of its people. *Worldview* refers to the outlook a culture has on the nature of the universe, the nature of humankind, the relationship between humanity and the universe, and other philosophical issues defining humans' place in the cosmos. Since prehistoric times, humans have made creation stories in order to explain their relationship to nature. This relationship can be subjugation to nature, harmony with nature or mastery over nature. Phrases like 'Nature as machine' and its variant 'Nature as storehouse' justify the exploitative relationship between Western civilizations and the environment, where nature is regarded as something that needs to be conquered. For example, the economic system of capitalism, which emphasizes profit and accumulation, definitely advocates conquering nature and making business out of it. In the United States, people make a clear distinction between humans and nature, with humans assuming a dominant role over nature, and valuing and protecting it. This viewpoint is evident in changing river courses to accommodate city planning.

In Saudi Arabia, humans are seen as part of nature and are supposed to live in harmony with it. This orientation is related to the Islamic view that everything in the world, except humans, is administered by God-made laws. The physical world has no choice but to be obedient to God. Humans, however, can choose to obey the law of God; in so doing, they will be in harmony with all other elements of nature. Japanese culture is also characterized by a love of and respect for nature; the Japanese believe that humans should live in harmony with nature. They cherish the beauty of nature through *hanami* (cherry blossoms) in spring and *momijigari* (maple leaves changing colour) in autumn, and practise traditional flower arranging known as *ikebana*. Harmony is a central concept in Japanese culture, influenced by Shintoism along with Buddhist and Confucian traditions. The traditional Japanese garden illustrates this harmonious relationship between humans and nature.

Activity orientation

The *activity orientation* addresses the question: What is the modality of human activity? This refers to the use of time for self-expression and play, self-improvement and development, and work. The activity orientation can refer to being, being-in-becoming and doing. Protestant cultures, such as in Britain, perceive paid work as essential: it is a dominant human activity that occupies a central place in human existence. Human work is understood as a duty that benefits both the individual and society as a whole. Many Americans believe that work should be separated from play, and that a feeling of accomplishment is the most important aspect of work. High value is placed on time and efficiency. In Arab cultures, earning a living through labour is not only a duty but a virtue, and is thus not separable from other aspects of human existence. In some religious cultures, praying is cherished and a prayer is considered to be more important for humans than work.

Time orientation

The *time orientation* answers the question: What is the temporal focus of human life? Cultures differ widely in their conceptions of time. Time orientation can be past, present or future. Past-oriented cultures emphasize tradition; present-oriented cultures stress spontaneity and immediacy; and future-oriented cultures emphasize the importance of present activities to future outcomes (Cooper et al., 2007). In Eastern Europe, the past plays an important part of the present. In Serbia, for example, past historical events are cited and justified for making important present-day political decisions. People enjoy talking about their past, and they perceive time through the past–present dimension. Many Western cultures view time in a linear fashion – past, present and future move in a line, in one direction. This attitude conceives of time as a commodity that can be spent, saved, borrowed and wasted. When time is considered as a tangible object, it becomes something to be managed and used responsibly. For example, time decides when Americans make their appointments, when they do their work and even how they spend their leisure time. Punctuality is important, and being late without a legitimate reason is considered bad manners. Similarly, the Swiss have a reputation for being as punctual and precise as their famous watches. The saying is: *Avant l'heure, c'est pas l'heure, après l'heure, c'est plus l'heure* (Before the hour is not yet the hour, after the hour is no longer the hour).

In other cultures, the past, present and future may not be as distinct. Mulder (1996) reports three different conceptions of time in Thai society. The first conception is characterized by continuity. This is the belief in continuity of life, traditions and the environment, from ancestors into endless future generations. In this sense, time stands still. Past, present and future are indistinct. The second conception is the 'modern' conception of time – instead of standing still, time in this conception moves ahead towards the future. For example, when a poor Thai farmer migrated to the city for a better life, she/he had to measure time in terms of working hours in a factory instead of in the field. The third is an animistic conception of time. Communities feel that they are controlled by a strong power beyond their control. Thus, they look for ways to manage the power through various means, including worship and animal sacrifices. Thai people worship the gods, who they believe will help villagers in return by sending rain when it is needed.

There are cultures that do not have a clear sense of time, and this is revealed in their language. For example, the Hopi language does not have verb tenses, but simply uses two words to express time: one meaning 'sooner' and the other meaning 'later'. The Hopi tribes live for the most part in northeast Arizona, and are well known for being very peaceful. Another example is the Pirahã, a small Amazonian tribe that has a limited language consisting of relatively few sounds and grammatical constructions. For some purposes (like hunting), the language is whistled. Their traditional language appears to have no precise numbers, no specific past tense and no written form. There is limited art in this culture and no precise concept of time. Their religion is animistic, and they make little reference to history or ancestors. The Pirahã do not (or did not in the past) have a desire to remember where they come from or to tell cultural stories. In the old days in Venice, similarly, there were clocks on public buildings that showed the position of the sun and moon along with the relative positions of Saturn, Jupiter, Venus, Mercury and Mars. Today, we can see clocks in public places in Venice that use Roman numerals to show the hours of the day.

PHOTO 5.2   A clock in a public place in Venice uses Roman numerals to show the hours of the day.

Human nature orientation

The *human nature orientation* addresses the question: What is the intrinsic character of human nature? Are we born good or evil, or a mixture of good and evil? The Puritan origins in the United States reflect a Christian view that people are born evil but have the potential to become good through self-control and self-discipline. Other contemporary views claim that humans are born with a mixture of good and evil, and thus have a choice to be either. Such a belief in rationality is consistent with the belief in the scientific method of inquiry, whereby truth can be discovered through human reasoning. In other cultures, such as Chinese culture, Confucianism teaches that humans are born free of evil. Buddhism emphasizes the spirituality and goodness of the individual, in what is a more inward-oriented philosophy. The Judaeo-Christian tradition claims that an understanding of the person is bound together with the belief that humans are created in the image of God, suggesting a close relationship between the concept of God and the concept of the person. Humans are seen as sinful, but they can be redeemed during the course of life, since God created humans endowed with intelligence and choice. The purpose of human life is to worship God by knowing, loving and obeying. In Hinduism, a person is defined by his/her membership of a caste, so it is difficult to practise equality for all persons.

Relational orientation

The *relational orientation* addresses the question: What is the modality of a person's relationship to others? It refers to perceptions of the self and the ways in which society is organized. It can be lineal, collateral and individualistic. In individualistic cultures, such as Canada, people are encouraged to accept responsibility as independent individuals. For example, in such cultures marriage is usually the decision of the individual, and romantic love tends to be the reason for marriage. In collectivistic cultures, such as India, marriage may be considered as too great a decision to be left to the individuals involved, because marriages present opportunities for familial alliances in a culture where families are very important. In such group-oriented cultures, individuals subordinate personal needs to their ingroup, particularly their family. If a Chinese youngster passes the national entrance exams and is offered a place in a good university, both parents and other members of the extended family feel they have been given face because honour is the collective property of the family. In the same way, all family members would feel they had lost face should a single member of the family commit a dishonourable act. Collectivistic cultures tend to be more caring for each other, as there is a strong sense of belonging to some collective – family, neighbourhood, village, class or organization. In Bosnia, for example, elderly people enjoy playing chess in a public square, which creates an atmosphere of collectivity.

DO IT!

In Western cultures, children's career paths are often their own choice, although they may seek advice from their parents. In many Asian cultures, the parents decide which career path their children will follow in the future. Interview two international students, one from an Asian culture and the other from a Western culture. Ask them who decided on their choice of university and the subject area they were to study; ask them to explain why. Then interpret your findings in terms of the value orientation theory. Write a one-page report and show it to the two students you interviewed to see how they respond to your report.

SCHWARTZ'S CULTURAL TAXONOMY

Shalom Schwartz developed another cultural values framework to understand the influence of cultural values on attitudes and behaviours, known as Schwartz's cultural taxonomy. Schwartz (1994: 88) defines values as the 'desirable goals, varying in importance, that serve as guiding principles in people's lives'. Like Hofstede, Schwartz attempted to identify national cultural dimensions that can be used to compare cultures by aggregating the value priorities of individuals. Unlike Hofstede, whose research focused on IBM employees, Schwartz's original research data were collected from teacher and student samples in 38 nations between 1988 and 1992. Schwartz (1999) proposes seven types of values on which cultures can be compared. They are conservatism, intellectual autonomy, affective autonomy, hierarchy, mastery, egalitarian commitment and harmony (see Table 5.1).

PHOTO 5.3   Elderly people in Sarajevo, Bosnia, enjoy playing collective games like chess in a public square.

Copyright © Zala Volčič. Used with permission.

TABLE 5.1   Schwartz's seven cultural taxonomies

Value type	Definition
Conservatism	A society that emphasizes close-knit harmonious relations, the maintenance of the status quo and traditional order.
Intellectual autonomy	A society that recognizes individuals as autonomous entities who are entitled to pursue their own intellectual interests and desires.
Affective autonomy	A society that recognizes individuals as autonomous entities who are entitled to pursue their own stimulation and hedonistic interests and desires.
Hierarchy	A society that emphasizes the legitimacy of hierarchical roles and resource allocation.
Mastery	A society that emphasizes the active mastery of the social environment and the individual's rights to get ahead of other people.
Egalitarian commitment	A society that emphasizes the transcendence of selfless interests.
Harmony	A society that emphasizes harmony with nature.

Source: Adapted from Schwartz, Shalom H. (1999) 'A theory of cultural values and some implications for work', *Applied Psychology: An International Review*, 48(1): 23–47, p. 29.

Those seven cultural value taxonomies were summarized into three dimensions, namely (1) autonomy versus embeddedness, (2) hierarchy versus egalitarianism and (3) mastery versus harmony. While each dimension represents a continuum of cultural responses, a culture's preference for one orientation of a given dimension means that the opposite end of the continuum is less important to that culture. Similar to Kluckhohn and Strodtbeck's premise that all cultures face universal problems that they must resolve, Schwartz (1999) argues that there are three issues that all societies face and must resolve.

The first issue is to define the nature of the relation between the individual and the group. Resolutions of this issue give rise to the cultural dimension that Schwartz calls *autonomy versus embeddedness*. In autonomy cultures, people are more independent; they find meaning in their own uniqueness; they are encouraged to express their own preferences, traits, feelings, opinions and motives. Cultures that value autonomy, such as France and Japan (Lustig and Koester, 2013), encourage people's independent pursuit of ideas, creativity, intellectual directions, curiosity and broad-mindedness. In contrast, cultures that are oriented towards embeddedness view the person as an entity embedded in the collectivity and finds meaning in life largely through social relationships. Identifying with the group and participating in its shared way of life are important. This outlook is expressed in values like conservatism, which emphasizes maintenance of the status quo, propriety, and restraint of actions that might disrupt the solidarity of the group or the traditional order. Nigeria, for example, is a country that values predictability, obedience to authority, maintenance of the social order and respect for tradition and elders' wisdom. It therefore exemplifies embeddedness.

The second issue that Schwartz identifies is to guarantee responsible behaviour that will preserve the social fabric. He labels this dimension *hierarchy versus egalitarianism*. Cultures that value hierarchy view the unequal distribution of social, political and economic power as legitimate and desirable. They prefer the use of power ascribed by hierarchical systems to ensure socially responsible behaviour, and compliance with the obligations and rules is emphasized. Countries like Thailand and Turkey, where power distance is relatively high, have a more hierarchical culture. On the other hand, cultures that value egalitarianism believe that responsible social behaviour can be induced by encouraging people to recognize one another as moral equals who share basic interests. People in more egalitarian cultures are socialized to a commitment to voluntary cooperation with others, to transcend selfish interests and to promote the welfare of others. Countries like Spain and Belgium belong to this category of more egalitarian cultures. The countries of the East European and Balkan cultural region, which have strong historical connections to the Ottoman empire and were deeply penetrated by communism, are relatively low in cultural egalitarianism and high in hierarchy.

The third universal issue that Schwartz identifies is the relation of humankind to nature. Resolutions to this issue give rise to the cultural dimension that he calls *mastery versus harmony*. Mastery cultures encourage people to actively control and change the world and to exploit it in order to advance personal or group interests. Think of the planned mass tourism industry in Spain that has aggressively built and transformed the Spanish coast, or the view in Germany, where one can be self-sufficient, self-assertive, daring, ambitious and successful. The emphasis is on getting ahead through self-assertion; ambition, success, daring and competence are valued. India and China are ranked high at the mastery end of the spectrum. A culture that values harmony with nature encourages acceptance and fitting harmoniously into the environment, as humans are viewed as an integral part of nature; unity with nature, protecting the environment and a world of beauty are valued. This cultural orientation is held by the dominant cultures in Italy and Mexico.

INTERCULTURAL COMMUNICATION ETHICS

Ethics is concerned with what is right or wrong, good or bad, and the standards and rules that guide our behaviour. Communication ethics involves how we engage in communication acts and the consequences of our communication behaviour (Chen and Starosta, 2005). When we engage in intercultural interactions, we make decisions about what is right or wrong, albeit sometimes unconsciously, and apply ethical principles. Ethics philosopher Martin Buber (2000) pointed out how important it is, within communication, to focus on the willingness

THEORY CORNER

CONDON AND YOUSEF'S MODEL

Condon and Yousef (1975) developed a value orientation model that extended Kluckhohn and Strodtbeck's value orientations to include six spheres of universal problems all humans face. These six spheres include the self, the family, society, human nature, nature and the supernatural, all of which are interdependent of each other. Condon and Yousef then derived 25 value orientations encompassed within the six spheres. They claim that all value orientations exist in every society, but the preferred response to the problem varies from culture to culture. For example, one value orientation under the sphere of the 'supernatural' is 'knowledge of the cosmic order'. In some cultures, people believe this order is comprehensible; in others they believe it is mysterious and unknowable; still others believe understanding it is a matter of faith and reason.

An illustration of Condon and Yousef's family value orientation is through Egyptian culture, in particular with regard to relationships. Egyptians place great value on relationships and they like to be surrounded by a network of relatives and friends. According to Begley (2015), relationships constitute one of the fundamental values of Egyptian culture. The flood cycles of life near the Nile make it important for Nile Valley inhabitants to maintain relational harmony so that a diverse group of people can share limited resources. In Egyptian collectivism, each person represents a social collective and sacrifices his or her needs for the greater good of that group. Family, social and business relationships are taken seriously. Kinship terms are used in various situations to reinforce positive connections among people. For example, when conversing, the first few questions that Egyptians ask guests are concerned with group affiliations: 'Where is your family?', 'Where is your father?', 'Where are your co-workers?' A relational focus is also reflected in the blurred boundary between social and business interactions. Egyptians often conduct lengthy business meetings without ever touching on business matters. There was an anecdote that a visitor learned the power of relations after waiting at an Egyptian embassy for five hours to get a visa. He later realized that the hotel owner's son could use his connection in the embassy to get the visa delivered to the hotel within half an hour after a single phone call. Relationships are a source of pleasure and are also a way to get things done in Egypt.

REFERENCES

Begley, Polly A. (2015) 'Communication with Egyptians', in L. A. Samovar, R. E. Porter, E. R. McDaniel and C. S. Roy (eds.), *Intercultural Communication: A Reader* (14th edn). Boston, MA: Cengage Learning. pp. 126–132.

Condon, John C. and Yousef, Fathi (1975) *An Introduction to Intercultural Communication*. Indianapolis, IN: Boffs-Merrill.

and ability of each participant to surrender self-interest in favour of experiencing the views, beliefs and convictions of the Other.

DO IT!

Intercultural sensitivity is a well-developed awareness of and ability to respond appropriately to cultural differences. Search the internet to locate an example where miscommunication or misunderstanding occurred between people from different cultures due to a lack of intercultural sensitivity. Analyse the problem and offer solutions.

Approaches to intercultural communication ethics

Debates on approaches to ethics have largely been about two approaches: universalism versus relativism. Proponents of *ethical universalism* believe that there are universal ethical principles that guide behaviour across all societies. Thus, what is wrong in one place will be wrong elsewhere, regardless of time and circumstance (Lowenstein and Merrill, 1990). The Geneva Convention standards on appropriate warfare and human rights groups who work across geographic and cultural borders can be considered as illustrative of this universalistic view. The problem with universalism is that universalist approaches attempt to ground ethics variously in religion, nature, history and reason, but largely fail because there is no agreement about what is religiously authoritative, natural, historical or reasonable (Evanoff, 2004).

Contrary to universalism, proponents of *ethical relativism* believe that ethics is closely related to motive, intuition and emotion. They believe that while people from different cultures share common needs, interests or feelings, their ways of acting upon these internal states vary because of cultural differences. Relativists deny the existence of a single universal set of values and norms, and instead believe that values and norms are relative to particular individuals or groups (Lowenstein and Merrill, 1990). Relativist approaches are connected with subjectivity in ethics, the preservation of local cultures and a multilinear model of cultural development that views all cultures as progressing along separate lines of development and diverging with respect to values and norms (Evanoff, 2004). Thus, ethical relativists would not judge another's behaviour by their own ethical standards, because they believe that adhering to one's own contextualized truths in intercultural interactions only leads to conflict. Nevertheless, relativism is not without criticisms. While acknowledging that various cultures construct ethical systems, cultural relativists fail to address how conflicts between cultures can be resolved.

Evanoff (2004) states that relativism seems progressive but is in fact conservative because it obligates us simply to accept the values and norms of other cultures instead of encouraging us to critically reflect upon them. He proposes a *communicative approach* to intercultural communication ethics as an alternative to both universalism and relativism. The communicative approach recognizes that humans are socialized into a particular set of cultural norms, but that they are capable of critically reflecting upon and changing those cultural norms. We are also able to critically review the norms of other cultures and make informed decisions about which of them are worthy of adoption or rejection. Ethical dialogue on intercultural communication can take place between specific cultures in specific contexts in relation to specific problems and specific individuals or groups. Thus, a communicative approach views criteria for judging ethical behaviour as dynamic and evolving. For example, we no longer find slavery acceptable, and we are in the process of creating ethical norms to deal with emerging issues such as euthanasia.

Principles of ethical intercultural communication

Bradford Hall (2005) argues that the controversy between universalism and relativism both enables and constrains creativity and stability in human societies. Therefore, a more appropriate way to examine intercultural communication ethics is to integrate both universal and relative perspectives (Chen and Starosta, 2005). Just as Hall claims that communication ethics is a combination of constraints and empowerment, one of the golden rules of communication ethics, which was originally based in religious philosophy, is to 'do unto others as you would have them do unto you'. Similarly, a famous Confucian maxim states, 'Never do to others what you would not like them to do to you'. In general, the principle of communication ethics includes respect, non-judgementalism, mindfulness and mutuality.

Respect refers to sensitivity to and acknowledgement of other people's needs and wants. Like mutuality, the golden rule with respect is to 'do unto others as you would have them do unto you'. The platinum rule goes one step further, stating that rather than treating others as you want to be treated, treat them as you think they would want to be treated. For example, religious practices vary widely across cultural and ethnic groups. Muslims fast at a certain time of the year to demonstrate their religious faith; some Buddhists do not eat red meat as an illustration of the religious principle of non-violence; whereas people in Hong Kong offer temple sacrifices of a piglet in return for a deity's protection. To be an ethical intercultural communicator means we need to respect the people who observe those customs and rituals even though we do not necessarily have to practise what other cultures do.

Non-judgementalism involves a willingness to express ourselves openly and to be open-minded about others' behaviours. The key to this principle is to see things as they are rather than as how we want them to be. This requires understanding other people's views, values and positions. Muslim women cover their head with a scarf in public to observe their religious beliefs; Chinese business people often give gifts to their business partners, not to bribe them but to show their desire to establish a good interpersonal relationship, because in China there is an overlap between personal and work relationships. Neither of these practices may be practised in your culture. The important point is to recognize and appreciate differences. Judging others' behaviour through one's own cultural lenses can risk basing one's own behaviour towards other people on false premises or stereotypes.

Mindfulness requires us to be open to new information and to be aware of more than one perspective (Guirdham and Guirdham, 2017). For example, Elliott (1997) examined the cross-cultural tensions created by the 1995 earthquake in Japan. When the Japanese government was slow to accept the assistance offered by the international community, the US media were quick to criticize what it perceived as ingratitude. However, Elliot uncovered the cultural assumptions that underlay the Japanese response, such as collective self-sufficiency, an emphasis on local action first, bottom-up decision making and a lack of emphasis on individual volunteerism. We are socialized into our own cultural rules and norms as we grow up, and hence we carry personal biases regarding what is or is not an appropriate way of handling certain situations. In the process of intercultural communication, we must be aware of these biases in order to understand other people's behaviour as it is.

Mutuality means we should locate a common ground for communication. We need to gain an understanding of the perspective of the other before making any ethical decisions. We also need to build relational empathy with the other party. A spirit of equality, inclusiveness and a supportive climate are conducive to successful communication outcomes. On the other hand, if either party demands that the interaction be conducted according to his/her own cultural norms, intercultural communication is unlikely be successful.

SUMMARY

- Hofstede's four cultural dimensions and the fifth dimension developed by Hofstede and Bond are used widely in cross-cultural research on organizations, individuals and communities, although they have attracted some criticisms.
- Kluckhohn and Strodtbeck's theory of value orientations claims to address some fundamental problems all societies face, but the variation of cultural values makes it impossible for a single list to be exhaustive.
- Schwartz's cultural taxonomies are summarized into three dimensions: embeddedness versus autonomy, hierarchy versus egalitarianism and mastery versus harmony.
- General principles that govern all ethical intercultural communication include respect, non-judgementalism, mindfulness and mutuality.

The debate around same-sex marriage, often referred to as marriage equality, is becoming increasingly complex. Despite advocates arguing that there is a growing level of support for marriage equality, the decision or desire to legally redefine 'marriage' is complicated by personal, social and religious reasons, as well as legal issues. Some cultures, including many religious groups, view the purpose of marriage as the reproduction and balanced upbringing of offspring, which these groups argue is not possible in same-sex relationships. These religious groups often cite Bible passages that support their view. On the other hand, those in favour of marriage equality maintain that it is a basic human right, and argue that the current legislation is discriminatory, based on sexual orientation. By mid-2013, 15 countries had enacted legislation allowing same-sex couples to marry, including Argentina, New Zealand, South Africa and, most recently, Australia. In other countries, such as Mexico and the United States, the debate continues nationally despite many states altering their legislation in favour of marriage equality. What is your view on same-sex marriage? Should the definition of marriage be universal or culturally specific?

Freedom of expression is essential for a vibrant public sphere that lies at the heart of democracy. The essence of democracy is that it protects civil and political rights and liberal, democratic governments recognize the right to free speech. However, along with freedom of expression comes the discussion of hate speech. Hate speech, in its broadest sense, includes verbal and nonverbal communication. It is hostile and malicious speech that has a biased motive and is directed towards a group of people because of some innate characteristics (Matsuda, Lawrence, Delgado and Crenshaw, 1993). These characteristics can include ethnicity, gender, colour, nationality, sexual orientation, race or physical disability. While freedom of speech reflects an open society, facilitating differences of opinion while respecting diversity and creativity, the right to freedom of expression is limited because democracies recognize that certain limits may, and sometimes must, be placed on these rights (Guiora and Park, 2017).

While incitement to violence is outlawed, hate speech is, in the United States for example, protected by the First Amendment doctrine. However, in many countries, the collective – rather than the liberal individualistic approach – prevails over the freedom of speech principle, allowing for direct (legal) intervention when it concerns racism and discrimination. As a result, and contrary to the US approach, many countries have adopted quite stringent legislation to counter hate speech and the incitement of racial and ethnic hatred. In some European countries, freedom of speech is more carefully weighed against other rights and protections. Their supposition is that hate speech causes harm to individuals as well as communities and the whole society. At an individual level, harm can be manifested in the form of sadness, pain, distress, loss of self-confidence, fear, shame, humiliation, isolation and hurt dignity; harm at the collective level occurs wherever groups of people are silenced.

With the prevalence and proliferation of the internet, hate speech is confronting and challenging contemporary societies in more and diverse ways. One of the greatest challenges on the internet has been to maintain the appropriate balance between the wish to control racist content and the protection of one's freedom of expression (Alam, Raina and Siddiqui, 2016). The fact that the internet is decentralized does not help. Besides, laws differ widely from country to country, ranging from the extremely liberal to the highly conservative. As Alam and colleagues (2016) point out, a number of laws have been formulated by the Indian Constitution to check and punish anybody indulging in spreading animosity in the media among individuals, ethnic groups, castes, religions and so on through words (spoken or written) or acts. The laws are particularly strict in instances where there is an attempt to outrage somebody's religious sentiments. However, a number of these laws have received heavy criticism because of instances where individuals and groups have misused the laws to settle personal scores. Additionally, some people do not seem to be aware of the existence of such laws.

Therefore, one of the greatest challenges confronting democratic decision makers is to determine to what extent hate speech on the internet should be tolerated in the context of freedom of speech (Guiora and Park, 2017). The internet is a limitless platform for information and data sharing. Social media, in particular, are where contentious public issues are now played out. Further, the internet is also a low-cost, high-speed dissemination mechanism that facilitates the spreading of hate speech, including violent and virtual threats (Anat and Matamoros-Fernández, 2016). In the past decade, legislation and regulatory policy were developed around the world to address explicit hate speech on public websites, and to distinguish between the criminalization of hate speech and the protection of freedom of expression. Today, social media define for themselves what hate speech is, set the accepted rules of conduct, and act on them (Anat and Matamoros-Fernández, 2016). Facebook both creates and enforces the criteria for the removal of hateful content. Thus, unlike the regulation of hate speech on websites by internet service providers, social media enjoy greater freedom to decide whether and how to regulate hate speech.

For example, in Spain, the extreme right comprises several fringe parties that hold nostalgic fascist agendas, such as Alternativa Española (AES), Movimiento Social Republicano (MSR), Democracia Nacional (DN) and FE-La Falange (Anat and Matamoros-Fernández, 2016). However, only two parties – España 2000 and Plataforma per Catalunya (PxC), whose agendas are more aligned with anti-immigration and new European right-wing populism – have gained electoral success in recent years. Despite their relative marginal electoral success, these parties have used the internet to reach new audiences, balance their under-representation in traditional media and create a stronger sense of community. One of the characteristics of such increased activity is the radicalization of the extreme-right parties' discourse against immigrants and minorities. There are numerous examples that are sexist, mysoginynist, racist, hurtful and deeply insulting. Anonymity triggers hatred and calls for violence and harm to others, whether they are individuals or groups.

Alam, Iftikhar, Raina, Roshan Lal and Siddiqui, Faizia (2016) 'Free vs hate speech on social media: The Indian perspective', *Journal of Information, Communication and Ethics in Society*, 14(4): 350–363.

Anat, Ben-David and Matamoros-Fernández, Ariadna (2016) 'Hate speech and covert discrimination on social media: Monitoring the Facebook pages of extreme-right political parties in Spain', *International Journal of Communication*, 10(3): 1167–1193.

Guiora, Amos and Park, Elizabeth A. (2017) 'Hate speech on social media', *Philosophia*, 1(2): 2–15.

Matsuda, Mari J., Lawrence, Charles R. III, Delgado, Richard and Crenshaw, Kimberlé W. (1993) *Words That Wound: Critical Race Theory, Assaultive Speech and the First Amendment*. Boulder, CO: Westview Press.

REFERENCES FOR CASE STUDY

1. Have you seen hate speech on the internet in your own language? If so, to which group does it tend to be directed?

2. Do you think that hate speech does harm not only to specific individuals who belong to particular ethnic and religious communities but also to a society that tolerates hate speech in the name of freedom of expression?

QUESTIONS FOR DISCUSSION

3. How should we draw the boundary between freedom of expression and hate speech?

4. Social media, such as Twitter, provide a powerful space for discourses of 'us' against 'them' to be generated. Can you think of some possible mechanisms to regulate hate speech on social media?

5. How can ethical communication principles be applied to communication on social media platforms?

FURTHER READINGS

Bergelson, Mira (2015) 'Russian cultural values and workplace communication patterns', in L. A. Samovar, R. E. Porter, E. R. McDaniel and C. S. Roy (eds.), _Intercultural Communication: A Reader_ (14th edn). Boston, MA: Cengage Learning. pp. 133–140.

This book chapter systematically examines some Russian cultural values. It explores some Russian worldviews, including Russians' views on emotionality, fatalism, judgemental attitudes and irrationality. The chapter emphasizes the importance of understanding how cultural values influence communication behaviour. Various communication patterns that can bring about misunderstandings or create conflict during interaction between Russians and US Americans are discussed.

Lee, Hyung-Seok and Park, Jin S. (2012) 'Cultural orientation and the persuasive effects of fear appeals: The case of anti-smoking public service announcements', _Journal of Medical Marketing_, 12(2): 73–80.

This study examined the extent to which one's individualistic traits moderate the persuasive effects of fear appeals in anti-smoking public service announcements. A total of 129 undergraduates in the United States and South Korea participated in an experiment. The results showed that individualists respond better to an anti-smoking public service announcement that emphasizes an individualistic fear appeal, whereas a public service announcement stressing a collectivistic fear appeal is more effective among collectivists.

Masumoto, Tomoko (2004) 'Learning to "do time" in Japan: A study of US interns in Japanese organizations', _International Journal of Cross-Cultural Management_, 4(1): 19–37.

This paper compared Japanese time orientations with US time orientations and found that US culture tends to focus on the future, with distinct boundaries between work time and personal time. Japanese culture, on the other hand, values tradition and 'longevity'; it is quite common for one employee to stay with the same company for more than 30 years. Many Japanese people may not separate work and non-work time, often staying late at the office without expectation of compensation. These different values of time could negatively affect international business communication.

Merritt, Ashleigh (2000) 'Culture in the cockpit: Do Hofstede's dimensions replicate?', *Journal of Cross-Cultural Psychology*, 31(2): 283–301.

This paper tests Hofstede's indexes of national culture by surveying 9,400 male commercial airline pilots from 19 countries. The data rendered significant replication correlations for all indexes. The successful replication confirms that national culture exerts an influence on cockpit behaviour over and above the professional culture of pilots, and that 'one size fits all' training is inappropriate.

Tsai, Jeanne L. (2000) 'Cultural orientation of Hmong young adults', *Journal of Human Behavior in the Social Environment*, 3(3–4): 99–114.

This study explored whether American-born and overseas-born Hmong young adults differed in interpreting cultural orientations. In total, 14 American-born and 32 overseas-born Hmong college students were asked what 'being Hmong' and 'being American' meant to them. Both groups reported being more oriented to American culture than to Hmong culture. Despite similarities in mean levels of orientation to Hmong and American cultures, American-born Hmong and overseas-born Hmong differed in their underlying models of cultural orientation.

In this video Professor Patrice Buzzanell describes critical empathy as a way of approaching cultural differences in communication and design. This video will help you to achieve the learning objective of appreciating the importance of ethical principles in intercultural communication. Watch it to see how critical empathy is applied in practice.

This video is available at http://study.sagepub.com/liu3e

SAGE VIDEO SOURCES

In the social jungle of human existence, there is no feeling of being alive without a sense of identity.

Erik Erikson, German-born American developmental psychologist, 1902–1994

6

IDENTITIES AND SUBGROUPS

LEARNING OBJECTIVES

At the end of this chapter, you should be able to:

- Define identities at the individual and collective levels.

- Explain the characteristics of cultural and national identity.

- Understand the theories of identity and identity negotiation.

- Analyse the relationship between identity and intercultural communication.

INTRODUCTION

Throughout our lives we identify with various social groups, and hence develop multiple identities. Identities can be studied at the individual or collective level. At the individual level, an individual uses characteristics that distinguish the self from others as members of categories, along with the specific relationships he or she has with others. At the collective level, the identification is based on group membership, and serves to make groups rather than individuals distinctive (Tajfel, 1978). Identification with and perceived acceptance into a group involves learning systems of symbols as well as values, norms and rules, which all express people's group or cultural affiliation. Racial identity, for example, is a type of identity at the collective level; it involves a group that characterizes itself or is characterized by others as being distinct by biological differences (even in the absence of actual biological evidence). In addition to race and culture, identities can be defined by gender, class, ethnicity, religion, sexual and political orientation, social group, occupation and geographic region, among others. Because of our multiple group memberships, we always engage in communicating with people from outgroups (groups we do not belong to). Humans in all cultures desire positive individual and group identities. Therefore, we negotiate identities through communication, particularly when we are positioned into groups that we do not want to be a part of.

This chapter focuses on identities and subgroups. We first define identities at the individual and collective levels. Then we describe the characteristics of cultural identities and national identities. Because identity is not only self-defined but also ascribed by others, sometimes our ascribed identity might not be the one we would like to use to categorize ourselves. In this situation, we negotiate identities, hence theories of identity and and identity negotiation are introduced. We next define subgroups and use three common subgroups as illustrations of subgroup identities, drawing on various historical and contemporary examples. These three subgroups are categorized by gender, ethnicity and religion. Finally, we discuss the relationship between identity and intercultural communication. Throughout the chapter, we emphasize that identity is not given and fixed, but rather is constantly negotiated, performed and reconstructed in the process of communication.

DEFINITIONS OF IDENTITIES AT THE INDIVIDUAL AND COLLECTIVE LEVELS

Identity gives us a sense of place (Castells, 1997). It is generally agreed that the term *identity* refers primarily to a person's subjective experience of himself or herself in relation to the world. Therefore, identity can be defined at personal and social levels.

Personal and social identities

We often use the term personal identity to define an individual in terms of his or her difference from others. The individual creates a self-image and responds to the image created. Others also expect the individual to act in accordance with his or her self-image. Personal identity consists of the things that highlight us as individuals and make us distinct from others who are similar in some ways. Aspects of personal identity include physical features, hobbies, interests, family relationships, social circles, as well as personal aspects of age, sex, nationality, religious affiliation, disability, sexual orientation and so forth. Part of our personal identity, such as sex and genetic characteristics, is given to us at birth. Other parts are developed during our childhood and continue to evolve throughout our lives as we are socialized into society. Personal identity gives individuals a sense of distinctiveness, even when they are in a crowd of similar people.

Individuals belong to various social groups and form identities based on membership of those social groups. We use the term *social identity* to refer to those parts of an individual's self-concept that derive from his or her membership in a group together with the value and emotional significance attached to the membership (Tajfel, 1978). Through this process, society is internalized by individuals on the basis of social categories. Social identities connect individuals to society through group memberships, which influence their beliefs, attitudes and behaviour in their relationships with members of other social groups (Hogg and Abrams, 1988). Social identities define us as group members and distinguish our groups (e.g., national groups, sports groups) from other, perhaps competing, groups. Social groups can be marked by ethnicity, culture, race, nationality, occupation or friendship circles. Moreover, people use their beliefs, attitudes, feelings and behaviours as prototypes to differentiate their own group from other ones. An important consequence of categorizing people (including self-categorization) based on group membership is drawing the boundary between ingroups and outgroups; some types of group (e.g., those with a strong group orientation) and some contexts (e.g., competition for scarce resources) can lead to sharper boundaries being drawn between ingroups and outgroups than others. Social identity influences how we live within diverse cultural contexts and how we connect to a range of social groups and institutions.

Cultural identity

Cultural identity refers to those social identities that are based on membership of a cultural group; they are our identification with and perceived acceptance by a cultural group, into which we are socialized and with which we share a system of symbols, values, behavioural norms and cultural traditions. Our cultural identity comprises elements such as physical appearance, racial traits, skin colour and language, and is formed through socialization. Cultural identity involves the emotional significance we attach to our sense of belonging to a culture (Ting-Toomey, 2005a). We are more aware of our cultural identity when we find ourselves in another culture than when we are in our own culture. The level of our cultural identification influences our behaviour. For example, Anglo-Australians who strongly identify with Australian culture may value freedom, a 'fair go' and independence more than those Anglo-Australians who only weakly identify with their culture. Cultural identity has value and salience content. Value content refers to the criteria that people hold to evaluate appropriate or inappropriate behaviour. In collectivistic cultures such as China it is considered polite for a smoker to offer cigarettes to those he or she is with at the time, but in the United States, it is less common for a smoker to make such an offer. Also, in China a smoker might start smoking in a public place (where smoking is permitted) without asking for permission from the friends he or she is with but who are not smokers; in the United States, such behaviour would be considered inappropriate. Behaviour that is perfectly acceptable in one culture may be considered selfish and impolite in another. A further example of the normative function of culture is coffee drinking. While coffee is a traditional morning drink in most places around the world, in Turkey people drink it almost as a dessert. Turkish coffee is, according to a local proverb, 'black as hell, strong as death, and as sweet as love'. Importantly, when paying in a coffee shop you never pay just for your own cup, you always pay for friends having a coffee together. The idea that each person of the group would pay for their own cup in a coffee shop is not common. The same goes for Italy: when enjoying coffee with friends or colleagues, one person always pays for everyone in the group and people may take turns to pay for the group at future gatherings.

Cultural identity salience refers to the strength of identification with a cultural group. A strong sense of affiliation indicates high cultural identity salience, whereas a weak sense of affiliation reflects low cultural identity salience. Cultural identity salience can be reflected consciously or unconsciously. For example, a person of Nigerian heritage may strongly uphold the commonly held collectivistic values of Nigerian culture, but might not identify strongly as a Nigerian in public contexts. The more our self-concept is influenced by our cultural values, the more likely we are to practise them in communication. Although cultural identity is often defined by one's nation, it is important to note that it is different from national identity. Cultural identity refers to the sense of belonging to one's cultural heritage, whereas national identity tends to refer to one's legal status in a specific nation (Ting-Toomey, 2005a).

National identity

National identity is characterized by one's individual self-perception as a member of a nation. Smith (2007) contends that national identity is a politically organized category that is reproduced and reinvented through different symbols, values, memories, myths and traditions that compose the distinctive heritage of a nation. The national flag that hangs outside government buildings in every country represents a symbol of national identity, because the national flag symbolizes the distinctive features of the nation. Every national flag has a historical story behind it, explaining what the symbols and colours on the flag stand for. Some of those stories might be based on historical facts, whereas others might be legends. Nevertheless, the stories are passed on from one generation to another. Every nation also has a national anthem, which communicates the history and identity of the nation.

National identity has two main features. First, it is based on a set of common characteristics that hold members of the nation together. These characteristics include a common descent, shared culture, language and common historical heritage, and a common legal and economic system (Smith, 2007). National identity creates feelings of national belonging: where you belong is where you feel safe, where you are recognized and understood, and where you are accepted 'among your own people' – they understand you, as you understand them; and this understanding creates a sense of shared identity.

Second, national identity always implies difference – it involves not only awareness of the ingroup (people from the same nation), but also awareness of others from whom the nation seeks to differentiate itself. Like other types of identity, national identity suggests similarity, unity and difference; it is salient in relation to other nations (Hutchinson, 1987). In order to distance ourselves from other nations, we create distinctive national markers. For example, France promotes itself as culturally and historically based; the United States prides itself on being freed from historical ties; Israel is known as the Holy Land, being holy for all Abrahamic religions, including Judaism, Christianity, Islam and the Bahá'í faith.

National identity has both political and cultural aspects. The political aspect is related to the presence of common political institutions, rights and duties, while the cultural aspect refers to people's sense of belonging to a common cultural heritage (Smith, 2007). A nation's history and myths of origin serve to reinforce the sense of national identity. For example, the Jewish myth is based on the notion of the 'Chosen People' and the story of Exodus; the Italians see themselves as descending uniquely from the Romans, and relate their identity to the history of Roman culture and the Catholic religion; Greek identity is founded on the belief that they are the direct descendants of the Ancient Greeks; Indians see their roots in the stories of Mahābhārata and Rāmāyana; in Japan the myth of origin starts with the legend of Emperor Jimmu (Seton-Watson, 1977). The historical accuracy of all these myths can easily be challenged. Nevertheless, the power of the myths helps to create a sense of national identity.

PHOTO 6.1   Bryggen, one of Bergen's and Norway's main attractions, was built after the great fire in 1702 and is included in the UNESCO World Heritage List.

Copyright © Shuang Liu. Used with permission.

As in every nation-state today, there are debates about national identity, and about who has it and who does not. For example, in Warsaw, one of the biggest gatherings of far-right activists in Europe in recent years was organized in November 2017. The march was mobilized by far-right groups in Poland as an annual event to celebrate Poland's independence from Russia, Austria and Germany at the end of the First World War. Some demonstrators chanted 'Pure Poland, white Poland!' and 'Refugees get out!'. Those exclusionary, xenophobic phrases and far-right symbols were combined with calls to regain 'national identity' in order to protect a Polish nation from non-Poles. Another example is Sweden. Sweden has undergone two somewhat contradictory political processes: the increasing presence of non-white and non-Western immigrants in the country, and the entry of the racist party Sweden Democrats (Sverigedemokraterna) into Parliament in September 2010. These developments challenged two seemingly incompatible constructions of Swedish identity – 'the old Sweden' (conceiving of Sweden as a homogeneous country) and 'the good Sweden' (framing Sweden as an anti-racist and feminist country), both of which ultimately constitute the 'double-binding power of Swedish whiteness' (Hübinette and Lundström, 2011: 43). These examples illustrate the political aspects of national identity.

DO IT!

Search the website to locate the lyrics of national anthems from three countries. Analyse the content of each to see what the lyrics tell you about the country and its people. Compare the themes revealed across the three countries and identify similarities and differences. In a one-page essay, reflect on the national identity of each country – what are the distinctive characteristics that define each nation, as reflected in their national anthems?

IDENTITY DEVELOPMENT AND IDENTITY NEGOTIATION

Rita Hardiman (2001) proposes that identity development follows several stages, based on her research on white people in Western cultures. The first stage is called unexamined identity, which is characterized by acceptance of the dominant norms and a lack of desire to look into one's identity. Following this is acceptance, a stage during which dominant group members internalize the identity imposed by the culture. In the third stage, redefinition, a re-interpretation of the dominant culture occurs and may be accompanied by attempts to openly challenge it. The fourth stage is integration, whereby white people connect themselves to a dominant culture that reflects an awareness of the special privilege accorded to them and an appreciation of the values of minority cultures. Of course, identity development may not necessarily follow a linear process, and each stage of identity development may not be achieved by all individuals.

Identity development through adolescence is an example. Psychologists often regard adolescence as a period of self-identity and growth, particularly in relation to the physical and social changes that teenagers go through during this time. Social identities are activated through self-categorization, particularly through comparison of oneself with others (Tajfel, 1978), and scholars believe that during adolescence young people undergo stages of identity development. Tanti and colleagues (2011: 556) argue that 'in most Western cultures, adolescents generally experience significant change in their social world during two major transitions that are clearly afforded by the prevailing social-cultural milieu': transition from primary school to secondary school, and transition from secondary school to university or work. Both of these transitions involve a marked period of discontinuity in the adolescents' social world. Teenagers may confront more diverse and heterogeneous social situations, and different roles, responsibilities and expectations in the different groups they are associated with. All these experiences give rise to the possibilities of new social group memberships and identities. In their study, Tanti and colleagues (2011) found that the stages of identity development among adolescents are shaped by the stereotyping of the groups they belong to (ingroups) as well as of the groups they do not belong to (outgroups).

Intercultural research shows that individuals develop an understanding of the world around them, learning the important societal rules, norms and behaviours appropriate to their cultural environment, between the ages of 14 and 18, and that such knowledge is crucial to cultural identity formation (Phinney, 1990). Children growing up in a multicultural environment may have their identity development disrupted because they have to move between cultures before they can be socialized in any one culture. For example, Hoersting and Jenkins (2011) reported that individuals who experience multiple cultural frameworks before the age of 14 are at an elevated risk of cultural homelessness. On the other hand, other scholars argue that immersion in more than one culture can help to develop cultural sensitivity and multicultural competence (LaFramboise, Coleman and Gerton, 1993). Studies on third-culture children (those who have spent a significant part of their developmental years outside the parents' culture) revealed mixed findings: for some participants, having mixed cultural identity enables them to move between two cultures without feeling disoriented; but for other participants, mixed cultural identities can lead to some level of identity confusion.

THEORY CORNER

COMMUNICATION THEORY OF IDENTITY

The communication theory of identity proposes that identity is formed, maintained and modified in communicative processes because a person's sense of self is defined and redefined in social interaction (Hecht et al., 2005). This communicative approach is largely informed by theories from the role identity theory in sociology and social identity theory in social psychology. Role identity theory explains the relationship between the individual and society on the basis of roles. Within this framework, a role refers to 'the functions or parts a person performs when occupying a particular position within a particular social context' (Schlenker, 1985: 18). Since a person's role involves a pattern of social behaviour that conforms to the expectations of others and to the demands of the context, role identities are formed in opposition to and in relation to others (Hecht et al., 2005). Individuals wield control over which role to perform in which situation, although this presentation of the self has various personal and social constraints. On the other hand, the premise of social identity theory is that identity formation is a product of social categorization (Hogg, 1993). Individuals form identities based on memberships of various social groups, and through this process society is internalized by individuals in the form of social identities. Social identity theory emphasizes the social aspects of identity and group processes over individual aspects, whereas role identity theory, from a sociological perspective, focuses on individual roles in the individual–society relationship.

Communication theory of identity complements role identity theory by acknowledging identity as relational, and at the same time utilizes the notion of group-based identities and categorization from social identity theory. However, it extends both fields by situating identity in social interaction. Specifically, first, the theory proposes that identity is formed when relevant symbolic meanings are attached to and organized in an individual through social interaction (role identity theory).

Second, it proposes that when people place themselves in socially recognizable categories, they validate through social interaction whether those categories are relevant to them (social identity theory). Thus, identity is formed and reformed through categorization in social interaction. In this sense, the communicative theory of identity views the group and social roles as important aspects of the self, and the categorization processes are one of the bases by which identity is established and enacted (Hecht et al., 2005).

REFERENCES

Hecht, Michael, Warren, Jennifer R., Jung, Eura and Krieger, Janice L. (2005) 'The communication theory of identity', in W. B. Gudykunst (ed.), *Theorizing about Intercultural Communication*. Thousand Oaks, CA: Sage. pp. 257–278.

Hogg, Michael (1993) 'Group cohesiveness: A critical review and some new directions', *European Review of Social Psychology*, 4: 85–111.

Schlenker, Barry R. (1985) 'Introduction: Foundation of the self in social life', in B. R. Schlenker (ed.), *The Self and Social Life*, New York: McGraw-Hill. pp. 1–28.

SUBGROUPS AND IDENTITIES

Within the larger cultural or national context, there are various subgroups to which we belong. Subgroup memberships give people a sense of identity and belonging, and mark the boundaries between the self and others or between ingroups and outgroups. As there are so many subgroups, it is not possible to cover all subgroups and identities in this chapter; we focus on three common subgroups and their associated identities as illustrations.

Subgroup defined by gender and gender identity

Gender identity is part of personal as well as social identity. The term 'gender' entails social roles established for the sexes, while the term 'sex' refers to a biological category, usually determined at birth. Gender is a social interpretation of biological sex and its associated cultural assumptions and expectations. All cultures divide some aspects of human existence into distinct male and female roles, but the content of gender roles – the norms for behaviour and the expectations and assumptions associated with them – vary across cultures. These characteristics may or may not be closely related to the biological differences between males and females.

Children develop gender-identity constancy by 5–6 years of age (Lee, 2000). Gender constancy is the concept that a child born as a girl will always be female, will adopt female roles and will grow up to be a woman. Similarly, a child born as a boy will adopt male roles and grow up to be a man. However, these roles have to be learned. The famous Swiss developmental psychologist Jean Piaget, who studied the development of gender identity by examining young children's everyday play interactions, found that by age 5, children tend to play with gender-specific toys. For example, girls tend to play more with dolls, while boys play more with Superman and Batman toys. Moreover, young boys play together in larger groups, while young girls prefer to play more in pairs and smaller groups. It is also during this period of early childhood that children become aware of stereotypical gender roles. For example, a girl may see her mother cook most of the meals at home, and thus learn that cooking is a woman's job; a boy may observe his father carrying out repairs around the house and from this observation start to perceive repairing things as a man's job. Early beliefs about gender roles reflect children's observations of what they see around them, in their family, at school, in the neighbourhood, through mediated channels such as TV, the internet, movies and computer games, and elsewhere in the social environment.

It is society that defines the gender roles we know as feminine and masculine. Masculinity in the West traditionally denoted strength and rationality, whereas femininity was traditionally associated with physical weakness, emotion and intuition. People perform their gender identities daily as a matter of routine. However, when we do not identify with the specific norms of our society, when our identity does not fit the dominant culture, or when we do not respond in socially accepted ways to our assigned identity, then we may be disparaged or discriminated against. Resisting an assigned identity can be extremely difficult since much of identity maintenance and expression takes place at a subconscious level. Moreover, the mass media, school, religion, the internet and other social agencies are creators of gender stereotypes which reinforce the gender roles we are supposed to inhabit. For example, males are often shown on television as strong and brave, powerful and dominant, whereas female characters often appear as submissive, emotional and primarily focused on romantic relationships. These media representations inform and influence our understandings and expectations of gender roles in the real world.

However, gender identity is not necessarily limited to male or female. In some societies there is a third gender, which is often used to refer to a person who performs the role of the opposite gender. The Native American *berdache* is defined as an individual with two spirits, both masculine and feminine. The *berdache* is believed to have supernatural powers. In India, the *hijra* are recognized as a special caste; they are born with male genitals, but do not accept specifically male or female gender roles. Instead, they identify themselves as *hijra*. In the Islamic culture of Oman, males who wear clothing that mixes masculine and feminine characteristics and who engage in sexual relations with males are called *khanith*; they are also categorized as people of a third gender. The *fa'afafine* of Samoa, the *fakaleiti* of Tonga and the *mahu* of Hawaii and Tahiti further illustrate that gender identity can be disconnected from gender roles. These people are males with a feminized gender identity, dressed in feminine attire and performing female-designated tasks. Importantly, these third-gender roles are accepted not only by the individuals themselves, but also by the wider society in which they live. For example, Samoa's social acceptance of *fa'afafine* has evolved from the long tradition of raising some boys as girls. In families with all male children, or in which the only daughter is too young to assist with the women's work, parents often choose one or more of their sons to help the mother. These boys perform women's work and are raised and dressed as girls.

PHOTO 6.2   Nesting dolls (matryoshka), a set of typically seven wooden dolls of decreasing sizes that all fit inside of each other, are very popular Russian souvenirs.

Copyright © Zala Volčič. Used with permission.

DO IT!

Despite legislation to prevent discrimination, individuals who identify as LGBT (gay, lesbian, bisexual and transgender) remain a target of exclusion in many parts of the world. Search the internet or local sources to locate an event organized by an LGBT community and talk to the people there about their views on stereotypes and prejudices against LGBT people. Write a brief report of your findings and include your view on what challenges face the LGBT community and individuals. Present your report to the class.

Subgroups defined by ethnicity and ethnic identity

Ethnicity can be based on national origin, race or religion. Ethnicity is different from race, but as a concept it is often used interchangeably with race. However, race is based on biological characteristics, while ethnicity is based on cultural characteristics shared by people of a particular race, national origin, religion or language. *Ethnic identity* refers to a sense of belonging to or identification with an ethnic group. Individuals associated with a particular ethnic group do not necessarily act in accordance with ethnic norms, depending on their level of identification. For example, many Australians identify their ethnicity based on the countries from which their ancestors came. Some Vietnamese refugees who came to Australia during the 1970s as adopted orphans may still identify themselves as Vietnamese, although they were brought up in an Anglo-Australian culture and may not even have a Vietnamese name. Thus, the content and salience of a person's ethnic identity reveals the significance of his or her ethnicity (Ting-Toomey, 2005a).

Gudykunst (2004: 81) states that 'it is the shared cultural characteristics that influence communication, not the biological characteristics associated with race'. In intercultural communication, therefore, it is our ethnic identification that influences our behaviour when we interact with others who are different from ourselves. For example, in Greek communities, family, friends and relatives form primary identification circles. Greek Australians are known to be group-oriented, as they perceive their universe in terms of the ingroup over the outgroup, with outgroup members often being viewed with suspicion and mistrust (Cooper et al., 2007). This does not necessarily suggest that membership in an ethnic group automatically translates into identification. As Alba (1990: 22) notes, 'individuals may be ethnic in their "identities" and still consciously reject their ethnic backgrounds'. Skin colour, for example, does not automatically guarantee ethnic identification (Ting-Toomey, 2005b). Tensions can exist between a person's physical attributes or ethnic origin and his or her psychological feeling of belonging to the ethnic group and the values he or she cherishes.

In addition to the value content, ethnic identity is also concerned with the issue of salience. Salience refers to the likelihood that an individual will acknowledge his or her identity in a given context. For example, ethnic identity can be demonstrated by adherence to traditions, customs, language or way of living. Many scholars today agree that ethnic identity is more of a subjective classification than an objective one. It is the extent to which group members feel emotionally bonded by a common set of values, beliefs, traditions and heritage (Ting-Toomey, 2005a). Second- or third-generation immigrants are less likely to feel as close a bond to their ethnic traditions as first-generation immigrants, even though they share the same physical attributes and may even use the ethnic language at home.

THEORY CORNER

INTERPELLATION

We like to think that, as individuals, our thoughts, behaviours and various other social attributes emerge from deep within the core of our being: we make and create them. At the same time, we recognize that society itself can structure how we think and act; it can shape our hopes and dreams, and even our self-understanding. Louis Althusser (1971), a French philosopher, describes the process whereby a society creates individuals as particular kind of people as a form of 'interpellation' or 'hailing' (as when someone calls out to you, asking you to respond). For Althusser, cultures interpellate or hail particular types of subject. When we come to recognize ourselves as the type of subject being called, the interpellation is successful. That is, we come to identify with the type of subject (or type of person), and in this respect our sense of identity comes not from within, but from the outside – our culture and society that are 'hailing' us.

However, when people are called by a category they do not want to identify with, they can act in a way to resist interpellation. For example, historically, racial discrimination against those marked as 'dark' gave rise to the well-known phenomenon of 'acting white'. This refers to a person's attempt to move out of the marked group into the majority or from a less powerful group to a more powerful one, in order to enjoy the opportunities and privileges reserved for the majority or powerful group members. Sasson-Levy and Shoshana (2013) conducted a cultural analysis of the practice of 'acting white' in Israel. In Israel, the phenomenon of ethnic passing is called *hishtaknezut* in Hebrew. The term refers to *Mizrahim* (Jews from North Africa and the Middle Eastern countries) who adopt the practices associated with Ashkenazim (Jews of European origin). While Ashkenazim in Israel are not considered ethnic in everyday discourse due to their whiteness, Mizrahim are generally marked as the Other, that is, of a disadvantaged ethnic group. In the Israeli context, acting white refers to mimicking the behaviour of the dominant (European) ethnic group. The prevalence of *hishtaknezut* illustrates the perpetuation of the ethnic order in Israel, which distinguishes between worthy social positions and unworthy ones from which one must escape to achieve social privileges.

REFERENCES

Althusser, Louis (1971) 'Ideology and ideological state apparatuses', in *Lenin and Philosophy and Other Essays*. New York: Monthly Review Press.

Sasson-Levy, Orna and Shoshana, Avi (2013) '"Passing" as (non)ethnic: The Israeli version of acting white', *Sociological Inquiry*, 83(3): 448–472.

DO IT!

Stereotypes affect the way people address each other. For example, ageism, as an example of the negative stereotyping of older people, is manifested in daily life through 'elderspeak' – a condescending form of talking that younger people sometimes use to talk to older people. Features of elderspeak include high vocal pitch, exaggerated up-and-down intonation (gushing speech), terms of endearment ('love', 'darling'), and over-inclusive 'we' (e.g., 'how are we feeling today, darling?'). Locate three older and three younger people and gather their views on 'elderspeak'. Do they all have negative views about it? Why or why not? Then write a brief report of your findings and present it to the class.

Subgroups defined by religion and religious identity

Religious identity is the sense of belonging based on membership of a religion. Religion is a powerful cultural institution. It interacts with economic, healthcare, political and education institutions (Dodd, 1998). The word 'religion' comes from the Latin word *religare*, which means 'to tie'. The implication is that religion ties members together to what is sacred. For many people worldwide, their religious traditions anchor them in the world. Although religious identity is closely related to religiosity, the two concepts are not the same. Religious identity refers to religious group membership, regardless of participation in religious activities, whereas religiosity often refers to both religious group membership and participation in religious events (Arweck and Nesbitt, 2010). Similar to ethnic groups, religious groups generally provide members with a repertoire of beliefs, values and worldviews as well as opportunities to socialize with ingroup members. Indeed, some religions, such as the Greek and Serbian Orthodox churches, are closely associated with specific ethnic or national groups. Religion also provides a set of basic (ethical) principles for members to observe. For example, Buddha's four virtues teach people to strive for benevolence, compassion, joy in others' joy, and equanimity. In the past, it was believed that one's religious identity was a social and cultural given, not a result of individual choice. In modern society, however, religion has become more a matter of choice and training, not simply a fact of birth. Many religious groups have been very successful in educating individuals in faith, whether through institutions such as the Catholic Church, spiritual leaders like Buddha or the teachings of the Bible, to mention just a few. Religious beliefs, values and worldviews shape an individual's self-concept.

Religious identity is often associated with a person's way of life. In many cultures, religious rituals such as rites of passage are important events in the life of the society. For thousands of years people have relied on religion to explain the workings of the world, and in some cases the next world. Many people feel a need to look outside themselves to seek help when addressing questions about mortality and immortality, suffering, the meaning of life and death, the creation of the universe, the origin of society, the relation of humankind to nature, even natural phenomena like floods and earthquakes. Religious traditions provide members with beliefs, values, norms and social participation in a community. 'A shared religion reinforces group norms, provides moral sanctions for individual conduct, and furnishes the ideology of common purpose and values that support the well-being of the community' (Haviland, Prins, McBride and Walrath, 2011: 576).

The majority of research on identity formation tends to be devoted to ethnic, gender and cultural identities; relatively less research has been conducted on religious identity. Previous research on religious identity has investigated various factors that can affect the strength of one's religious identification over time, such as gender, ethnicity and generational status. For example, Hirchman (2004) studied the religious identity of adolescents in immigrant families and found that immigrant youths reported higher levels of religious identity than adolescents from non-immigrant families. These findings support the argument that the emotional, social and spiritual support of religious groups can help immigrants to overcome the stress associated with the transition to a new cultural environment. Religious identity is perceived differently by different people. Some see themselves as belonging to a single community that provides them with a firm direction in life; others live in situations where they see themselves as members of various groups. Religious people who have not been raised within a single religious tradition since childhood (converts or children of intercultural marriages) may have to deal with the complexity of identifying with more than one religious identity (Kimball, 2002). Religious prejudice, if not managed properly, can lead to conflict and hatred between different religious groups.

THEORY CORNER

IDENTITY NEGOTIATION THEORY

Identity negotiation theory, proposed by Stella Ting-Toomey (2005a), emphasizes particular identity domains as being influential to our everyday interactions. Individuals acquire and develop their identities through interaction with others, as it is in this way that we acquire the values,

(Continued)

beliefs, norms and styles governing communication behaviour. Identity negotiation theory posits identity as a reflective self-image constructed during the process of communication. The means of negotiating cultural identity is described as 'a transactional interaction process whereby individuals in an intercultural situation attempt to assert, define, modify, challenge, and/or support their own and others' desired self-images' (Ting-Toomey, 2005a: 217). Identity negotiation is present through all communication interactions, as communicators simultaneously attempt to evoke their own desired identities and challenge or support others' identities. Intercultural communication requires the mindful process of attuning to self-identity issues as well as being consciously aware of and attuning to the salient identity issues of others.

When people first meet and interact, they are likely to try to establish respective identities as well as projecting their own desired identity according to situational requirements. As an example of its application, Huang (2011) analysed the communication behaviours of tour guides, whose job requires them to constantly predict and meet the expectations of their customers. With growing tourism across China, it has become vitally important for tour guides to balance or negotiate identities in order to ensure that their communication with international tourists is appropriate and effective. As Huang argues, tour guides already have pre-conceived perceptions of themselves and their expected role; they may also have formed certain stereotypes of tourists from different parts of the world. However, those pre-existing expectations of their customers and their own anticipated role as tour guides may not match. Huang's study revealed that tour guides from China place more emphasis on ethnic identity when interacting with foreign tourists than on professional identity or personal identity. Therefore, identity negotiation has to take place during the initial communication between tour guides and tourists.

REFERENCES

Huang, Ying (2011) 'Identity negotiation in relation to context of communication', *Theory and Practice in Language Studies*, 1(3): 219–225.

Ting-Toomey, Stella (2005a) 'Identity negotiation theory: Crossing cultural boundaries', in W. B. Gudykunst (ed.), *Theorizing about Intercultural Communication*. Thousand Oaks, CA: Sage. pp. 211–233.

IDENTITIES AND INTERCULTURAL COMMUNICATION

In his famous work 'Negotiating Caribbean identities', Stuart Hall (2001: 123) claims that 'identity is a narrative; the stories that cultures tell themselves about who they are and where they came from'. Identities are externally and internally defined – we are created by ourselves and by others at the same time. Our perceptions of self and others influence how we communicate with others.

Identities and intercultural relations

Our appearance, values, dress and language all reveal who we are, and subsequently influence our relationships with others. Theorists of intercultural communication have studied the dominant Western racial category of 'whiteness' in many different ways. They have analysed structural advantage, which is linked to (white) privilege but is not equivalent to it. They have also examined cultural activities that mark white identity. To understand the factors underlying racial identity means to explore new ways of understanding racial identifications as complex social meanings, rather than as objective biological categories. This means that, although the existence of visible racial traits is relevant to racial identity, the significance of such traits is always embedded in specific socio-historical relations of power. For example, hair has a power to shape personal and collective identities in the lives of African-American women in the United States, as it represents a particular racial subgroup. Banks (2000) conducted interviews with over 50 black girls and women between 1996 and 1998 to explore the political complexities of African-American hair and beauty culture. Banks argues that hair shapes black women's identities and their feelings about race, gender, class, sexuality and images of beauty. Since mainstream Western images of beauty do not include tight black curls, the decision of many African-American women to straighten their hair and to use pressing combs reflects a devaluation of their natural hair.

Gudykunst (2004) contends that our social identities emerge from the tension between the need to be seen as similar to and fit in with others and the need to be seen

PHOTO 6.3 In front of the Macedonian state parliament in Skopje stand different statues from an ancient period, representing Macedonian national identity and its ancient roots.

Copyright © Zala Volčič. Used with permission.

as unique and different from others. People demand both inclusion and differentiation in identity validation. Identity conflicts may arise in intercultural situations if one is not treated in the way one expects. Argent (2003) writes that feeling or being made to feel different is a major issue for adopted children, particularly those from cultural backgrounds different from their parents, or for those with a disability. For an adopted child, the stigma of not living with the birth family, as well as living as a cultural minority, may require a long psychological and cultural adjustment. Many children adopted from minority groups have to conform to the demands of the dominant culture, which means internalization of dominant norms, assimilation into the dominant culture and acceptance of that culture's identity. Similarly, communication between those subgroups defined by socioeconomic class may present problems because the most basic class distinction is between the powerful and the powerless. If people from social classes with greater power attempt to retain their own positions in a culture, intergroup communication is unlikely to be successful.

Intercultural communication researchers, such as Young Kim (2008), propose that contact between cultures enables the emergence of intercultural personhood. People who are in an intercultural personhood accept that contact between cultures and people can lead to the development of intercultural identity. Such a development process involves individualization and universalization of one's self–other orientation (Kim, 2008). Individualization refers to a feeling of certainty about one's place in the world. Universalization stands for one's mental outlook when it recognizes the relative nature of values and of the universal aspects of human nature (Kim, 2008). Through individualization and universalization, individuals who undergo the process of intercultural transformation cultivate a mindset that integrates, rather than separates, cultural differences. Moreover, an intercultural person rejects treating culture as given, fixed and external, but instead understands it as an unfinished product and is open to values and practices of culturally different others.

Developing intercultural identity

Individuals who acquire an intercultural identity are willing to negotiate these differences. They are able to reach intercultural agreements, and they desire to integrate diverse cultural elements and achieve identity extension. In particular, they want to go beyond an 'unexamined identity' (Hardiman, 2001), which is the stage of acceptance of the dominant norms and a lack of willingness to look into one's identity and reconstruct or negotiate it. One of the widely known approaches to developing intercultural identity is the *Developmental Model of Intercultural Sensitivity* (DMIS), which was created by Milton Bennett (1986, 1993) as a framework to explain people's reactions to cultural difference. Bennett's argument is that one's experience of cultural difference becomes more complex as one's competence in intercultural relations increases. He observed that individuals confront cultural difference in certain predictable ways as they learn to become more competent intercultural communicators. He organized these observations into six stages of sensitivity to cultural differences, moving from ethnocentric, which characterizes the first three stages, to ethnorelative, which characterizes the last three stages. Table 6.1 summarizes the characteristics of all six stages.

TABLE 6.1   Stages of sensitivity to cultural differences

Sensitivity	Stages	Characteristics
Ethnocentric	Denial	One's own culture is experienced as the only real one. Other cultures are avoided by maintaining psychological and/or physical distance.
	Defence	One's own culture is experienced as the only good one. The world is organized into 'us' and 'them', where we are superior and they are inferior.
	Minimization	Elements of one's own worldview are experienced as universal. People expect similarities and they may insist on correcting others' behaviour to match their expectations.
	Acceptance	One's own culture is experienced as equal to others. Acceptance does not have to mean agreement – cultural difference may be perceived negatively, but the judgement is not ethnocentric.
	Adaptation	The experience of another culture replaces perception and behaviour appropriate to that culture. One's own worldview is expanded to include worldviews from others. People may intentionally change their behaviour to communicate more effectively in another culture.
Ethnorelative	Integration	One's experience of self includes the movement in and out of different cultural worldviews.

Source: Adapted from Bennett, Milton J. (1993) 'Towards ethnorelativism: A developmental model of intercultural sensitivity', in M. Paige (ed.), *Education for the Intercultural Experience.* Yarmouth, ME: Intercultural Press. pp. 343–354.

The DMIS has been used in constructing a competent intercultural identity that aims at understanding other cultures holistically. An open-minded intercultural communicator interacts actively with strangers and does not exclude other possibilities beyond the established cultural boundary. Effective intercultural communication requires both openness to culturally different others and a willingness to negotiate differences. Thus, an intercultural person makes an attempt to abandon cultural stereotypes, prejudices or ethnocentrism and to engage in a dialogue with others. As cultural differences presuppose a need for coordination, intercultural identity negotiation should be interpreted as a process of informing, learning and compromising in order to reach intercultural consensus. Only when difference is recognized can we start to reach out towards each other.

SUMMARY

- Identities can be defined at individual and collective levels. Throughout our lives we develop membership groups and subgroups and form multiple identities.
- Identities are not always self-defined; they can be ascribed by others. Sometimes we do not want to be in the identity categories we are ascribed; then identity negotiation may take place.
- Today's world necessitates processes of identity construction and identity negotiation, as opposed to the slower, more traditional processes of taking on identity.
- The Developmental Model of Intercultural Sensitivity (DMIS), created by Milton Bennett, functions as a framework to explain the reactions of people to cultural differences.
- Intercultural identity can be developed through openness to culturally different others and a willingness to negotiate differences.

JOIN THE DEBATE

IS IDENTITY WHAT WE HAVE OR WHAT WE PERFORM?

Some scholars argue that we act out different identifies according to situational characteristics; hence identities are performance. Immigrants, for example, have to move between heritage and national cultures, and as they do so they take on different identities (e.g., Greek, Greek American, American). Others argue that the core of our identities remains stable across multiple contexts, although our behaviour may change. Our identities, which are based on categories such as ethnicity, race or the physical characteristics associated with ethnicity or gender, are often considered stable across different contexts. However, research has found that people from ethnic minority groups can adopt the strategy of passing (e.g., acting white) in order for others to categorize them as being part of the dominant group they would otherwise not belong to. This strategy may be permanent, but it can also change from one situation to another – for example, acting white in public, but reverting to another identity at home with the family. In addition, nowadays people can choose to change hair and skin colour or even biological sex through surgery or hormone replacement therapy. Is identity what we have or what we perform? Can we always choose our identity? How can we resist the identities that have been ascribed to us by others but that we do not want to have?

Nation branding is a communication strategy that national governments employ to build and maintain a country's strategic advantage (e.g., geographical location, natural resources, culture, economic standing or technology) through managing and controlling the image they project to the world (Dinnie, 2016). As such, nation branding creates and communicates a particular version of national identity, with the purpose of attracting investment, tourism, trade and talent in order to successfully compete with a growing pool of national contenders for a shrinking set of available resources (Aronczyk, 2008). Many governments have invested in nation branding in order to strengthen their country's influence, improve its reputation or boost tourism, trade and investment. For example, in 1998 the British *Cool Britannia* campaign attempted to move Great Britain from the traditional image of Queen, rain, aloofness and snobbery to a cool image of the country. Other examples of branding include attempts to globally promote a national (visual) image and transform it into a commodity. Colombia is branded as *Café de Colombia*; Switzerland is powerfully represented by its delicious chocolates and cheese; Brazil is promoted by samba dancing, carnival, sex, magic, sports, adventure and music; Poland has *The Natural Choice*; Turkey has *Welcome to Friends*. Such nation branding represents a marketable representation of differences, which emphasizes national distinctiveness and even exoticism.

In the Australian context, one of the most, if not *the* most, prominent nation branding campaign was created by the Australian Government's Building Brand Australia programme, namely *Australia Unlimited*. This was a slogan once used by the late Queensland premier Joh Bjelke-Petersen (1911–2005), who was the longest-serving premier of Queensland (1968–1987). In 2009 the Australian Government hosted a series of discussions about the importance of Australia's international image for exporters, and the ways in which industry could benefit from and contribute to updating the Building Brand Australia campaign, which is a government initiative administered by Austrade, the national government agency responsible for promoting Australian trade, investment and education. Those conversations led to a commitment of AU$20 million (approximately US$14 million) over the subsequent four years for the Building Brand Australia programme. The Australia Unlimited campaign was designed by M&C Saatchi following industry consultation, a public tender and extensive international and domestic research, which confirmed a need and desire for a contemporary and consistent way to present Australia internationally, especially in a business-focused context (Australian Government, 2017). At the heart of the Australia

CASE
STUDY

USING
NATIONAL
IDENTITY
TO BRAND
AUSTRALIA

Unlimited concept is the idea that Australia's development has been forged through its enterprising spirit – the resilience, creativity and unquenchable desire of Australians to succeed, no matter what the challenge may be. The logo, two boomerang-shaped arrows, represents the Australian coastline and symbolically conveys the nation's unlimited potential for growth (Khamis, 2012). According to the Australian Trade and Investment Commission, the programme was tested among 14,000 people in 12 markets and was found to effectively project an image of Australia as a confident and globally engaged business partner (Australian Government, 2017).

Using digital content platforms, the Building Brand Australia programme asked Australia's exporters, internationally focused business leaders, 1 million-strong expat community and growing alumni around the world to tell meaningful Australian stories of achievements. For example, the promotion video 'Australia is a land with unlimited potential' (www.australiaunlimited.com/brand-australia/articles/Corporate/2015-australia-unlimited-video), produced in 2015, uses familiar Australian faces (e.g., a chef, scientist, the prime minister, a sports star, a doctor) and familiar places (e.g., a tourist site in an Indigenous community, a top university, the Outback) to showcase excellence across business, culture, design, education, environment, food, science and technology. In addition to covering achievements in various industries, diversity in Australia's population is featured in the video, which includes people with different skin colour, religious dress and ethnic background. These faces communicate the values Australia places on diversity, multiculturalism, equality and 'fair-go'.

Of course, the Australia Unlimited campaign also features the stereotypical image of Australia. For instance, beer and Akubra hats are often associated with Australia as examples of unofficial national symbols. Other things commonly considered Australian are the country's natural assets, including its unique plants and animals, such as gum trees, koalas and kangaroos (Austin and Fozdar, 2016). Australia Unlimited is not simply about how Australians see themselves, that is, their national identity, but also about how Australia wants itself to be seen by others globally. As a national identity, Australia is more than just its friendly people, spectacular environment, sun-drenched beaches and stunning landscapes; it has more to offer. Contemporary Australia is a confident, creative and outward-looking nation, with a strong economy and an abundance of talented people. At the same time, it is a nation rich in cultural, scientific and business talent, driving the country forward with creativity and passion. Despite some criticisms of its over-emphasis on trade and marketing, the Australia Unlimited campaign successfully creates a brand identity of Australia as a cosmopolitan and technologically adept nation.

Aronczyk, Melissa (2008) '"Living the brand": Nationality, globality and the identity strategies of national branding consultants', *International Journal of Communication*, 2(1): 41–65.

Austin, Catherine and Fozdar, Farida (2016) 'Australian national identity: Empirical research since 1998', *National Identities*. Published online 17 October. DOI: 10.1080/14608944.2016.1244520.

Australian Government (2017) *Australia Unlimited*. Australian Trade and Investment Commission. Accessed 23 December 2017 at: www.australiaunlimited.com.

Dinnie, Keith (2016) *Nation Branding: Concepts, Issues, Practice* (2nd edn). New York: Routledge.

Khamis, Susie (2012) 'Brand Australia: Half-truths for a hard sell', *Journal of Australian Studies*, 36(1): 49–63.

1. What are the official symbols (e.g., the flag, national emblem, national anthem) of Australia that you know, and what are the unofficial ones (e.g., elements of dress, speech, locations) that you know?

2. What is your understanding of Australianness? Where is the source of your knowledge of Australia? Has it changed over time?

3. What does this case study tell you about the link between national identity and nation branding?

4. How is your country branded and why? What do you see as the advantages and disadvantages of branding your country in this way?

5. Can you give an example of your own to illustrate how national identity is commercialized in nation branding to produce benefits for economic development?

**Grimson, Alejandro (2010) 'Culture and identity: Two different notions',
Social Identities, 16(1): 61–77.**

This article provides a conceptual distinction between 'culture' and 'identity', forming an essential precondition for analysing social processes. The article enriches our understanding of culture by incorporating decisive contributions from theories on national identity. Culture and nation are highly complex, both dealing with heterogeneous and conflictive entities. The author asserts that culture and identity allude to analytically different aspects of social processes. Therefore, it is necessary to analyse cultural and identity aspects separately.

Housley, William and Fitzgerald, Richard (2009) 'Membership categorization, culture and norms in action', *Discourse & Society*, **20(3): 345–362.**

This article examines the extent to which membership categorization analysis (MCA) can inform an understanding of reasoning within the public domain where morality, policy and cultural politics are visible. The article demonstrates how specific types of category device are a ubiquitous feature of accountable practice in the public domain where morality matters and public policies intersect. Furthermore, the authors argue that MCA provides a useful tool for analysing the mundane mechanics associated with everyday cultural politics and democratic accountability.

Sfard, Anna and Prusak, Anna (2005) 'Telling identities: In search of an analytical tool for investigating learning as a culturally shaped activity', *Educational Researcher*, **34(4): 14–22.**

This article attempts to operationalize the notion of identity to justify the claim about its potential as an analytic tool for investigating learning. The authors define identity as a set of reifying, significant and endorsable stories about a person. These stories, even if individually told, are products of a collective storytelling. Data were obtained from a study of the mathematical learning practices of a group of 17-year-old immigrant students from the former Soviet Union. The authors argue that learning may be considered as closing the gap between actual identity and designated identity.

Usborne, Esther and Taylor Donald M. (2010) 'The role of cultural identity clarity for self-concept clarity, self-esteem, and subjective well-being', *Personality and Social Psychology Bulletin*, **36(7): 883–897.**

This article proposes that a clear cultural identity provides the individual with a clear prototype with which to engage the processes necessary to construct a clear personal identity and, by extension, to achieve self-esteem and well-being. Data were collected from samples of undergraduate students, Anglophone Quebecers, Francophone Québécois, Chinese North Americans and Aboriginal Canadians. The findings show that cultural identity clarity was positively related to self-concept clarity, self-esteem and were markers of subjective well-being.

Volčič, Zala and Andrejevic, Mark (2011) 'Nation branding in the era of commercial nationalism', *International Journal of Communication*, **5: 598–618.**

This article applies critiques of branding and marketing to a case of nation branding in Slovenia. The authors reviewed recent development of nation branding as a global phenomenon and then explored the details of one such campaign in post-socialist Slovenia. The case study illustrates the ways in which nation branding enjoins the populace to 'live' the national brand, and to promulgate it nationally and internationally in the name of taking responsibility for the homeland's economic development.

In this video Professor Michael Bamberg challenges the idea that identity is static. The video will help you to achieve the learning objective of understanding identity negotiation. Watch it to see how Professor Bamberg explains how identity can be managed and mediated depending on the context.

This video is available at http://study.sagepub.com/liu3e

**SAGE VIDEO
SOURCES**

Man acts as though he were the shaper and master of language, while in fact language remains the master of man

Martin Heidegger, German philosopher, 1889–1976

7

VERBAL COMMUNICATION AND CULTURE

LEARNING OBJECTIVES

At the end of this chapter, you should be able to:

- Describe the components and characteristics of language.

- Explain how language shapes our thoughts and behaviour.

- Analyse communication styles and gender differences in verbal communication.

- Appreciate the relationship between language and identity.

INTRODUCTION

Language is an integral part of human lives, and thus has a powerful influence on people's ability to communicate interculturally. The term 'language' may refer not only to spoken and written language, but also to 'body language', although the latter is usually called nonverbal behaviour or nonverbal communication by communication scholars. In this chapter, we will focus on spoken and written language, that is, on verbal codes. People use language to convey their thoughts, feelings, desires, attitudes and intentions, as well as information about the world. We learn about others through what they say and how they say it; we learn about ourselves through how others react to what we say (Bonvillain, 2014). Verbal communication has been studied by scholars from a variety of disciplines, including anthropology, psychology, sociology, political theory and human geography, bringing diverse theories and perspectives into the study of communication and culture. Linguists are key contributors to intercultural communication; they address the question of what is unique about human language in particular, sometimes along with aspects of the voices that accompany language. Whether we speak English, French, Swahili, Dutch, German, Japanese, Slovene, Hindi, Arabic or any one of the numerous languages of the world, the important role language plays in communication holds true.

This chapter concentrates on the relationship between language and culture. We first describe the components and characteristics of language. One particular key feature of verbal communication is that, unlike most nonverbal communication, we are not limited to describing the here and now, but we can and do talk about the past, future or abstract and imaginary things – even impossible things. Next, we explain how language shapes our thoughts and behaviour. We discuss the relationship between language, meaning, perception and reality through the influential Sapir-Whorf hypothesis of linguistic relativity. The chapter then analyses communication styles across cultures, including gender differences in verbal communication. Finally, the chapter examines the relationship between language and identity. We emphasize the integral relationship between language and culture, as well as the important role language plays in influencing how we see ourselves, how we see others and how we relate to those who speak or do not speak our own language.

THE COMPONENTS AND CHARACTERISTICS OF VERBAL CODES

A verbal code comprises a set of rules governing the use of words in creating a message, along with the words themselves. We acquire or learn the rules and contents of our native language (or languages) as we grow up; thus, we can express our thoughts, emotions, desires and needs easily in our native language. The study of language begins with identifying its components and how they are put together.

The components of human language

While studying human language, linguists focus on sound, structure and meaning. Lustig and Koester (2013) identified five interrelated components of language: phonology, morphology, syntax, semantics and pragmatics. Collectively, knowledge of each aspect of the language system provides us with a holistic understanding of the nature of human language.

Phonology explores how sounds are organized in a language. The smallest sound unit of a language that can distinguish meaning is called a phoneme. The phonological rules of a language determine how sounds are combined to form words. For example, the phonemes [k] and [au] can be arranged to form the word 'cow' [kau] in English. Mastery of any language requires the speaker to be able to identify and pronounce different sounds accurately. This may prove difficult for second-language speakers, particularly those whose native language does not have a similar sound system to the new language.

Morphology refers to the combination of basic units that carry meaning (morphemes) to create words. For example, the word 'happy' consists of one morpheme, meaning to feel cheerful. The word 'unhappy' contains two morphemes: happy and the prefix 'un' meaning 'not' or the 'opposite'. Used together, they refer to a feeling akin to sadness. Morphemes, and the ways in which they are combined, differ across cultures. In the English language, prefixes or suffixes constitute morphemes as well as individual words, whereas in tonal languages, such as Chinese, tones are morphemes and the meaning of units depends on the tone with which the word is pronounced. Turkish combines many morphemes through prefixes and suffixes to convey complex meanings, whereas French tends to use several words to do this.

Syntax concerns the grammatical and structural rules of language. We combine words into sentences according to grammatical rules in order to communicate. In English and other languages of the Indo-European family, people change the tense of a verb by adding a suffix or prefix or changing the morpheme. In German, prepositions are often placed at the end of a sentence, whereas in French they are placed before nouns or noun phrases. Every language has a set of grammatical rules that govern the sequencing of words. Mastery of another language means knowing those grammatical rules in addition to building a stock of vocabulary.

Semantics refers to the study of the meanings of words, and the relationships between words and the things they refer to. A command of vocabulary is an essential part of linguistic proficiency in any language. When we learn a second language, we devote much time to memorizing words and their meanings, concrete or abstract. However, just memorizing words and their dictionary meanings is often insufficient for successful intercultural communication, because meaning often resides in a (cultural) context.

Pragmatics is concerned with the impact of language on human perception and behaviour. It focuses on how language is used in a social context. The pragmatic analysis of language goes beyond its structural features and concentrates on the social and cultural appropriateness of language use in a particular context. For example, a fairly direct communication style is preferred for resolving interpersonal conflicts in South Africa or Germany; a more indirect approach tends to be favoured in South Korea, where the preservation of harmony is strongly valued.

THEORY CORNER

STRUCTURAL LINGUISTICS

Linguists have developed descriptive and explanatory tools to analyse the structure of language. *Structural linguistics* views language as a coherent system whereby every item acquires meaning in relation to the other items in the system. The rise of modern structural linguistics came largely through the influence of the Swiss linguist Ferdinand de Saussure (1857–1913) in the early twentieth century. De Saussure claims that meaning resides within the text (de Saussure, 1983). Within each language system, spoken or written words (the *signifier*) attribute meaning to objects, concepts and ideas (the *signified* – mental pictures produced by the signifier) in the construction of reality. The relation between signifier and signified is based on convention. For example, the linguistic sign 'dog' (signifier) represents 'a four-legged, barking domestic animal' (signified). We recognize the meaning of the word 'dog' from its difference from other similar-sounding words, such as 'hog' and 'doe', which produce different mental pictures. We also use the difference between dog and similar concepts, such as 'cat' and 'rabbit', as well as opposing concepts, such as 'human', in comprehending meaning. De Saussure compared language to a game of chess, noting that a chess piece in isolation has no value and that a move by any one piece has repercussions for all the other pieces. Similarly, the meaning of a unit in a language system can be discerned by examining the items that occur alongside it and those which can be substituted for it (de Saussure, 1983).

The structural approach dominated linguistics in the United States in the mid-twentieth century, when the prime concern of American linguists such as Leonard Bloomfield was to produce a catalogue of the linguistic elements of a language and a statement of the positions in which they could occur. However, critiques of de Saussure's model argue that abstract concepts like justice, truth and freedom cannot be tied directly to the outside world, and that they mean different things to different people. Linguists and social psychologists therefore identify two types of meaning: denotative and connotative. *Denotation* refers to the literal meaning of a word or an object and is basically descriptive. This is the kind of meaning we find in a dictionary. For example, a denotative description of a Big Mac would be that it is a sandwich sold by McDonald's that weighs a certain number of grams and is served with certain sauces. *Connotation* deals with the cultural meanings that become attached to a word or an object. The connotative meaning of a Big Mac may include certain aspects of American culture – fast food, popular food, standardization, lack of time and lack of interest in cooking. Because connotative meanings are often emotionally charged, we may make mistakes about the messages we think we are sending to others. Hence, researchers have noted that the connotative meaning may differ across languages or cultures even when the denotative meaning is the same.

REFERENCE

de Saussure, Ferdinand (1983) *Course in General Linguistics*. Edited by C. Bally and A. Sechehaye, translated and annotated by R. Harris. London: Duckworth.

The characteristics of verbal codes

It is important to stress that communication is symbolic, but not all symbols are linguistic. In linguistics, symbols represent a subcategory of signs, and like signs, they are not completely arbitrary. The *symbol* of justice, a pair of scales, cannot be replaced by just any symbol, such as a chariot (de Saussure, 1983). Symbols, like gestures or cries, may be shared with other animals. There are significant limits on the messages such symbols can communicate; these messages are mostly formed on the basis of a stimulus and are related to the present, without reference to the past, future or imaginary situations. However, the relationship between a linguistic symbol (such as the word 'cow') and its *referent* (a four-legged animal that gives milk) is completely arbitrary; there is nothing 'cowy' about the word 'cow', and the same referent is called 'vache' in French. There is no natural relationship between a word and its referent.

Although languages differ, there are some characteristics shared by all of them. Neuliep (2017) identified five common characteristics. First, all languages have some way of naming objects, places or things. Second, all languages have a way of naming action. Third, all languages have a way of stating the negative, constructing interrogatives and differentiating between singular and plural. Fourth, all languages have a systematic set of sounds, combined with a set of rules for the sole purpose of creating meaning and communicating, with no natural or inherent relationship between the sounds and their accompanying alphabet. Fifth, all languages have a set of formal grammatical rules for combining sounds and sequencing words to create meaning.

LANGUAGE, THOUGHTS AND BEHAVIOUR

The language we speak affects how we see things around us, how we think and act in the world, as well as how we want to be seen by others based on what we say and do. Language learning is an essential part of the education process in almost all schools, regardless of culture. As Dan Slobin (2000: 110) writes, 'Children in all nations seem to learn their native languages in much the same way. Despite the diversity of tongues, there are linguistic universals that seem to rest upon the developmental universals of the human mind'. Scholarly debates have centred on the issue of whether language is innately programmed, requiring only minimal environmental stimuli to trigger it, or whether language is actively learned through the general learning mechanisms present while children are growing up. We can divide the language acquisition debate into two contrasting views: nativists versus constructivists (Hoff, 2001).

Noam Chomsky's universal grammar

Nativists such as Chomsky argue that language acquisition involves triggering these models, so that only the details of a particular language must be learned (Chomsky, 1980). Noam Chomsky (1975) claimed that all human languages share a universal grammar that is innate in the human species and culturally invariant. Just as humans are programmed to walk upright, so too are human minds equipped with a set of pre-programmed models that are triggered when exposed to the surrounding language. Chomsky says that language is as much a part of the human brain as the thumb is a part of the human hand. One of the most remarkable features of any language's rule structure is that it allows speakers to generate sentences that have never before been spoken. Chomsky refers to this aspect of language as *generative universal grammar*. From a finite set of sounds and rules, speakers of any language can create an infinite number of sentences, many of which have never before been uttered. The commonalities between different languages are so strong that Chomsky and other linguists are convinced that the fundamental syntax for all languages is universal, and that particular languages are simply dialects of the universal grammar.

Constructivists, grounded in the work of Piaget, oppose the idea that there is a universal grammar. They argue that language acquisition involves unveiling the patterns of language, and thus requires interaction with a structured environment (Piaget, 1977). A famous language acquisition debate between Chomsky and Piaget took place in 1975 at the Abbaye de Royaumont near Paris, nearly 200 years after the wild boy of Aveyron was found in France. The wild boy of Aveyron lived his entire childhood in the forests and lacked any language before he was found. Piaget saw the wild boy and his mind as an active, constructive agent that slowly inched forward in a perpetual bootstrap operation; Chomsky viewed the boy's mind as a set of essentially pre-programmed units, each equipped with its rules that needed only the most modest environmental trigger to develop. As Hoff (2001) points out, both sides are right, and indeed the line between nativists and constructivists is not clear-cut. Language may be natural behaviour, but it still has to be carefully nurtured.

The Sapir-Whorf hypothesis

Philosophical debates surround the question of the extent to which our perception is shaped by the particular language we speak. *Nominalists* argue that our perception of external reality is shaped not by language but by material reality. Any thought can be expressed in any language and can convey the same meaning. *Relativists* believe that our language determines our ideas, thought patterns and perceptions of reality (Hoff, 2001). A classic example to illustrate the relativists' view that language shapes our perception of reality is the existence of numerous Eskimo words for 'snow', whereas in English there are fewer words for this concept. The relationship between language and thought is well captured in the *Sapir-Whorf hypothesis*, which proposes that language and thought are inextricably tied together, so that (in the original and strongest version of the hypothesis) a person's language determines the categories of thought open to the person. In his book *Language, Thought and Reality* (1956: 239), Whorf states that 'We cut up and organize the spread and flow of events as we do largely because, through our mother tongue, we are parties to an agreement to do so, not because nature itself is segmented in exactly that way for all to see'.

Edward Sapir (1884–1939), a famous linguist and anthropologist, published a paper that changed the face of the study of language and culture. He argued that the language of

PHOTO 7.1 Beverly Hills is more than a place name; it symbolizes Hollywood stars, expensive houses, upscale shopping streets and extravagant lifestyles.

a particular culture directly influences how people think, and speakers of different languages see different worlds. In 1931, Benjamin Lee Whorf (1897–1941) enrolled in Sapir's course on Native American linguistics at Yale University. In his study of the Hopi language, Whorf learned that in Hopi, the past, present and future tenses must be expressed differently from English, as the Hopi language does not have verb tense. This led Whorf to believe that people who speak different languages are directed to different types of observations of the world. Sapir and Whorf's ideas received great attention and became known as the Sapir-Whorf hypothesis.

Sapir and Whorf claimed that a cultural system is embodied in the language of the people who speak the language. This cultural framework shapes the thoughts of the language's speakers. We think in the words and the meanings of our language, which in turn is an expression of our culture. The Sapir-Whorf hypothesis has two versions: strong and weak. The strong version of the hypothesis, or linguistic determinism, posits that the language one speaks determines one's perception of reality. The weak version of the hypothesis, or linguistic relativity, makes the claim that native language exerts an influence over one's perception of reality. The differences among languages are thus reflected in the different worldviews of their speakers.

Consider some examples of how language categorizes our world. In Chinese there are no single words that are equivalent to the English words 'uncle' and 'aunt'. Instead, Chinese has different words for one's father's elder brother, younger brother, mother's elder brother and younger brother, other different words for elder or younger brother-in-laws, and so forth. This diversity of terms may suggest that the interpersonal relationships between an individual and his or her extended family are more complex and perhaps more important in China than in English-speaking countries. Arabic has many words for 'camel', whereas English has few. The word 'moon' is masculine in German (*der Mond*), feminine in French (*la lune*) and neither masculine nor feminine in English (which does not use word gender for nouns). Also, if you speak a language where you must decide on a form of second-person address (you) that defines your social relationship to your interlocutor – such as Spanish *tu* ('you' for friends and family) versus *usted* ('you' for those with whom you have no close connection) or French *tu* versus *vous* – you must categorize every person you talk to in terms of the relevant social dimensions. This kind of categorization can even vary within the same language. For example, French speakers in Belgium are more likely to call others *tu* than they are in France. In English, this distinction has largely disappeared, but there are still areas (e.g., Yorkshire) where it persists.

Language categorizes our experiences without our full awareness. Only when an individual learns a second language and moves back and forth between the first and second language does the person become aware of the influence that language has on perception. The Sapir-Whorf hypothesis does not imply that people of one culture cannot think of objects for which another culture has a plentiful vocabulary (Neuliep, 2017). Rather, the fact that we do not think of certain concepts or objects in such specificity may mean that such distinctions are less important to our culture. It is worth noting that this same thing applies to the specialized languages of different professions. For example, medical doctors, lawyers and academics have extensive vocabularies marking their areas of expertise; they learn these terms and the concepts and relationships underlying them as they learn their profession. Thus, the Sapir-Whorf hypothesis shows that language, thought and culture (including professional and other types of subculture) are closely connected. Language, as a part of culture, affects how we perceive the world, and thus influences the meanings that are conveyed by words.

DO IT!

UNESCO's *Atlas of the World's Languages in Danger* lists roughly 600 languages as critically endangered or dying. Scholars argue that at least 100 languages around the world have only a handful of speakers – from *Ainu* in Japan to *Yagan* in Chile. Search the internet to locate one language that is on the verge of dying or has already disappeared. Find out the reason for its disappearance and what cultural knowledge might have been lost along with the disappearance of that language. Write a one-page report on what you have learned.

THEORY CORNER

PIDGINS AND CREOLES

Pidgins and creoles are formed as a result of contact between languages and culture. *Pidgins* are formed and used when two communities that do not share a common language come into contact and need to communicate. This is very common, especially in trade or other business activities. Common pidgins based on English, French, Spanish and Portuguese are used in the East and West Indies, Africa and the Americas. A pidgin has a simplified grammatical structure, a reduced lexicon (vocabulary) and refers mainly to a small set of contexts – it is about situational

(Continued)

use (McWhorter, 2003). For example, a line taken from a comic strip in Papua New Guinea is 'Fantom, yu pren tru bilong mi. Inap yu ken helpim mi nau'. Its translation is 'Phantom, you are a true friend of mine. Are you able to help me now?'. In this case, many of the words are based on English, but local languages have a strong influence on morphology and syntax. Pidgin is not a native language to those using it, but is a code system developed for a specific purpose. When a pidgin is passed on to future generations who acquire it as a first language, it can develop and become a creole.

A *creole* is a new language developed from the prolonged contact of two or more languages. It is a language that expands and regularizes its structural systems, and the next generation learns it as their first language. A creole develops a grammar, morphology, lexicon, phonetics and phonology: English-based creoles contain words like 'banan' (banana), 'chek' (check), 'maket' (market). A creole is a full, linguistically complex language in its own right: examples include Hawai'ian creole English and Louisiana creole French (McWhorter, 2003).

It is important to understand the social histories of the speakers of varieties of these languages. Shapiro (2012) investigated the socio-historical development of Chinese pidgin Russian, its phonology, morphology, syntax, typology and vocabulary. Initially developing on the Russian–Mongolian border around the trade city of Kyakhta, Chinese pidgin Russian later spread along the Russian–Chinese border. Shapiro analysed travelogues, newspapers, phrasebooks, dictionaries and texbooks from the 1770s onwards. His findings showed that because the Chinese were adamant about not allowing foreigners to learn Chinese, they required Chinese businessmen and shop assistants in Kyakhta to learn Russian. However, the 'Russian' they taught and made their own material for was Russian written in Chinese characters! Russian merchants adapted to 'try to fit in with this broken speech known by the name of Kyakhta trade language' (Shapiro, 2012: 6). In his analysis, Shapiro unravelled Chinese interpretations of Russian phonetics, semantics and grammar, which were all written in Chinese characters. He also examined Russian interpretations of Chinese phonetics, semantics and grammar, all of which were written in Cyrillic.

REFERENCES

McWhorter, John (2003) *The Power of Babel: A Natural History of Language.* New York: Perennial/HarperCollins.

Shapiro, Roman (2012) 'Chinese pidgin Russian', in A. Umberto (ed.), *Pidgins and Creoles in Asia*. Amsterdam and Philadelphia, PA: John Benjamins. pp. 1–58.

CULTURAL VARIATIONS IN VERBAL COMMUNICATION

Cultural variation in verbal communication is reflected in communication styles, including differences between males and females in communication. People from different social or cultural groups may experience similar events; however, there are vast differences in the ways in which they use language to interpret their experiences.

Cultural variation in communication styles

Communication style refers to how language is used to convey meaning to others. Recognizing the differences in communication styles can help us understand the cultural differences underpinning the verbal communication process. Two leading communication researchers, Gudykunst and Ting-Toomey (1988), identified four communication styles: direct/indirect, elaborate/succinct, personal/contextual and instrumental/affective. Successful communication not only depends on what is said, but also on how the message is communicated.

The dimension of *direct/indirect communication style* stands for the extent of explicity expressed in a message. A *direct communication style* is one in which the speaker's needs, wants, desires and intentions are explicitly communicated. Conversely, an *indirect communication style* is one in which the speaker's true intentions or needs are only implied or hinted at during the conversation. Research indicates that indirect styles are more likely to be used in collectivistic cultures, such as in Japan, China, South Korea and Hong Kong, where harmony is considered important for maintaining good interpersonal relationships. By comparison, Western or individualistic cultures generally prefer a direct communication style. As an example, an American student asked his Nigerian friend to give him a lift on an evening when the Nigerian had made a commitment to babysit his niece so that his sister could go to work. However, instead of saying 'Sorry I cannot do it', the Nigerian replied by talking about how his sister could perhaps stay home instead of working that night. The American student felt confused as to what his Nigerian friend was trying to say. In American culture, if such a request for a lift is inconvenient, one would simply respond by saying 'Sorry, I can't do it'. However, in collectivistic cultures like Nigeria, it is not considered polite to say 'no' to a friend – but it is the responsibility of the person who made the request to figure out that it is not appropriate to ask for the favour. The differences in expectations of appropriate communication styles can lead to misunderstandings between speakers.

The dimension of *elaborate/succinct communication style* is concerned with the quantity of talk a culture values, and reflects a culture's attitudes towards talk and silence (Martin and Nakayama, 2001). The *elaborate style* involves the use of rich, expressive and embellished language in everyday conversation. For example, rather than simply saying that someone is thin, a comment such as 'she is so thin that she can walk between rain drops without getting wet' embellishes and colours the statement. Arab, Middle Eastern and African-American cultures tend to use metaphorical expressions in everyday conversation. In the *succinct communication style*, simple assertions and even silence are valued. The elaborate style tends to characterize individualistic cultures, in which the direct communication style is preferred. Conversely, in collectivistic cultures, where the indirect communication style is favoured, communicators are sometimes expected to figure out the meaning conveyed by contextual cues, rather than asking direct questions.

The dimension of *personal/contextual communication style* refers to the extent to which the speaker emphasizes the self as opposed to his or her role. Gudykunst and Ting-Toomey (1988) define the *personal communication style* as one that amplifies the individual identity of the speaker. This style is often used in individualistic cultures, which emphasize individual goals over those of the group. Person-centred communication tends to be informal and is reflected by the use of the pronoun 'I'. On the other hand, the *contextual communication style* is oriented by status and role. Formality and power distance are often emphasized. The contextual communication style is often seen in collectivistic cultures where one's role identity and status are highlighted. For example, instead of using 'you' for all persons, as is the case in English, in Japanese there exists an elaborate system of linguistic forms that are used to communicate respect to people of different ranks or social status.

The dimension of *instrumental/affective communication style* is related to whether communication is sender-focused and goal-oriented or receiver-focused and process-oriented.

PHOTO 7.2   Names of popular tourist places in Beijing, like Silk Street, have been translated into English; however, 'Silk' – the English translation – is a rough sound equivalence of the Chinese name (Siu Shui), not a concept equivalence.

Copyright © Shuang Liu. Used with permission.

The *instrumental style* is goal-oriented and sender-focused. The speaker uses communication to achieve an outcome. The *affective communication* style is receiver-focused and process-oriented (Gudykunst and Ting-Toomey, 1988). Speakers using affective communication styles are more concerned with the process of communication than the outcome. For example, in an organization where the boss explicitly tells a subordinate what to do and why, communication is instrumental. Instrumental and affective communication styles can also be related to the individualism–collectivism cultural dimension. In collectivistic cultures people are more conscious of the other person's reactions, and attempt to sense meaning by situational cues, so that an affective style tends to be preferred. An instrumental style, on the other hand, is often seen in business and other professional contexts, particularly in Western cultures where verbal explicitness is valued.

DO IT!

In group assignments, students sometimes experience conflict among group members due to the allocation of tasks to members, or different opinions on how the assignment should be written. In such situations, students in the group might adopt a passive communication style (avoiding expressing their opinions or avoiding any response to hurtful messages), an aggressive communication style (expressing their opinions or advocating for their needs in a verbally abusive way that violates the rights of others), or an assertive communication style (declaring their opinions and advocating for their needs without violating the rights of others). Discuss with a classmate who has experience with group assignments the costs and benefits of the three ways of communication. How much are these tied to the culture of the students? Summarize your discussion and present it to the class.

Gender differences in communication

In her seminal work *Language and Woman's Place*, Robin Lakoff (1975) argues that women and men speak differently, since boys and girls are socialized separately. Deborah Tannen (1990), a discourse analyst, further claims that men and women express themselves differently because they have different cultures. In her influential 'two-cultures' theory, she states that men usually use verbal communication to report about the world. A report is a specific way to communicate in order to maintain independence and status in a hierarchical social order. Women, however, use verbal communication for rapport, in order to establish a human connection. It is a way of establishing connections and negotiating relationships. Moreover, on the question of who talks more, the usual stereotype is that women are talkers and men are doers (Mohanty, 2003). On the other hand, academic research shows that men tend to speak more often in public and they tend to speak longer in meetings (Tannen, 1994).

Gender differences in verbal communication are a complex and controversial combination of biological differences and socialization. Many linguists argue that language defines gender. Think of words such as 'businessmen', 'chairman' and 'mankind', in which there is a generic male implication. In subtle ways like this, language reinforces social stereotypes (Ardizzoni, 2007). For example, women are often defined by appearance or relationships; furthermore, the use of the titles 'Miss' and 'Mrs' designates a woman's marital status. On the other hand, men are more commonly defined by activities, accomplishments or positions. In general, it is gender studies scholars who explore issues of sexuality, power, language and marginalized populations, and point to the increasingly complex and murky binary oppositions between male and female language. Some gender studies scholars also attempt to introduce politically correct language, which is claimed to be calculated to provide a minimum of offence, particularly to racial, cultural or other identity groups. In the light of the public (verbal) sexual harassment cases in 2017, from powerful Hollywood producer Harvey Weinstein to journalists Charlie Rose and Bill O'Rilley to politicians such as Al Franken, many argue that we need a neutral language and rules about how to speak and what to say, especially in the workplace.

Gender-neutral language, which was originally suggested by feminist language reformers in universities during the 1970s, is a verbal communication style that discourages common usages that are thought of as sexist, such as the use of masculine pronouns in referring to persons of either sex. Consequently, a number of new words have been coined, such as 'chairperson' or 'spokesperson', as substitutes for the older male-oriented words in common usage. Feminists hope that by paying attention to gendered details in language, the language of the whole society can gradually be reformed, and people develop more positive attitudes towards equality between the sexes (Gauntlett, 2002). The term gender-neutral language is also known as 'inclusive language', 'gender-inclusive language, 'gender generic language' and 'non-discriminatory language'. In gender-neutral languages such as English there is no grammatical marking for most nouns, whereas in gender-grammatical languages, such as French and German, a gender is assigned to every noun. Even in the latter languages, people in general are often described using masculine words, and there has thus been a movement aimed at making language more gender-inclusive.

Language barriers in translation and interpretation

When cultures that speak different languages come into contact, translation is critical but always imperfect. *Translation* refers to the process of converting a source text, either spoken or written, into a different language. For example, ethnic shops often put up signs in both the national language and their ethnic language to attract customers. *Interpretation* refers to the process of verbally expressing what is said in another language. Interpretation can be simultaneous, with the interpreter speaking at the same time as the original speaker, or consecutive, with the interpreter speaking only during the breaks provided by the original speaker (Lustig and Koester, 2013). Cultural differences in word usage make translation a difficult task, and two translators rarely agree on the exact translation of any given source text. Translation and interpretation raise issues of authenticity and accuracy, as well as the subjective role of the translator or interpreter.

It is very difficult, if not impossible, to translate an entire text word-for-word from one language to another, because different languages may convey views of the world in different ways. Problems of translation arise due to a lack of equivalence in vocabulary, idiomatic expressions, connotational meaning, experience and concepts (Jandt, 2016). This is one reason why machine translators (like Google Translate) often make little sense. One example is that after a major US corporation introduced a new breakfast cereal in Sweden, the company was distressed to discover that the cereal's name translated roughly as 'burned peasant' in Swedish (Dumitrascu, 2017). On the other hand, word-for-word translation can result in awkward (sometimes hilarious) expressions that puzzle people from both sides. Here are examples of some awkward translations:

- On the menu of a Swiss restaurant, 'Our wines leave you nothing to hope for'.
- In a Copenhagen airline office, 'We take your bags and send them in all directions'.
- Outside a Hong Kong tailor shop, 'Ladies may have a fit upstairs'.
- On the box for a toothbrush at a Tokyo hotel, 'Give you strong mouth and refreshing wind'.

In addition to lexical equivalence, experiential equivalence can cause problems in translation. If an experience does not exist in a cultuwwwwwre, it is difficult to translate words or expressions referring to that experience in that culture's language. For example, the literal translation of an expression in Hong Kong is 'Touch the nail on the door'. It actually means 'No one was home when you went to the house'. The meaning of this expression dates back to ancient China when upon leaving their houses, people would hammer a nail on the door instead of locking it. Thus, if a visitor touched the nail when trying to knock on the door, the visitor would know that no one was home. The literal meaning of 'touch the nail on the door' would not be easily understood by people from another culture in which this practice has never existed. To translate it into another language, the translator has to offer an explanation either by using a word-for-word translation or by using a different set of words to capture the meaning. Translation problems like these raise the issue of the role of the translator or interpreter.

We tend to consider that translators or interpreters simply convert the source text into the target language. The assumption is that anyone who knows two languages can act as a translator, but the example of 'touch the nail on the door' shows that language proficiency alone does not make a good translator. Knowledge of history and culture plays a significant role in how well or accurately a message from one language is translated into another. Translation involves more than finding linguistic equivalence; conceptual, idiomatic and experiential equivalence are also key factors in comprehending messages, particularly in intercultural situations.

PHOTO 7.3   A café in Skopje, Macedonia, uses English, Italian, Macedonian and Albanian to attract customers who speak different languages.

THEORY CORNER

DISCOURSE

Discourse not only refers to the speech and writing of people, but also reflects the social systems of the society in which it occurs. In contemporary societies, our lives are strongly governed by the political environment, the economy, different public and private institutions, and the media. Fairclough (2003) points out that discourses represent not only the world as it is (or rather is seen to be), but also the possible worlds we imagine or that we project to be. These imagined or projected social worlds constructed by the social discourses can be different from the actual world. Often, people act in accordance with their imagined world rather than the actual world out there. Moreover, discourses are important in constructing and framing our identities, since the sense of who we are is constructed, articulated and made meaningful to others through our interactions with others either at the personal or social level.

Scollon, Scollon and Jones (2012: 8) propose that we have been formally or informally socialized into various discourse systems. Discourse systems contain 'ideas and beliefs about the world, conventional ways of teaching other people, ways of communicating using various kinds of texts, media, and "languages", and methods of learning how to use these other tools'. They also believe that we can only interpret the meanings of public texts like road signs, notices and brand logos by considering the world that surrounds them. Thus, discourse is engaged and mediated in the situated actions of the everyday practices of social actors. Discourse acts as 'a regulating body' that establishes what can be said and what cannot be said in a given historical moment in a given society. For example, discourse in relation to refugees is one of the most important discourses in contemporary society. At the national and international levels, this discourse is itself a space for debate, about issues such as what rights receiving countries should grant refugees, how many refugees a country should take per year, in which part of the country refugees should settle, and how the receiving country can strike a balance between exercising humanitarian effort and maintaining the sustainability of its economy and the living standards of its citizens. These are just some of the questions debated in public discourse.

REFERENCES

Fairclough, Norman (2003) *Analysing Discourse: Textual Analysis for Social Research*. London: Routledge.

Scollon, Ron, Scollon, Suzanne W. and Jones, Rodney H. (2012) *Intercultural Communication: A Discourse Approach* (3rd edn). London: Wiley-Blackwell.

LANGUAGE AND THE DISCURSIVE CONSTRUCTION OF IDENTITY

The language we speak defines our world and our identity. As a Czech proverb goes, 'Learn a new language and get a new identity'. From childhood, we take for granted that our name describes who we are. The language we speak has an impact on how we define ourselves and others as well as how we relate to those who speak or do not speak our own language.

Language and national identity

The sense of national unity is concerned with the integrity of the national language, territory and religion. A contemporary interest in linguistic homogeneity is often traced to the eighteenth-century German philosopher Johann G. Herder, who claimed that language expresses the inner consciousness of the nation, its ethos, its continuous identity in history and its moral unity. Nationalists defend their national language against foreign 'pollution' in the belief that moral degeneration will follow. For example, language is seen as one of the most important markers of Serbian national identity, since it is understood as preserving, bearing and passing down memories over the centuries (Volčič, 2005). Interestingly, majority groups in multicultural societies like the United States and Canada can become threatened by other languages, so that significant groups have asserted the dominance of their languages through English-only (in the United States) and French-only (in Quebec) movements (Barker et al., 2001).

Other scholars argue that living in a global world and multicultural societies, 'there is no need for all citizens of a nation to be native speakers of a single language, and absolutely no need for a nation's language to be clearly distinct from others' (Barbour, 2002: 14). The fact remains that every nation faces some kind of language dilemmas. For example, Louw (2004a) writes extensively about *Afrikaans*, the first language of 5.9 million people, mostly in South Africa and Namibia. But by the end of the twentieth century, English had replaced Afrikaans as the dominant state language. With the ending of apartheid in 1994, Afrikaaners became a South African minority group, marginalized within a political process geared to 'black empowerment'. Westernized black South Africans have deployed English as a language of state administration and lingua franca, further marginalizing Afrikaans. Today, only three of South Africa's languages are important print media languages, namely, English, Afrikaans and Zulu. Nearly all South Africans are multilingual, being fluent in at least the two main languages of their area, but often understanding many more. In this way, South Africa is similar to the highly multilingual country of India, which has 22 official languages (including English), but literally hundreds of languages and dialects (Sachdev and Bhatia, 2013). It is uncommon for an Indian not to speak several languages, yet communication across regions can still be problematic.

When Ireland, Israel and Slovenia became independent nation-states, each country asserted its own distinct national language: Irish (Gaelic), Hebrew and Slovene, respectively. In the case of Israel, a dead language, Hebrew, was brought back to life and modernized as a way of marking the new nation as distinctive; in Ireland, a language spoken by relatively few people (Irish) is now a required subject at school. In Sweden, the national identity has for a long time been perceived by many as a monolingual and homogeneous one (Godin, 2006). Throughout the centuries, the Swedish language has played a major role in the unification of the country and the creation of a sense of national identity. However, twentieth-century globalization led the homogeneous Swedish society to welcome immigrant workers and refugees among its citizens, and people from different cultures did not share the same native language as the majority. Godin argues that it is not a surprise to find questions regarding language at the centre of national identity in the public sphere in Sweden.

Language and ethnic identity

Language is a vital aspect of any ethnic group's identity. Often, immigrant groups maintain their cultural heritage and identity by using their native language in their new cultures and teaching them to their children. Identity based on ethnic language also hinges on the assumption that one's linguistic community is acceptable in a number of ways. The degree of prestige, acceptability and importance attached to a group's language is known as *ethnolinguistic vitality* (Reid and Giles, 2010). When you are faced with an ethnic or cultural group obviously different from your own, this encounter may be brief and unpleasant if you have the feeling that your ethnic or cultural group is being put down. Since language is one of the most clear-cut and immediate ways by which people discursively construct their identity, it is quite easy to see how your confidence can suffer if your language is disparaged.

The language or dialect we speak also influences the way we are perceived by others. The fact that someone speaks another language or speaks our language with a foreign or regional accent influences our social attitudes towards that speaker. Considerable evidence indicates that speech patterns, dialect and accent serve as cues that cause listeners to assign certain attitudes or characteristics to another person. Dodd (1998) related an anecdote illustrating the relationship between language and identity: When a student who came from a rural area of the United States entered a large North American university, he was informed by his mass media professors that his rural accent was inappropriate for broadcasting. This student adapted to 'standard' speech to meet the norms favouring standard American patterns of speech. When he went home for Thanksgiving, his mother would not let him into the house because when he knocked and called out, she did not recognize his voice. Her response was that he had to start 'talking right' or he would not be allowed entry. This dilemma, common for people who participate in two or more different cultures or subcultures, is illustrative of how important our language is as an aspect of our identity and of our group membership.

Moreover, there is a strong desire in many parts of the world to retain and enhance local or regional languages that may once have been common but are now spoken only by a few people; this is a good example of glocalization (local and global at the same time). A key concern is that, because language encodes so much of culture, when the language is lost the culture goes with it. The Catalonia region in north-eastern Spain is seeking independence (after a political referendum in 2017). Catalan is not a dialect of Spanish, but a language that developed independently out of the Latin spoken by the Romans who colonized the Tarragona area. It is spoken by roughly 9 million people in Catalonia, Valencia, the Balearic Isles, Andorra and the town of Alghero in Sardinia. Today, institutes like the School of Oriental and African Studies in London and the Mercator Institute in the Netherlands are devoted to research on minority and endangered languages in efforts to preserve them. Similarly, people in many countries are using political and social action to enhance the status of local languages, including reinstating the teaching of these languages at school (Everett, 2002). For example, speakers of Welsh and Irish have mobilized over the past decades to achieve a higher status for their languages, and they have been successful to a significant extent. The indigenous language is now a required subject in Welsh and Irish schools, along with English and other languages. As a result, the number of speakers of these languages is increasing, and the languages themselves are adapting new vocabulary and structure to accommodate the modern world. In the same vein, in Friesland (part of the Netherlands and home of the Mercator Institute), students are required to study all their subjects in Dutch, Frisian and English at school; the rationale is that they will know a world language, the national language and their regional language, and will thus broaden their identity.

DO IT!

Search the internet to find out approximately how many people speak your native language. Think about how it makes you feel when you hear a foreigner speak your language with a different accent, or when you hear a different dialect of your language. How might the accent of a second-language speaker bias your judgement of the intellectual competence, educational level and so on of the person? Write down your views in no more than one page and share your views with your classmates.

SUMMARY

- Language comprises a set of symbols shared by a community to communicate meanings. Children learn the rules of their language and are productive and creative in their language acquisition.
- The language we speak influences how we perceive and categorize the world around us. The Sapir-Whorf hypothesis highlights the close connections between language, thought and culture.
- Communication styles vary across cultures. Cultural rules govern speaking, listening and turn-taking behaviours.
- Gender differences are reflected in the use of language. The preference for gender-neutral or inclusive language may depend on the cultural context.
- Language is an integral part of our personal, social, ethnic and national identities because the language we speak marks our cultural and social boundaries.

JOIN THE DEBATE

DO 'THE LIMITS OF MY LANGUAGE' MEAN 'THE LIMITS OF MY WORLD'?

Language shapes our perception of reality, our attitudes towards others and others' perceptions of us. Ludwig Wittgenstein (1889–1951) played a key role in twentieth-century analytic philosophy and language studies. His work continues to influence current philosophical thought on topics as diverse as logic and language, perception, ethics and religion, aesthetics and culture. In one of his most influential works, *Tractatus Logico-Philosophicus* (1922/2001), Wittgenstein writes that 'The limits of my language are the limits of my world' ('Die grenzen meiner sprache sind die grenzen meiner welt'). This statement invites different interpretations. One way to construe it would be to think of how your own world is limited by your language. Would you agree that we know what we know because we have words for this knowledge in the language we speak? If you agree, what limits do you think this places on our thinking? If you disagree, how do you think we can have knowledge without the appropriate words to express it?

CASE STUDY

CULTURE JAMMING

Activists, artists and citizen groups around the world now use the language of different media and information technologies to gain visibility and voice, present alternative or marginal views, share their own DIY information systems and content, and otherwise resist, talk back to or confront dominant commercial cultures (Lievrouw, 2011). For the last 20 years or so, a practice called 'culture jamming' has grown in popularity and sophistication around the world. Culture jamming aims to disrupt consumer culture by using a particular type of language while transforming corporate advertising with subversive language and specific kinds of messages (Dery, 1999). Culture jammers, for example, hoax corporate language or spoof mass media messages in a way that counteracts dominant meaning in order to negate their impact or success. Culture jammers want to expose and challenge the way we think about politics, ourselves and our relationship to consumer products.

Culture jamming is conceptually inspired by the technique of electronically interfering with (i.e., 'jamming') radio or television broadcast signals for military or political purposes, and it comprises a variety of strategies and tactics (Carducci, 2006). These include subvertising (parodies of advertising messages while playing with language); product re-engineering; billboard resignification; public performance or protest; altering corporate messages, products and/or identities; parodying or satirizing corporate or other institutional communications, artefacts and images; and otherwise appropriating or mimicking corporate or other institutional references or frames, usually in critique (Carducci, 2011).

The origin of the term 'jamming' dates to the beginning of the twentieth century when, as a means of protesting against hard working conditions and low wages, factory workers in Europe would throw their wooden clogs into the machinery, thereby jamming or clogging the work in an act of sabotage (Dery, 1999).

Culture jamming is also known as a 'meme'. A meme is a unit of information (an image, an idea, an object, etc.) that serves to reproduce culture in the same way that a gene serves to reproduce an organism. Interrupting, engaging with and redirecting the system of cultural reproduction through using and reappropriating language is one of culture jamming's main objectives (Lievrouw, 2011).

Culture jamming is often directed against major brands, trademarked products and advertisements as these symbols are seen to represent the growth of corporate control over all aspects of contemporary life. For example, image-intensive social networking sites, such as YouTube and Flickr, have greatly expanded the reach of culture jamming practices. The activist group Billboard Liberation Front (BLF) is one of the best-known examples of 'subvertising'. BLF has intervened in corporate marketing communication campaigns since 1977. Its first project was to alter the billboard message of a cigarette brand (by playing with language) from 'I'm realistic. I smoke Fact' to 'I'm real sick. I smoke Fact' (Carducci, 2011: 405). BLF produced new letters in a type font, character size and colour to mimic the original text and glued them over existing printed copies, making it virtually impossible to perceive that the message was not the one intended by the advertiser (Carducci, 2011). The intervention was intended to point out that no tobacco cigarette is healthy, not even those marketed as 'low tar' or 'low nicotine'.

Another example is the Guerrilla Girls, another New York-based group of media activists. The group comprises feminist artists who wear gorilla masks to protect their identities while engaging in feminist resistance to patriarchal representations of gender in art and the historical exclusion of women artists in the West. They pay attention to the way advertisers depict women and minorities. For example, images of impossibly thin female fashion models are 'skulled' to link them to disordered eating behaviours. Culture jammers want to unveil how using female sexuality to sell a product is highly problematic. A further well-known example is the 'hacktivism' of Jonah Peretti (Carducci, 2011). Responding to an online promotion from Nike in early 2001 offering to customize its products with a personalized message, Peretti ordered a pair of shoes with the word sweatshop on them. The aim was to use the company's own product to resist and protest its exploitative labour practices. A series of email exchanges ensued when the company declined to supply the product as ordered. These emails were circulated on the internet and different mainstream media, drawing far more attention to the issue of Nike's labour policies than would have been possible if Peretti had simply worn the shoes in public (Carducci, 2011).

Culture jammers want us to think about economic externalities, such as environmental crises and global social inequality (Lievrouw, 2011). Culture jamming has been an effective method of using language to raise awareness of issues of public concern. It has played an active role in the development of what has come to be termed transnational civil society (Carducci, 2011). Culture jamming remains one of the most popular media strategies of the global justice movement. Pro-environment and anti-sweatshop movements regularly use culture jamming and its language in their campaigns.

REFERENCES FOR CASE STUDY

Carducci, Vince (2006) 'Culture jamming: A sociological perspective', *Journal of Consumer Culture*, 6(1): 116–138.

Carducci, Vince (2011) 'Culture jamming', in D. Southerton (ed.), *Encyclopedia of Consumer Culture*. Thousand Oaks, CA: Sage. pp. 406–407.

Dery, Mark (1999) *Culture Jamming: Hacking, Slashing and Sniping in the Empire of Signs.* Amsterdam: Grove Press.

Lievrouw, Leah (2011) *Alternative and Activist New Media.* Oxford: Polity Press.

1. Can you think of some examples of culture jamming from your own culture, for example in television commercials?

2. Google and Facebook ads are now measured on 'a cost-per-click basis'. Advertisers are charged not by how many people see their ads, but by how many people click on them. Do you think that culture jammers need to readjust some of their methods, such as 'ignoring ads' in the digital era?

3. Do you think that making it harder for corporations to gather information about our consumption habits could be a tool of culture jamming?

4. Many critics of culture jamming say that the political agenda of jammers compromises the counter-culture fun. Do you agree with this view or not, and why?

5. Do you think we need an organized, social activist effort to counter the bombardment of consumption-oriented messages in the mass media? Why, or why not?

QUESTIONS FOR DISCUSSION

FURTHER READINGS

Duranti, Alessandro (2015) *The Anthropology of Intentions: Language in a World of Others*. **Cambridge: Cambridge University Press.**

This book explores the relevance of intentions in making sense of what others say when they use language. Through the careful analysis of data collected over three decades in US and Pacific societies, Duranti demonstrates that, in some communities, social actors avoid intentional discourse, focusing on the consequences of actions rather than on their alleged original goals. In other cases, people speculate about their own intentions or guess the intentions of others, including in some societies where it was previously assumed they would avoid doing so.

Fairclough, Norman (2003) *Analysing Discourse: Textual Analysis for Social Research*. **London: Routledge.**

This book is about how language works to maintain and change power relations in contemporary society, and how understanding these processes can enable people to resist and change them. It is a critical introduction to discourse analysis as it is practised in linguistics, sociology and cultural studies. The author shows how concern with the analysis of discourse can be combined with an interest in broader problems of social analysis and social change.

Pantos, Andrew J. and Perkins, Andrew W. (2013) 'Measuring implicit and explicit attitudes toward foreign accented speech', *Journal of Language and Social Psychology*, **32(1): 3–20.**

This paper reported a study that examined language attitudes to foreign and US accented speech. A total of 165 undergraduate students from an American university participated in the study. Results showed that participants' implicit attitudes favoured the US-accented speaker over the Korean-accented speaker. However, they showed a pro-foreign accent bias on explicit measures. The authors concluded that because explicit attitudes are more controllable, listeners can hypercorrect implicit attitudes if they suspect those attitudes could reflect a socially unacceptable bias.

Rusi, Jaspala and Coyleb, Adrian (2010) 'My language, my people: Language and ethnic identity among British-born South Asians', *South Asian Diaspora*, **2(2): 201–218.**

This study explores how a group of second-generation Asians (SGA) understood the role language had played in defining their identity. Qualitative thematic analysis was undertaken in 12 interviews with SGAs. Four superordinate themes are reported, entitled 'Mother tongue and self', 'A sense of ownership and affiliation', 'Negotiating linguistic identities in social space' and 'The quest for a positive linguistic identity'. Participants generally expressed a desire to maintain continuity of self-definition as Asian, primarily through the maintenance of the heritage language.

Schnurr, Stephanie and Zayts, Olga (2017) *Language and Culture at Work. New York: Routledge.*

This book examines the discrepancy between colleagues' beliefs about linguistic practices and their actual verbal behaviours when going about work. The authors analysed authentic workplace data (including interaction and interview data) from different practitioners in Hong Kong, a multicultural metropolis where expatriates work with locals everywhere. The book proposes a new, integrated framework for researching culture at work from a sociolinguistic perspective.

In this video Professor Deborah Borisoff explains the reasons underlying the differences in gender-based communication styles. The video will help you to achieve the learning objective of analysing gender differences in communication. Watch it to see how – and why – men and women communicate differently.

This video is available at http://study.sagepub.com/liu3e

SAGE VIDEO SOURCES

The most important thing in communication is hearing what isn't said.

Peter F. Drucker, American-Austrian Management Consultant, 1909–2005

8

NONVERBAL COMMUNICATION AND CULTURE

LEARNING OBJECTIVES

After this chapter, you should be able to:

- Identify the characteristics of nonverbal communication.

- Describe the functions of nonverbal communication.

- Explain the different types of nonverbal codes and their application.

- Appreciate the influence of culture on nonverbal communication.

INTRODUCTION

Human communication frequently involves more than the use of a verbal code. *Nonverbal communication* broadly refers to the use of non-spoken symbols to communicate a message. We use *nonverbal codes* as a means of communicating with others, sometimes consciously and other times below the level of conscious awareness. It is important to recognize that our nonverbal communication – facial expressions, gestures, eye contact, posture and tone of voice – can speak louder than words. Those nonverbal codes can continue to communicate our thoughts and feelings, even when we stop speaking or when we are silent. Sometimes the meaning conveyed by words and nonverbal behaviour may differ or even contradict each other. In circumstances where mixed messages are received, the listener often chooses to believe the nonverbal, because these channels are perceived to be harder to control, perhaps even unconsciously used. On the other hand, when the nonverbal message is consistent with that conveyed by words, it can increase trust, clarity and rapport between communicators. Therefore, it is important to learn about nonverbal communication, because such knowledge can make you more sensitive not only to the nonverbal cues of others you interact with, but also to your own. Mehrabian (1982) estimates that 93 per cent of the meaning we convey is carried through nonverbal communication channels and only 7 per cent of the meaning is carried through words. Mehrabian's numbers are not well supported by data, and other scholars dispute them. Nevertheless, scholars agree that a very significant amount of communication is nonverbal. Effective communication requires that we understand the central role of nonverbal behaviour as part of our communication competence.

This chapter focuses on nonverbal communication and how it influences intercultural communication. Given the amount of research on nonverbal behaviour and communication, we must focus strongly on culture, and leave the discussion of other aspects of this fascinating area to books specifically on nonverbal communication. We first define nonverbal communication and provide a brief history of the study of nonverbal behaviour. Next, the chapter identifies the similarities and differences between verbal and nonverbal codes and explains the characteristics and functions of nonverbal codes. We describe different types of nonverbal codes, including body movement (kinesics), vocal qualities (paralanguage), the use of time (chronemics), space (proxemics), artefacts, dress and smell (olfactics), using various examples to illustrate their application. Finally, this chapter shows the close link between culture and nonverbal communication. The chapter highlights the importance of understanding how culture influences nonverbal behaviour in achieving positive intercultural communication outcomes.

CHARACTERTISTICS AND FUNCTIONS OF NONVERBAL COMMUNICATION

The study of nonverbal communication dates back at least to the time of Charles Darwin, who believed that facial expressions such as smiles and frowns are biologically determined. Although body language as a form of communication has been recognized since the time of Aristotle, and many thinkers in different cultures have written about it, it is the anthropologist Ray Birdwhistell who is recognized as the originator of the scientific study of body language – kinesics. In 1970, Birdwhistell published a book reviewing two decades of his work entitled *Kinesics and Context*, in which he argued that nonverbal communication, like spoken language, has its own set of rules, some of which are universal and some of which vary across cultures. Ekman and Friesen's (1971) early research on facial expressions also illustrates the universality of many emotional expressions. For example, fear is indicated in most or all cultures by a furrowed brow, raised eyebrows, wide-open eyes, partially open mouth and upturned upper lip. Based on subsequent research and observations, scholars have become convinced that, although all humans share basic emotions, such as fear, happiness, anger, surprise, disgust and sadness, the rules governing the display of these emotions vary from culture to culture.

Characteristics of nonverbal communication

Verbal and nonverbal communication often take place simultaneously. In the West, we tend to use verbal behaviour to convey the literal or cognitive content of a message (what is said), whereas the nonverbal component of the message communicates more of the affective content (feelings connected to the words). The affective content accounts for much of the meaning we derive from verbal communication because unspoken messages sometimes deliver more reliable and meaningful information than words alone (Hwang and Matsumoto, 2017). Hence, nonverbal codes can influence how a verbal message is interpreted. While we normally have some control over the words we say, we may inadvertently (or deliberately) reveal our true feelings through nonverbal behaviour. Blushing, for example, is very hard to control. Other nonverbal cues may also be involuntary. On the other hand, some nonverbal behaviour is as easy to control as words, although we do not tend to believe this – take, for example, a smile to indicate that our words are not really true or serious. Thus, we can also lie with our bodies as well as with our words.

However inseparably verbal and nonverbal codes are linked in a communication event, the difference between the two types of code is significant. Neuliep (2017), following from Hockett's (1960) early work on the design features of human language and how they differ from nonverbal behaviour, identified three ways in which verbal and nonverbal codes differ. First, the verbal language system is based primarily on symbols (things that stand for their referents but are not part of the referents), whereas the nonverbal system is sign-based (the parts of referents that are used to stand for them) to a greater extent. A second way in which the nonverbal system differs from its verbal counterpart is that its sending capacity is more restricted. For example, it is difficult to communicate about the past or future through purely nonverbal codes – likewise, it is hard to communicate nonverbally without seeing or hearing the other person (although devices like emoticons do some of this work). A third difference is that verbal codes have a formal phonetic (sound) system and syntax (structure and grammar) to govern usage, whereas there are fewer formal rules governing the use of nonverbal code systems. In fact, sign languages and semaphore communication are classified as verbal because they do have such formal rules. Different types of nonverbal behaviour can be categorized, but these categories are more loosely defined than those for verbal codes.

The meanings of nonverbal behaviour are also usually less precise than those of verbal codes and are only made clear within a particular cultural and situational context. It is important to remember that these three differences are a matter of degree, rather than kind – for example, verbal codes are made up almost entirely of conventional symbols, whereas nonverbal codes are a mix of symbols and signs. This use of symbols and display codes in nonverbal as well as verbal behaviour, combined with the commonly held belief that nonverbal behaviour is not learned but 'natural', creates the potential for misunderstanding both in the same culture and across cultures. This is especially likely in the latter case, where communicators may not share the interpretation of either verbal or nonverbal codes.

THEORY CORNER

EXPECTANCY VIOLATION THEORY

Expectancy violation theory was developed by Judee Burgoon (1978) to study nonverbal behaviour. The theory assumes that humans anticipate certain behaviour from the people with whom they interact. These expectancies may be general – pertaining to all members of a language community – or particularized – pertaining to a specific individual. When expectancies are violated, the violation can exert significant impact – either positive or negative, depending on whether the expectancy violation is positive or negative – on the communicators' impressions of one another and on the outcomes of their interactions. Based on various experiments, Burgoon concludes that people evaluate communication with others in either a positive or negative way, depending on their expectation of the interaction and their evaluation of the communicator. A positive evaluation is often directed towards attractive, powerful or credible others, while negative evaluation is more likely to be associated with unattractive or less powerful individuals. Initially, the theory was concerned only with spatial violations, but since the mid-1980s it has been applied in a range of communicative situations, including rhetoric, visual appearance, eye contact, online versus offline interactions, and marital and intercultural communication.

One interesting example of its application was Jennifer Bevan's (2003) study, which adopted expectancy violation theory to examine the link between sexual resistance and the negative violation of the resisted partner's expectations. Data were obtained from 307 university students in the United States. Participants read eight sexual resistance scenarios and then judged the realism and frequency of occurrence of the scenario in their own close relationships and the messages' directness and strength. The findings indicated that hypothetical sexual resistance from a long-term dating partner is a more negative and more unexpected violation than hypothetical rejection from a cross-sex friend. When a participant is hypothetically rejected by way of direct communication from his or her close relational partner, such a violation is perceived as more relationally important than indirect sexual resistance. Bevan argues that, as sexual encounters generally occur in situations with high levels of emotional sensitivity and vulnerability, partners' behaviour may be influenced by different sexual goals, with the result that each partner believes that their expectations have been violated. The prior history of an interaction, however, is likely to affect whether one partner decides the other's action is an expectancy violation.

REFERENCES

Bevan, Jennifer L. (2003) 'Expectancy violation theory and sexual resistance in close, cross-sex relationships', *Communication Monographs*, 70(1): 68–82.

Burgoon, Judee (1978) 'A communication model of personal space violation: Expectation and an initial test', *Human Communication Research*, 4: 129–142.

DO IT!

We expect certain nonverbal behaviours to accompany certain spoken words. For example, a teacher from Western Europe would expect a student to engage in direct eye contact during a conversation and might be surprised or upset if eye contact did not occur. Can you think of an occasion where a 'breach' of expected nonverbal behaviour like this would be accepted? Describe the occasion to a classmate from a cultural background different from yours and see what his or her response is. Compare similarities and differences.

Functions of nonverbal codes

Knapp and Hall (1997) identified six primary functions of nonverbal communication: to repeat the message sent by the verbal code; to contradict the verbal message; to be a substitute for a verbal message; to complement a verbal message; to accentuate the verbal message; and to regulate verbal communication.

Repeat a verbal message. We use nonverbal codes to repeat what has been said on another channel. For example, you may wave your hand while saying goodbye to a friend, as waving is a common nonverbal symbol for goodbye. Similarly, when someone asks us for directions, it is very likely that we will use our hands to point out the direction while explaining it in words. Verbal and nonverbal communication are usually used simultaneously, which helps us greatly in understanding other people and in sending clearer messages ourselves.

Contradict a verbal message. Nonverbal messages may, however, contradict verbal ones. For example, imagine that your friend is proudly showing you a new dress she has bought. You think the dress is awful and unflattering on her, but do not wish to hurt her feelings. Unfortunately, while telling her you think the dress looks beautiful, you may also inadvertently frown or use your hands too abruptly. When verbal and nonverbal codes contradict, people tend to believe the nonverbal message because it is considered to be less controlled and more revealing of our true feelings.

Substitute for a verbal message. Hand gestures in particular can be used as a substitute for a verbal message in noisy places or in a situation when a common language is not shared. Police officers use gestures to direct the traffic flow. In tourist-populated marketplaces, sellers and buyers can use nonverbal symbols to bargain for goods if they do not speak the same language. In radio station recording studios, the director must use gestures to indicate to the speaker when to start or stop speaking. In addition, some messages that are difficult to express in words can be communicated nonverbally. For example, you can keep looking at your watch to indicate to your visitor that it is time to go.

Complement a verbal message. A nonverbal message can complement a verbal message; that is, it can add information to the verbal message. For example, a man involved in a car accident may be able to use gestures to describe the accident to the police, while simultaneously conveying the same message in words. A student may jump up and down while saying how happy she is with a final grade. A mother may place a finger to her lips while whispering to her child to keep quiet in a puppet theatre.

Accentuate a verbal message. Although accentuating and complementing are similar, the former specifically increases or decreases the intensity of a message. For example, a manager may pound his fist firmly on the table to emphasize his feelings while saying 'No' to an unreasonable request for a pay rise from an employee. A child might say 'I love you' while giving you a kiss on the cheek. Alternatively, a colleague may use a neutral tone of voice to *lower* the intensity of positive (or negative) words. In these cases, nonverbal codes accent the emotions conveyed by verbal messages because they add more information to them.

Regulate verbal communication. We can use nonverbal codes to tell others to do or not to do something. A mother may use a stare to stop the naughty behaviour of her children in public places. We use voice inflection, head nods and hand movements to control the flow of conversation or to direct turn taking. In fact, conversational speech is mainly regulated – in terms of who gets to speak, for how long and when – by nonverbal behaviour in the voice (intonation, pausing) and body (forward lean, gaze, smiling).

THEORY CORNER

HIGH-CONTEXT AND LOW-CONTEXT CULTURES

Edward Hall (1976) divided cultures into *high-context* and *low-context* categories. This dimension refers to the extent to which we gather information from the physical, social and psychological context of an interaction (high-context) as opposed to the explicit verbal code (low-context). This dimension represents a continuum in which some cultures (e.g., China, the UK, France, Ghana, Japan, Korea) orient to the high-context end of the spectrum whereas others (e.g., Germany, Scandinavia, Switzerland, the United States) are at the low-context end. According to Hall and Hall (1990: 183–184), high and low context refer to 'the fact that when people communicate, they take for granted how much the listener knows about the subject under discussion. In low-context communication, the listener knows very little and must be told practically everything. In high-context communication, the listener is already "contexted" and does not need to be given much background information.'

For people in high-context cultures, meaning is largely implicit either in the physical setting or in shared beliefs, values and norms. The context provides a lot of information about the culture's rules, practices and expectations. Thus, information about background and procedures is not

(Continued)

overtly communicated; instead, listeners are expected to know how to interpret the communication and what to do. Thus, information and cultural rules remain unspoken, as the context is expected to be a cue for behaviour. High-context cultures generally have restricted code systems, in which speakers and listeners rely more on the elements of the communication setting for information than on the actual language – interactants look to the physical, social, relational and cultural environment for information. In high-context cultures, where meaning is more often conveyed by nonverbal and contextual cues, silence rather than talk can be used to maintain control in a social situation. For example, in Europe, the Finns place a high value on silence, and it is not unusual to pass a companionable evening in Helsinki with virtually no words exchanged at all. By contrast, people in low-context cultures rely on words to create and interpret meaning. Information to be shared with others is explicitly explained in the verbal message, procedures are also explained and expectations are discussed.

REFERENCES

Hall, Edward T. (1976) *Beyond Culture*. New York: Doubleday.

Hall, Edward T. and Hall, Mildred R. (1990) *Understanding Cultural Differences: Germans, French, and Americans*. Yarmouth, ME: Intercultural Press.

DO IT!

Select three popular politicians (at least one of them a woman) in your country. List some features of body language that these three politicians often use to communicate power (e.g., posture, arm movements). Write down your answers. Talk to a classmate from a different cultural background from yours and see whether her or his interpretation of these 'power communicating movements' is similar to or different from yours. Discuss whether there are any gender-specific nonverbal behaviours that tend to be used by the female, but not the male, politicians. Write up your discussion and reflections in a short essay.

TYPES OF NONVERBAL COMMUNICATION

It is impossible to categorize all the different types of nonverbal communication behaviour. Not only are they too numerous, but often several types of nonverbal behaviour from seemingly different categories can be used by the same person simultaneously. In this section, therefore, we examine the seven categories that are most relevant to intercultural communication: kinesics, proxemics, chronemics, haptics, physical appearance and dress, paralanguage and olfactics.

Kinesics: body movement

Kinesics refers to gestures, hand and arm movements, leg movements, facial expressions, eye contact and posture. Ekman and Friesen (1969) developed a system that organized kinesic behaviour into five broad categories: emblems, illustrators, affect displays, regulators and adaptors.

Emblems are primary hand gestures that have a direct literal verbal translation; these gestures blur the boundary between verbal and nonverbal communication. Within any culture there is usually a high level of agreement about the meaning of a particular emblem. For example, making a circle with one's thumb and index finger while extending the other fingers is emblematic of the word 'OK' in the United States, but it stands for 'money' in Japan and signifies 'zero' in Indonesia.

Illustrators are typically hand and arm movements that function to complement or accent words. Thus, illustrators serve a metacommunicative function; they are messages about messages. For example, a person might describe the size of a crocodile she saw while using hand gestures to illustrate its length. An illustrator that is widely used in the Balkans is a double head nod to emphasize and support views expressed in words.

Affect displays primarily refer to facial expressions that communicate an emotional state. Through facial expressions we can communicate an attitude, or feelings of disgust, happiness, anger or sadness. Some facial expressions are universal (e.g., a smile indicates pleasure and happiness in every culture), but the specific meaning attached to a facial expression or other affect display – even one as universal as smiling – must be linked to its context. For example, a shop assistant may smile at customers to show friendliness and politeness; a mother may smile at her baby to show affection; a student who is unable to answer a question from the teacher may smile to cover her embarrassment. All these expressions need to be interpreted in context.

Regulators include behaviours and actions that govern or manage conversations. We may use eye contact, silence and head nodding during conversation to show interest and to indicate turn-taking. If a teacher asks a question and the student does not wish to respond, the student can look away to indicate a reluctance to speak. However, it is worth noting that silence during a conversation may not always communicate disinterest. In high-context cultures, silence may signify agreement or satisfaction with the conversation; in some situations however, particularly in low-context cultures, silence may indicate disagreement or hostility.

Adaptors are kinesic behaviours that are used to satisfy physiological or psychological needs. For example, scratching an itch satisfies a physiological need, while adjusting one's glasses before speaking may satisfy a psychological need to calm down. These behaviours help people to adapt to their environment. The interpretation of any kinesic behaviour depends on its context and the other communication that takes place at the same time. For example, sitting with arms and legs tightly crossed may mean that the person is feeling cold (e.g., at a train station), defensive (e.g., during an argument) or nervous (e.g., waiting for a job interview).

THEORY CORNER

EVOLUTIONARY THEORY OF EMOTION

Emotion can speak volumes about a communicator. An understanding of how emotion is displayed helps us to improve the quality of our social interaction and relationships. As a pioneer of emotion theory, Charles Darwin (1998/1872) believed that emotions and their expressions are functionally adaptive and biologically innate. In particular, he claimed that facial expressions are the residual actions of more complete behavioural responses. For example, humans express anger by furrowing the brow, tightening the lips and displaying the teeth because these expressions are the residual reflection of an attack response – the full response appears among many mammals, including other primates. Darwin also believed that all humans, regardless of race or culture, possess the ability to express emotions on their faces in similar ways. Based on his study, in which he observed the muscle actions involved in emotion, Darwin concluded that muscle actions are universal and that their antecedents can be seen in the expressive behaviour of non-human species as well.

Facial expressions are one of the most commonly observed nonverbal expressions, because the face is a fundamental and primary medium through which emotions are expressed and managed in social interactions. Darwin's evolutionary theory of emotion paved the ground for the development of the coding systems that are used in the identification of facial expressions. According to this work, the emotions that have been empirically shown to be universally expressed and recognized in the face are anger, contempt, disgust, fear, happiness, sadness and surprise. These are called 'basic emotions'. Matsumoto and Willingham (2006) examined the facial expressions of 84 judo athletes from 35 countries at the 2004 Olympic Games. They observed the immediate emotional reactions on the faces of winners and losers at the completion of their final medal match and found them consistent with the prototypical expressions of basic emotions. In particular, winners displayed genuine smiles, while losers displayed sadness, disgust, anger and other negative emotions. While recognizing that some facial expressions are universal, Matsumoto and Willingham also pointed out that culture guides people to socially modify their facial expressions in order to smooth social interactions.

REFERENCES

Darwin, Charles (1998/1872) *The Expression of Emotions in Man and Animals*. New York: Oxford University Press.

Matsumoto, David and Willingham, Bob (2006) 'The thrill of victory and the agony of defeat: Spontaneous expressions of medal winners of the 2004 Athens Olympic Games', *Journal of Personality and Social Psychology*, 91(3): 568–581.

Proxemics: the use of space

Proxemics refers to the use of space, including territory, which stands for the space that an individual claims either permanently or temporarily. For example, it is very likely that you have sat in the same seat in a lecture theatre from the beginning of the semester, even though you do not have assigned seating. If someone takes that seat before you, you may feel as if that person has taken 'your spot'. The study of proxemics includes three aspects of space: fixed features, semi-fixed features and personal space (Hall, 1966). The size of one's office, a fixed feature of space, communicates status and power, while semi-fixed features of space – the movable objects within an office, such as furniture and

PHOTO 8.1   The M&M's shop uses the brand's red and yellow characters with funny facial expressions to attract customers.

Copyright © Shuang Liu. Used with permission.

decorations – can communicate the degree of openness of the occupant as well as status and power. Some people prefer to have their desk facing the door, which may make visitors feel welcome but may also communicate a barrier between the visitor and the resident of the office. Others prefer to put high bookshelves near the entrance to block the view in and out, which may make people feel the person is less accessible.

Personal space refers to the distance within which people feel comfortable when interacting with others. We use space to communicate, and the size of this space is not only culturally determined but also influenced by the relationship of the communicators. People from Latin America or the Middle East often feel comfortable standing close to each other, while people from European countries or North America prefer a relatively greater distance between them. Lovers stand closer to each other during a conversation than do colleagues. Unwanted or unexpected intrusions often cause the 'invaded' individual to feel uncomfortable or even irritated. Khan and Kamal (2010) compared reactions to an invasion of personal space in a group of postgraduate students in Pakistan. The male participants tended to reach for their mobile phone more frequently than the female participants, while the female participants tended to display more compensatory behaviours, such as moving away. Based on the findings from their study, along with a great deal of other similar research, when an individual's personal space is invaded by a stranger or someone with whom he or she does not have a close personal relationship, the resulting effects are mostly negative.

Chronemics: the use of time

Chronemics refers to the use of time. Our concept of time may influence our communication behaviour. A meeting in an African village does not begin until everyone is ready. A 45-minute wait may not be unusual for a business appointment in Latin America, but it would probably be insulting to a North American business person. Differences in the conception of time can cause frustration in intercultural communication. For example, an American professor complained about the long staff meetings when he taught at a university in Hong Kong. Unlike his experience of staff meetings in the United States, those he attended in Hong Kong did not seem to follow the agenda items in a linear way. Often, even upon reaching the seventh item on the agenda, a question raised by someone could bring the discussion back to the second item on the agenda. Decisions were not made by majority vote, but rather by consensus by those present at the meeting. Thus, each staff meeting commonly lasted for over two hours, which this American professor considered an inefficient use of time.

Different conceptions of time lead people to attempt to do only one task at a time or to multi-task. Hall (1976) categorizes time orientations into monochromic and polychronic. People with a *monochronic* time orientation, characteristic of many Western cultures, view time as linear, much like a progressive path, with a beginning and an end. They also believe that this 'path' has discrete compartments. Therefore, people should do only one thing at a time. To a Westerner, time can be bought, saved, spent, wasted, lost or made up, and observing clock time is important. In contrast, *polychronic* cultures view time as cyclical and people attempt to perform multiple tasks simultaneously. To an Arab, observing clock time is irreligious because only God can determine what will or will not happen. Offices in Arabic cultures may have large reception areas where several groups of people all conduct their affairs at the same time. To someone from a culture with a monochronic time orientation, this arrangement may appear counter-intuitive and confusing. Of course, the division between monochronic and polychronic time orientations is frequently not clear-cut. People are capable of both orientations, depending on the context.

Haptics: the use of touch

Haptics refers to the use of touch, the most primitive form of communication. Touch sends myriad messages – for example, protection, support, approval or encouragement. As usual, when, where and whom we touch, and what meanings we assign to touch, differ widely across cultures. The amount of touch also varies with age, sex, situation and the relationship between the people involved. North American culture generally discourages touching by adults except in moments of intimacy or in formal greetings (e.g., hugging or hand shaking). Similar culturally defined patterns of physical contact avoidance are found in most cultures in Asia and Northern Europe. In so-called Mediterranean cultures, touch is extremely important, and people frequently use touch during a conversation or a meeting.

Hall (1966) distinguishes between high- and low-contact cultures. High-contact cultures are those that tend to encourage touching and engage in touching more frequently (e.g., Southern and Eastern Europe). Anglo-Celtic cultures are considered to be low-contact cultures. Even within a low- or high-contact culture, the cultural and social rules governing touch vary. People from Islamic and Hindu cultures typically do not touch with the left hand, because to do so is a social insult. The left hand is reserved for toilet functions. Islamic cultures generally do not permit touching between genders, but touch between people of the same gender tends to be acceptable. In many Western cultures, touching between people of the same sex may be interpreted by others as a sign of homosexuality, but in other cultures this practice is normal for everyone.

Physical appearance and dress

Interpersonal communication is often preceded by the communicators' observations of each other's physical appearance. People can wear a particular type of clothes, or change other aspects of their physical appearance, to communicate culture, religion, status, power,

PHOTO 8.2   Dim sum at a Chinese restaurant where people enjoy tea and dim sum (yam cha).

Copyright © Shuang Liu. Used with permission.

personality, self-esteem and social identity (Keblusek, Giles and Maass, 2017). For example, the traditional costume for the Hausa-Fulani people in Nigeria is characterized by bright colours. Men's traditional outfit consists of a wide-sleeved robe called 'babban riga'. It is floor-length, with long wide sleeves. This garment is very popular among Nigerian men for formal occasions. Hausa-Fulani men also wear a headdress called a 'fula', which is a round cap. Women's traditional attire consists of colourful wrappers called 'abaya' with matching blouses.

In most cultures people consciously manipulate their physical appearance in order to communicate their identity. In ancient Chinese culture, women had to bind their feet at a young age, because small feet symbolized beauty. Plastic surgery is another example of using physical appearance to communicate messages. According to the American Society for Aesthetic Plastic Surgery (2017), surgery accounted for 56 per cent of the total expenditures on aesthetic cosmetic procedures in 2016 and Americans spent more than $15 billion during the calendar year on aesthetic cosmetic procedures. The most popular procedure in 2016 was liposuction, with 414,335 procedures being performed. As noted by Zebrowitz and Montepare (2008), in Western societies women are expected to look beautiful because they are considered 'to embody' beauty. Consequently, many women believe they must conform to society's notion of beauty, as it is reinforced as their 'role'.

DO IT!

Collect several advertisements for cosmetic products for men in your culture (e.g., facial cream, moisturizer, etc.). You might search the internet or websites of some cosmetics companies or shops to locate the advertisements. Construct a table and compile information of the types of products advertised, the character used to promote the product and the message being communicated in the advertisement (e.g., looking bright or youthful). Based on your analysis, in a one-page essay explain how masculine beauty is constructed by these advertisements and how the concept resonates with stereotypes in your society.

Paralanguage: quality and characteristics of the voice

Paralanguage refers to the vocal qualities that accompany speech. Arguably, paralanguage carries as much information about emotions, attitudes and regulation of the interaction as all the non-vocal channels put together. Certainly, our use of the telephone for every kind of conversation – even suicide-prevention counselling – suggests that, if we are sensitive to paralanguage, we can get most of the information contained in a message. Thus, it is surprising that this type of nonverbal behaviour has received relatively less attention than non-vocal behaviours, perhaps because paralanguage is so closely connected to words and spoken language (Siegman and Feldstein, 2014).

Paralanguage can be divided into two broad categories: voice qualities and vocalizations (Knapp and Hall, 1997). Voice qualities include elements like pitch, volume, tempo, rhythm, tone, pausing and resonance of the voice. Vocalization includes laughing, crying, sighing, yelling, moaning, swallowing and throat clearing. Some scholars also include as paralinguistic vocalizations back-channel utterances such as *um*, *ah*, *ooh*, *shh* and *uh*, although other scholars categorize these as verbal behaviour – once again, the boundary between verbal and nonverbal behaviour is blurred. Silence is also considered by some (but not all) to fall within the domain of paralanguage. People may use silence to show respect, agreement or disagreement, apathy, awe, confusion, contemplation, embarrassment, regret, repressed anger, sadness and myriad other things. We interpret a speaker's feelings and emotions based partly on our perception of the variations in vocal quality. The same words said with different vocal qualities convey different meanings, as illustrated in the example below:

Mark, you are going to marry Hillary (A declarative statement of a fact.)

Mark, you are going to marry *Hillary*? (A question to convey that I thought you were going to marry someone else.)

Mark, you are going to marry Hillary! (An exclamation to express excitement.)

Mark, are *you* going to marry Hillary? (A question to express surprise, e.g., I thought someone else was going to marry her.)

Mark, *are* you going to marry Hillary? (A question to get confirmation: I thought you just liked her, not loved her.)

Cultural differences are reflected in people's use of paralanguage. Speaking loudly indicates strength and sincerity to Arabs, authority to Germans, but impoliteness to Thais and a loss of control to the Japanese. The Lebanese proverb 'Lower your voice and strengthen your argument' also emphasizes the value that this culture places on controlling one's voice in a conversation. The use of vocal segregates (e.g., um, uh) may communicate interest, uncertainty, attention, acceptance or hesitation, and their meanings vary across cultures. In China, people may use 'um' or 'hai' (for Cantonese speakers) to indicate 'yes' or 'I see' while the other person is speaking. This vocal segregate is used to encourage the other speaker to continue talking, rather than to suggest a change of turn. The appropriateness of vocal qualities is also judged based on gender. For example, laughing loudly is common and acceptable for American women, but it might not be considered as such in Thailand. In ancient China, women had to cover their mouth with a handkerchief when they were laughing to indicate good manners and politeness.

Olfactics: the use of smell, scent and odour

Olfactics refers to humans' perception and use of smell, scent and odour. Compared with other types of nonverbal code, the study of olfactics has received less academic attention. Research evidence shows that there is a universal preference for some scents that may have biological and evolutionary roots. For example, the fragrances of jasmine, lavender and roses tend to communicate a soothing and pleasant feeling to people; the perfume industry makes billions of dollars a year by capitalizing on these scent preferences.

Smell can also be used to communicate position, social class and power. Anthony Synnott (1996) claims that odour is used to categorize people into social groups of different status, power and social class, because the meanings attributed to a specific scent give it social significance. Synnott argues that perceived foul odours are one of the criteria by which negative identities are attributed to some social or ethnic groups. If a well-dressed man carrying a briefcase and smelling of a high-quality aftershave gets into the lift of an office building, others in the lift are more likely to think he is someone who holds a management position, rather than being an ordinary office worker. Nevertheless, people's smell preferences are not universal, but vary across cultures. For example, the Dogon people of Mali find the scent of onions very attractive, and young men and women rub fried onions all over their bodies (Neuliep, 2017); the smell of onion from a person's mouth is considered bad breath in many other cultures.

INFLUENCE OF CULTURE ON NONVERBAL COMMUNICATION

People hold expectations about the appropriateness of others' nonverbal behaviour. These expectations are learned, and thus vary across cultures. Interactants from different cultural backgrounds have to learn each other's expectations regarding appropriate nonverbal behaviour. This section uses Lustig and Koester's (2013) three cultural variations in nonverbal communication as a framework to discuss the relationship between culture and nonverbal communication.

Cultural variation in repertoire of behaviour

Culture embodies a repertoire of nonverbal behaviour and provides rules governing appropriate and inappropriate behaviour on certain occasions (Lustig and Koester, 2013). Body movements, gestures, posture, vocal qualities and spatial requirements are specific to a particular culture. For example, shoulder shrugging is commonly used by Westerners when something is not understood, whereas in some Asian cultures this body movement is almost never used; the same feeling is often expressed by shaking one's head. Another example is *yum cha* – an important part of Chinese culinary culture, particularly for people from Hong Kong and Guangdong Province. In *yum cha* etiquette, it is customary for one person (people at the table take it in turns) to pour tea into other people's cups before filling their own. The nonverbal behaviour to thank the person who has poured tea into your cup is to tap the table with three or two fingers. Finger tapping is also known as finger *kou-tou*; this is a gesture to thank someone in the traditional Chinese style. A story has it that the historical significance of this gesture can be traced to the Qing Dynasty. When visiting south China on an incognito inspection visit, the emperor went to a teahouse with his companions and guards. To disguise his identity, the emperor joined others at the table in taking turns to pour tea. His companions could not kneel down and kowtow to show gratitude for this great honour, because doing so would reveal the identity of the emperor. Instead, they tapped three fingers on the table to represent their bowed head and their prostrated arms. Up to this day, tapping one's fingers remains the ritual expression of gratitude to someone when being served tea.

PHOTO 8.3   The Arc de Triomphe is one of the most famous monuments in Paris, honouring those who fought and died for France in the French Revolutionary and Napoleonic Wars.

Copyright © Shuang Liu. Used with permission.

Cultural variation in display rules

Every culture has rules which govern when and in what context certain nonverbal expressions are required, permitted, preferred or prohibited. Display rules govern such things as how far apart people should stand during a conversation, where and whom to touch, when and with whom to use direct eye contact, how loudly one should speak, and how much one should show his or her feelings (Lustig and Koester, 2013). For example, Arab men kiss each other on both cheeks in greeting; Chinese men often shake hands; Japanese men bow; Malaysians put their palms together in front of the chest. One behaviour, the eyebrow flash (a quick raising and lowering of the eyebrows), is almost universally used when friends or acquaintances encounter each other in the street. Some people believe that this behaviour is innate. Nevertheless, Japanese people rarely use it. Display rules are different across cultures even for universal or quasi-universal behaviour like this.

A good place to observe cultural variations in display rules is the arrival terminal of an international airport. Westerners tend to greet their loved ones with hugs and kisses, whereas Asians tend to be more reserved and may hug each other but will generally not kiss each other in public places. To illustrate this point, think of any kind of public space and observe how different people from different walks of life (different gender, class, race, etc.) display their nonverbal communication. What is allowed in, for example, museums, is telling. In Europe, complete silence is desirable while visiting art galleries and admiring art. Silence is an accepted behaviour in this context, whereas in other cultures it is interpreted as a mark of distress.

Cultural variation in attributing meanings to nonverbal behaviour

Lustig and Koeter (2013) pointed out that interpretation of the same behaviour varies across cultures. In Western countries, it is common to see people smile at strangers or passers-by in the neighbourhood, while this facial expression may be interpreted as strange in Singapore or in other Asian countries, where people do not often initiate conversations with strangers. On one occasion in China during the peak travel time (before the Chinese New Year), posters were displayed in railway stations advising travellers not to speak to strangers. In Australian universities, it is very common to see students wearing rubber sandals (called flip-flops in the UK and US) in the classroom; in China, shoes that look like slippers are regarded as improper footwear in the classroom. The same kinds of cultural differences apply to nonverbal behaviour like gestures – even emblems. For example, pulling down on your lower eyelid with one finger means 'my eye' in English (and in French) – that is, 'I don't believe you'; the same gesture, *Chashm* (my eye) in Farsi, means 'I promise'.

Culture and nonverbal behaviour are inseparable. Unlike verbal codes, however, there is little grammar for nonverbal codes that foreigners can learn to make intercultural communication easier. Members of a particular culture learn the norms for appropriate and inappropriate nonverbal behaviour through the process of socialization. In addition, the application of these rules usually occurs outside conscious awareness. We become aware of our culture's rules and norms mainly when we see them broken. Consequently, when we communicate with people whose repertoire of nonverbal codes differs from our own, misunderstandings are almost certain to occur. Violation of nonverbal rules or misinterpretations of nonverbal codes can lead to negative attitudes or even conflict. It is important, therefore, for us to be alert to differences in nonverbal codes in intercultural communication, to monitor our own use of nonverbal codes, and to be observant of the rules governing the use of nonverbal codes of other people.

SUMMARY

- Unlike verbal codes, there is no formal grammar governing the use of nonverbal codes. These rules are learned as part of a culture's socialization process.
- Nonverbal communication often takes place simultaneously with verbal communication; however, if the messages from the two contradict one another, people tend to believe the nonverbal because it is believed to be less controlled and thus more likely to reveal the true feelings of the speaker.
- Nonverbal codes are used to repeat the message sent by the verbal code, contradict the verbal message, substitute for a verbal message, complement a verbal message, accentuate the verbal message and regulate the verbal communication.
- There are seven major types of nonverbal code systems: kinesics, proxemics, chronemics, haptics, physical appearance and dress, paralanguage and olfactics. They have different functions and are culture-specific.
- Although there is evidence that some nonverbal codes have universal meanings (e.g., facial expressions of fear or anger), how behaviour is displayed and the circumstances in which it is appropriate vary from culture to culture.

JOIN THE DEBATE

Nonverbal behaviours, which often accompany verbal communication, can 'speak' volumes in a very powerful way. When we lie, for example, our body language sometimes gives away our true feelings and intentions, irrespective of the content

CAN WE LIE WITH
OUR BODY
LANGUAGE?

of our words. Nonverbal specialists often apply the concept of norming when analysing videotapes to see whether the nonverbal cues are consistent with the verbal content. These specialists believe that there are always tell-tale signs when someone is lying, often referred to as 'nonverbal leakage' or 'hot spots'. Eye contact, blinking, shoulder movement, posture, crossing and uncrossing ankles, and tapping feet are all indicators that can give away even the most accomplished liar. However, the mere presence or absence of these behaviours does not necessarily indicate lying, and nonverbal cues vary across individuals. Indeed, detection of lying through nonverbal cues is not always accurate, even when the observers are highly trained. Some scholars argue that, with the exception of a small number of people who give themselves away, it is extremely difficult to detect lying in interpersonal communication by any means. Can you give examples where you have successfully lied by using body language? What behaviour did you use? Have you ever been able to detect others who were lying by using their nonverbal behaviour? How did you do it? Is it possible to lie with our body language?

CASE STUDY

NONVERBAL BEHAVIOUR IN POLITICS – THE CASE OF VLADIMIR PUTIN

Using the appropriate and effective nonverbal codes to communicate is important for all politicians, especially when they are public speaking, networking, or undertaking media appearances and fund-raising activities. Nonverbal communication is extremely effective in creating a particular type of desirable political image, and this has an important role in international and national politics. That 'we do not communicate by words alone' is an important first lesson for politicians: facial expression, voice, accent, silence, colour, body movements, posture, touching, smell, use of objects, sense of place and time, dress, accessories used, and walking style are all part of the nonverbal communication codes that politicians employ. When voters are evaluating political leaders they make use of information other than the content of the politicians' speeches, and this information is often obtained from nonverbal communication. Politicians learn that the same words uttered in different tones of voice, with variations in loudness, pitch, pause and tempo, can have very different effects on an audience. Populist politicians, from Berlusconi in Italy to Sarkozy in France, Orban in Hungary, Trump in the United States and Putin in Russia, use nonverbal communication deliberately. They learn how important it is to know when to look or not to look at each other, when to stand close or further apart, when to face each other more or less directly, and when to move their bodies.

Research has identified three main dimensions of nonverbal behaviour among politicians: a positiveness dimension, a responsiveness dimension and a potency or status dimension. These are very basic dimensions that we use constantly in interpersonal and intergroup judgements, and they have been extensively studied in many contexts since the 1950s. Concrete behaviours within these dimensions emerge at several nonverbal communication levels. For example, politicians can use their voice, gestures or body movements to be perceived as friendly, interested, competent, compassionate, powerful or superior. One can demonstrate sympathy towards another person on the positiveness dimension by smiling, nodding or touching that person. Responsiveness is related to nonverbal communication that demonstrates the other's importance for the politician. Maintaining eye contact, for example, is a concrete behaviour on this dimension that politicians use frequently. Finally, nonverbal behaviour indicating potency or status is used to demonstrate social control. Politicians expand their size and presence, and take up a lot of space, by using gestures or body movements or by speaking with a loud voice (Tavanti, 2012). In politics, it has become legitimate to show aggressive feelings within culturally prescribed limits.

One of the leading politicians in the world, Vladimir Putin, is famous for his effective use of nonverbal communication. He appears very much in control of his 'brand' image of masculinity: strong, fashionable, with decisive looks, charismatic posture and confident walk (Foxall, 2013). He was elected Russian President in March 2000. Despite being seen as mishandling the Kursk submarine disaster in 2000, and an increase in Chechen terrorist attacks in Russia (including the Nord-Ost theatre siege in Moscow in 2002), Putin was re-elected President for a second term in March 2004. After serving as Prime Minister between 2008 and 2012, Putin was again elected President in March 2012 and yet again in 2018, making him the longest-serving president in Russian history. As the President (2000–2008 and 2012–present) and a former member of the KGB (translated into English as the Committee for State Security, which was the main security agency for the Soviet Union from 1954 until its collapse in 1991) between 1975 and 1991, he is widely seen as the authoritarian face of Russia in the 'New Cold War' (Foxall, 2013). When he stood down as President in April 2008, owing to the Russian Constitution forbidding more than two consecutive terms, Putin enjoyed approval ratings of 84 per cent. Since 2016, he has entered into the United States' political spaces as well, with open statements supporting Donald Trump during the 2016 US elections.

Putin offers a rich case for exploring how nonverbal communication is used to convey masculinity and power. Putin uses nonverbal communication, and his body in particular, as a key element in building his identity. He is a judo expert, and frequently poses in front of the cameras dressed in his judo outfit and his black belt. His holiday photographs are regularly published by the Kremlin, and he is often photographed semi-naked while on holiday. Other politicians use this same behaviour; there were pictures of UK Prime Minister Tony Blair talking on the phone wearing swimming trunks in 2002 and 2006, and a bare-chested Barack Obama (then Senator of Illinois) body surfing in Honolulu in 2008 (Foxall, 2013). The former Australian Prime Ministers Bob Hawke and Tony Abbott were both frequently photographed running along the beach or in other informal activities in very brief swimming costumes. Photos of Putin show him dressed in fatigues, fingerless gloves, a bush hat and chic sunglasses, riding horses, rafting down a river, fishing for grayling and off-roading in a sport utility vehicle. These photographs of Putin help to reflect and perpetuate the stereotypically masculine discourse about what it means to be a leader in contemporary Russia.

Some commentators claim that Putin uses his body very openly during his public performances. He uses the centre of his chest, which is an important nonverbal gesture to indicate that we are openly expressing what we think. In comparison to the other topics, a close analysis of his nonverbal communication shows a distinctive nonverbal behaviour (displaying a high amount of aggressiveness) when he addresses topics related to the domestic financial crisis. Putin's hand gestures are also used very differently in speeches about the financial crisis compared with other topics (Tavanti, 2012). Thus, Putin is able to convey nuanced – but always masculine – attitudes to different topics and in different contexts.

REFERENCES FOR CASE STUDY

Foxall, Andrew (2013) 'Photographing Vladimir Putin: Masculinity, nationalism and visuality in Russian political culture', *Geopolitics*, 18(1): 132–156.

Tavanti, Marco (2012) 'The cultural dimensions of Italian leadership: Power distance, uncertainty avoidance and masculinity from an American perspective', *Leadership*, 8(3): 287–301.

QUESTIONS FOR DISCUSSION

1. What are the effects of politicians' different nonverbal behaviour styles on their image?

2. Do you agree that the appearance of both the speaker and the surroundings are vital to convey a message successfully?

3. Body language, and particularly facial expressions, can provide important information that may not be contained in verbal communication. Can you think of any examples when particular politicians have used this kind of nonverbal behaviour?

4. Politicians' style of clothing can demonstrate their mood, levels of confidence, interests, age, authority, values and beliefs, and their sexual identity. Do you think clothing is an important aspect of nonverbal communication? How does it function?

5. Do you think that the position of the feet may also transmit interest or disinterest to the communicated person or the topic?

FURTHER READINGS

Bonaccio, Silvia, O'Reilly, Jane, O'Sullivan, Sharon L. and Chiocchio, François (2016) 'Nonverbal behavior and communication in the workplace: A review and an agenda for research', *Journal of Management*, 42(5): 1044–1074.

This article reviews the literature on nonverbal behaviour, particularly as it applies to the organizational context. The authors discuss several areas in the organizational sciences that are ripe for further explorations of nonverbal behaviour, for example personnel selection and performance appraisal, teams, trust and motivation. The article provides information on the methods used to study nonverbal behaviour in laboratory and field contexts.

Burgoon, Judee K., Guerrero, Laura K. and Floyd, Kory (2009) *Nonverbal Communication*. New York: Routledge.

This book, authored by three well-known scholars in nonverbal communication, examines both the features and the functions that comprise the nonverbal signalling system. Drawing on classic and contemporary research and theory from multidisciplinary areas, the book discusses both knowledge about and the application of nonverbal communication in a practical way. The book is suitable for students who are particularly interested in exploring nonverbal communication in lived experiences.

Demir, Müge (2011) 'Using nonverbal communication in politics', *Canadian Social Science*, 7(5): 1–14.

This article discusses the effect of nonverbal communication in voter perceptions of political rhetoric. When people are evaluating political leaders they take note of some features of nonverbal communication. The tone of voice, dress style, accessories, body posture and facial expressions, among other aspects of nonverbal communication, are argued to be much more effective, easier to recall and more persuasive than the written or spoken communication of political leaders. This article addresses the question: How do political leaders use nonverbal communication to effectively create their political image and make an impact?

Manusov, Valerie (2017) 'A cultured look at nonverbal cues', in L. Chen (ed.), *Intercultural Communication*. Boston, MA/Berlin: De Gruyter. pp. 239–259.

This chapter reviews cross-cultural research in the area of culture and nonverbal cues. The chapter identifies the communicative functions of some primary nonverbal cues, such as the use of space, physical appearance and time, and explains how they are enacted differently across cultural groups. These communicative functions include the expression of emotion, identity displays and relational messages, among others. The author challenges the assumption that nonverbal cues can make up a 'universal language' for people from different cultural groups who interact with one another.

McDaniel, Edwin R. (2015) 'Japanese nonverbal communication: A reflection of cultural themes', in L. Samovar, R. Porter, E. McDaniel and C. S. Roy (eds.), *Intercultural Communication: A Reader* (14th edn). Boston, MA: Cengage Learning. pp. 242–252.

This chapter uses Japanese culture as an example to illustrate how nonverbal communication practices function as a reflection and representation of cultural themes common to Japanese society. They include group orientation, hierarchy, social balance, formality and humility. The hierarchical nature of Japanese society and the cultural pressure for social harmony increases the reliance on nonverbal behaviours. The chapter demonstrates how cultural influences can subtly shape a society's communication conventions.

SAGE VIDEO SOURCES

This video explores the function of vocal cues, facial expressions, and eye contact. It will help you to achieve the learning objective of understanding the function and application of different types of nonverbal codes. Watch the video to see how the functions of nonverbal codes change across context and message.

This video is available at http://study.sagepub.com/liu3e

Recognize yourself in he and she who are not like you and me.

Carlos Fuentes, Mexican writer, 1928–2012

9

IMMIGRATION AND ACCULTURATION

LEARNING OBJECTIVES

At the end of this chapter, you should be able to:

- Understand immigration as a major contributor to cultural diversity.

- Explain culture shock and reverse culture shock.

- Critically review acculturation models.

- Identify the communication strategies that facilitate cross-cultural adaptation.

INTRODUCTION

It goes without saying that our society is becoming more culturally and linguistically diverse by the day. An important contributor to cultural diversity is the migration of people. Some undertake voluntary migration and others are forced to do so: immigrants, refugees, asylum seekers, businesspeople, international students and so on. Globalization and communication technologies not only redefine the mobility of people in contemporary societies, they also delineate new parameters for interpreting immigration. Historically, immigration referred to the restricted cross-border movements of people, emphasizing the permanent relocation and settlement of usually unskilled, often indentured or contracted labourers who were displaced by political turmoil and thus had little option other than resettlement in a new country. Today, growing affluence and the emergence of a new group of skilled and educated people have fuelled a new global movement of migrants who are in search of better economic opportunities, an enhanced quality of life, greater political freedom and higher expectations. These people, known as skilled migrants, form an integral part of the modern-day immigrant population. In addition, refugees and asylum seekers, usually from countries and regions in political turmoil, war, conflict or economic crisis, constitute a significant number of the displaced people in the world. Statistical data from the Pew Research Center (2016) revealed that nearly one in 100 people worldwide are displaced from their homes. This is the highest share of the world's population that has been forcibly displaced since the United Nations High Commissioner for Refugees (UNHCR) began collecting data on displaced people in 1951. Relocated into the legal and political institutions of the settlement culture, immigrants and refugees aspire to a high quality of life, a good education for themselves or their children, autonomy in their choice of work and economic stability. These goals, however, have to be achieved alongside a journey of acculturation, a process through which immigrants adjust into the settlement culture. This journey not only involves a mental reconciliation of sometimes incompatible pressures for both assimilation into the settlement culture and differentiation from it, but also affects immigrants' economic survival in the settlement country.

This chapter discusses the immigration and acculturation of mainly immigrants. First, we provide a historical review of immigration as a key contributor to cultural diversity, along with discussions of multiculturalism and its differentiated benefits for host nationals and immigrants. The chapter then defines and explains the concepts of diaspora and transnationalism. Next, we explain culture shock and reverse culture shock, as experienced by people who are in cultural transition. We critically review the dominant models of acculturation and use examples to illustrate their application. Finally, the chapter identifies a range of personal, social, cultural and political factors that shape acculturation processes and outcomes as well as communication strategies to facilitate immigrants' cross-cultural adaptation.

IMMIGRATION AND CULTURAL DIVERSITY

Human migration is more than 1 million years old and continues in response to complex human cultural and existential circumstances. In modern times, profound changes in the world's political and economic order have generated large movements of people in almost every region. Viewed in a global context, the total world population of immigrants, that is people living outside their country of birth or citizenship, is huge. More than a decade ago, Massey and Taylor (2004: 1) wrote that if migrants, estimated at some 160 million, were united in a single country, they would 'create a nation of immigrants'. By 2015, the number of international migrants, or persons living in a country other than where they were born, reached 244 million (including almost 20 million refugees) for the world as a whole, which is a 41 per cent increase compared to the year 2000, according to data presented by the United Nations (2016).

Migrants and refugees

Following the lifting of restrictions on race-based immigration in the 1950s and 1960s, Asians and Africans began to migrate in large numbers to North America, Australasia and Europe. There has also been substantial migration from Latin America into the United States, and significant labour migration into newly industrialized nations, such Korea, Malaysia and Singapore, during the 1970s and 1980s (Brubaker, 2001). In Europe, the countries with the highest emigration rates until 1960 were Italy, Spain, Portugal, former Yugoslavia and Greece (Vukeljic, 2008). There is widespread consensus among migration scholars that since the 1980s, migration has become one of the most important factors in global change (Castles, 2000). According to a report from the International Organization for Migration (2006), the number of international migrants is thought to have reached between 185 and 192 million in 2005, an upward trend that is likely to continue. A salient feature of the Asia Pacific system is the increasing scale and significance of female migration (Ehrenreich and Russell-Hochschild, 2002). For example, the massive economic development of Malaysia, which began after the implementation of the New Economy Policy (NEP) in the 1970s, provided widespread opportunities for the employment of local and foreign workers (Chin, 2003). The higher wages and status of industrial work attracted many Malaysian women to the workforce, which has created problems in household labour. To resolve this, Malaysians hire low-wage female domestic workers from other countries, such as the Philippines and Indonesia. Consequently, the number of foreign maids increased from a few hundred in the 1970s to around 228,000 in 2010 (Asrul Hadi, 2011).

Forced migration, such as migration due to war, violence, civil unrest, economic dislocation and political persecution, creates another category of migrants: refugees and asylum seekers.

The plight of refugees has gained new prominence, with the number of displaced people hitting a record high across the world of 65.6 million in 2016 (UNHCR, 2018). This figure is more than the population of the UK, is an increase of 300,000 on the year before, and is the largest number ever recorded, according to the UNHCR. Of the more than 70,000 refugees who have been admitted to the United States in the fiscal year 2016, the largest numbers have come from the Democratic Republic of the Congo, Burma and Syria (Pew Research Center, 2016). Syrian refugees currently attract significant attention globally, as they are a visible by-product of regional power struggles and a reminder to Americans of the threat terrorism poses (Glaser, 2016). Around 12.5 million (six in ten) Syrians are now displaced from their homes, up from less than 1 million in 2011, according to a Pew Research Center (2016) analysis of global refugee data. Displaced Syrians worldwide include those internally displaced within Syria, refugees living in neighbouring countries and those relocated to other countries, such as Canada and the United States, and those in Europe awaiting a decision on their asylum application. European Union countries plus Norway and Switzerland received a record 1.3 million refugees in 2015. About half of the refugees in 2015 trace their origins to just three countries: Syria, Afghanistan and Iraq. Among the destination countries, Germany, Hungary and Sweden together received more than half of the asylum seeker applications in 2015 (Pew Research Center, 2016).

Diaspora and transnationalism

Regardless of reasons for migration, migrants form diaspora communities in the settlement country. The term *diaspora* is based on the Greek terms *speiro*, meaning 'to sow', and the preposition *dia*, meaning 'over'. The Greeks used diaspora to mean migration and colonization. In Hebrew, the term initially referred to the settling of scattered colonies of Jews outside Palestine after the Babylonian exile, and came to have a more general connotation of people settled away from their ancestral homeland. The meaning of diaspora has shifted over time and now refers not only to traditional migrant groups, such as Jews, but also much wider communities comprised of voluntary migrants living in more than one culture. Diasporas are not temporary; they are lasting communities. Such a community maintains cultural identification with members outside the national borders of space and time in order to live within the new environment (Clifford, 1997).

Many migrants today build social networks that cross geographic, cultural and political borders. Basch, Schiller and Blanc (1994) used the concept of *transnationalism* to refer to the process by which migrants forge and sustain multi-stranded social relations that link together their societies of origin and settlement. Immigrants who develop and maintain multiple relationships – familial, economic, social, organizational, religious and political – spanning borders are referred to as transmigrants. As migrants maintain contacts across international borders, their identity is not necessarily connected to a single country. One implication is that migrants continuously negotiate identities between 'old' and 'new' worlds, creating new configurations of identification with home in both places. For example, until recently, Syrian food was hard to find in Toronto. Because of the recent influx of more than 50,000 Syrian refugees to Canada, including around 11,000 in Toronto, Syrian cuisine is becoming very popular there. The food spaces range from cafés to farmers' markets or Syrian women sharing traditional recipes from home with the wider public. Toronto is a city whose culinary landscape is framed by its immigrant foods (more than half of all Torontians are foreign-born), and the emergence of Syrian cooking shows how food can build a bridge between two or more homelands (Sax, 2018).

PHOTO 9.1   A scene in downtown Sydney showing the diverse population in the city.

Copyright © Shuang Liu. Used with permission.

DO IT!

Some people argue that cultural diversity in an immigrant-receiving country can pose a threat to the cultural uniqueness of that country and people. Interview a student with an immigrant background in your country and a student who was born and grew up in your country. Ask about their views on the benefits and threats that immigration may bring to the national culture of the country. Summarize their views and present your findings to the class.

Attitudes towards multiculturalism

In immigrant-receiving countries, tensions between ethic and national cultures are constantly evident. At the same time as a country maximizes the benefits of cultural diversity, it is aware of the potential threats that the existence of different cultural practices might pose to the uniqueness of the national culture. Immigrants everywhere form associations to maintain their ethnic cultural heritage and to promote the survival of their languages within mainstream institutions. On the other hand, people from the national culture express concerns about the threat that incoming immigrants pose to mainstream cultural values, the existing political and economic power structure, and the distribution of employment opportunities. For example, in both Germany and France, there is growing anxiety about the withdrawal of immigrant groups into their home cultures and their increasing unwillingness to integrate into the larger national culture. Situations like this raise the question of whether multiculturalism poses a threat to cultural identity.

Countries adopt different policies regarding diversity. The melting-pot ideal used to be the dominating discourse of immigrant identity in Australia and the United States. People with this ideal take the view that national identity should be a blend of all the cultures – a melting pot – so that differences between 'us' and 'them' are reduced in the hope that 'we' become more like 'them', and 'they' see us as less alien and more like them (Zubrzycki, 1997). Over time has come the realization that a multitude of ethnic cultures can coexist in a given environment, retaining their original heritage while functioning in the mainstream culture. This led to a change of perspective from the 'melting pot' to the 'salad bowl' to depict contemporary American society (Ogden, Ogden and Schau, 2004). Similarly, Canada has been described as a mosaic of cultural groups to reflect the distinguishable constituent parts of multiple cultures there. The survival of ethnicity has directed scholars' attention towards understanding how immigrants integrate into the host society. When immigrants interact with people from the mainstream culture, they move not only between languages but also between cultures. Central to this culture-switching process is their relationships to the ingroup (their ethnic group) and outgroup (the mainstream cultural group). The settlement country's attitudes to cultural diversity play an important role in influencing immigrants' strategies to participate in the mainstream culture.

The concept of multiculturalism has been a subject of debate among the public and scholars. Multiculturalism stresses the importance of recognizing cultural diversity within a given social and political environment. However, the promotion of multicultural coexistence can lead to group distinctions and threaten social cohesion (Berry, 2001). Berry and Kalin (1995) argue that groups are more in favour of multiculturalism when they see advantages for themselves. The *ideological asymmetry hypothesis* (Sidanius and Pratto, 1999) suggests that hierarchy-attenuating ideologies such as multiculturalism appeal more to low-status groups than to high-status groups, because the existing status hierarchy tends to be more beneficial for members of high- rather than low-status groups. For minority and lower status groups, multiculturalism offers the possibility of maintaining their own culture and at the same time obtaining higher social status in society. Majority group members, on the other hand, may see ethnic minorities and their desire to maintain their own culture as a threat to mainstream cultural identity and their higher status position. Thus, multiculturalism has more to offer to majority than to minority groups.

The question is about the extent to which immigrants can maintain access to their ethnic language, religion, customs and traditions, and ethnic organizations without posing a threat to the overall political unity of the host society. Studies conducted with Asian immigrants in Australia showed that they tend to view multiculturalism as a greater benefit than do Anglo-Australians, who see it as more of a threat (Liu, 2007). The perceived threat to one's own culture from another culture is one of the greatest stumbling blocks in intercultural relations (Bygnes, 2013). Such fears interfere with diplomatic relations, business cooperation and interpersonal relations between members of different cultures, and can even lead to wars between nations. The fears may also lead to prejudice by people in one culture against those in another. When people feel their cultural identity is threatened, they reject others.

The arrival of immigrants as new settlers also brings changes to the host cultural environment. As pointed out by Sayegh and Lasry (1993: 99), it is difficult 'to imagine a host society which would not be transformed after immigrants have been accepted as full participants into the social and institutional networks of that society'. Thus, both the immigrant group and host nationals undergo psychological and sociocultural adjustment as a result of the presence of culturally distinctive others. Under some circumstances, psychological adjustment for members of the majority may be even more difficult than that experienced by immigrants. The reason is that immigrants, in many cases, are aware of the need to adjust to their host cultural environment as soon as, if not well before, they set foot in the host country. People in the mainstream cultural group, however, are not likely to be so well-prepared to accept or adjust to the changes in their lives brought about by the immigrant population. Hence, it is important to take into consideration both ethnic minorities and the majority group or groups, because the lack of accommodating attitudes in either group may hamper the realization of a positively diverse society.

THEORY CORNER

INTEGRATED THREAT THEORY

A significant amount of research indicates that the perception of threat plays an important role in prejudice towards outgroups in general and immigrants in particular. *Integrated threat theory*, advanced by Walter Stephan and colleagues (1999), identified four domains of threat: realistic,

(Continued)

symbolic, negative stereotypes and intergroup anxiety. Realistic threat concerns the threat to the political and economic power and well-being of the ingroup. Immigrants are likely to evoke such a threat, as they need jobs and may also require additional resources from the host society. Symbolic threat concerns group differences in values, beliefs, morals and attitudes, which may lead to prejudice against members of outgroups. Negative stereotypes serve as a basis for negative expectations concerning the behaviour of members of the stereotyped group. For example, when migrant group members are perceived to be untrustworthy, mainstream group members may feel threatened when interacting with them. The fourth type of threat, intergroup anxiety, refers to people's feeling of being personally threatened in intergroup interactions because they are concerned about negative outcomes for themselves, such as being embarrassed, rejected or ridiculed. Interacting with immigrants is often difficult for people from the host culture because of differences in language and cultural values, and this adds to intergroup anxiety in interaction.

Following a number of terrorist attacks in the early twenty-first century, including the September 11 attacks in the United States, the 2002 nightclub bombings in Bali and the 2005 bombings in London, Muslims across the world have increasingly been perceived as a threat to security and targets for hostility. As an example of the application of the integrated threat theory, Stephen Croucher (2013: 50–51) studied the effects of growing Muslim populations in the UK, France and Germany, where Muslims are increasingly becoming 'victims of prejudice and hate'. He applied the integrated threat theory to examine the relationship between host nationals' perceptions of Muslims' motivation to fit in the host culture and the level of perceived threat from them. The findings revealed that when members of the national culture feel a threat, either real or symbolic, they are more likely to believe that the immigrant group does not want to integrate. In addition, the economic and political context strongly affects the perceived level of threat from immigrants. Muslim immigrants were considered a higher threat, both symbolic and real, in the UK and France, where both unemployment and anti-Muslim rhetoric is high. People in Germany, on the other hand, saw Muslims as less of a threat.

REFERENCES

Croucher, Stephen M. (2013) 'Integrated threat theory and acceptance of immigrant assimilation: An analysis of Muslim immigration in Western Europe', *Communication Monographs*, 80(1): 46–62.

Stephan, Walter G., Ybarra, Oscar and Bachman, Guy (1999) 'Prejudice toward immigrants', *Journal of Applied Social Psychology*, 29(11): 2221–2237.

DO IT!

Governments differ in the degree of cultural diversity they are ready to accept. Search the internet for the immigration policies of three countries from different regions of the world – for example, Europe, North America and Asia. Find out what the rules are for accepting immigrants and refugees, and the requirements for becoming a citizen of the country. Compare the similarities and differences. Share your findings with a classmate who has also looked at three different countries.

CULTURE SHOCK AND ACCULTURATION

Although the reasons for migration vary, all migrants undergo adjustment during cultural transition and face the same task of moving between their home culture and the mainstream culture of their new country. Immigrants' ability to develop a sense of belonging in the new country, where they feel somewhat out of place (at least upon arrival), is crucial to their psychological well-being.

Culture shock and reverse culture shock

Culture shock refers to the feelings of disorientation and anxiety that a sojourner experiences due to his or her inability to adjust to a new cultural environment (Furnham and Bochner, 1982). It occurs in social interactions between sojourners and host nationals when familiar cultural norms and values governing behaviours are questioned in the new cultural environment. Adler (1975) notes that culture shock is a psychological and social process that progresses through several stages. For some people it may take several weeks to overcome psychological stress; for

PHOTO 9.2   A celebration of Buddha's birthday in Brisbane.
Copyright © Shuang Liu. Used with permission.

others the frustration of culture shock may last as long as a year. Symptoms of culture shock include depression, fatigue, helplessness, anxiety, homesickness, confusion, irritability, isolation, intolerance, defensiveness and withdrawal, and all are indicators of psychological stress.

The most widely known model of culture shock is the U-curve model, based on the work by Oberg (1960) and Lysgaard (1955) in relation to expatriate sojourners, whose reactions were characterized by increased levels of depression and anxiety related to doubt over how to live in a new cultural environment. The initial stage of culture shock, usually called the honeymoon stage, is characterized by the intense excitement associated with being somewhere different and unusual. The new arrival may feel euphoric and excited with all the new things he or she is encountering. The second stage is called disintegration, when frustration and stress begin to set in due to the differences experienced in the new culture. The new environment requires a great deal of conscious energy that was not required in the old environment, and this leads to cognitive overload and fatigue. Communication difficulties may occur. In this stage, feelings of discontent, impatience, anger, sadness and feelings of incompetence may appear. The third stage of culture shock is called the reorientation or adjustment phase, which involves the reintegration of new cues and an increased ability to function in the new culture. Immigrants start to seek solutions to their problems. A sense of psychological balance may be experienced, which initiates an evaluation of the old ways versus the new. The fourth stage of culture shock is labelled the adaptation stage. In this stage, people become more comfortable in the new culture as it becomes more predictable; they actively engage in the culture with their new problem-solving and conflict resolution tools, with some success. The final stage is described as biculturalism, where people are able to cope comfortably in both the home and new cultures. This stage is accompanied by a more solid feeling of belonging as people have recovered from the symptoms of culture shock.

Intercultural scholars have applied the concept of culture shock to understand the cross-cultural adjustment process in general. For instance, in a longitudinal study on the cross-cultural adaptation of 35 international students studying in New Zealand, Ward and her colleagues (1998) found that psychological and sociocultural problems were greatest at the beginning of a sojourn. Similarly, in a study of 500 Korean immigrants residing in the United States, Park and Rubin (2012) reported that longer residence was associated with better adaptation. The longer the sojourners stay in the new culture, the more likely they are to develop sociocultural and linguistic competence as they become more experienced in dealing with their new lives. In addition, a large body of culture shock research has been conducted in the multidisciplinary field of international management studies to inform expatriate selection and training as well as issues related to international relocation and repatriation (Kraimer, Bolino and Mead, 2016).

Culture shock can also be experienced by people who return to their home country after an extended stay in a foreign culture. Such an experience is referred to as *reverse culture shock*.

In early work, Gullahorn and Gullahorn (1963) extended the U-curve model to the W-curve model to account for reverse culture shock, which may cause greater distress and confusion than the original shock experienced in the new culture. In reverse culture shock, the home culture is compared adversely to the admired aspects of the new culture. Since people do not want to admit that they are having difficulty readjusting to the home culture, the re-entry process often involves suffering in silence. Upon first returning home, there is a sense of relief and excitement about being back in familiar surroundings, seeing old friends and family, and eating familiar food. However, to the surprise of everyone, especially the returning expatriate, a sense of depression and a negative outlook can follow the initial re-entry cycle. Several factors contribute to the downturn phase. First, upon re-entry to the home culture, there is a felt need to search for a new identity. Second, the home culture may look so negative at times that the re-entering person longs for the 'good old days' in the host country where she or he lived for the previous period. Third, the old values, beliefs and ways of thinking and living with which the person was once familiar may have changed, resulting in a sense of loss or ambiguity. Finally, people too may have changed over the intervening years; resuming deep friendships with old friends may not be automatic. For example, Chiang (2011) conducted a study on 25 young Taiwanese who emigrated to Canada and New Zealand with their parents as children in the 1980s and 1990s, but had returned to Taiwan. The findings showed that these returnees reported encountering reverse culture shock, and more than half of the participants expressed a desire to move back to the place to which they had emigrated.

The U-curve and other similar models have been criticized for oversimplifying the complex cross-cultural adjustment process and failing to reflect the range of factors at play. Scholars argue that cross-cultural adjustment should be seen as a multidimensional concept instead of a unitary, linear phenomenon, as suggested by classic models of culture shock. Fitzpatrick (2017) pointed out that culture shock should be viewed as a dynamic, discourse-based concept that is created through universal cultural processes but influenced by contextual factors, rather than as a set of the immutable characteristics of a given group of people based on cultural stereotypes. He further argues that culture shock is more about how individuals deal with the changes in their lives in a particular context as they engage in social behaviours and construct discourse around their behaviours and experiences. Research on culture shock, therefore, needs to seek to identify the possible causes of disorientation, stress and anxiety due to cultural transition, and to highlight the resources and strategies that can influence cross-cultural adjustment.

DO IT!

Talk to some international students at your university, some whose native language is English and others whose native language is not English. Ask them what kind of culture shock symptoms they experienced when they initially arrived in the country and started university, and whether they find speaking English helpful in overcoming culture shock. Write one paragraph about the role of language in culture shock, and share it with the classmates you have talked with to get their feedback.

Acculturation models and critiques

Acculturation refers to the changes that cultural groups undergo when 'groups of individuals having different cultures come into continuous first-hand contact, with subsequent changes in the original cultural patterns of either or both groups' (Redfield, Linton and Herskovits, 1936: 149). Acculturation is often marked by physical and psychological changes that occur as a result of the adaptation required to function in a new and different cultural context. The most widely applied model of acculturation was developed by John Berry (1980). According to his model, immigrants are confronted with two basic issues: maintenance of their heritage culture and maintenance of relationships with the host society. On this continuum, acculturation orientations include a positive value placed on both the heritage and the new culture (integration), a negative value placed on the old and a positive value placed on the new (assimilation), a positive value on the old and a negative value on the new (separation), and a negative value on both cultures (marginalization). For example, individuals who wish to maintain their ethnic traditions and at the same time to become an integral part of the host society are *integrationists*. *Marginalization* refers to individuals devaluing their cultural heritage but not having significant psychological contact with the host society either. Marginalized people may feel as though they do not belong anywhere or, in a more positive variant of this orientation, they may reject ethnic identity and host cultural identity. Bourhis, El-Geledi and Sachdev (2007) refer to such people as *individualists*. *Assimilation* and *separation* both refer to rejecting one culture and living exclusively in the other. Many immigrants move between these orientations and over time gravitate to one, most commonly integration or assimilation.

A plethora of studies have identified integration as the most preferred acculturation strategy (Ward, 2008), because it offers immigrants the opportunity to keep their ethnic cultural practice while maintaining a positive relationship with the host society. Integration probably benefits immigrants most, as among other advantages it provides them an opportunity to raise their social status. However, it is difficult, if not impossible, to upgrade the status position of their whole ethnic group. Efforts to achieve a positive social and cultural identity are therefore often focused on integrating into the mainstream cultural group, rather than remaining as a member of the foreign outgroup. Evidence from previous research also indicates that the integration strategy is linked to good psychological adjustment, a sense of belonging and a feeling of acceptance.

A shortcoming of Berry's original model is that it places the emphasis in acculturation on minority or immigrant groups, based on the assumption that immigrants have the freedom to pursue the acculturation strategy they prefer in the host society. In reality, host-culture attitudes can exert a strong influence on how immigrants experience the acculturation process (Kosic, Mannetti and Sam, 2005). Like immigrants, members of a host society also develop acculturation attitudes (Rohmann, Florack and Piontkowski, 2006). For them, acculturation centres on whether they want immigrants to maintain their heritage culture, and how much they value intergroup contact. Their acculturation attitudes, in a model analogous to Berry's but referring to the host culture, are referred to as integration, assimilation, segregation and individualism (Bourhis et al., 1997). Discordance between majority and minority acculturation attitudes leads to negative outcomes, such as stereotyping, prejudice and discrimination (Zagefka and Brown, 2002). Moreover, most acculturation research is about change in minorities, rather than reciprocal change in people from the mainstream population. For example, Nguyen and Benet-Martínez (2013) found that 65 per cent of the studies included in their meta-analysis were about minorities in the United States, but not acculturative change in the dominant American population.

Other criticisms of Berry's linear model are reflected in the call for examining acculturation at the level of the family, because acculturation is a process rather than a variable, and as such it is dynamic and multidimensional, extending beyond the static models (Tardif-Williams and Fisher, 2009). These scholars believe that in addition to the large body of scholarship on macro-level contexts of acculturation, such as cultural, socio-political and economic, there is a need for more longitudinal research that focuses on the day-to-day experiences in which cultural meanings are negotiated. Other attempts to address the limitations of the linear acculturation models are reflected in adding more complexity to the model.

THEORY CORNER

BICULTURAL IDENTITY INTEGRATION

Many people are now exposed to more than one culture and become bicultural or multicultural. These bicultural/bilingual individuals may be international students, expatriates, business people, immigrants, refugees, foreign-born migrants or children of interracial marriages. As a result, biculturalism and bilingualism have been attracting increasing attention in research in the field of cross-cultural psychology and intercultural communication. One influential theoretical concept in this field was *bicultural identity integration* (BII), developed by Benet-Martínez and colleagues.

(Continued)

Bicultural individuals differ in how they combine and negotiate their two cultures. Benet-Martínez and Haritatos (2005) conducted a study using a sample of Chinese-American biculturals to unpack the construct of BII; that is, the degree to which a bicultural individual perceives his or her two cultural identities as 'compatible' versus 'oppositional'. The BII measure has two components: distance (versus overlap) and conflict (versus harmony) between one's two cultural identities or orientations. High BII people identify with both heritage and mainstream cultures, see them as compatible and complementary, see themselves as part of a combined, blended cultural being (e.g., 'I keep the Chinese and American cultures together), and feel good about all this. Low BII people also identify with both cultures, but they are more likely to feel caught between the two cultures, and prefer to keep them separate (e.g., 'I feel conflicted between the Chinese and American ways of doing things').

Bicultural individuals engage in a process called cultural frame switching, where they shift between their two cultural interpretative frames in response to cues in the social environment. However, although extensive research has investigated the differences *between* cultural groups, relatively less is known about cultural switching processes *within* multicultural or bicultural individuals. For example, how do bicultural individuals organize and move between their various cultural orientations without feeling disoriented? Cheng, Lee and Benet-Martínez (2006) conducted a study to examine how cultural priming affects the cultural frame switching of individuals with high and low levels of bicultural identity integration, using a sample of 179 first-generation and 41 second-generation Asian-American biculturals. They used an implicit word-priming task that included one of four types of words: (a) positive words associated with Asians, (b) negative words associated with Asians, (c) positive words associated with Americans or (d) negative words associated with Americans. The findings indicated that when exposed to positive cultural cues, biculturals who perceived their cultural identities as compatible (high BII) responded in culturally congruent ways, whereas biculturals who perceived their cultural identities as conflicting (low BII) responded in culturally incongruent ways. The opposite was true for negative cultural cues. These results confirmed that the cultural frame-switching process is different depending on one's level of BII, and that both high and low BIIs can exhibit culturally congruent or incongruent behaviours under different conditions.

REFERENCES

Benet-Martínez, Verónica and Haritatos, Jana (2005) 'Bicultural identity integration (BII): Components and psychosocial antecedents', *Journal of Personality*, 73: 1015–1050.

Cheng, Chi-Ying, Lee, Fiona and Benet-Martínez, Verónica (2006) 'Assimilation and contrast effects in cultural frame switching (CFS): Bicultural identity integration (BII) and valence of cultural cues', *Journal of Cross-Cultural Psychology*, 37: 742–760.

STRATEGIES OF CROSS-CULTURAL ADAPTATION

Cross-cultural adaptation refers to the process of increasing one's level of fitness in a new cultural environment (Kim, 1988). A number of factors influence the level of anxiety, distress and frustration experienced by sojourners or new immigrants, hence appropriate communication strategies are needed to facilitate cross-cultural adaptation.

Factors influencing cross-cultural adaptation

Similarity between host and home cultures. The degree of similarity between the host and home cultures of immigrants can predict the acculturation stress experienced by them. For example, Sudanese immigrants in Australia experience significantly larger psychological and cultural distance compared to those from New Zealand. In addition to physical appearance and language, cultural traits such as beliefs and values may also set one group of immigrants apart from others. The early Chinese settlers in Australia in the 1840s were resented because they were efficient, hardworking and economically competitive, and were therefore viewed as a threat to the livelihoods of European migrants (Ang, 2000). Increasing cultural distance encourages immigrants to remain psychologically located within their ethnic groups.

Ethnic support. Immigrants extend their connection to their home culture through various types of ethnic associations, including religious groups. Ethnic community networks also provide valuable support for immigrants in adjusting to the new culture. For example, a number of studies have identified social networks as a critical part of the entrepreneurial activities of immigrants in many countries. When immigrants relocate from the home country, they bring with them significant attachments to their home culture. They also extend this attachment in the host country by connecting to ethnic social networks, which provide an initial cushion for negotiating a sense of

PHOTO 9.3   Halloween, an American festival, is celebrated in Hong Kong.
Copyright © Annie Liu. Used with permission.

place, as evidenced in ethnic residential concentration in certain areas. Ethnic social support can therefore create a space where immigrants can bridge cultural distance and gradually build connections with the mainstream culture.

Personal characteristics and background. Demographic factors such as age, native language and education, personal experience such as previous exposure to other cultures, and personality characteristics such as extraversion may all influence cross-cultural adaptation outcomes. Younger migrants generally adapt more easily than older ones, particularly when they are also well educated. However, there are studies that have not found age to be a significant predictor of acculturation outcomes (Park and Rubin, 2012). Scholars argue that the lack of host language proficiency is one of the main barriers that sojourners face during cross-cultural adaptation (Berry, 2005). Previous exposure to other cultures also better prepares a person psychologically to deal with the stress and frustration associated with settling in a new culture.

Mainstream media. When mass media portray an ethnic group, the image they create about that ethnic group becomes a common category that others may use to describe the group members. Because of this effect, mass media can serve as a contributor to perpetuating or diminishing stereotypes of certain minority groups (Mastro and Greenberg, 2000). This role of the mass media in activating and perpetuating stereotypes is particularly significant when the audience either has little direct experience with the group or lacks other sources of verification. For example, the negative media representation of Muslims contributes to hostile attitudes towards this group in many countries. When negative stereotypes are perceived to be real, prejudice is a likely outcome. An ethnic group's perception of how they are portrayed in the mass media will affect their attitudes to the mainstream culture and subsequently their desire to integrate.

Ethnic media. In addition to exposure to mainstream media, ethnic minorities also have access to ethnic media such as newspapers and TV programmes in their native language, accessible in their host country. Ethnic media have both intragroup and intergroup functions. As an intragroup function, ethnic media promote ethnic group cohesion not only through their news stories, but also via the ethnic language they use. As an intergroup function, ethnic media can help immigrants to learn about the host culture through their familiar language. Past studies have found that ethnic minorities, especially during the early stages in the new culture, may avoid interpersonal encounters when they can instead use mediated channels such as newspapers in their native language as alternative sources of learning about the new cultural environment and people. Ethnic media, therefore, can play a positive role in facilitating immigrants' cross-cultural adaptation.

Intergroup contact. The amount of interpersonal contact between immigrants and host nationals can influence the process of cross-cultural adaptation. Contact between groups has long been considered to be an important strategy for improving intergroup relations.

Pettigrew (1997) examined the responses of over 3,800 majority group members from France, Great Britain, the Netherlands and Germany, and found that intergroup contact played a critical role in reducing bias. Appropriate and friendly intergroup contact may translate into more positive perceptions and may also strengthen ingroup identification by creating positive feelings about it. Potentially negative stereotypes created by the mass media may also be reduced by more frequent intergroup contact. Intergroup contact or intercultural friendships can facilitate immigrants' cross-cultural adaptation.

Political and social environments. The host culture's political and social environment has a major impact on adjustment to new cultural surroundings. Specific outgroups are more (or less) welcome in a culture. Negative attitudes towards immigrants can indicate rejection of a minority group and can establish impermeable social boundaries (Bourhis et al., 1997). Liebkind and Jasinskaja-Lahti (2000) compared experiences of discrimination on psychological distress among a large sample of 1,146 immigrants representing seven ethnic groups (Russian, Ingrian/ Finnish, Estonians, Somalis, Arabs, Vietnamese and Turks) in Finland. They found that, across the sample, self-reported experiences of discrimination were highly predictive of psychological well-being. Factors affecting the degree of tolerance of particular outgroups include the social or political policies of the mainstream culture, such as political representation, citizenship criteria, language requirements and employment opportunities.

THEORY CORNER

THE INTEGRATED THEORY OF COMMUNICATION AND CROSS-CULTURAL ADAPTATION

A widely applied model of cross-cultural adaptation from the field of intercultural communication is Young Y. Kim's integrative theory of communication and cross-cultural adaptation. Kim (2001: 31) explains that cross-cultural adaptation is interactive and fundamentally communicative; it is 'the dynamic process by which individuals, upon relocating to new, unfamiliar or changed cultural environments, establish (or re-establish) and maintain relatively stable, reciprocal and functional relationships with those environments'. According to this model, adaptation is a progressive series of positive and negative experiences, rather than a smooth, continuous process. This process can be pictured as a coiled spring, which stretches and grows but is pulled back by its own tension. In the initial phase of cross-cultural adaptation, migrants may experience 'draw-back' as they

(Continued)

undergo stress in their interactions with the mainstream culture. As they grow more accustomed and comfortable with the mainstream culture, they experience a 'leap forward'. This process is explained as a stress, adaptation and growth dynamic that is a continual, cyclical process of cultural learning and intercultural transformation achieved through communication. Interaction may be interpersonal (e.g., interacting with particular individuals in the host culture) or mass-mediated (e.g., reading or watching or listening to mass media, which may afford a less risky form of interaction for immigrants), but it is always communicative.

In respect of how the process of acculturation unfolds over time, the integrative theory of communication and cross-cultural adaptation suggests that change over time takes place as a result of the challenges experienced in the host environment. These challenges cause stress, which in turn evokes adaptive change through learning and internal reorganization. The 'growth' referred to in the stress, adaptation and growth dynamic is the development of a more effective functionality in the new environment, referred to as functional fitness; also known as sociocultural adaptation. This model adds to Berry's models in that it highlights how individual predispositions (preparedness for change, ethnic proximity and adaptive personality) and the mainstream cultural environment (receptivity, conformity pressure and ethnic group strength) influence and are influenced by communication (communication competence, interpersonal communication with host members and access to ethnic interpersonal and mass communication), which in turn affects sojourner adaptation.

REFERENCE

Kim, Young Y. (2001) *Becoming Intercultural: An Integrative Theory of Communication and Cross-Cultural Adaptation*. Thousand Oaks, CA: Sage.

Communication strategies to facilitate cross-cultural adaptation

Immigration invariably means having to live in more than one culture. Consequently, people engage in communication with three types of audience: members of the mainstream culture, people from the home country, and their children who have grown up in the new culture. First, migrants have to learn how to communicate with members of the mainstream culture. This involves learning about a new culture and the practices and discourses of this host culture. Consistent research shows that integration is most preferred by migrants and host nationals, although sometimes an individual can adopt more than one strategy depending on the situational requirements. Second, migrants do not completely separate themselves from the home culture. Engaging with the home culture can take the form of remaining part of it by keeping in regular contact with people from the home country. Some immigrants, for example Vietnamese refugees who arrived in Australia in the 1970s, may lose touch with the old country due to the prevailing conditions there. If this happens, they will eventually only have a historical understanding of the 'home' country. Third, migrants have to learn to 'translate' between their old culture and their children's hybridized culture. Learning to cope with their children's hybrid culture is part of the daily routine of older generations of immigrants.

These myriad relationships require immigrants to adopt strategies to integrate into the settlement country. Successful cross-cultural adaptation is related not only to the psychological and social well-being of the immigrants, but also to their economic survival. Part of the process of acculturation is learning survival skills, including how to use banking services, where to go shopping, when to eat, how to work and rest, and how to use public transport. Building intercultural friendships can be helpful as it not only gives immigrants local guidance, but also increases the opportunity for intergroup contact, hence promoting intercultural understanding. It is not uncommon to find many migrants remaining within a network of their own ethnic group, not being aware that the best way to become acquainted with another culture is to establish relationships with members of that culture. Further, cross-cultural adaptation also requires immigrants to learn to accept differences.

As intercultural communicators, we should try to understand and interpret the things we experience as they are within a particular cultural context, rather than using our own cultural norms as the only judgement criteria. Regardless of how well we have prepared ourselves before entering a new culture, there will always be moments when we experience culture shock, encounter difficulties or feel frustrated at our own incapacity to accomplish our goals. Therefore, a positive attitude towards the new culture is something migrants should carry with them throughout the cross-cultural adaptation process.

SUMMARY

- The cultural diversity that migrants bring to the settlement country creates challenges for both immigrants and host nationals. Not only the migrant group but also the host nationals need to undergo psychological and sociological adjustment.
- Immigration is no longer a one-way journey. Many immigrants today build social networks across geographic, cultural and political borders, thus engaging in the process of transmigration.

- All people moving to a new culture experience culture shock, the process of which can be divided into several stages. Returning migrants may experience reverse culture shock, too.
- Orientations to heritage and host cultures can result in four acculturation orientations (or variations of them): assimilation, integration, separation and marginalization. The outcomes of acculturation can be influenced by a range of personal, social, cultural and environmental factors.

JOIN THE DEBATE

TO WHAT EXTENT SHOULD IMMIGRANTS BE ENCOURAGED TO MAINTAIN THEIR HERITAGE CULTURE?

People move to other cultures for different reasons, including joining family, for further study, or in search of humanitarian protection or employment opportunities. For example, almost 1.5 million migrants over the age of 15 have settled in Australia since 2000. As the global number of migrants increases, the debate over the maintenance of heritage cultures remains at the forefront. A 'melting pot' versus a 'salad bowl' is a commonly used metaphor when discussing managing diversity in multicultural societies. While we enjoy the benefits of cultural diversity and encourage migrants to keep their heritage and cultural traditions and practices (particularly their language and customs) so that they can pass these on to future generations, we also hope that the endorsement of diversity will not create a threat to the uniqueness of our own culture. The questions is: To what extent should we encourage migrants to maintain their heritage and cultural practices without creating a threat to the unity of the mainstream culture? What difference does context (e.g., public versus private) make? What other factors make a difference, and what difference do they make?

CASE STUDY

REFUGEES IN EUROPE

Refugees constitute a special category of migrants. According to the UNHCR, a refugee is someone who has been forced to leave his or her country because of persecution, war or violence. As such, a refugee has a justified fear of persecution for reasons of race, religion, nationality, political opinion or membership in a particular social group. The term 'asylum seeker' is often used interchangeably with 'refugee', but it refers to something different under law. An asylum seeker is a person who has sought protection as a refugee, but whose claim for refugee status has not yet been assessed. Under international law, a person is a 'refugee' as soon as he or she meets the definition of refugee, whether or not the claim has been assessed.

In 2015, more than a million refugees and asylum seekers came into Europe, mostly from Syria, Afghanistan and Iraq. The movement of people had been mainly driven by violent conflicts in the Middle East and Africa. Refugees were fleeing wars, persecution and unrelenting poverty. The majority crossed the Mediterranean Sea by boat, but some of them made their way overland via Turkey and the Balkans. Many reports pointed to the tremendously difficult and dangerous journey (Taub, 2016). For example, refugees on their way to Europe had to deal with circumstances such as newly erected fences, walls and border restrictions. The Libya to Italy crossing continues to be exceptionally dangerous, and the route has claimed the lives of 1 in every 92 persons who have tried to cross illegally, according to data from the International Organization for Migration (IOM, 2006). Since 2014, an average of 3,500 people have died each year trying to make the journey to Italy from North Africa (Campbell, 2017). The boats are overcrowded and become unseaworthy. Most of the boats sink just 20 to 40 miles from the Libyan coast.

The influx of such a large number of refugees in recent years has created a huge challenge to European social structures, as European countries have struggled to cope with the new challenges in the shorter term (e.g., how to organize emergency campsites for refugees) and in the longer term (e.g., how to help refugees to integrate, learn a new language and navigate through the education system for their children). The huge numbers of refugees and the issues related to their integration into host societies also poses difficulties. What happens depends on how well prepared local communities are for accommodating the newcomers. On the other hand, many refugees have undergone severe trauma and suffer from distress, anxiety or mental illness after their arrival in the destination country. The loss of social networks, separation from family members, a lack of language proficiency of the settlement country, fear of repatriation, and the unstable political environment in the home country, among other factors, all play a role in perpetuating psychiatric symptoms, particularly depression.

The arrival of refugees also creates economic challenges for the receiving countries. In Europe, there are hot debates about who can and should accept refugees, because of the disproportionate burden faced by some countries, particularly the destination countries (Greece and Italy) where the majority of migrants have been arriving. In 2015, Germany suggested that all EU states should accept mandatory quotas to spread the refugees EU-wide. France, Italy and Greece supported Germany's suggestion, but EU leaders as a whole decided on a voluntary scheme. Great Britain, however, argued that refugees should claim asylum when they reached their first safe destination. There also continues to be a division within the EU countries over how best to help with resettlement. Germany, for example, has been welcoming to refugees and asylum seekers. German Chancellor Angela Merkel pledged to Syrians that if they could manage to reach Germany, they could apply for asylum seeker status there. She stressed the need to fulfil Germany's international humanitarian duty. According to the *New York Times* (28 April 2017), the German government spent €14.5 billion (approximately US$15 billion) on refugees in 2016. About $1.5 billion of expenditures went to different reception centres and was spent on housing and government-provided food or stipends, and $2.2 billion went towards the provision of education and training, such as courses on intercultural communication that are being offered around Germany. These courses in particular address concerns over integration (or the lack of it), particularly in the large German cities. Refugees in Germany are required to take roughly 700 hours of classes in the German language and culture. When they pass a language test, they are eligible to get a job and stay in the country permanently.

Similarly, Sweden has received large numbers of refugees. At the peak of the European migrant crisis in 2015, more than 160,000 people arrived in Sweden seeking asylum; this is a high number of refugees to accommodate for a country with a population of fewer than 10 million. Sweden particularly invested in accepting refugees. The government itself, along with citizens' groups that are a part of a strong civil society, is extremely active in reaching out to newcomers. For example, the Department of Invitations is a creative programme where Swedes and new arrivals are 'matched' and have dinner together at the host's home. It aims to connect fluent Swedish speakers to refugees who want to improve their language skills while sharing a home-cooked meal.

According to *European Parliament News*, a dialogue was held between the Commission and the different organizations that have been working at the local level in the area of culture to discuss the role of culture in promoting the inclusion of refugees. They agreed that there is an urgent need to find strategies that will allow large numbers of refugees fleeing conflict and war zones to be included in European societies while preserving their cultural roots. Different proposals focus on culture as a factor in helping refugees to recover from trauma, develop communication skills and feel empowered. Proposals are also being put forward for conflict resolution and prevention, and mutual understanding.

Campbell, Zach (2017) 'Abandoned at sea', *The Intercept*, 1 April, https://theintercept.com/2017/04/01/europe-keeps-its-rescue-ships-far-from-the-coast-of-libya-where-thousands-of-refugees-have-drowned.

Taub, Ben (2016) 'The journey from Syria', *The New Yorker*, www.newyorker.com/news/news-desk/the-journey-from-syria-part-one.

1. What factors can influence migration flow and what effects can immigration have on receiving countries?

2. What factors can influence a change in immigration policy in countries receiving refugees and asylum seekers?

3. When refugees enter a new country they often feel 'out of place'. What roles could intercultural communication play in helping them to integrate into the host country?

4. Do you view Europe as a 'Liberal Europe', committed to moral humanitariansm, or do you see Europe as a 'Fortress Europe', committed to expelling refugees and asylum seekers? Why?

5. The refugee issue has shaped the political discourse in Europe. Can you think of any examples in other countries or regions where recent flows of refugees have triggered public debates?

Bjarnason, Thoroddur (2009) 'London calling? Preferred emigration destinations among Icelandic youth', *Acta Sociologica*, 52(2): 149–161.

Preferred emigration destinations among adolescents reflect the images and stereotypes of countries that continuously emerge in a multitude of local and global discourses and from concrete experiences with other countries. This study found that, if they wish to leave Iceland, female adolescents are more likely to move to other Nordic countries, particularly Denmark. Male adolescents, however, preferred English-speaking countries that have a reputation for economic or military power, such as the United States or the UK.

Bygnes, Susanne (2013) 'Ambivalent multiculturalism', *Sociology*, 47(1): 126–141.

Multiculturalism is a fiercely debated subject, and this article argues that ambivalence is a central feature of people's perspectives on societal diversity. Focusing on interviews with the leaders of three Norwegian social movement organizations, the study found that despite the leaders' very different organizational and political vantage points, they share a common ambivalence towards multiculturalism. This study provides an important supplement to analyses aimed at classifying specific political preferences on multiculturalism.

Crippen, Cheryl and Brew, Leah (2013) 'Strategies of cultural adaption in intercultural parenting', *The Family Journal*, **21(3): 263–271.**

This article discusses the potential issues arising when intercultural couples raise children. Twenty-one participants were interviewed regarding their parenting experiences as part of an intercultural couple. The study identified the diverse strategies that were used by intercultural parents to negotiate diversity. These strategies of adaptation included assimilation, cultural tourism, cultural transition, cultural amalgamation and dual biculturalism.

Fitzpatrick, Frank (2017) 'Taking the "culture" out of "culture shock" – a critical review of literature on cross-cultural adjustment in international relocation', *Critical Perspectives on International Business*, **13(4): 278–296.**

This paper aims to examine culture shock in international management studies and cross-cultural research. It argues that the use of the concept is based on a flawed understanding of culture and proposes an alternative perspective to help organizations prepare their employees for overseas assignments. The paper claims that culture shock is not about culture, but rather about the dynamics of context and how sojourners deal with life changes in cross-cultural adjustment.

West, Alexandria, Zhang, Rui, Yampolsky, Maya and Sasaki, Joni Y. (2017) 'More than the sum of its parts: A transformative theory of biculturalism', *Journal of Cross-Cultural Psychology*, **48(7): 963–990.**

This paper provides theoretical arguments for a transformative theory of biculturalism that aims to unify existing research on bicultural individuals' experiences. The paper reviews the existing literature on acculturation and links specific identity negotiation processes to unique products within the basic psychological domains of self, motivation and cognition. The authors argue that the way bicultural individuals negotiate their cultures and identities may result in unique psychological and social products that go beyond the additive contributions of each culture, justifying the need for a new transformative theory of biculturalism.

In this video Professor Tina Harris talks about her work in interracial communication. The video will help you to achieve the learning objective of identifying communication strategies to facilitate cultural adjustment. Watch it to see how Professor Harris distinguishes interracial communication from intercultural communication.

This video is available at http://study.sagepub.com/liu3e

SAGE VIDEO SOURCES

If civilization is to survive, we must cultivate the science of human relationships – the ability of all peoples, of all kinds to live together, in the same world at peace.

Franklin D. Roosevelt, 32nd President of the United States, 1882–1945

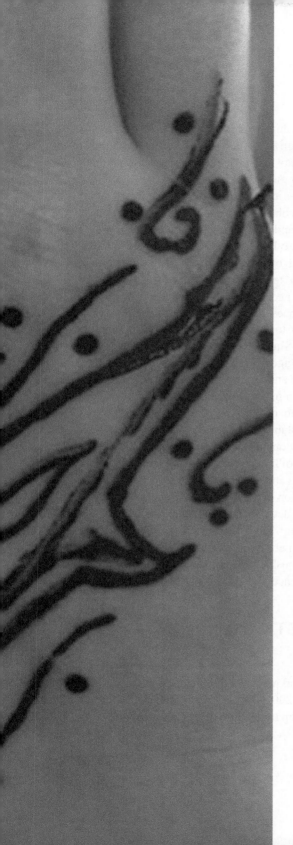

10

INTERCULTURAL AND INTERGROUP RELATIONS

LEARNING OBJECTIVES

At the end of this chapter, you should be able to:

- Understand the dimensions and characteristics of human relationships.

- Identify the conditions and stages for human relationship development.

- Apply the theories of intergroup and intercultural relationships in practical contexts.

- Evaluate the influence of culture on human relationship development.

INTRODUCTION

Initiating and maintaining personal and social relationships is an essential part of human life. We are connected to others in a variety of ways – through social networks, ethnic communities, friends, family, organizations and online social platforms – and we define ourselves and evaluate others through these relationships. American psychologist William Schutz (1966) states that humans satisfy the basic needs of inclusion, affection and control through communication. *Inclusion* is a sense of belonging or of being involved with others, as well as of including others in our activities. *Affection* refers to sharing emotions, and to showing love to and being loved by others. *Control* refers to people's ability to influence others, themselves and the surrounding environment, along with the desire to be influenced by others (or not). Although people from all cultures engage in initiating, maintaining or terminating relationships with others throughout their lives to mutually satisfy their social needs, how those social needs are met is influenced by culture. For example, cultural differences are reflected in showing deference. Indians and Japanese are more likely than Americans to act deferentially in the presence of authority figures (Savani, Morris and Naidu, 2012). Similarly, Thai younger adults tend to increase respect, politeness and deference norms as the age of their interlocutors increases from young to middle-aged and older people (Ota, McCann and Honeycutt, 2012). They rarely use first names to address elderly people, which is common in Western cultures.

This chapter discusses the influence of culture on developing and maintaining human relationships with culturally different people. We explain the dimensions and characteristics of human relationships. Next, we describe the conditions and stages of human relationship development. The chapter then introduces the theories of human relationships, including social exchange theory, the similarity attraction paradigm and anxiety/uncertainty management theory. Examples are provided to illustrate the application of those theories. Finally, the chapter discusses the influence of culture in human relationship development and maintenance, drawing on examples from different cultures regarding friendship, family and romantic relationships as well as relationships developed through social media networking sites. We emphasize in this chapter that although the development of human relationships is a universal phenomenon, how we develop and maintain human relationships is influenced by culture.

DIMENSIONS AND CHARACTERISTICS OF HUMAN RELATIONSHIPS

A human relationship can be defined as an interactional process of connecting ourselves with others in a network of social needs (Chen and Starosta, 2005). Some connections occur because of kinship, family or marriage; others exist due to group memberships, such as religion, class, ethnicity and political affiliation; still others are created because of shared interests or goals, such as relationships between colleagues, friends or people in an online social network.

Dimensions of social relationships

Harry Triandis (1977) suggests four universal dimensions of social relationships: association–dissociation, superordination–subordination, intimacy–formality and overt–covert, as summarized in Table 10.1.

TABLE 10.1   Four dimensions of social relationships

Dimension	Behaviours
Association–dissociation	*Association behaviours* include helping friends, cooperating with colleagues and supporting others' ideas or actions, whereas *disassociation behaviours* are illustrated in verbal or nonverbal behaviours such as fighting or avoiding the other person.
Superordination–subordination	Examples of *superordinate behaviours* are a supervisor giving orders to workers; *subordinate behaviours*, in contrast, involve employees obeying orders from the above.
Intimacy–formality	*Intimate behaviours* can be seen in a person's self-disclosure, such as revealing personal attitudes and feelings, touching and expressing emotions; *formality behaviours* include sending written invitations or displaying other formal communication behaviour.
Overt–covert	*Overt behaviours* are visible to others, such as touching, whereas *covert behaviours* are not visible (e.g., evaluating the behaviours of others).

Source: Adapted from Triandis, Harry C. (1977) *Interpersonal Behavior*. Monterey, CA: Brooks/Cole. p. 277.

Triandis (1984) pointed out that although these four dimensions are universal, the degree to which they are manifested varies across cultures. Association behaviours refer to people helping, cooperating with and supporting others' ideas or actions, whereas disassociation behaviours include fighting or avoiding others. However, people in every culture can engage in both association and dissociation behaviours depending on the contexts and the nature of the relationship. Superordination–subordination behaviours can be explained in terms of Hofstede's power distance dimension. In high power distance cultures like Japan and the Arab countries, subordination and superordination are viewed as natural and acceptable. However, in low power distance cultures like Austria, Denmark and Sweden, equality between people is treasured. In general, individuals in subordinate cultures are deferential to those in power. This is expressed, for example, in the bowing customs observed in Japan and Nepal: one bows deeply to a superior, who may merely nod in return. The intimacy–formality dimension refers to the degree of contact people in a given culture desire. Edward Hall (1966) called cultures that display a high degree of affiliation 'high-contact' cultures and those that display a low degree of affiliation 'low-contact cultures'. In high-contact cultures, people stand closer and use more touching when interacting than in low-contact cultures, where people may feel more comfortable standing farther apart during a conversation. The overt–covert dimension, as Triandis (1984) indicates, refers to the level of tightness or looseness in a culture. Cultures towards the tight or covert end of the continuum are characterized by more role-bonded relationships; an example is the caste system observed in India. Tight cultures tend to be more collectivistic and high-context. On the other hand, cultures at the loose or overt end of the continuum are characterized by fewer role-bonded relationships. Loose cultures tend to be more individualistic and low context. One explanation is that contextual cues play a greater role in communication between tightly bonded people than between loosely bonded people.

An important domain of social relationships is intergroup relations, which can be intercultural if the groups are from different cultures. Research on intergroup relations is primarily in the field of social psychology, which concerns perceptions, attitudes and behaviours humans express when they think of themselves and others as members of social groups (Hogg, 2003). All humans belong to many types of social group, ranging from circles of friends to larger social categories such as gender and race. When people think and act as group members, they tend to accentuate similarities between themselves and members of their own groups, and exaggerate differences between members of their own group and other groups (social categorization). People also tend to evaluate others differently, depending on whether they are members of one's own groups (ingroups) or members of other groups (outgroups). We typically show a tendency to evaluate ingroup members more positively and make more positive attributions for their behaviours, as compared to how we evaluate outgroup members – this tendency is called ingroup favouritism (Hogg, 2003). When intergroup relations are harmonious, members of different groups are less likely to emphasize differences between ingroups and outgroups. However, when there is conflict, outgroup differences are accentuated, and intergroup conflict increases when there is more prejudice held against outgroup members.

THEORY CORNER

SIMILARITY ATTRACTION PARADIGM

The *similarity attraction paradigm* was proposed by Byrne (1971). The basic premise of this paradigm is that, if we perceive that our attitudes are similar to those of other people, we are attracted to them, because the similarity in attitudes validates our view of the world. Research applying the similarity attraction paradigm has found consistent support for the proposition that people are more likely to be attracted to strangers whom they perceive to be similar to them, for example those who have similar values. However, actual similarities in attitudes and self-concepts may not be related to our attraction to another person; rather, people are attracted to others based on *perceived* similarity. Think about the similarity you have with your own ethnic group that makes you want to form relationships with them, and how a lack of perceived similarity with members of other ethnic groups influences your communication with them. In the initial stages of getting to know strangers, people tend to focus on general attitudes and opinions. As they get to know each other better, they search for similarities in worldviews or core values.

As an example to test the theory, Tidwell, Eastwick and Finkel (2013) applied the similarity attraction paradigm to examine the effects of actual and perceived similarity simultaneously during an initial face-to-face encounter in speed-dating sessions. Using a sample of 187 college students who attended one of the eight speed-dating sessions, the researchers calculated actual and perceived similarity for each pair based on questionnaire responses obtained before the event and after each date. Overall, the study found no evidence that actual similarity predicted romantic liking. However, participants who perceived similarity, both specific and general, with their speed-dating partners indicated strong levels of romantic liking. This study demonstrates that actual similarity is a weaker and less consistent indicator of romantic attraction than perceived similarity in a speed-dating context.

REFERENCES

Byrne, Donn (1971) *The Attraction Paradigm*. New York: Academic Press.

Tidwell, Natasha D., Eastwick, Paul W. and Finkel, Eli J. (2013) 'Perceived, not actual, similarity predicts initial attraction in a live romantic context: Evidence from the speed-dating paradigm', *Personal Relationships*, 20(2): 199–215.

Dimensions of interpersonal relationships

Lustig and Koester (2013) identified three dimensions of interpersonal relationships: control, affiliation and activation. Control (like the control dimension in Schutz's theory) involves power: the level of control we have over others, ourselves and the environment is dependent on the amount of power we have to influence people. Similar to Schutz's (1966) needs for inclusion and affection, Lustig and Koester (2013) define affiliation as the degree of friendliness, liking, social warmth or immediacy that is communicated between people. People from high-contact cultures, such as those of the Mediterranean region and Latin America, tend to show affection more openly by touching more frequently during conversations, standing closer to each other, and using more emotional expressions. Activation refers to the ways people react to the world around them. Some people seem very energetic, excitable and quick; others value and exude calmness, peacefulness and a sense of inner control (Lustig and Koester, 2013). For example, Germans compare themselves to a symphony orchestra because of its emphasis on rules, regularity and punctuality. Italians use opera as a cultural metaphor to define themselves because of its emphasis on emotion, drama and the lyrical use of language. Most Italians tend to engage in more animated conversations by using expressive hand gestures and vivid facial expressions, whereas Chinese tend to be more reserved and not reveal much of their feelings through facial expressions. The Chinese are taught to avoid extremes in communication; being neutral is considered a virtue. How a particular trait is perceived or displayed in a specific culture, therefore, must be interpreted against the beliefs, values, norms and social practices of that culture.

Characteristics of human relationships

Human relationships enable us to understand others and test our stereotypes about others, particularly people from outgroups whose cultural or social norms we are not familiar with. Chen and Starosta (2005) identified five characteristics of human relationships. First, human relationships are dynamic. They develop and are transformed through communication. Second, human relationships are hierarchical. Based on the level of intimacy or closeness, human relationships can be arranged in a hierarchical order ranging from strangers to intimate friends. The required degree of inclusion, control and affection varies depending on the hierarchical order of the relationship. Third, human relationships are reciprocal. Reciprocity occurs when individuals in a relationship network can satisfy each other's social needs. Fourth, human relationships are unique; they are rule-governed, with different rules for different types of relationships. Fifth, human relationships are interdependent and irreplaceable. Individuals in a human relationship network connect to each other and share emotions with each other. Sometimes our self-concept is strengthened by the confirmation we receive from others, but at other times our self-perception is at variance with others' perceptions of us. Moreover, human relationships are irreplaceable in that one person's place in the relationship network is not replaceable by another person.

People in relationship networks, particularly interpersonal relationships, continually try to maintain balance amid changing circumstances and seemingly opposing needs (Lustig and Koester, 2013). Leslie Baxter (1988) refers to the basic contradictions in human relationships as relationship dialectics, using a term borrowed from Hegel, a German philosopher from the nineteenth century. She identifies three dialectics, or points of tension, that lead to growth in interpersonal relationships; in turn, these have implications for intercultural relations (see Table 10.2).

TABLE 10.2   Dialectics in interpersonal relationships

Dialectics	Definition	Cultural implication
Autonomy–connection	The extent to which individuals want a sense of separation from others (autonomy) or a feeling of attachment to others (connection).	Culture teaches its members the appropriate range of autonomy and connection when communicating with others (e.g., individualistic versus collectivistic cultures).
Novelty–predictability	The dynamic tensions between people's desire for change (novelty) and stability (predictability) in their interpersonal relationships.	The level of uncertainty avoidance in a culture suggests the range of desired novelty and predictability.
Openness–closeness	The extent to which individuals want to share (openness) or withhold (closeness) personal information.	Collectivistic cultures encourage openness to ingroup members but closeness to outgroup members.

Source: Adapted from Baxter, Leslie (1988) 'A dialectical perspective on communication strategies in relationship development', in S. W. Duck (ed.), *Handbook of Personal Relationships: Theory, Research, and Interventions*. New York: Wiley. pp. 257–273.

CONDITIONS AND STAGES OF RELATIONSHIP DEVELOPMENT

Charles Berger and Richard Calabrese (1975) propose that relationships develop in three phases. In the entry phase, communication is governed by a set of social norms. The communication patterns in this stage are structured, and the content focuses mostly on demographic information. Our interactions with strangers or those whom we meet for the first time are examples of this entry phase. The second phase is personal. Communication content in the personal phase goes beyond the superficial (e.g., the weather or sharing demographic information), and may include information on personal problems, attitudes and opinions. The relationship between interactants becomes more intimate, and the communication styles they use are often more informal and relaxed. The third stage of relationship development is the exit phase. In this phase, the relationship begins to deteriorate and the frequency of interaction decreases. Interactants are no longer interested in maintaining the relationship and tend to avoid communicating.

Like Berger and Calabrese, Irwin Altman and Dalmas Taylor (1973) proposed *social penetration theory* to explain the development of relationships through the exchange of information. This theory states that, as an interpersonal relationship develops, the interpersonal exchange of information moves from superficial and impersonal to intimate and personal. The depth of information exchange reflects one of four stages of relationship development: orientation, exploratory affective exchange, affective exchange and stable exchange. The orientation stage is characterized by superficial information exchange about weather or demographic information. The exploratory affective stage involves an exchange of information on the periphery of our personalities, such as who you are and how you evaluate yourself (e.g., intelligent or hardworking). In the affective exchange stage, people feel more comfortable exchanging opinions and attitudes, such as 'I think Jenny is too bossy and arrogant'. At the stable exchange stage, an intimate relationship is developed and people freely express their true feelings. The frequency and amount of interaction also increase as the relationship develops. A key concept in the social penetration theory is *self-disclosure*, which refers to the process of revealing personal information that another person would be unlikely to discover through third sources.

Although self-disclosure is used in almost all cultures as a means of developing relationships, cultural norms and values govern the degree to which it is acceptable in interpersonal relationships. For example, US Americans generally feel comfortable sharing family problems or tensions with colleagues. In Chinese culture, self-disclosure about family problems is only expected to take place between close friends or relatives. As Xi describes (1994: 155), 'For Americans, self-disclosure is a strategy to make various types of relationships work; for Chinese, it is a gift shared only with the most intimate relatives and friends'. On the other hand, cultural norms govern what content is considered private and what is public (or appropriate for self-disclosure). For example, in Hong Kong, it is common to ask about one's income and age, even when meeting for the first time; in England, however, people are hesitant to reveal such private information – in this case, norms about self-disclosure are reversed.

PHOTO 10.1   Home-made Slovenian deserts for Christmas at a Slovenian's home in Los Angeles to showcase the link to Slovenian cultural traditions.

Copyright © Zala Volčič. Used with permission.

The emergence of the internet has opened a new context for self-disclosing to others. Researchers have begun to study gender effects on self-disclosure in online environments and have reported gender differences in self-disclosure in cyberspace. Trammell, Tarkowski, Hofmokl and Sapp's (2006) content analysis of 358 Polish blogs identified gender differences in the type of information communicated. Their findings showed that women tend to provide a record of the day, discuss a memory and communicate intimate feelings or thoughts more often than men, whereas men discuss hobbies or interests more often than women. Men and women were similar in providing information about current events in society, current projects, feelings and thoughts towards or about something, family and friends, intimate details about their life and expressions of gratitude.

DO IT!

Think about norms governing self-disclose in your culture, for example what type of personal information is considered appropriate to share with a friend or to ask a friend to share with you in your culture (e.g., age, income, religion, romantic relationships). Talk to a classmate from a different culture from your own and ask the person about the appropriateness of sharing the personal information you feel comfortable sharing with friends in your culture. Compare differences and identify some potential consequences if a violation of the expected level of self-disclosure should occur between communicators from the two cultures. Share your views with the classmate you have talked to.

THEORY CORNER

SOCIAL EXCHANGE THEORY

Social exchange theory aims to explain the conditions for the development of interpersonal and intercultural relationships. Developed by John Thibaut and Harold Kelley, the basic assumption of this theory is that individuals establish and continue social relations on the basis of their expectation that such relations will be mutually beneficial (Kelley and Thibaut, 1978). When people enter a relationship, they usually evaluate the rewards they are likely to gain and the costs they are

(Continued)

willing to pay. If the perceived rewards are greater than the costs, or the reward:cost ratio is more favourable than those in other relationships the people could enter (alternatives), they will continue to develop the relationship. If not, people may leave the existing relationship and seek a new one. Our culture provides an implicit theory about what is considered as important in what types of relationship. Social exchange theory, therefore, is based on the assumption that all individuals are rational beings, and human decisions are made based on the consideration for the highest net benefit in the circumstances.

The rewards of human relationships can be expressed in the form of satisfaction, happiness, self-esteem, acceptance and friendship. The costs may involve money, time, unhappiness, dissatisfaction, losing face and frustration. Corcoran (2013) applied social exchange theory to explain religious behaviour, arguing that religious behaviour can be understood as social exchange. These exchanges can be between individuals and their god(s), usually through an intermediary such as a religious representative or institution. Corcoran (2013: 342) believes that the benefits or rewards from these exchanges are largely 'other-worldly'. In other words, the reward received is not necessarily immediate or tangible, but often is expected in an afterlife. People tend to seek assurance about these rewards before committing themselves to a religion. This assurance reduces uncertainty and increases the likelihood of participation in religious exchanges (benefits). A range of personal, social and cultural factors can affect the levels of certainty (e.g., the likelihood of receiving the promised reward) and subsequent religious exchange behaviour (e.g., donation to the religious institution).

REFERENCES

Corcoran, Katie E. (2013) 'Divine exchanges: Applying social exchange theory to religious behavior', *Rationality and Society*, 25(3): 335–369.

Kelley, Harold H. and Thibaut, John W. (1978) *Interpersonal Relations: A Theory of Interdependence*. New York: Wiley.

CULTURE AND HUMAN RELATIONSHIP DEVELOPMENT

Culture governs what constitutes appropriate or acceptable behaviours regarding a certain relationship. Moreover, our interpretation of the same type of relationship may also vary across cultures. For example, friendship is universal to all cultures, but who can be called a friend may differ depending on the culture. In Australia, the term 'friend' can be used to refer to neighbours or colleagues, or even someone whom a person has just met. The boundaries between ingroups and outgroups in Australia may not be as sharp as they are in some collectivistic cultures. For collectivistic cultures like the Greek culture, the line between ingroups and outgroups is much sharper. Cultural differences are also reflected in what is considered to be private or intimate information. In Hong Kong, it is perfectly appropriate to ask a married acquaintance about his wife; in the United Arab Emirates, this would be considered a major breach of social etiquette. In Bosnia and Herzegovina, people like to say that they 'breathe' political and historical discussions. In Korea, however, similar topics would be avoided. In Taiwan, discussion about income and religion among colleagues is acceptable; in Slovenia and many other parts of Europe, such information is only shared with close friends or family members.

Yum's model of human relationships

June Yum (1988) proposed a relationship model comparing differences between North Americans and East Asians. The model identifies five types of relationship: particularistic versus universalistic, long-term versus short-term, ingroup versus outgroup, formal versus informal, and personal versus public.

Particularistic versus universalistic relationships. The subject of particularistic relationships was originally proposed by John Condon, an intercultural communication scholar, in the 1970s. Condon (1977) notes that in a culture where particularistic relationships are desired, people maximize differences in age, sex and status, and encourage mutuality and interdependency. Particularistic societies tend to be more hierarchical and human relationships are established in accordance with levels of social hierarchy. Communication is governed by specific cultural rules concerning whom to talk to, what to talk about, and when and how to talk about it in specific social contexts. Yum (1988) found that particularistic relationships are practised more in East Asian countries. This is also true in other parts of Asia. For example, because marriage in Sri Lanka means an alliance of two families, couples usually come from a similar social class. There is a Chinese metaphor 'Bamboo door matches bamboo door and wooden door matches wooden door', which implies that the matching couple need to come from 'matching doors' (status and family background).

In contrast, in cultures where universalistic relationships are desired, people establish interpersonal relationships based on rules of fairness and equality. Yum (1988) found that universalistic relationships are practised by North Americans. To them, the development of an interpersonal relationship relies on the principle of equality, not hierarchy. The rules governing ways of addressing people, for example, illustrate the level of hierarchy in a society. Employees in Australia may address their bosses using their first names, whereas such a practice is not common in companies in Malaysia. People in universalistic societies, such as Canada, Sweden, Denmark and Norway, believe that laws and regulations are written for everyone to follow and must be respected all the time. For people in particularistic societies, such as China, South Korea, Venezuela and Russia, the nature of the particular relationship in a given situation may determine how people act in that situation. The relationship might be more important than following the rules.

Long-term versus short-term relationships. Long-term relationships are preferred in East Asian cultures, where a social reciprocity is viewed as centrally important. People in these cultures tend to feel indebted to others. For example, Koreans always try to return a favour from friends with much more than they received. This practice is intended to maintain the existing relationship over a long period of time or permanently. When friends go out for a meal, often one person pays the bill for the whole group – the shared understanding is that, as friendship is considered long-lasting, there will be many opportunities in the future for each person to reciprocate in a like manner. The same friendship practices are seen in other parts of the world. In Slavic cultures, friends pay for everyone in a friendship circle, and each person paying only for himself or herself seems rude. The Anglo-Celtic custom of 'shouting' in pubs – each person buying a round of drinks – has some similarities. But in this case the expectation is that everyone will buy a round in turn on the same occasion (which, of course, can result in far too much to drink); in this case, there is less expectation of permanence in the relationships, but the same expectation of reciprocity and generosity.

Yum (1988) found that short-term and symmetrical reciprocity is characteristic of North Americans' interpersonal relationships. Commitment to long-term interpersonal relationships is not considered so important. In cultures where short-term relationships are commonly practised, people consider freedom and independence as important, and the flexibility to initiate or terminate relationships as an individual choice is valued. Hence, it is a common practice for North Americans to split the bill when having a meal with friends. The value placed on long-term versus short-term relationships is also reflected in communication styles. For example, Australians are usually direct when they need to say 'no' to friends – although they usually give an excuse or reason for refusal and are not as direct as Dutch or German people. However, the Japanese tend to say 'maybe' or 'that would be somehow hard' instead of a direct 'no'.

Ingroup versus outgroup relationships. The boundary between ingroups and outgroups is very clearly drawn in East Asian cultures. To East Asians, ingroup membership ties suggest similarity, trust and affinity, ultimately leading to the development of close interpersonal relationships. On the other hand, the boundary between ingroup and outgroup members is less clearly defined for North Americans, the British and other Western Europeans, who establish relationships to fit specific contexts. They feel comfortable being affiliated with a relatively large number of groups, even though relationships based on these affiliations are often brief (Condon and Yousef, 1975).

The boundary drawn between ingroups and outgroups can create challenges for managers in the business context, particularly in workplaces comprised of ethnically diverse employees and where group work is required. Managers realize that employees need to work in groups in order to maximize the use of resources, increase work productivity, and thus increase competitive advantage. For example, the mobile phone company Motorola depends highly on workgroups to produce innovative mobile phones (Katzenbach and Smith, 2003). However, evidence suggests that a diverse group may encounter difficulties in functioning due to differences such as culture, religion and ethnicity. Research shows that similarities, rather than differences, in demographic backgrounds 'strengthen in-group prototypes, identification and thus adherence to group norms' (Hogg and Terry, 2000: 127). Thus, the benefits of diversity, such as a breadth of ideas and skills, must always be balanced against the cost in terms of shared attitudes and perspectives.

Formal versus informal relationships. The practice around formal and informal relationships in a society depends on the hierarchical structure of the society. In hierachical cultures like those of East Asia, relationship development is more formal than in more horizontal cultures like North America. East Asians are more comfortable with initiating a relationship using a third party as a go-between. This can also avoid embarrassment or loss of face if the other party does not desire to enter into the relationship. Directly initiating a relationship characterizes horizontal cultures, where interactions are usually less formal. For example, it is common for Australians at social functions to approach strangers and introduce themselves by saying, 'I'm [their name]...', unlike in Hong Kong, where more commonly a go-between would say, 'Let me introduce my friend to you...'. Even so, in less formal cultures this kind of introduction can be a source of great tension; for example, Australians (and people from other cultures with informal relationship structures) at a business gathering in Hong Kong might be in great doubt about whether it is appropriate to introduce themselves to someone

PHOTO 10.2 Mehndi or henna in Indian tradition is applied to the hands and feet during special Hindu festivals and Hindu weddings to symbolize joy, beauty, spiritual awakening and offering.

they want to meet. Further, conversation starters such as questions about money or personal questions such as 'what do you do for a living?' and 'do you have kids?' might be common in some Asian cultures. In France, however, this is considered rude – one needs to ask questions on broader topics, such as culture, art, food, music, philosophy, architecture and popular events.

Personal versus public relationships. Yum notes that an overlap between personal and public relationships characterizes East Asian cultures. Gift-giving at negotiation meetings is a common practice in Chinese business culture – it is not a sign of bribery, as some view it, but an attempt to build trust and a good relationship so that smooth and cooperative transactions in the future can be expected. Because of the blurred boundary between personal and public relationships in Asian cultures, people tend not to separate the issue from the person. Thus, if someone criticizes a suggestion made by a manager, the manager may view the criticism as a personal attack. At meetings, therefore, people in Asian organizations are cautious about bringing up negative comments about managers or leaders.

In contrast, an emphasis on privacy, individualism, autonomy and self-reliance encourages Westerners to keep public and personal relationships separate. Westerners may argue with or criticize each other at a meeting, but they laugh and chat over drinks after the meeting – they separate the issue from the person. Moreover, gift-giving is not a tradition among Western business people. Together, these behaviours may make the Chinese business partners feel that they are not respected or have not been 'given face'. On the other hand, the Westerners may feel that their Chinese counterparts are too slow to 'get down to business' and spend too much time on things unrelated to business, such as giving gifts.

DO IT!

A frequent complaint by Chinese business people about their Western counterparts is that in business negotiations, Westerners are more 'money-minded' than 'people-oriented'. Westerners tend to start business negotiations by going immediately to the business at hand, without showing much interest or concern for their Chinese counterpart's personal life. Interview one Asian student (Chinese, Japanese, Singaporean, etc.) and another student from a Western culture to gather their views on 'small talk' (talking about family or personal matters other than the business) at the beginning of a business negotiation. Identify cultural differences and draw on Triandis's model to explain the source of barriers in a summary. Present your summary to the two students you interviewed to get their feedback.

Friendship, romantic relationships and family relationships

Friendship is one of the most important interpersonal relationships people develop with others, and it usually involves high levels of intimacy, self-disclosure and involvement. Although friendship is universal across cultures, our interpretation of the term varies from culture to culture. We choose our friends based on shared interests, goals and liking. Because friendship is voluntary, it usually occurs between people who are similar in important ways. Thais are likely to view a person as a whole, and a friend is accepted either completely or not at all. Nigerians expect friends to be involved in all aspects of each other's lives, to anticipate each other's needs and to provide advice on various matters when needed. The language people use to describe their friends can reflect underlying cultural values about the meaning and importance attached to the friendship. For example, among Mexicans, friends are referred to as a brother or a sister, suggesting collectivistic cultural values and a lasting bond. In Australia, friends are referred to as 'mates', but not as brothers and sisters.

DO IT!

Write down what you consider to be the significant characteristics of friendship and the important aspects of choosing a friend. Analyse the criteria to see how many of your preferred qualities are determined or influenced by your culture. Show your list to a classmate from another culture and find out to what extent she or he agrees with you and why. Write a paragraph on the influence of culture on choosing a friend and present it to the class.

Romantic relationships are another important type of interpersonal relationship, or in some cultural contexts inter-family relationship, that are also influenced by culture. There are enormous differences in cultural beliefs, values, norms and social practices about love, romance, dating and marriage. Casual dating for romance among Americans is not viewed as a serious commitment that will necessarily lead to marriage (Lustig and Koester, 2013). If the lovers choose to get married, it is because of their love for each other. Although family members may be consulted before a final decision is made, the choice to marry is primarily made by the couple themselves. Marrying for economic, social or political reasons seems improper to most people. In India, casual dating relationships for romantic expression among unmarried individuals are not common. Marriage is usually arranged by the parents with the consent of the couple. For example, an Indian speech pathologist who works in Sydney asked his mother in India to find him a wife. His mother compiled a list of 14 women whom she believed would be suitable, and her son went back to India for three days and picked one from the list. After consent had been obtained from the girl's parents, a wedding ceremony was held in India. At that point, the couple knew very little about each other; it was not until nine months after the marriage when the wife joined her husband in Sydney that the couple began to get to know each other and develop affection. Similar patterns of familial arrangement can also be found in Muslim cultures, where romantic love is believed to be something that develops after marriage, not before.

With increasing cross-border movements and intercultural contacts, the rate of interracial marriage has dramatically increased since the latter decades of the twentieth century in the Americas, East and South-East Asia, Europe, Australia and New Zealand. For example, the number of interracial marriages in the United States increased by more than 1,000 per cent between 1960 and 2002 (Zhang and Kline, 2009). One notable world trend is the frequency with which people of Chinese ancestry are marrying people from other cultural groups. This has been attributed to the large diaspora of Chinese people across the world, and the notable excess of young Chinese men relative to young Chinese women (Jones and Shen, 2008). Intercultural couples often struggle to resolve different cultural beliefs about what constitutes a good couple relationship, and how partners need to communicate. Cross-cultural scholars argue that individualism–collectivism is a key cultural dimension that influences interpersonal behaviour. The notion of romantic love can be seen as meeting the individualistic needs of self-expression and discovery, in that it provides romantic partners with the opportunity to explore their emotional selves (Hiew, Halford, van de Vijver and Liu, 2016). However, it has been argued that there is less need for love and intimacy in couple relationships in collectivistic societies, as these are shared across the broader family network (Dion and Dion, 1993).

Family relationships are also characterized by cultural variations. Among members of European cultures, family life is primarily confined to interactions between parents and children. Members of the extended family rarely live together in the same household or take an active part in the daily lives of the nuclear family members. In China, family is the primary means through which a person's social life is extended.

PHOTO 10.3   In a pre-wedding ceremony of the Indian Christian community, the bride to be is given milk – a symbol of fertility.

Copyright © Pradip Thomas. Used with permission.

For example, Chinese children's first friendship is usually with the children of their parents' colleagues or friends. In the Netherlands, family can be peripheral to the social networks that children establish, although school networks are a strong source of friendship and often include partners and children. Moreover, the roles of family members are more clearly defined in Asian cultures. Gender roles, for example, are well defined in Sri Lanka, where men make major decisions, provide for the family and are the head of the household. Women are expected to take care of the family and perform household duties, although nowadays more and more women join the workforce and work side by side with male colleagues. Due to the change in tradition and the effects of globalization, arranged marriage is not as common now, but there is still significant pressure on couples not to divorce, as to do so reflects badly upon the whole family.

The individualism–collectivism dimension is reflected in the perceived boundaries of the family relationship. While individualistic cultures emphasize family members' independence, autonomy and self-sufficiency, collectivistic cultures emphasize the interdependence of family members throughout the lifespan. For example, US spouses have been found to desire stronger boundaries around their relationship (less sharing of information and acceptance of advice from others), reflecting the US perception of the couple as a separate system. In contrast, in China the marital relationship is considered a continuation of the parents' family, rather than a separate system. The term 'extended family' is not used in many collectivistic cultures, as all relatives are considered to be part of the family. In addition, network members' approval and the belief that a potential partner will support one's parents have been found to have more influence on Chinese than American marital intentions and relationship commitment (Zhang and Kline, 2009).

Parent–child relationships, too, are influenced by cultural values. In collectivistic cultures like Japan, Korea, India and China, parents play a pivotal role in making decisions for children, including the choice of university, profession and even marital partner. For example, in the movie *Bend It Like Beckham* (2002), the Indian girl's (Jess) parents felt they should decide which career path their children would follow. Thus, they wanted Jess to go to university to study medicine, even though it was her personal desire to become a professional football player. In individualistic cultures, children are taught from their early years to be independent, to make their own decisions and to plot their own career paths. The parents' role is to support their children in achieving their goals, although, once again, this can be a source of great tension if the parents do not approve of the child's career choice. In Chinese families, it is not uncommon to see grown-up children, even after they are married, still live in the parental home. Some parents encourage their married sons to live with them so that they can take care of them. In contrast, children in Western cultures are encouraged to move out of the family home when they become adults.

In the case of interracial marriage, when one partner comes from a low-context culture and the other from a high-context culture, the high-context partner can misinterpret the low-context spouse's remarks, assuming that they mean more than they say explicitly, whereas the low-context partner who is not sensitive to indirect cues can miss their high-context culture partner's messages altogether (Hiew et al., 2016). Furthermore, when a partner from a collectivistic culture uses indirect communication (e.g., 'Are you thirsty?'; 'Shall we get something to drink?'), it may be seen as manipulative by a spouse from a low-context culture, whereas an explicit statement of wants and needs by a spouse from an individualistic culture (e.g., I want an orange juice) may appear demanding, rude and selfish to collectivistic partners. In a similar vein, when conflicts arise in relationships comprised of an individualistic and a collectivistic partner, partners are likely to engage in different conflict resolution strategies based on different cultural expectations. Chen (2017) draws upon the Chinese philosophy of *yin* and *yang* to emphasize the importance of developing cultural synergy, whereby people build common ground for resolving conflicts. In Chinese culture, *yin* characterizes the internal or negative nature of things whereas *yang* stands for the external or positive side. Together, they represent the two united but opposite principles in nature, such as the moon and the sun, female and male, dark and light, cold and hot, and passive and active. Although sometimes in conflict, *yin* and *yang* are complementary and work together to create the world. In a similar vein, intercultural persons play the role of both mediator and transformer; they are capable of promoting and integrating potentially incompatible cultural elements, transforming them and initiating mutual growth.

THEORY CORNER

ANXIETY/UNCERTAINTY MANAGEMENT THEORY

Anxiety/uncertainty management theory was developed by William B. Gudykunst (2004). It is based on uncertainty reduction theory, proposed by Charles Berger and Richard Calabrese (1975). Anxiety/uncertainty management theory posits that effective interpersonal and intercultural communication is a function of how individuals manage the anxiety and uncertainty they experience when communicating with others. Uncertainty refers to individuals' inability to predict and/or explain others' feelings, attitudes and behaviour. Anxiety is the affective equivalent of uncertainty. It stems from feeling uneasy, tense and worried about what might happen, and is based on a fear of potentially negative consequences. Because intercultural communication involves people from dissimilar cultures, there is always the possibility of uncertainty. The reduction of uncertainty leads to an increase in both the amount of communication and the level of interpersonal attraction. If the amount of uncertainty present in initial interactions is not reduced, further communication between the people is unlikely to occur.

Uncertainty can give rise to ethnocentric thinking and encourage a reliance on stereotypes. Kirk Johnson and colleagues (2010) conducted a critical discourse analysis on transcripts of the on-air conversations between journalists in national and cable television news broadcasts that were made during the second week after Hurricane Katrina devastated New Orleans in 2005. The 65 news programmes contained inter-journalistic discourse about African Americans in New Orleans. The findings showed that unfamiliarity with the African-American community created anxiety and uncertainty for reporters covering the post-Katrina devastation. The stressful nature of covering the crisis and the unfamiliar cultural terrain gave rise to ethnocentric and stereotypical thinking expressed in talk between journalists. These findings provide support for uncertainty management theory, which proposes that exposure to unpredictability and unfamiliar settings can cause individuals to think in ethnocentric and stereotypical ways. Hence, effective communication requires that the interactants have the ability to reduce and manage uncertainty, particularly during their initial encounter with each other.

REFERENCES

Berger, Charles R. and Calabrese, Richard J. (1975) 'Some explorations in initial interaction and beyond: Toward a developmental theory of interpersonal communication', *Human Communication Theory*, 1: 99–112.

Gudykunst, William B. (2004) *Bridging Differences: Effective Intergroup Communication* (4th edn). Thousand Oaks, CA: Sage.

Johnson, Kirk A., Sonnett, John, Dolan, Mark K., Reppen, Randi and Johnson, Laura (2010) 'Interjournalistic discourse about African Americans in television news coverage of Hurricane Katrina', *Discourse & Communication*, 4(3): 243–261.

SUMMARY

- Humans develop different types of relationships to fulfil the need for inclusion, control and affection.
- Social exchange theory, social penetration theory, the similarity attraction paradigm and anxiety/uncertainty management theory are used to explain interpersonal and intercultural relationship development.

- People from different cultures may have very different interpretations of various types of relationships and the rules governing appropriate behaviour in them.
- Yum's work identifies five dimensions on which differences between East Asians and North Americans (and members of other cultures) can be compared in terms of interpersonal relationships.
- Culture influences the development and maintenance of various types of interpersonal relationships, including friendships, romantic relationships and families.

JOIN THE DEBATE

IS THE INTERNET A SUSTAINABLE SITE FOR BUILDING INTERCULTURAL ROMANTIC RELATIONSHIPS?

Communication technologies allow us to initiate relationships with other people via the internet. With the development of social networking sites, online dating sites like eHarmony and other online communication tools, creating intercultural relationships via the internet is easier than it ever has been. For example, online dating services allow subscribers from different countries to build personal profiles and to contact or be contacted by other users, with a view to developing romantic relationships. Online dating sites, therefore, are an important site for developing intercultural romantic relationships, in so far as the romantic relationship raises the issue of cultural norms and practices. Some argue that it is impossible to establish a meaningful relationship with somebody you only meet online, whereas others believe that online relationships are not that different and it is easier for you to 'be yourself' online than in a face-to-face encounter. This is in part because an online encounter is non-threatening to face, should there be clashes in cultural beliefs and values between the communicators. However, there are issues that need to be addressed on online dating sites. An issue that has received increasing attention in recent years is that online dating sites create the possibility of deception. Some people have been found to use fake profile photographs to showcase their physical attractiveness; others have been reported to lie about their marital status or financial situation. There are many reported cases in which one partner made use of the intercultural dating site to 'fake' a relationship in order to obtain a visa to the country that they would otherwise not be able to enter. Online deception has a serious negative effect on the victim, such as financial loss or emotional trauma, and can even lead to suicide. Do you think that online dating sites are a sustainable platform for developing romantic relationships between people of different cultural backgrounds? Why or why not? What is your view about developing online romantic relationships?

India is a country of extreme diversity, with multiple languages, religions, castes and classes. Over 500 languages and 6,000 dialects are spoken across the country, and the diverse cultures and religions shape wedding traditions. India's dominant wedding traditions are difficult to categorize, especially on the basis of religion. Essentially, India is divided into two large regions with regard to Hindu kinship and marriage practices: the north and the south. Additionally, various ethnic and tribal groups in the central, mountainous north and eastern regions follow a variety of other practices. Generally speaking, in most parts of north India the Hindu bride goes to live with strangers in a home she has never visited. In contrast, marriages between cousins (especially cross-cousins; that is, the children of a brother or sister) and even between uncles and nieces (especially a man and his elder sister's daughter) are common in south India. Among Muslims in both the north and the south, marriage between cousins is encouraged.

For an Indian, marriage is a great watershed in life, marking the transition to adulthood. Generally, this transition occurs as a result of the efforts of two families, if not a whole community. Arranging a marriage is a critical responsibility for parents and the extended family of the bride and groom. Marriage alliances entail the redistribution of wealth as well as building and restructuring social relations between two families. It is 'marry me, marry my family'. Some parents begin marriage arrangements at the birth of their child. In the past, Indians were likely to marry at a young age; in smaller communities, such as in Rajasthan, children under the age of 5 could be united in marriage. Legislation which mandates minimum marriage ages has been introduced over the past decades, but such laws have had limited effect on actual marriage practices.

Arranged marriage still remains a preferred way for many Indians to enter into matrimony (Arranged Marriage, 2018). In an arranged marriage, parents and other relatives decide on a life partner that they deem suitable for their child. Even in the twenty-first century, around 85 per cent of Indians prefer to marry the boy or girl chosen by their family, rather than choosing their life partners themselves (Arranged Marriage, 2018). In a typical arranged marriage, the parents send out word that they are looking for a match for their child through their social networks, including friends, neighbours and relatives. They may also employ a local matchmaker, who keeps a database of marriageable individuals from the local neighbourhood. Once a match is established, the elders of the family first meet at a neutral place to judge the suitability of the couple. Criteria for a suitable match include religion, caste, culture, horoscope, profession and physical appearance.

After the suitability of the match is confirmed, the groom's family visits the bride's family to see the bride and finalize the marriage. Elders of both families are seated and the bride-to-be is brought in, often dressed in fine clothes and jewellry. If the groom's family considers the girl suitable for their son, they inform the girl's family through the matchmaker. If all goes well, the marriage talks proceed, solidify and move towards the formalization of the match, which is an engagement. This happens only after families on both sides have agreed that this is the best match possible for their child. Subsequently, a date is fixed where the formal announcement of the match and impending wedding is to take place.

Although the practice of arranged marriage has remained in India, the whole procedure has been modernized, thanks to the advent of communication technology. Computers, websites and portals have taken over the job of traditional matchmakers, with computer programs predicting matches for individuals (Arranged Marriage, 2018). The criteria for matches have also changed. For example, in urban areas, working women are often preferred as better matches. Emphasis is put on education and values, rather than only on efficiency in the domestic arena. The prospective partners are allowed to interact more freely nowadays, over the telephone or even face to face. The concept of courtship has gained favour, with the couple having the opportunity to get to know each other, sometimes for as long as a year before the marriage date. In rural regions, however, these changes have not occurred as fast as in urban areas.

Indian weddings symbolize not only the joining of the couple, but also the alliances of two families. To illustrate the family theme, many customs involve family members on both sides. Indian weddings are multi-day events, and it is not uncommon for middle- or upper-class weddings to have a guest list of over 500 people. The wedding is typically divided into three parts: pre-wedding, main wedding and post-wedding. The pre-wedding includes all the preparations and a party the night before, where the two families can meet each other, dance and have fun. In a typical Hindu wedding, a *pandit* (a wise man with knowledge in Hinduism), who has selected the day of the wedding based on the bride and groom's horoscopes, conducts a prayer with family members to provide the couple with a happy married life (Hindu Wedding, 2018).

The wedding altar (*mandapa*) is built on the wedding day, and the groom is welcomed by his future mother-in-law. His feet are then washed, and milk and honey are offered to him. An Indian groom typically wears a turban with a veil of flowers to protect him from evil spirits. At the wedding ceremony, the bride's parents give her away to the groom. The couple commit to each other in front of the sacred fire, and then the couple take the seven vows of commitment to the marriage. The bride's saree is tied to the groom's scarf to symbolize the union of the souls (Indian Wedding Traditions, 2018). Finally, seven married women from the bride's side pass by the couple and whisper blessings in the bride's right ear. The post-wedding ritual comprises the welcoming of the bride at the groom's house and a reception. The bride's mother-in-law places a vessel filled with rice at the entrance to the house. When the bride arrives, she is supposed to spill the rice by touching it with her right foot, to signify wealth and that the bride accepts her new responsibility.

Arranged marriage. Accessed 24 January 2018 at: www.culturalindia.net/weddings/arranged-marriage.html
Hindu wedding traditions. Accessed 24 January 2018 at: www.theknot.com/content/hindu-wedding-traditions
Indian wedding traditions and customs. Accessed 24 January 2018 at: www.beau-coup.com/indian-wedding-traditions.htm

REFERENCES FOR CASE STUDY

1. What does a wedding generally signify in Indian culture?

2. How has the concept of matchmaking changed over time? What is your view of this practice?

3. Some cultures and religions (e.g., Judaism and Hinduism) place people under a lot of social pressure to marry within the culture, but many individuals nonetheless find love across cultural boundaries. What is your view on out-of-culture marriage?

4. What are some reasons for choosing not to date interculturally? Are there any reasons (apart from romance itself) for choosing to date interculturally?

5. What beliefs, thoughts, feelings and attitudes should couples have in common? What differences can continue to exist between couples without threatening the marriage?

QUESTIONS FOR DISCUSSION

FURTHER READING

Chan, Darius K. S. and Cheng, Grand H. L. (2004) 'A comparison of offline and online friendship qualities at different stages of relationship development', *Journal of Social and Personal Relationships*, **21(3): 305–320.**

This article compares the qualities of online and offline friendships at different stages of relationship development. Participants consisting of 162 Hong Kong internet users were asked to think of two friends, one they knew through face-to-face interactions and one they knew through the internet, and then describe the qualities of their offline and online friendships. Results revealed that offline friendships involved more interdependence, breadth, depth, understanding, commitment and network convergence than online friendships.

Hiew, D., Halford, K., van de Vijver, F. R. and Liu, S. (2016) 'Communication and relationship satisfaction in Chinese, Western and intercultural Chinese–Western couples', *Journal of Family Psychology*, **30(2): 193–202.**

This paper reports on a study that compared Chinese, Western and intercultural Chinese–Western couples' communication and examined how culture moderated the strength of association between communication and relationship satisfaction. Communication of 33 Western couples, 36 Chinese couples and 54 intercultural Chinese–Western couples when discussing a relationship problem was recorded. The findings showed that relationship satisfaction was associated with low rates of negative behaviours and high rates of positive behaviours across cultural groups, and these associations were particularly evident in problem discussions.

Neville Miller, Ann and Samp, Jennifer A. (2007) 'Planning intercultural interaction: Extending anxiety/uncertainty management theory', *Communication Research Reports*, **24(2): 87–95.**

This article reports on a study that applied the theory of anxiety/uncertainty management to examine the notion of mindfulness in intercultural and intracultural interactions, tolerance for ambiguity, attributional confidence and interaction anxiety. Participants were 108 female Caucasian-American college students who responded to a videotape of either an American or a Korean confederate with whom they believed they would be holding a conversation. Interestingly, this study found that there was no significant difference in the complexity of plans prior to conversational engagement between intercultural and intracultural situations.

Russell, Kate (2011) 'Growing up a third culture kid: A sociological self-exploration', *Human Architecture*, 9(1): 29–42.

The author gives an account of her experiences as a third culture kid, moving every few years between cultures. She writes that: 'Growing up overseas and mainly outside of mainstream American culture has shaped me in ways that I am still discovering.' In particular, she discusses experiencing culture shock when returning to her country of citizenship and the relative notions of 'home'. She also reveals her coping strategies, including involving herself in extracurricular activities and volunteering.

White, Mark H. and Landau, Mark J. (2016) 'Metaphor in intergroup relations', *Social and Personality Psychology Compass*, 10: 707–721.

This paper provides a review of the common metaphors that people use in intergroup contexts. These metaphors, which draw on knowledge of such familiar experiences as physical cleansing and warmth sensations, are not mere figures of speech, but have a systematic and practically important influence on intergroup attitudes and behaviour. The paper shows that reliance on metaphor contributes to prejudice, stereotyping and discrimination. On the other hand, the paper suggests that researchers and politicians can harness the power of metaphor to promote intergroup harmony and peace.

SAGE VIDEO SOURCES

In this video Professor Howard Giles discusses the history and the many facets of the field of intergroup communication. The video will help you to achieve the learning objective of applying theories of intergroup and intercultural relationships in practical contexts. Watch it to learn more about intergroup communication and Communication Accommodation Theory.

This video is available at http://study.sagepub.com/liu3e

Peace cannot be kept by force; it can only be achieved by understanding.

Albert Einstein, German-born theoretical physicist, 1879–1955

11

INTERCULTURAL AND INTERNATIONAL CONFLICTS

LEARNING OBJECTIVES

At the end of this chapter, you should be able to:

- Identify different types of conflict and sources of conflict.

- Describe the stages of the conflict process.

- Recognize the influence of culture on conflict management.

- Develop the communication strategies to effectively resolve conflicts.

INTRODUCTION

The growth in intercultural contact increases opportunities for understanding, but also possibilities for misunderstanding between people, groups, communities, organizations and nations. If misunderstanding or miscommunication goes unmanaged, *conflict* can be the result. The word '*conflict*' has the Latin roots '*con*', meaning 'together', and '*fligere*', meaning 'to strike'. In order to 'strike together', the conflicting parties have to be linked in an interdependent manner. Putnam and Poole (1987: 552) define conflict as 'the interaction of interdependent people who perceive opposition of goals, aims, and values, and who see the other party as potentially interfering with the realization of these goals'. This definition highlights three key elements of conflict: incompatible goals, the interdependence of the parties involved and communication. It is unrealistic to expect a life without conflict, because conflict permeates all social relationships, even among those from the same cultural background. When we factor in cultural differences, the possibility for conflicts to occur can increase, because our approaches to conflict management are also culture-bound. Individuals from different cultural groups bring with them diverse and complex value assumptions, expectations, and verbal and nonverbal communication rules and norms that govern the conflict process. However, conflict, if resolved constructively, can lead to new ways of thinking and can deepen relationships. Therefore, it is important for us to identify the sources of conflict and find resolutions that lead to positive outcomes.

This chapter concentrates on intergroup and intercultural conflicts and conflict resolution through effective communication. We first define the different types of conflict and identify their potential sources. Next, the chapter describes the stages of the conflict development process; of course, not all incidents of conflict undergo all the stages. We then discuss the influence of culture on conflict management styles. Finally, we present communication strategies to constructively manage conflicts. Conflict styles are communication behaviours; in fact, communication is the means by which conflicts are socially conducted, and the instrument through which conflicts are resolved. As culture acts as the guide and predictor of communication, conflict in intercultural settings must be viewed in terms of culture and communication. Throughout the chapter, we highlight the importance of cultural sensitivity in conflict management and remind you that culturally inappropriate responses can result in unrealistic expectations, frustration, anger, hatred, damage to relationships, and even war between nations.

DEFINING CONFLICT TYPES AND IDENTIFYING POTENTIAL SOURCES OF CONFLICT

Just as any relationship development occurs at different levels, so too does conflict. Whether communication is cooperative or competitive depends on what is shared, perceived and experienced between the parties – individuals, groups, communities, organizations, nations and so forth.

Types of conflict

Conflict can be defined by the levels at which it occurs, ranging from interpersonal to international conflict; in many cases, a single conflict may happen at more than one level (e.g., inter-ethnic, interpersonal, interorganizational, and intercultural). At the individual level, conflict occurs between two (or several) individual people when they disagree with each other, or when they compete for something (often scarce resources); such conflict is defined as *interpersonal conflict*. For example, two co-workers competing for promotion to a higher position that is available to only one person in the same workshop, where each believes that the other person does not deserve the position, may engage in interpersonal conflict. *Intergroup conflict* occurs when two groups perceive disagreements over resources, power, territory, and the like. In an organization, intergroup conflicts may occur between aggregates of people, for example between the sales and supplies departments or between management and unions. *Interorganizational conflict* involves disputes between two or more organizations; in this case, the organizations themselves enter intergroup disputes. For example, different energy suppliers may engage in interorganizational conflict when they are competing for a larger market share. *International conflicts* refer to disputes and hostilities between nations, even leading to wars fought between nations over political governance or territorial disputes. In the context of intercultural encounters, *intercultural conflict* involves perceived or actual incompatibility in the goals, interests, resources, values, expectations, processes or outcomes between two or more people from different cultures (Ting-Toomey, 1994). Intercultural conflict can be at interpersonal and/or international levels.

THEORY CORNER

AFFECTIVE, COGNITIVE AND GOAL-ORIENTED CONFLICT

Conflict can be categorized as affective, cognitive and goal-oriented (Amason, 1996). Affective conflict arises from interpersonal tension and is largely emotional in nature. When affective conflict arises, disagreements are incompatible and detrimental to personal and group relationships.

(Continued)

Cognitive conflict arises from disagreements between two parties in relation to viewpoints, attitudes and opinions. Some scholars argue that cognitive conflict can be beneficial if it is managed constructively. For example, workers who disagree on solutions to a problem in the workplace can learn ideas, opinions and arguments from each other, and the organization can benefit from a better solution to the problem. In goal-oriented conflicts, people disagree about goals over either a preferred future – where conditions, relationships and needs must be met – or expectations about their opponents' behaviour. In real-life situations, a conflict can be affective, cognitive and goal-oriented at the same time.

An example of goal-oriented conflict in Turkey was presented in Cafnik's (2010) work. With the slow decline of the Ottoman Empire at the end of the nineteenth century, and later on with the occupation of Ottoman regions by the Allies in the aftermath of the First World War, domestic conflicts over the future of the Ottoman Empire started. A Turkish national movement was established and fortified, which led to the war of independence and finally to the establishment of the Republic of Turkey in 1923. Mustafa Kemal Atatürk, a distinguished military commander, became Turkey's first president. This change in leadership also changed more than 600 years of monarchical rule based on Islamic beliefs and laws in Turkey, which became a secular nation. After this goal had been achieved, Atatürk and his supporters fought for specific goals: state control over all educational institutions and the abolition of religious courts. Because the rural regions did not change as fast as the urban areas, two parallel cultures soon began to exist within Turkey. One was a Westernized, secular, urban culture with a small but powerful elite, and the other was a local, traditional culture connected to Islam. According to Cafnik (2010), this goal-oriented conflict was reflected in Turkey's state politics.

REFERENCES

Amason, Anne C. (1996) 'Distinguishing the effects of functional and dysfunctional conflict on strategic decision-making: Resolving a paradox for top management teams', *Academy of Management Journal*, 39: 123–148.

Cafnik, Petra (2010) *The Veil which Shows and Hides: Turkish Women between Modernity and Tradition*. Nova Gorica, Slovenia: University of Nova Gorica.

Conflict, particularly at the intergroup and international levels, can also be categorized by intensity. High-intensity conflicts at the national or international level involve a series of intense battles between military forces adopted by at least one party, or even involve the threat of nuclear weapons. On the other hand, low-intensity conflicts do not involve the use of armed forces. According to the Heidelberg Institute for International Conflict Research (HIICR, 2016), while more than 90 per cent of the conflicts reported by the HIIRC in 2016 were categorized as involving low levels of violence (i.e., they were low-intensity), the number of high-intensity conflicts has increased in recent years. Violent conflicts have occurred in Pakistan, India, the Philippines, Mexico and Myanmar, which witnessed three intrastate conflicts on the level of limited wars. Pakistan's intrastate war against the Tehrik-e-Taliban and other Islamist militant groups has continued unabated for more than ten years and involves a full-scale war in the region (HIICR, 2016). In Mexico, high levels of violence are evidence of the claim that this is the deadliest nation in the world after Syria – there were 23,000 homicides in Mexico in 2016 (Navitski, 2017). The violent conflicts pose a profound threat to public life in Mexico.

THEORY CORNER

TRANSITIONAL JUSTICE

Transitional justice refers to a range of approaches that cultures undertake to deal with the legacies of widespread or systematic human rights abuse, as they move from a period of violent conflict or oppression towards peace, democracy, the rule of law, and respect for individual and collective rights (Simič and Volčič, 2013). It also refers to the short-term and often temporary judicial and non-judicial mechanisms that address the legacy of conflicts during a specific culture's transition away from conflict or authoritarian rule. In making a transition towards peace, cultures must confront the painful legacy of the past in order to achieve a holistic sense of justice for all citizens, to establish or renew civic trust, to reconcile people and communities and to prevent future abuses (Simič and Volčič, 2013). The major approaches to transitional justice include domestic and international prosecutions of perpetrators of human rights abuse; determining the full extent and nature of past abuses; providing reparations to victims of human rights violations, including compensatory, rehabilitative and symbolic reparations; promoting reconciliation within divided communities; and constructing memorials and museums to preserve the memories of the past. All of them have communication at their core.

An application of transitional justice is illustrated in Jeffery's (2013) study on the violent conflict in the Solomon Islands. According to his study, in late 1998 the Solomon Islands were plunged

(Continued)

into a period of violent civil conflict, triggered by grievances, injustices, ethnic tensions and economic insecurities. The conflict continued until the middle of 2003, leaving some 200 people dead, more than 20,000 displaced from their homes, and numerous others subjected to torture, rape, fear and intimidation. On 24 July 2003, the Australian-led Regional Assistance Mission to the Solomon Islands (RAMSI) arrived in the capital, Honiara. In an attempt to restore law and order, RAMSI facilitated the arrests of more than 700 individuals who were accused of committing serious offences, including murder and human rights violations. Although RAMSI's actions created the initial impression of swift justice for human rights violations, questions emerged regarding whether a 'reconciliation' approach (a bottom-up method involving local community associations and churches, for example) might have been a better way to help post-conflict recovery. Jeffery's study shows the importance of a culturally informed transitional justice plan to bring about the best outcomes. In this case, the key impact of good intercultural communication may have been missed due to the reliance on a top-down approach.

REFERENCES

Jeffery, Renee (2013) 'Enduring tensions: Transitional justice in the Solomon Islands', *The Pacific Review*, 26(2): 153–175.

Simič, Olivera and Volčič, Zala (2013) *Transitional Justice and Civil Society in the Balkans*. New York: Springer.

Sources of international and intercultural conflict

The sources of conflict are myriad, ranging from differences in beliefs and values and incompatible goals to prejudice and historical grievances. This section discusses three common sources: racial violence, inter-ethnic and inter-religious hatred, and disputes over political, territorial and economic issues.

Racial violence. Racial violence is on the rise against vulnerable groups like immigrants, asylum seekers and refugees in all parts of the world, according to reports of the HIICR (2016). Racial violence is defined as a complex and enduring social problem that exists in many forms at the institutional, interpersonal and individual levels. Racism maintains or exacerbates inequalities in power, resources or opportunities based on race. According to Van Dijk (2004: 41), 'racism is a system of ethnic/racial inequality, reproduced by discriminatory social practices, including discourse at the local (micro) level, and by institutions, organizations and overall group relations on the global (macro) level, and cognitively supported by racist ideologies'. During Israel's 2014 bombardment of Gaza and the 2016 Russian aerial bombardment of the rebel-held Syrian city of Aleppo, young women and children came to international attention for sharing their stories of extreme prejudice and discrimination in those war zones. In particular, Farah Baker, a 16-year old Palestinian girl, became known in the international media for her analysis of surviving extreme racial discrimination during Israel's occupation and bombing of Gaza.

Racial conflicts have been documented in many parts of the world. In South Africa, the racial policy of apartheid was constructed by the white minority and dominated South Africa until 1992 (Louw, 2004b). Apartheid maintained white people's political and economic supremacy and led to interracial conflicts in South Africa. In the United States in 2015, the social movement known as *Black Lives Matter* (BLM) became a prominent voice in calling for racial justice. BLM came into existence after George Zimmerman was acquitted for the killing of 17-year-old Trayvon Martin. Alicia Garza, in an attempt to articulate her pain and frustration with the verdict, posted what she described as a 'love letter to Black folks on Facebook'. A more recent example of racial violence in the United States is 'The Unite the Right' rally in Charlottesville, Virginia, in 2017. This event triggered a United Nations (UN) Committee charged with tackling racism to urge the Trump administration to 'unequivocally and unconditionally' reject discrimination. Anastasia Crickley, chair of the UN Committee, wrote: 'We are alarmed by the racist demonstrations, with overtly racist slogans, chants and salutes by white nationalists, neo-Nazis, and the Ku Klux Klan, promoting white supremacy and inciting racial discrimination and hatred' (Siddique and Laughland, 2017).

DO IT!

Visit a webpage of the United Nations at http://www.un.org/en/about-un/. Search for information on where the UN is currently taking action on racial conflicts. Choose one country as your case study. Identify the source of the racial conflict and the steps that are being taken to alleviate it. How successful has the UN action been? And what are the main reasons for the success or lack of success? Report your findings to your class.

Inter-ethnic and inter-religious hatred. Many examples of hostility against ethnic minorities and religious groups have been documented: discrimination against Roma in Europe, Muslims in India, Christians in the Arab world, Kurds in Iraq, Houthis in Yemen, Bahais in Iran, Protestants and Catholics in different parts of Ireland, and so forth. Jitpiromsri (2008) studied violent conflicts in Thailand's southern border provinces. These provinces, plagued by political, religious and intercultural conflicts, were annexed to Thailand in the 1900s. More than 80 per cent of the population in these provinces were Malay Muslims who demanded independence. Since the new resurgence of violence in 2004, around 3,000 people had been killed and 4,986 injured by 2008. Some inter-ethnic and inter-religious conflicts are based on centuries-old antagonisms, often arising from long-standing grievances against certain ethnic and religious groups. For example, tensions between Muslims and Orthodox Christians in the Balkan region have been ongoing since the Turks conquered Serbia and the rest of the Balkans in the fourteenth century (Colovic, 2002). The defeat of the Christian armies in the famous Battle of Kosovo in 1389 has been perceived as the epitome of Serbian sacrifice, and the theme of the Serbs defending Christian Europe against Islamic expansionism has been appropriated into Serbian history. The Serbs are not alone in this; ethnic and religious prejudice rooted in historical grievances lies at the heart of much of the conflict in this region, particularly in Bosnia (Volčič & Simič, 2016). For example, Mostar is a city in Bosnia and Herzegovina, famous for its ancient bridge. The elegant bridge was designed by the Ottoman (Turkish) architect Mimar Hayruddin and completed in 1566. In 1993, during the Bosnian war, it was destroyed by the Croatian army as a way of destroying part of Bosnia's Muslim history. Today, the city remains divided between Croats (mainly Catholics) and Bosnians (mainly Muslims).

Conflicts arising from prejudice against certain ethnic and religious groups are also illustrated by the disputes between the Mexican government and Mexican Indian farmers, known as Zapatistas (Zapatista National Liberation Army) after the nineteenth-century agrarian leader Emiliano Zapata. Few international events over the last decade have captured the global imagination as much as the Zapatista uprising in Chiapas, Mexico, in 1994. The impoverished Indian farmers, led by the rebel leader, Subcomandante Marcos, advocated a rebellion against the Mexican government with minimal violence, to change the oppressive economic and political conditions. At that time, the Mexican government was creating an image of the country as socially and economically stable, but the Zapatistas argued that poverty, landlessness, inadequate healthcare, illiteracy and governmental corruption were ruling Mexico. They fought for land, justice,

PHOTO 11.1   The historic bridge in Mostar divides Croats (mainly Catholics) and Bosniaks (mainly Muslims).

Copyright © Zala Volčič. Used with permission.

democratic reforms and the end of Mexico's one-party state (McCowan, 2003). In this case, historical antagonism between poor Mexican Indian farmers and the Mexican government led to new forms of hostility and hatred.

Inter-ethnic hatred as a result of ignorance is clearly illustrated by the continuing practices of anti-Semitism. Anti-Semitism refers to a negative perception of Jews (Office for Democratic Institutions and Human Rights; ODIHR, 2008). Historically, rhetorical and physical manifestations of anti-Semitism have been directed towards Jewish individuals or their property, Jewish community institutions and their religious facilities. Examples of contemporary anti-Semitism can be found in the media, at schools, in workplaces and in the religious sphere. According to the Anti-Semitism Worldwide Report (2016), anti-Semitic manifestations have become an increasingly pervasive phenomenon in European countries. A more extreme example of conflict due to inter-ethnic hatred was the violence in Rwanda. Between March and April 1994, around 1 million ethnic Tutsis were slaughtered by the other main ethnic group, the Hutus (Simič, 2010). The genocide in Rwanda was the most brutal and devastating after the Holocaust during the Second World War, and it received widespread media attention.

The term Islamophobia, which refers to a fear of anything Muslim, frequently appears in the media. Over the last 20 years or so, in various countries, including Afghanistan, Turkey, Algeria, Singapore, the Netherlands, the UK, Bosnia and Canada, Islamic female clothing and the interpretation of Islamic law have become the focus not only of political debates and legal battles but also of political aggression. For example, the Netherlands is known as one of the most tolerant nations in the world, but the murder of the extreme right-wing Dutch filmmaker Theo van Gogh in 2004 by a Muslim immigrant of Moroccan origin, Mohammed Bouyeri, challenged this image (Buruma, 2007). At the time of the murder, van Gogh collaborated with Ayaan Hirsi Ali in making the film *Submission* (2004), which attempted to demonstrate that the Qur'an considers women to be fundamentally inferior to men. Ayaan Hirsi Ali is a Somali refugee and former Muslim who argues against Islam in the name of women's emancipation. Following the murder of van Gogh, a number of mosques were assaulted with racist symbols and an Islamic school was burnt down. The conflicts that have arisen from inter-ethnic and inter-religious hatred are longstanding and deeply rooted in many countries. As such, resolving them is necessarily a long and multifaceted process.

DO IT!

Interview one person who is from a conflict region (e.g., South Africa, Mexico, Pakistan, Syria). Ask the person whether or not he or she believes that an international agency like the United Nations can help to prevent or resolve conflicts in their region and why or why not. Then reflect on whether conflict prevention agencies have the power, or the right, to move a country or region from ongoing conflict to durable peace. Write a one-page report on your interview and your reflection. Present it to class.

THEORY CORNER

ORIENTALISM

Orientalism is the title of the book by Edward Said, a well-known Palestinian scholar, which was published in 1994. The concept refers to a specific kind of discourse that fosters the difference between the familiar (Europe, the West, 'us', the democratic and civilized) and the strange (the Orient, the East, 'them', the uncivilized and barbaric). Based on his analysis of the works of painters, historians, linguists, archaeologists, travellers and colonial bureaucrats, Said argues that European domination is not only about political and economic interests, but also about cultural power. *Orientalism* rests upon four dogmas. First, the Orient is undeveloped and inferior, while the West is rational, developed, humane and superior. Second, the Orient lives according to rules inscribed in their sacred texts, rather than in response to the changing demands of life. Third, the Orient is eternal and uniform, and the people are incapable of defining themselves, thereby justifying the vocabulary used by the West to describe them. Finally, the Orient is either something to be feared (e.g., Islamic terrorism) or to be controlled by pacification, occupation or development.

Scholars have applied Said's theory of Orientalism to explain how this discourse creates stereotypes, and how politics is significantly intertwined with discourses. One illustration comes from the Balkan region: Maria Todorova (1997) discusses the historical construction of Balkan identity and its representation as the Other of the Western world. She believes that, in the same manner as the Orient, the Balkans became 'the Other' of Europe. Furthermore, while the Orient has been constructed by the West as the Other, the Balkans are the dark side of Europe itself; they represent the darkness within. Overall, the discourse of Orientalism represents a clear example of the discourse of the Other. Although this discourse is now less acceptable in the political communication of Western countries, it has been and remains pervasive in the media. Films, television and other entertainment media show many subtle examples of Orientalism in their depictions of conflict between Western Europeans and Asian or Eastern Europeans – one needs only to think of movies like the James Bond series to find this. Orientalism as a theory also describes the subtle ways in which hatred (which may be unpalatable in its overt form) can be transmitted through many communication channels.

REFERENCES

Said, Edward (1994) *Orientalism*. New York: Vintage Books.

Todorova, Maria (1997) *Imagining the Balkans.* New York and Oxford: Oxford University Press.

DO IT!

Watch the internationally acclaimed Iranian film *Separation* (2011), directed by Asghar Farhadian. This film powerfully deals with interpersonal and intercultural conflicts in the family. Write down the sources of conflicts identified in the film. Can you think of another film set in your own culture that represents family conflict? Identify the sources of conflict in that film and compare the sources of family conflicts in the two films.

Disputes over political, territorial and economic issues. Intercultural and international conflict can arise from disputes over territory, economic control over resources, inequalities, and cultural disputes over language and religion. For example, the violent conflict in Palestine represents a dispute over territory. Historically, the most fundamental bonding among various Jewish groups was the Zionist dream of building a Jewish state in Palestine, the Promised Land, as the traditional saying 'Next year in Jerusalem' shows (Hestroni, 2000). Zionists began buying land and settling throughout Palestine in the late nineteenth century and continued until and after the establishment of Israel in 1948. Zionists thought of Palestine as desolate and empty, despite the fact that a large number of Palestinians lived there. This point is especially important in understanding the continuing conflict between Jews and Arabs over this land, with each side seeing it as their people's homeland. The conflict did not cease with the establishment of Israel in 1948, but continues up to the present day, and is the basis for a great deal of intercultural conflict throughout the region. Meanwhile, the land has become a central component in Jewish identity and Israeli national identity.

In other parts of the world, many conflicts and even wars are fought over the protection of sovereignty of territory claims. For example, there are over 750,000 bunkers in Albania. These were built under the Communist dictator Enver Hoxha, who ruled Albania from the end of the Second World War until his death in 1985. These cement and steel, mushroom-like lookouts were an attempt to protect communist Albanian territory against its perceived enemies and foreign powers.

PHOTO 11.2   Bunkers in Albania were built to protect communist Albania against its enemies and foreign powers.

Copyright © Zala Volčič. Used with permission.

In addition to territorial claims, international and intercultural conflict can occur as a result of prohibitions on speaking one's own language. For example, the rise in status and usage of the English language coincided with the gradual disappearance of the Welsh language, supported by state institutions. In one instance, Welsh children were forced to speak English at school and were punished for speaking Welsh. In recent times, a movement for the resurgence of the Welsh language, accompanied by Welsh nationalism, has reversed this decline to some extent. Today, the number of speakers of Welsh as a first language is rising. The devolution of political power in the UK has meant that the Welsh language now has a higher status and is supported by state institutions in Wales. This has helped in the revival of Welsh. Now cultural icons like Bryn Terfel and Katherine Jenkins promote Welsh identity throughout the world, demonstrating the possibility of a peaceful and communication-based, rather than violent, reclaiming of cultural status.

Economic issues can also underlie intercultural and international conflicts. Such conflicts are often expressed through cultural differences and through blaming minorities (e.g., refugees) for economic pressure in a society. The prejudice and stereotypes that lead to such conflict frequently result from perceived economic threat and competition. In a study conducted in Australia, Liu (2007) found that Anglo-Australians viewed cultural diversity and equal societal participation as more of a threat than a benefit, compared with Asian immigrants. In particular, Asian immigrants were viewed by Australians as a burden on the economy of the host country and a threat to host nationals in a competitive job market. In Europe, Hungarians, who face a migration crisis, blame asylum seekers and migrants for their economic problems. In 2016, it was reported that one of Hungary's right-wing politicians described the arrival of asylum seekers in Europe as 'a poison', saying that his country did not want or need 'a single migrant'.

Political, territorial and economic disputes begin when a society fails to provide reasonable equality for various groups of citizens. Towards the end of the last century, scholarly works in the area of intercultural and international conflicts became prominent in addressing the relationship between conflict and concepts such as identity, culture, history and the nation-state. Many of them addressed these relationships in the aftermath of the immense social changes in the world at the end of the twentieth century. For example, the fall of the Berlin Wall, the collapse of the Soviet Union, the end of apartheid in South Africa and the civil war in the Balkans signified the end of an era marked by high tensions between nations advocating different concepts of social order and development. Today more than ever, there are claims for the recognition of ethnic and cultural identities in rapidly changing international cultural environments, fuelled by increasingly complex flows of cultural and economic goods (Volčič and Simič, 2016).

CONFLICT STAGES AND CONFLICT MANAGEMENT

Individuals, groups or nations do not move suddenly from peaceful coexistence to conflict. Rather, as Louis Pondy (1967) indicates, conflict develops and subsides in stages. Conflict management strategies are informed by our approaches to conflict and the underlying assumptions.

Conflict development stages

According to Pondy, the first phase, latent conflict, involves a situation in which the conditions are ripe for conflict, because incompatibilities and interdependence exist between the two parties. The second phase, perceived conflict, occurs when one or more of the parties believe that incompatibilities exist. It is possible to have latent conflict without perceived conflict. For example, two ethnic groups may have different value orientations about the relationship between humans and nature. This difference in worldviews may not be an issue for either group, unless there is a need for them to reach a consensus about, for example, the political rights of refugees. During the third phase, felt conflict, the parties begin to formulate strategies about how to deal with the conflict, and to consider outcomes that may or may not be acceptable. These strategies and goals are enacted in communication during the manifest phase. Finally, the last phase discussed by Pondy is conflict aftermath, which emphasizes that conflicts can have both short-term and long-term consequences. Even after a manifest conflict is concluded, the conflict can change the nature of the interactants' relationship and functioning in the future. Table 11.1 summarizes the characteristics of each stage of conflict development.

An illustration of the development of a conflict is the dispute between German nudists and Polish puritans on the Baltic Sea Island of Usedom (Boussouar and Mailliet, 2008).

TABLE 11.1   Stages of conflict development

Stages	Characteristics
Latent conflict	Conditions are ripe for conflict because incompatible goals and interdependence exist between parties.
Perceived conflict	One or more parties believe incompatible goals and interdependence exist.
Felt conflict	Parties begin to focus on conflict issues and formulate strategies to deal with the conflict.
Manifest conflict	Conflict and conflict strategies are enacted through communication between parties.
Conflict aftermath	Conflict seems 'settled'. However, it has short-term or long-term effects on the relationship between the conflicting parties.

Source: Adapted from Pondy, Louis R. (1967) 'Organizational conflict: Concepts and models', *Administrative Science Quarterly*, 12: 296–320.

Straddling the border between Germany and Poland, Usedom is divided into German and Polish parts. For over 50 years nudist beaches have been the norm on the German side, as naked bathing is not considered unusual in Germany (latent conflict). However, the removal of border controls between Germany and Poland as part of the Schengen agreement in January 2008 has enabled Polish people to stroll along the leafy coastal paths to nearby German towns, so they notice the nude beaches (perceived conflict). Many are shocked by what they see (felt conflict). For the Polish people, sunning nude where people go walking is unacceptable. Poland is approximately 80 per cent Catholic, which has influenced their views on nudist bathing. A Polish national remarked: 'It's horrible, we would never bathe naked, we are Catholic.' While nude bathing can lead to a fine in Poland, for Germans of all ages who enjoy swimming and sunbathing on naturist beaches, the disapproving glances from Polish walkers are incomprehensible and intrusive (manifest conflict). Hence, the island of Usedom has become the site of a culture clash – the centre of a conflict of values. Both Poles and Germans cheered in December 2007 when the barbed-wire border was dismantled as part of the Schengen agreement; the cultural walls, however, are more difficult to demolish. As a temporary resolution, authorities put up signs marking the boundaries of the nudist beach in both German and Polish (conflict aftermath). Clearly, if this conflict is not managed properly, in the long term it may have international repercussions.

Conflict management

Intercultural research identifies two major approaches: conflict as normal (which views any type of conflict as an opportunity to grow and as a chance to develop and build relationships) and conflict as destructive (which views conflict as unproductive, negative, destructive and dangerous for relationships). Augsburger (1992) summarizes four main assumptions underlying each approach (see Table 11.2).

TABLE 11.2   Conflict approaches and assumptions

Approach	Assumptions
Conflict as normal	Conflict is normal and useful.
	All issues are subject to change through negotiation.
	Direct confrontation is valuable.
	Conflict always represents a renegotiation of contract, a release of tensions and a renewal of relationships.
Conflict as destructive	Conflict is a destructive disturbance to peaceful situations.
	The social system should not be adjusted to the needs of its members; rather, members of a society need to adapt to the established values.
	Confrontations are destructive and ineffective.
	Agents involved in a conflict should be disciplined.

Source: Adapted from Augsburger, David (1992) *Conflict Mediation across Cultures*. Louisville, KY: Westminster/ John Knox Press.

Blake and Mouton (1964) first classified five conflict management styles: avoiding, competing, accommodating, compromising and collaborating. *Avoiding* is physical withdrawal or refusal to discuss the conflict. *Competing* is linked to the use of power to gain one's objectives, even though it means ignoring the needs of the opponent. Competing is highly assertive and does not require cooperation. The outcome of this strategy is that you win and the other person loses (or vice versa). *Accommodating* refers to behaviours that conceal or play down differences by emphasizing common interests. If you chose to apply an accommodating strategy, you would sacrifice your own interest to satisfy that of the other party; that is, you lose, at least to some extent, and the other party wins. *Compromising* aims to find a midpoint between the opposing parties – both parties involved in a conflict try to work out a solution so that everyone gets something, although no party will get everything. Compromising involves both assertiveness and cooperation, and is a popular way to resolve conflicts because neither side wins or loses. In the *collaborating* strategy, conflict agents are encouraged to find a solution where both sides can win. It is considered the ideal way to handle conflict in most situations, but it is not often used because it requires much time, a willingness to negotiate, assertiveness and cooperation, and not all conflicts have win-win solutions.

Here is an example to illustrate the application of the five conflict strategies in resolving an interpersonal conflict in workplace. Imagine that your boss has informed you that your advertising firm has just signed a contract to produce a television commercial for a toy manufacturing factory. You and one of your colleagues need to work on Saturday in order to get the draft proposal ready for a meeting with your client on Monday. However, neither you nor your colleague wants to work on the weekend because you both have other plans. If you want to maximize your own interest, you could exercise your power as the project team leader to force your colleague to work long hours on Saturday, while you stay home fulfilling your personal commitments (a strategy of competition). On the other hand, if you wish to sacrifice your own interest in order to show concern for your colleague who has a birthday party scheduled over the weekend, you could come to the office to work instead of your colleague (an accommodating strategy). Finally, you could talk with your colleague to see whether you could each work for half a day or evening and free some time over the weekend to accomplish the task, which might (or might not) allow you both to complete your personal plans as well (a compromising or, if you are lucky, collaborating strategy). The application of different conflict styles requires different levels of assertiveness and cooperation from the conflict parties. Overall, it is important to remember that interpersonal conflict can reinforce relationships and even build teamwork; it can encourage open communication and increase productivity. The five conflict management strategies can be applied in other types of conflict situation, such as intergroup, international and intercultural conflicts.

INFLUENCE OF CULTURE ON CONFLICT MANAGEMENT

Individuals from different cultural groups bring with them different culturally governed communication styles and distinctive norms to evaluate appropriate or inappropriate behaviour. Hence, the way in which conflicts are resolved can vary considerably from culture to culture. These differences relate to the degree to which disagreement is acceptable, the extent to which conflict is tolerated, the preferred means of dealing with conflict, and the moment when intervention is needed. Culture shapes perceptions and the choice of alternatives, and it influences conflict outcomes (Chen, 2017). Understanding how culture influences conflict management strategies helps us to achieve better outcomes.

Cultural dimensions and conflict management

Ting-Toomey (2005b) identified the individualism–collectivism dimension (also see Chapter 5) as one of the key cultural variables in the management of intercultural conflict. Cultures that emphasize individualism and competition, like the Netherlands and Germany, often view conflict positively, whereas collectivistic cultures that emphasize collaboration, cooperation, harmony and conformity, like Greece and Turkey, generally see conflict as negative. In any conflict there are different levels of engagement, as well as different aspects that are elevated. Thus, determining what gets acknowledged and what gets resolved is the first step in conflict management (Fisher-Yoshida, 2005). In individualistic cultures, independence, freedom, privacy and self-esteem are considered important; thus, conflict strategies tend to be goal-oriented, focusing on problem solving, and communication is direct. On the other hand, in collectivistic cultures people are willing to sacrifice some personal interest in order to maintain good relationships with others during conflict, and may choose accommodating or avoiding communication styles.

The Amish see conflict as a source of distress to their community. This collectivistic culture, which descends from a German utopian religious movement that became established in the Midwest region of the United States during the eighteenth century, is an anomaly in the very individualistic larger society of which it is part. Legal and personal confrontations tend to be avoided because the use of force is discouraged in the Amish culture. This approach works well within the Amish community, but it can be a source of conflict when Amish people interact with other Americans. Similarly, in Chinese culture, harmony in social relationships (interpersonal, intergroup, interorganizational or international) is valued. A Chinese saying 'Everything prospers in a harmonious family' reflects the belief that conflict should be reduced, if not avoided, as it disturbs harmony in the group. In collectivistic cultures like the Amish and the Chinese community, people often avoid direct confrontation in a conflict situation and may instead seek to use a third party in order to avoid direct confrontation and save face. Third-party intervention may be informal, such as when a friend is asked to intervene. This 'peacemaking' approach to conflict values harmony and protection of face in conflict resolution.

Cultural context and conflict management

Conflict management strategies are not meaningful unless they are understood in the context of culturally learned expectations (Chen, 2017). It is important to interpret behaviour in terms of its intended expectations and values, which are consistent with its context because context stimulates, sustains and supports behaviour. Conflict strategies that are not sensitive to each culture's unique context are not likely to succeed. Merry (1989) describes how mediation practices across cultures are dependent upon context, where the process rather than the substance of agreement becomes the focus. In every culture, there are 'conflict transformers' who help disputants to think in new ways about the conflict, in an atmosphere of mutual respect. For example, an elder or the chief of a village may be brought in to resolve a dispute between two villages or between two villagers. Mediation also occurs between two nations. The promise of a Palestinian nation, for instance, was 'born' at the signing of the Oslo Accords on 13 September 1993 (Oslo I) – a pledge of peace between Israel and the Palestinians – as a result of mediation by the international community. Subsequently, between then and the outbreak of the Second Intifada seven years later, state-building and development efforts were significant in the territories. This example illustrates the potential positive outcome when conflict management takes context into consideration.

Cultural values and conflict management

Conflict management, to a certain extent, is negotiation in order to reach a solution that satisfies both sides. Lewicki, Saunders, Barry and Minton (2003) identified eight aspects through which cultural values can exert influence on the effectiveness of negotiation: (1) the way the negotiation is defined; (2) the parties at the negotiating table; (3) the protocol that is followed; (4) the style of communication; (5) the time frame; (6) the perception of risk; (7) whether the negotiation is on a group or individual basis; and (8) the way the agreement is shaped and enforced. These factors highlight the intricacies of addressing conflicts when the parties involved frame the conflict according to different cultural values. For example, in individualistic cultures, conflicts can be resolved directly through face-to-face negotiations. In more collectivistic cultures, this may not be possible. Rather, a third party may need to perform a type of shuttle diplomacy between the conflicting parties, guiding them towards a resolution. It is worthy of mention that third-party intervention is employed in both individualistic and collectivistic cultures, but the nature and role of the third party is different. In more individualistic cultures, the third party is usually a neutral mediator who guides the resolution process without adding his or her own beliefs. In collectivistic cultures, the mediator is more likely to be a known and trusted person who is expected to recommend the desired course of action.

Cultural sensitivity and conflict management

Culture influences how conflict is perceived and interpreted; effective intercultural conflict management therefore requires intercultural sensitivity. Ting-Toomey (1994) provides specific suggestions for effective conflict management in individualistic and collectivistic cultures. For people from individualistic cultures operating in a collectivistic cultural context,

Ting-Toomey provided seven suggestions to help manage conflict effectively: (1) understand the opponent's face-maintenance assumptions in order to keep a balance between humility and pride and between shame and honour in communication; (2) save the opponent's face by carefully using informal consultation or a go-between to deal with low-grade conflicts before they fall irrevocably into face-losing situations; (3) give face to opponents by not pushing them into a corner with no leeway for recovering face; (4) avoid using too much verbal expression and learn how to manage conflicts by effectively reading implicit and nonverbal messages; (5) be empathetic by listening attentively and respecting the opponent's needs; (6) put aside the explicit and direct communication skills practised in the West and learn to use an indirect communication style; and (7) tolerate the opponent's tendency to avoid facing the conflict by being patient, thereby maintaining a harmonious atmosphere and mutual dignity. These strategies have been widely applied in academic research and practice.

Communication strategies for conflict management

Communication is the means through which conflict is defined, managed and resolved. Intercultural knowledge is crucial in successfully managing conflicts, and failures in intercultural communication are likely to exacerbate both the intensity and the length of conflict (Jitpiromsri, 2008). Based on the literature, we propose the following communication strategies for conflict management, particularly in intercultural settings.

Focus on common ground and reduce disagreement. Intercultural conflict occurs because of an incompatibility in goals, interests, resources, values, expectations, processes or outcomes. Our attempts to establish and maintain intercultural relationships sometimes fail because others dislike what we like, or vice versa. One way to restore balance in the relationship is to seek commonalities by emphasizing a shared goal of accomplishing a task, or a common desire to restore peace or get a fair share of the resources. Emphasis on common ground fosters positive attitudes which, in turn, can ease tension and reduce negative feelings or stereotypes.

Practise relational empathy. Relational *empathy* refers to seeing the issue from the perspective of the other party. Relational empathy skills, such as active listening, form the starting point for the conflict management process (Chen, 2017). Mindful listening involves the process of interpreting the attitudes, emotions and values underpinning the spoken messages. To understand our own and others' deeply held cultural values and to engage those values in a culturally appropriate way are important in effective conflict management. This strategy is easily forgotten in intergroup conflicts, but it is essential to the resolution of these disputes.

Develop a positive communication climate. Conflict is more likely to be resolved effectively in a positive communication climate. During the process of conflict negotiation, both parties should avoid emotional presentations such as angry or insulting remarks. Another way to build a good communication climate is to deal with one issue at a time. Although intercultural conflicts can be the result of historical grievances and long-standing hatred, bringing up too many unresolved issues at one time may obscure the present question or escalate the conflict.

SUMMARY

- Conflict is pervasive in all human relationships and occurs at the interpersonal, intergroup, interorganizational and international levels. Intercultural conflict can occur at any or all of the levels.
- Potential sources of intercultural and international conflict include racial violence, inter-ethnic and inter-religious prejudice, and disputes over political, territorial and economic issues.
- Conflict develops in stages, and there are five conflict management strategies: avoiding, competing, accommodating, compromising and collaborating.
- Culture influences our approaches to conflict and conflict management strategies. It is important to develop culturally appropriate communication strategies for managing conflict effectively.

JOIN THE DEBATE

CAN CELEBRITIES PROMOTE HUMANITARIAN CAMPAIGNS IN REGIONS WHERE THERE IS CONFLICT OR WAR?

Every year, the United Nations embarks on myriad campaigns to address humanitarian concerns, potential human rights violations, international law, development, and peace and security. Sparked by the wish to commemorate the 22 lives lost on 19 August 2003 during the bombing of the UN headquarters in Baghdad, the UN established an annual World Humanitarian Day (WHD) on 19 August 2009. In 2012, the UN enlisted music celebrity icon Beyoncé to sponsor the humanitarian campaign. For this campaign, Beyoncé released a single entitled 'I Was Here', which she performed in front of the UN General Assembly for WHD 2012. The performance was subsequently released as a music video that remains extremely popular and influential throughout the world. The campaign aimed to engage at least 1 billion people around the world in small acts of kindness to help less fortunate people, such as people suffering from natural disasters, conflict and violence. While celebrity involvement is seen as favourable, especially by agencies such as the UN and the World Economic Forum, as well as by Western non-governmental organizations that have embraced celebrities as promoters of their activities, criticism has emerged concerning celebrities' lack of legitimacy and accountability in international politics. The most common critique is that the celebrities fail to address the underlying structural issues of the society. Thus, scholars continue to have very mixed opinions on the potential use of celebrity activism in promoting humanitarian campaigns to help people suffering from the aftermath of conflict, violence and even war. Do you think that musicians such as Beyoncé can truly contribute to our understanding and awareness of global poverty, racial conflict and violence?

CASE STUDY

CELEBRITY ACTIVISM IN WAR-TORN SOCIETIES

There is an ongoing debate regarding the suitability of using celebrities for humanitarian activism in a post-conflict context, although this idea is not new. Goodwill Ambassadors have been used by the United Nations for more than 50 years. UNICEF appointed Danny Kaye, an American actor, singer and comedian, as its first Goodwill Ambassador in 1953, and the UN agency has since recruited celebrities such as Whoopi Goldberg, Ricky Martin, Jackie Chan and David Beckham, among others, as international ambassadors and advocates for its causes. When Kofi Annan was appointed UN Secretary General in 1997, he was particularly interested in recruiting Hollywood celebrities as Goodwill Ambassadors in order to promote the UN's diplomatic agenda and to draw attention to development causes. His decision to employ more than 400 UN Goodwill Ambassadors by 2007, and to create a new type of celebrity activist programme, *Messengers of Peace*, signalled a new era for the UN. This era was heavily reliant upon popular trust in celebrity culture, amounting to a kind of public relations revolution within international diplomatic spaces. Annan's hope was that celebrities would possess the power to help end violent conflicts or, at the very least, shape international public opinion in support of UN missions, draw attention to its activities, and raise awareness about the suffering of others during different conflicts (Wheeler, 2011).

Celebrity and global fame were Angelina Jolie's primary qualifications for being appointed to the United Nations High Commission for Refugees (UNHCR) as a celebrity diplomat in 2001 (Cooper, 2008). Jolie is both a Hollywood sex symbol and a globally famous figure. Throughout her career, Jolie's image has been transformed from that of a Hollywood wild woman to an international celebrity peace ambassador. She was reported to be heavily involved in celebrity activism in Africa, Cambodia, Pakistan, Ecuador and Bosnia (Repo and Yrjölä, 2011). In 2001, Jolie still played the sexy action hero Lara Croft in *Tomb Raider*, but she decided ten years later to become a passionate and emotional witness of human suffering. Endorsing diverse international campaigns and causes, she also directed the highly acclaimed 2011 film *In the Land of Blood and Honey*, which is about war rapes in Bosnia and Herzegovina. In 2017, Jolie directed the film *First They Killed My Father*, a Netflix drama about the experiences of a young girl whose family was torn apart by the Khmer Rouge. During 1975–79, when the Khmer Rouge ruled Cambodia, it was responsible for some of the worst mass killings in world history. The brutal regime claimed the lives of up to 2 million people. Despite the mixed reviews of the film, Jolie has repeatedly said that her intention was to create a visual explanation of what happened during the genocidal wars.

Today, many celebrities have become well-recognized global activists in helping to bring peace to war-torn regions. In Bosnia and Herzegovina, for example, during and after the war in the 1990s, Bono, Richard Gere, Bianca Jagger, Princess Diana and Mia Farrow, among others, used their celebrity to campaign for peace there. Wheeler (2011: 58) suggests that this 'celebritization of international politics' has led to celebrities becoming more politically active, linking 'high politics with a more populist approach to cultural citizenship' (note that in the 1960s Jane Fonda used her celebrity to help turn public opinion in the United States against the Vietnam war, so this kind of celebrity activity is not new).

The value of celebrities as activists is drawn from their public and media images, with the symbolism of their value as a 'media star' easily transferred to diplomacy, and vice versa. For example, Arnold Schwarzenegger seamlessly moved from movie star to Governor of California in the United States; Ronald Reagan had earlier gone from movie and TV actor to California Governor to US President (he was labelled by supporters as 'the great communicator'); in 2016, Donald Trump moved from a reality show, *The Apprentice*, to become President of the United States (with a 'You're fired!' tagline).

Diplomacy scholars such as Cooper (2008) pointed out that celebrity diplomats have become enormously successful in mobilizing attention, channelling support and influencing international public policy, because celebrity diplomats employ innovative practices and are a part of the unofficial public diplomacy during and after conflicts. On the other hand, critical scholars see the emergence of celebrity activism as linked to the emergence of a post-democratic order, in which politics is transformed into a media spectacle that is only to be performed in front of an audience, while public opinion is reshaped and manipulated (Moyo, 2009). According to these accounts, the celebrity holds out a false promise of the power of the individual to influence social change, thereby reinforcing a reductionist and individualist politics. These scholars see celebrity activism as not promoting communication and peace, but only the celebrities themselves.

Cooper, Andrew F. (2008) *Celebrity Diplomacy*. London: Paradigm.
Moyo, Dambisa (2009) *Dead Aid*. New York: Farrar, Straus and Giroux.
Repo, Jemima and Yrjölä, Riina (2011) 'The gender politics of celebrity humanitarianism in Africa', *International Feminist Journal of Politics*, 13(1): 44–62.
Wheeler, Mark (2011) 'Celebrity politics and cultural citizenship: UN Goodwill Ambassadors and Messengers of Peace', in L. Tsaliki, C. A. Frangonikolopoulos and A. Huliaras (eds.), *Transnational Celebrity Activism in Global Politics: Changing the World?* Bristol: Intellect. pp. 45–61.

REFERENCES FOR CASE STUDY

1. What are your views on celebrity activism? Are there any unintended consequences of celebrity activism? If so, what are they, and how can they be avoided or minimized?

2. In your opinion, what is the association between celebrities' appearance in the media and their role in politics?

3. One comment often heard in post-conflict regions is that 'Law and order is here but peace is not in our hearts'. Do you think peace agreements can help stop violent conflicts? Why or why not?

4. What role can the mass media play in helping to restore peace and order in post-conflict regions?

5. What communication strategies can be employed to help people in post-conflict regions to 'forgive and forget'?

QUESTIONS FOR DISCUSSION

Boutton, Andrew (2016) 'Of terrorism and revenue: Why foreign aid exacerbates terrorism in personalist regimes', *Conflict Management and Peace Science*, 3(4): 1–26.

This article examines counter-terrorism aid and argues that the effects of foreign aid on terrorism will be conditional on recipient political incentives. Using a variety of data on regime type, terrorist attacks and terrorist group duration, the study found that in personalist regimes, US aid significantly increases levels of terrorist

FURTHER READINGS

activity. This paper contributes to the literature linking foreign aid and terrorism by considering domestic politics as an important determinant of counter-terrorism aid effectiveness.

Chouliaraki, Lilie (2006) *The Spectatorship of Suffering.* **London: Sage.**

This book is about the relationship between the spectators in Western countries and the distant sufferer on the television screen – the sufferer in Somalia, Nigeria, Bangladesh, India, Indonesia, but also from Paris, New York and Washington, DC. The book addresses the issue of whether the media can cultivate a disposition of care for and engagement with the faraway Other, and whether television can create a global public with a sense of social responsibility towards the distant sufferer.

Goodman, Amy and Moynihan, Denis (2012) *The Silenced Majority: Stories, Uprisings, Occupation, Resistance, and Hope.* **New York: Haymarket Books.**

This book provides a vivid record of the international events, conflicts and social movements shaping contemporary society. It presents writing and the daily work at the grassroots public TV/radio news hour *Democracy Now*, which is carried on more than 1,000 stations globally and at democracynow.org, and casts in stark relief the stories of the silenced majority and the major conflicts taking place today: the war in Afghanistan, climate change, racism and class conflict.

Li, Fabiana (2016) *Unearthing Conflict.* **Durham, NC: Duke University Press.**

This book analyses the aggressive expansion and modernization of mining in Peru since the 1990s to tease out the dynamics of mining-based protests. Li traces the emergence of the conflict by discussing the smelter-town of La Oroya, where people have lived with toxic emissions for almost a century, before focusing her analysis on the relatively new Yanacocha gold mega-mine. Li uncovers the mechanisms through which competing parties create knowledge, assign value, arrive at contrasting definitions of pollution, and construct the Peruvian mountains as spaces under constant negotiation.

Peters, John D. (2001) 'Witnessing', *Media, Culture & Society,* **23(6): 707–723.**

This article deals with questions of conflict, trauma, media, communication and witnessing. The long history of puzzlement and prescription about proper witnessing that developed in oral and print cultures is a rich resource for reflection about some of the ambiguities of audiovisual media. Peters traces the genealogy of the different discursive domains through which witnessing has been historically constituted: law, theology and atrocity. He makes a critical distinction that enables 'bearing witness' to be distinguished from 'eye-witnessing'.

This video features Professor Linda Putnam, who discusses the evolution of conflict management studies, highlights some trends within the field, and explains the centrality of communication. It will help you to achieve the learning objective of understanding the influence of culture on conflict management. Watch the video to learn more about the application of different conflict management strategies.

This video is available at http://study.sagepub.com/liu3e

SAGE VIDEO SOURCES

The media's the most powerful entity on earth. They have the power to make the innocent guilty and to make the guilty innocent, and that's power. Because they control the minds of the masses.

Malcolm X, American black leader, 1925–1965

12

MASS MEDIA AND CULTURAL CHANGE

LEARNING OBJECTIVES

At the end of this chapter, you should be able to:

- Identify the relationship between communication technology and global media in the digital age.

- Describe how social media have changed the way we communicate with each other.

- Explain the impact of (digital) media-constructed social reality and media effects.

- Understand the influence of mass media on cultural change.

INTRODUCTION

Mass media are all around us, playing a significant role in producing and representing our cultures. The word 'medium' (plural, media) in communication refers to a device or physical channel that carries message signals back and forth between communicators. We use a plural verb here – 'media are' – in order to underline the diversity of media forms and formats. Almost all aspects of our everyday life – from food to clothing, housing, education, entertainment and transportation – are affected by the mass media. Media not only bring us news, but also function as sources of education, entertainment and identity construction. McLuhan (1964) states that as the hammer extends our arm and the wheel extends our legs and feet, the mass media extend our connection to parts of the world where our physical bodies cannot reach. By extending our connections to the rest of the world, mass media can promote better understanding, appreciation and connections between different cultures and facilitate intercultural communication. Mass media can also achieve the opposite: increasing misunderstanding, fear, antagonism and fake news through the repetition and manipulation of negative stereotypes about ethnic origin, age, gender, sexuality and religion.

This chapter focuses on the relationship between mass media, including digital media, and cultural change. We first describe the relationship between communication technology and mass media in the digital age. The role of social media in changing the way we communicate is also discussed. We often judge others by the type of media they consume – the newspapers they read, the television programmes they watch, the internet sites they visit and the social media they use. The chapter explains the media-constructed social reality and media effects, including how media shapes our perception of others and our own identities. Finally, the chapter discusses the influence of media on cultural change. We highlight that media effects on the people and society need to be interpreted within the context of culture.

COMMUNICATION TECHNOLOGY AND MASS MEDIA IN THE DIGITAL AGE

The mass media in the digital age are shaped by communication technology. Just think of social networking websites that have become an integral medium for communicating within and across cultures. However, media do not operate in a vacuum: they are always tied to political and economic systems. The interactions among media, politics, culture and communication technology are precisely what shapes the daily lives of people in the contemporary digital society.

Communication technology and global media

Mass media, even radio and film with their broad reach, were largely local and national until well into the twentieth century. Increasing connections and interdependencies among institutions and people direct our attention to media globalization as a central phenomenon of the contemporary era. In particular, the rapid spread of digital media has been credited with many worldwide social, political, cultural and economic changes. The global media culture has manifested itself through a variety of signifiers, such as Pokémon Go, McDonald's fast food, Coca-Cola, MTV, the Kardashians, YouTube, and even beauty contests such as 'Miss World'. The international reach of media has opened exciting new vistas of a global village. Television, satellite dishes, computers and the internet open new borders around the world. Mass media have become a vehicle for globally relevant events. This feature testifies to the overwhelming success of the mass media, which allow people around the world to witness and experience the same event simultaneously: the Olympic Games, crises, famine, war, conflicts, hurricanes, terrorist attacks and presidential elections.

The rise of global media is closely tied to technology. Two media technologies – radio and motion pictures – contributed very significantly to the rise of global media. As early as 1914, 85 per cent of the world film audience was watching American movies (Gupta, 1998). More recently, satellite broadcasting and the internet have reduced the geographic distance of mass communication. Star-TV, for example, remains one of the most popular regional satellite and cable television operations in the world. Its coverage reaches from the Arab world to South and East Asia. It carries global US and British channels, as well as Mandarin and Hindi channels, targeting regional audiences. The varieties of language and culture define a new type of geo-cultural television market that stands between the US-dominated global market and national/regional television markets.

THEORY CORNER

CULTURAL STUDIES

The cultural turn in media studies dates back to the first half of the twentieth century. Cultural studies scholars are interested in the role culture plays in both preserving and transforming social relations. Whereas the study of art, music or literature has a history of focusing on formal or

(Continued)

aesthetic elements, the cultural studies approach is more interested in the relationship between cultural products (e.g., popular music, movies and radio) and the societies that create and circulate them. Moreover, cultural studies scholars tend to focus on those popular cultural forms that are not traditionally studied in academic settings, such as popular TV shows, rap music and romance novels (Turner, 2003). Examples of cultural studies projects are analyses of the reaction of audiences in the Middle East and the Netherlands to the TV show *Dallas*, the reasons that women read romance novels, and the way reality TV portrays changes in the way we think about privacy.

Cultural studies scholars who study reality TV attempt to place the reality TV trend within a broader social context. They interrogate issues of gender, race, sexuality and class. Reality TV shows like *Big Brother*, they suggest, promote an almost exhibitionist lifestyle in which work is living and living is work. Consumers turned producers actively participate in the process of production without having any control over the means of production. Even so, one of the crucial elements of reality TV is the way in which it has contributed to the diversity seen on television. Although reality TV offers more representations of gender, class and religions than most other mainstream television, scholars have been quick to criticize the ways in which reality TV has reinforced existing gender, sexual and racial stereotypes. For example, Banet-Weiser and Portwood-Stacer (2006) explored the complicated cultural work that female reality TV participants perform, not only in relation to beauty, femininity, nationhood, class and race, but also in relation to sexuality. They argue that reality shows are informed by cultural narratives about heterosexuality that equate happiness and success with normative ideals of sexual attractiveness.

REFERENCES

Banet-Weiser, Sarah and Portwood-Stacer, Laura (2006) 'I just want to be me again! Beauty pageants, reality television and post-feminism', *Feminist Theory*, 7(2): 255–272.

Turner, Graeme (2003) *British Cultural Studies: An Introduction* (3rd edn). London: Routledge.

Internet technology and social media

Social media have changed the way we communicate. Facebook has become ubiquitous, with over 2 billion active monthly users worldwide. Today around seven in ten Europeans use social media to connect with one another, engage with news content, share information and entertain themselves. In Indonesia, the average time a person spends on social media per day is three hours and sixteen minutes, whereas people in the Philippines spend an average four and a half hours on social media per day (Nguyen, 2017). In 2005, just 5 per cent of American adults used at least one type of social media. By 2012 that share had risen to half of all Americans, and today 75 per cent of the public use some type of social media. A majority of American adults (62 per cent) get news on social media. Two-thirds of Facebook users in the United States receive news on the site, and nearly six in ten Twitter users get news on Twitter (Pew Internet, 2017). Along with the benefits of social media, there are drawbacks. Around the world, concerns over privacy online are being expressed. Many fear they have lost control over their personal information and many worry whether government agencies and major corporations can protect the customer data they collect and sell (Pew Internet, 2017).

PHOTO 12.1   Television is the most popular medium in Istanbul, Turkey.

Copyright © Zala Volčič. Used with permission.

The widespread use of social media has given rise to new forms of monitoring, data mining and aggregating strategies designed to monetize the huge volumes of data such usage produces. Social media monitoring and analysis industries, experts and consultancies have emerged offering a broad range of social media intelligence and reputation management services. Such services typically involve a range of analytical methods (sentiment analysis, opinion mining, social network analysis, machine learning and natural language processing). An example of social media is Facebook, which started in 2004 as a social networking site for students at Harvard University, where its co-founders attended university. It started as a game called Facemash that allowed users to rate fellow classmates against one another by giving them two photos and deciding whether they were 'hot or not'. It changed into Facebook a year later, taking its name from the standard publication that is issued to incoming students at some universities that allow students to learn about one another (a university Facebook typically has a photograph of each incoming student and some basic information about where they are from and where they went to high school). The online version made this function interactive: people could find out about each other and post and share information about themselves. As a general rule, technologies that allow people to communicate with one another and socialize tend to be very successful, as indicated by the rise of emails, which had originally been almost an afterthought addition to the internet, but rapidly became one of its 'killer apps'. Something similar might be said of Facebook, which has a phenomenal rate of growth: it took only eight years for the Facebook platform to attract over 2 billion registered users and become one of the most well-known sites on the internet (Miller, 2011). If it were a country, Facebook would be the third largest country in the world, which means that it already unites users from many parts of the world and serves as a new way of keeping in touch and extending social networks across large geographic spaces.

Similarly, YouTube – founded only a year after Facebook in 2005 – rapidly turned into another internet phenomenon by allowing users to upload videos to share with others. As a convergence medium between the internet and TV, YouTube has highlighted a series of contradictions between traditional broadcasting and digital narrowcasting (Bratich, 2015). YouTube has influenced television, but at the same time this new medium imitates the rules of the old media. The original goal was both to allow users to generate their own videos to show online and to find ways to share clips of videos by other users and by professional media organizations of one kind or another. YouTube has played a role in allowing media moments to 'go viral', as in the case of the video of *Britain's Got Talent* contestant Susan Boyle, whose rendition of 'I Dreamed a Dream' from the musical *Les Misérables* received tens of millions of hits and helped gain her international fame and million dollar recording contracts.

YouTube is also credited with the discovery of pop idol Justin Bieber, and has created a tier of producers who are able to support themselves from the popularity of their online videos. At the same time, it has allowed the international sharing of an eclectic mix of political events, disasters, popular music videos and home videos (Snikars and Vonderau, 2009). Since its purchase by Google in 2006 for $1.65 billion, it has worked hard to commercialize its content and to address some of the concerns of copyright holders, who have sued the company for using their content without permission. As demonstrated by the most popular videos on the site, the most prevalent use is for short bites of entertainment: the music video for the pop song 'Gangnam Style' by South Korean artist Psy, for example. The most popular amateur user-generated video is called 'Charlie Bit My Finger', which shows two British toddlers playing with each other. The video, originally uploaded by the children's father to share with their godfather in the United States, has gone on to receive more than half a billion views. Thus, YouTube has helped create a new kind of international celebrity and allowed people from around the world to share videos with one another, whether for the purposes of politics, entertainment or information.

DO IT!

Interview five of your classmates from as many different cultures as you can. Ask them the following questions: Do you agree that YouTube and online video services have yielded new patterns of television watching? Do you believe that YouTube could serve as an intercultural video library? Do you think we should question celebratory accounts of the democratizing, participatory possibilities of social media? Write a summary of your findings and share it with your class.

MASS MEDIA OWNERSHIP AND CONTENT

The ownership of a media outlet can have an impact on the balance and bias in media coverage of that particular media outlet. In media research, questions related to the relationship between media ownership and content fall into the area of the political economy of media. Media political economy scholars address questions such as: Who owns and controls the mass media? What impact does this ownership and control have over media content and on the broader society? Where does the funding for the mass media come from, and where do the profits go? Does advertising affect journalists and editorial policy? Do mass media rely too much on information provided by government or industry? These are just a sample of the questions being asked by media scholars.

The political economy of media

The term political economy in media research is often associated with questions about the domination of state or economic power in media spheres. Scholars of the political economy of media investigate processes regarding the privatization, concentration, commercialization and deregulation (where the market replaces the state) of media. For example, they are interested in the conditions in which individuals can own many media corporations, and the consequences this has on democratic practices and media choices. These scholars claim that, globally, media are heavily dominated by a handful of gigantic media corporations and transnational corporations. The most important of these are Disney, Time Warner, Viacom and News Corporation.

The political economy of media scholars report that, globally, the trend of media conglomeration has been steady and that it continues. For example, in 1983, 50 corporations controlled most of the American media, including magazines, books, music, news feeds, newspapers, movies, radio and television. By 1992 that number had dropped by half. By 2000, six corporations had ownership of most media, and today five dominate the industry: Time Warner, Disney, Rupert Murdoch's News Corporation, Bertelsmann of Germany and Viacom (Democracy on Deadline, 2017). In the Eastern European media landscape there are reports of the Russian government's media activities, as it is becoming a major and fearsome player in the region's media market. And in some other parts of the world, such as North Korea, media remain strictly controlled by the government. According to the British Broadcasting Corporation (BBC, 2017), the press and broadcasters there are all under direct state control and deliver only flattering reports about North Korea's leader, Kim Jong Un. Economic hardship and famines are not reported at all. Ordinary North Koreans caught listening to foreign broadcasts risk harsh punishments, such as forced labour. North Korea also has a minimal internet presence.

When it started, the internet was celebrated and embraced as a liberating force *from* corporate-owned media. But over time even online news sites, as well as radio, television, newspapers and magazines, became owned by the small handful of media conglomerates. In estimated numbers, 80 per cent of the top 20 online news sites are owned by large media companies. Time Warner owns two of the most visited sites: CNN.com and AOL News, while Gannett, which is the twelfth largest media company, owns USAToday.com along with many local online newspapers (Democracy on Deadline, 2017). Scholars in the political economy of media have made consistent efforts to investigate the extent to which our view of the world is shaped by the concentration of power in certain media corporations, and the resulting impact this has on informed participation in our democratic societies. For example, The Walt Disney Company is now one of the six largest mass media corporations in the world, owning media production companies, studios, theme parks, television and radio networks, cable TV systems, magazines and internet sites. Focusing on an image of magic, joy and fun, its products are welcomed by parents, teachers and children alike, and are a powerful force in creating children's culture. However, some commentators have raised concerns about the role of Walt Disney movies in constructing children's imaginary worlds (Wasko, 2001).

DO IT!

Pick one online daily newspaper in your country. For five days, read its front-page cover stories carefully. Construct a table and divide the news you find into international, national and local news items. Count the items under each category and then compare the content across categories. In addition, search for information on who owns the newspaper. Write down your answer to the question: 'Is there a relationship between media ownership and the types of stories covered in this newspaper?'

Unity and diversity in media content

There are two ways of conceptualizing the relationship between global and local media. One way posits that media flow from 'the West to the Rest', resulting in global homogeneity of products, lifestyles, cultures, identities, tastes and attitudes. For example, television programming not only offers entertainment, but also reflects the sheer power and influence of global corporate culture. It shapes lifestyles and values, and replaces lost traditional institutions, communities, clans, family and authority. The mass marketing of culture takes place through satellite cables, mobile phones, YouTube, social media and the internet. All over the world, people of all ages are exposed to the same music, sporting events, news, soap operas and lifestyles. Young people in the so-called 'Third World' countries are the largest consumers of this global culture. The success in broadcasting global information may also have unintended, negative effects: the same media that inform globally also dominate globally. Some observers see media as a support system for one culture to dominate another culture – an uneven process called hegemony (Jandt, 2016). The argument is that mass media can unobtrusively influence the thinking and values of a specific society, while audiences willingly consent to the dominant meanings (Bratich, 2015).

Global media flows bring about *cultural hybridization* (Kraidy, 2005). The process and impact of media convergence and globalization can be seen in a number of transnational television channels launched in the past few years. Many of these channels seek to target ethnic groups beyond their national borders. Examples include CBC TV, Greek Cypriot Satellite Television, which broadcasts in Greek; Zee TV, which broadcasts in Hindi across Asia; Med TV, which targets the Kurdish population in Europe; MBC, Al-Jazeera, TRT and Al-Arabiyya, which broadcast in Arabic across the Middle East and North Africa and are watched by Arabs around the world; and TRT-INT, which targets the Turkish population across Europe.

Jeong, Seul-Hi and Sang-Gil (2017) write about the popularity of Korean dramas which have been televised across Asia since the late 1990s. From this time, the 'Hallyu' (or Korean Wave) has evolved into a global phenomenon, which is a strong indication of the transnational circulation and consumption of (South) Korean popular culture. They specifically analyse how and why Korean media shows are popular in Indonesia. While television channels can become the agents for a new global corporate vision, internet technology also contributes to the hybridization of culture by connecting people across the world. By the same means, the computer age also introduces subtle damage. Like video, film and global entertainment, the internet has the potential to become a substitute for human interaction, community and civic life, as adults and children alike spend ever more hours surfing, chatting and shopping online. We live in a media-saturated world.

THEORY CORNER

CRITICAL MEDIA THEORY

The term *critical media theory* is often associated with the Frankfurt School. Adorno (2001), a key critical media theorist from the Frankfurt School, developed the term 'culture industry' to call attention to the industrialization and commercialization of culture. The Frankfurt School

(Continued)

was formed by scholars working in different disciplines, from psychology to history: Max Horkheimer, Theodor W. Adorno, Herbert Marcuse, Leo Lowenthal and Erich Fromm. Because of the Nazi regime they had to leave Germany and emigrated to the United States. While in exile there, members of the Frankfurt School experienced the rise of media culture in film, popular music, radio and television. They argued that media are largely commercially produced and controlled by big corporations, and thus by commercial imperatives in subservience to the system of consumer capitalism. They believed that media produce content in order to cultivate, maintain, organize and utilize the audience as a product.

Critical media theory offers a useful framework for studying behaviours like cyberbullying. Cyberbullying generally refers to bullying through the use of technology such as the internet and mobile phones (Perren et al., 2012). Cyberbullying comes in diverse forms, such as sending insulting, rude or threatening messages, spreading rumours, revealing personal information, publishing embarrassing pictures, or excluding someone from online communication. Research shows that boys and girls are differentially affected by cyberbullying. For boys, only higher exposure to antisocial media content was found to predict higher levels of victimization over time (Baldry, Farrington and Sorrentino, 2017). On the other hand, girls are more likely to experience gender-based harassment and are more negatively affected by the messages (Perren et al., 2012). Perren and colleagues found that girls report with greater frequency that they feel their reputation is affected by the cyberbullying they experience, that their concentration is affected, that bullying influences their ability to make friends, that it makes them want to bully back, and that it induces suicidal thoughts. Moreover, research has demonstrated that there is a significant overlap between traditional bullying and cyberbullying, such that most young people who are cyberbullied also tend to be bullied offline in other ways (Perren et al., 2012).

REFERENCES

Adorno, Theodor W. (2001) *The Culture Industry: Selected Essays on Mass Culture* (2nd edn). London and New York: Routledge.

Baldry, Anna C., Farrington, David P. and Sorrentino, Anna (2017) 'School bullying and cyberbullying among boys and girls: Roles and overlap', *Journal of Aggression, Maltreatment & Trauma*, 26(9): 937–951.

Perren, Sonja, Corcoran, Lucie, Cowie, Helen, Dehue, Francine, Garcia, D'Jamila, McGuckin, Conor and Sevcikova, Anna (2012) 'Tackling cyberbullying', *International Journal of Conflict and Violence*, 6(2): 283–293.

MEDIA CONSTRUCTION OF SOCIAL REALITY AND MEDIA EFFECTS

In his book *Public Opinion* (1922), Walter Lippmann described an island where a handful of French, English and Germans lived in harmony just before the First World War. A British mail steamer provided their only link with the outside world. One day, the ship brought news that the English and French had been fighting the Germans for over six weeks. For those six weeks the islanders, technically enemies, had acted as friends, trusting the pictures in their heads. Lippmann's simple but important point is that we must distinguish between reality (the outside world of actual events) and social reality (our mediated knowledge of those events), because we think and behave based not on what is but on what is perceived to be. The importance of the mass media as sources for those 'pictures in our heads' leads us to question how closely the media world actually resembles the world outside.

Media and the construction of social reality

Scholars now largely accept that reality is socially and culturally constructed, understood and mediated. Mass media are one of the critical agents in this social construction of reality. Media content may be based on what happens in the physical world, but it singles out and highlights certain elements over others. Reality is necessarily manipulated when events and people are relocated into news or prime time stories. In doing this, the media can emphasize certain behaviours and stereotype people. One of the most obvious ways in which media content structures a symbolic environment is simply by giving greater attention (e.g., more time, space and prominence) to certain events, people, groups and places than to others. The media can thus be used to manufacture consent, legitimize political positions or cultivate a particular worldview. This is defined as the 'CNN effect' – the ability of television pictures to influence people so powerfully that important military and political decisions can be driven by the pictures rather than by policies (Robinson, 1999). In some instances, a nation may decide to support a decision to go to war with another country where they have never been and about which they have very limited knowledge, except for what they have learned from the mass media. This is not new. For example, the Spanish–American war at the beginning of the twentieth century was propelled by an unsubstantiated (and probably false) US media report (from the then media mogul William Randolph Hearst) that the battleship *Maine* had been blown up by a Spanish mine in Havana (Robinson, 1996).

The pervasiveness of celebrity coverage dominates magazines, television and newspapers. Magazines and specialist 'insider' television programmes routinely present detailed information about celebrities' personal lives and everyday routines – romantic

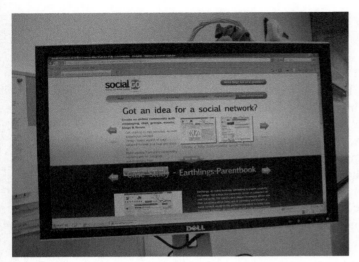

PHOTO 12.2   Social media sites have become an important platform for sharing news and even personal information.

Copyright © Shuang Liu. Used with permission.

involvements, shopping habits, trips, leisure activities and family issues – rather than their professional lives. In Brazil, for example, even though the fascination with celebrities is a relatively new phenomenon, the growing number of media outputs dedicated to fame, such as reality TV programmes, talk shows, websites and magazines, has greatly increased the coverage of celebrities in the national market (Turner, 1994). Among Brazil's 15 weekly magazines in 2015, 11 had mainly celebrity-oriented content. As such, media have a fundamental role in the construction of the famous: models, entertainers, athletes, hair stylists, fashion designers, as well as anyone directly related to them, such as spouses, children and even pets. Gessen (2017) explains how in Russia, media are under political and economic control. She also writes about how independent journalism is disappearing, how Russian media dominantly support Putin's authority, how media focus on celebrities, and the consequences these processes have on democracy.

The media play a crucial role in constructing symbolic social reality, to which we have no direct access. Tuchman (1978) analysed the role of news in the construction of social reality. In her view, news is simultaneously a record and a product of social reality. The final news story contains only part of the actual event covered, but in the eyes of a reader, viewer or listener it is timely and accurate. Had it not appeared in a news item, it might have no reality for the audience. At the same time, audiences make their own meaning in order for a story to make sense to them. Thus, the news source is socially constructed as a reliable basis upon which assumptions of truthfulness are made.

Research on media effects

Research on media effects is central to understanding the role of the media in constructing social reality and in understanding how audiences make sense of different media products.

Media effects on the audience. Audience analysis deals with audience tastes, preferences, habits and demographics. For example, this type of research studies why we like particular radio programmes more than others. One of the most commonly applied models for audience research is uses and gratifications theory, which was first formulated in the 1940s. Uses and gratifications studies ask the question 'What do people do with the mass media?' rather than 'What do media do to people?'. David Morley (2000) interviewed families about their television viewing to reveal the impact of gender on who uses the remote-control, programme choice, viewing style and amount of viewing. In his study, men and women offered different accounts of their viewing habits, in terms of their power to choose what and how much they viewed and their viewing styles. In his recent work, Morley (2017) investigates new types of audience (watching television on their mobile phones) and looks at how the mobile phone has been used differently in cultures and places where the social, demographic, technological and political assumptions of the rich North and West do not apply. Purnima Mankekar (2015) explores viewing habits in India. She discusses how viewers actively engage and interpret Indian TV, with an eye on relations of power within the nation and family. Audience studies have been crucial in promoting the idea that audiences are not passive, but active agents in media consumption.

Audience studies have also been highly influential in studying media effects on immigrants. Immigrants have always been quick to use the mass media in order to reduce the geographic and spatial distances between the host country and their home country. While radio, video recorders and films once served as the primary tool of maintaining contact with immigrants' culture of origin, it has now become common to find personal websites for immigrant communities (or diasporas), where images of the homeland are presented and important information about the homeland is relayed. Kolar-Panov's (1997) research on the use of video recorders (VCRs) and video letters among the Croatian and Macedonian communities in Australia showed the role of media in framing immigrants' cultures. News of the horrific events occurring in the former Yugoslavia, received by the immigrants through these diasporic channels, influenced the nature of their homeland connections.

PHOTO 12.3   On the wall of the School of Communication at Hong Kong Baptist University is the motto, *Truth is Virtue*, to remind future journalists of the principle of reporting.

THEORY CORNER

CULTIVATION THEORY

George Gerbner's *cultivation theory* postulates a relationship between heavy television viewing and people's worldview. Specifically, he suggests that exposure to vast amounts of violence on the screen conditions viewers to view the world as an unkind and frightening place. For almost two decades, he headed an extensive research programme that monitored the level of violence on television, classified people according to how much TV they watched, and compiled viewers' perceptions of risk and other sociocultural attitudes. His cultivation explanation of the findings is one of the most cited and debated theories of mass communication (Griffin, 2006). Gerbner regards television as the dominant force in shaping modern society, and believes that television's power comes from the symbolic content of the real-life drama frequently broadcast on television. In his view, television programmes dominate the symbolic environment, telling most of our stories most of the time.

The relationship between violent narratives and fear of crime is a major focus of cultivation theory. It has been argued that the stereotypical representation of sexual crime and its victims on television may cultivate fear of crime and fear of sexual assault. One study of the portrayal of women as victims of sexual assault on television was conducted by Custers and Van den Bulck (2013). They aimed to examine the relationship between television exposure and fear of sexual violence in women. Data were collected from 546 Flemish women in March 2010 by means of a standardized self-administered questionnaire. Findings showed that there was an indirect relationship between frequency of television viewing and fear of sexual violence. The level of fear of sexual violence was predicted by perceived risk, perceived control and perceived seriousness. The authors criticized the excessive amount of sexual violence in television content for its possible effect on women's fear of crime in real life.

REFERENCES

Custers, Kathleen and Van den Bulck, Jan (2013) 'The cultivation of fear of sexual violence in women: Processes and moderators of the relationship between television and fear', *Communication Research*, 40(1): 96–124.

Griffin, Erin (2006) *A First Look at Communication Theory* (6th edn). Boston, MA: McGraw-Hill.

Media effects on agenda-setting. Researchers on *agenda-setting* propose that mass media focus our attention on certain aspects of life, and in doing so, set the agenda for us. Maxwell McCombs and Donald Shaw (1972) proposed agenda-setting theory in the 1970s. They believe that mass media have the ability to transfer the salience of items on their news agendas to the public agenda. The theory has two interconnected points: it affirms the power of the press, while still maintaining that ultimately individuals are free to choose. Like the early Erie County voting studies (Berelson, Lazarsfeld and McPhee, 1954), the focus of agenda-setting is on election campaigns. The theory argues that there is a cause-and-effect relationship between media content and voters' perceptions. Although they did not use the largely superseded magic bullet conception of media influence, McCombs and Shaw ascribed to broadcast and print journalism the significant power to set the public's political agendas. Media may not exert a direct and instant influence on public opinion. However, news coverage of politics has been shown to have a wide range of subtle, but still powerful, effects on what the public thinks about important issues. As McCombs and Shaw suggested, the media may not be successful in telling people what to think, but there is much evidence to suggest that they are successful in telling people what to think *about*.

Numerous empirical studies have been conducted to test the match between the media's agenda and the public's agenda. Agenda-setting scholars claim that while the media definitely do not have the power to tell audiences specifically what to think, they are able to tell audiences what to think about (Newbold, 1995). As Piers Robinson (1999) suggests, the most useful way to conceptualize the CNN effect is to view it as an agenda-setting agency. Mohamed Sacirbey, Bosnian ambassador to the United Nations, once remarked: 'If you look at how humanitarian relief is delivered in Bosnia you see that those areas where the TV cameras are most present are the ones that are the best fed, the ones that receive the most medicines. While on the other hand, many of our people have starved and died of disease and shelling where there are no TV cameras' (Seib, 1997: 90). When images of starvation, anarchy and human misery appear on television screens, television becomes the *de facto* 'must-do-something' framework for everyone, including international policy-makers.

Media effects on identity construction. Scholars have explored the important role of the mass media in the historical development of national cultures and identities (Morley and Robins, 1995). Media and cultural production have a key role in reconstituting national, religious, gender and ethnic identities. The influential work of Benedict Anderson (1983) proposes that print capitalism is essential in promoting the creation of national imagined communities. The widespread dissemination of newspapers and novels creates an awareness of the 'steady, anonymous, simultaneous experience' of communities of national readers (Anderson, 1983: 31). The notion of simultaneity in time and a clearly defined national space is crucial to the construction of national consciousness today. Newspapers connect dispersed citizens with the land, people and discourses of a nation. The ritual of reading the newspaper or watching the national news on TV continues to be an essential element in the construction of a national community.

In addition, most countries treat broadcasting as a national public resource with a unique responsibility to represent and support the national culture. A classic example is the BBC, which is known for its balanced and high-quality programming that reflects diversity of topic, equality in representation and independence from outside governmental, religious or commercial influence. However, the belief in a single national identity that is itself based on a culture, religion and way of life that we all belong to is changing. Today, we belong to a world that is a vast cultural market from which we can pick and choose our preferences for music, fashion, food and so on. We belong to many subcultural groups, and hence we have multiple identities. This is especially so because we live in a so-called 'digital culture' that denotes the multiple ways in which we engage with digital media and technologies in our daily lives in different cultural contexts.

DO IT!

Choose one media outlet (e.g., print newspaper, TV, online media) that you primarily use to consume news. Select one salient news item concerning local residents and follow it for five days. Follow a social media forum that you are part of or familiar with. Observe whether the same issue has received the same level of salience as in the mainstream media outlet. Explain the similarities and/or differences observed in terms of media agenda-setting.

MASS MEDIA AND CULTURAL CHANGE

That the reality presented by the media is socially constructed has two important implications: first, we can understand the media as a debating ground for our system of values and beliefs; second, we can think of media effects not as simple, direct effects, but as a much wider part of the cultural fabric (Dodd, 1998). Mass media influence cultural change through cultural learning.

Mass media and cultural learning

Media create awareness. The mass media serve an awareness function, creating interest in an event or idea through reporting about its existence (Dodd, 1998). Such was the case with the use of chemical weapons in Syria, which brought instant world attention and led to international condemnation.

Media set agendas. Agenda-setting inevitably occurs because the media must be selective in reporting news and other events. News outlets, as gatekeepers of information, make choices about what to report and how to report it. Thus, what the public knows about current affairs at any time is largely a product of media gatekeeping. For example, the extensive coverage in the Australian media of the plight of struggling pensioners made this issue a public priority, and policy-makers had to address the ensuing public concern.

Media promote stereotypes. The media play a major role in constructing and maintaining stereotypes. They can create and reinforce stereotypes regarding old age, sexuality, religion, war, parenthood and myriad other aspects of human life. News programmes can help to erase misunderstandings on issues vulnerable to stereotyping. Conversely, entertainment in movies, theatres and television may inadvertently reinforce negative stereotypes. The representation of Indigenous people in Australia has often been the subject of criticism because when Indigenous people are present in news reports, they tend to be linked to violence, gambling, crime or alcoholism.

Media accelerate change. The mass media serve as accelerators for change, creating a climate in which change can more easily occur (Dodd, 1998). For example, what we regard as elements of a healthy lifestyle have changed considerably over the years, at least partially due to advertising campaigns against smoking, and eating fast-food and promoting regular exercise. In the same way, news coverage of issues like global warming, climate change and the energy crisis has functioned as an accelerator for changes in people's behaviour, which is evident in the current concern for energy consumption and the preservation of natural resources.

Mass media and intercultural communication

By looking at examples of how media and culture interrelate, we can understand the importance of media in the intercultural communication context and be aware of the need to develop skills in understanding media and culture.

Be conscious of ways in which the media may have affected your perceptions of a particular group. We need to keep up to date about current events and understand the source of our personal feelings. This can assist you in your intercultural communication.

Use media as a tool for understanding culture. Mass media can open our eyes to what is considered important in a culture. We cannot personally experience some cultures fully, but we may have an opportunity to interact with people from those cultures. Learning about other cultures can improve our understanding of that culture and hence assist us in interacting with its members. The mass media can play a significant role in culture-learning.

Broaden background knowledge. We need a broad knowledge of cultures other than our own. A common criticism of recent mass communication or journalism graduates is that they lack the background knowledge to carry out more than a superficial interview. Their articles will be superficial or incorrect or even offensive if they do not have an understanding of the influence of culture and context within which the reported events occurred. The same thing applies to everyone when they interact with another culture.

SUMMARY

- Communication technologies have enabled the globalization of media products. Social media have become crucial dominant platforms for news consumption and circulation.
- Mass and social media can promote social learning by giving prominence to certain issues, people and places. They can promote stereotypes of disadvantaged groups, such as ethnic minorities and Indigenous people.
- Research on media effects is central to understanding the role of the media in constructing social reality and in understanding how audiences make meanings out of different media products.
- Media-constructed social reality shapes our view of the world around us and influences our perception of others.
- Mass media contribute to cultural change in a society. As media and culture interrelate, we need to interpret media effects within a cultural context.

JOIN THE DEBATE

WHAT ARE THE PARENTS' ROLES IN YOUNG CHILDREN'S USE OF DIGITAL MEDIA?

Digital media create various opportunities for young children (aged 2–8 years) in terms of helping to develop academic and social skills and creativity. In some parts of the world, the internet may facilitate children's interaction and communication with relatives who do not live in close proximity. However, while the internet brings many benefits, it can also be risky for young children, especially considering their cognitive and emotional development. Parents introduce their children to smartphones or tablets for educational, entertainment as well as 'babysitting' purposes. Recent data suggest that the penetration rate of mobile devices among families with children aged 8 and below is as high as 50 per cent in the EU countries and approximately 75 per cent in the United States. The immediacy and interactivity of mobile technology make it possible for children to operate the devices with minimal assistance from adults. On the one hand, mobile phones provide opportunities from which children can benefit (enhancing literacy); on the other hand, they also pose online risks (violent and sexual content, online advertising) which raise concerns among parents of young children. Should parents accompany and interact with children during 'media time'? Do you think parents should set boundaries around children's media consumption, or should others take responsibility for this? What strategies should be used by parents and schools or child caretakers to monitor children's media consumption to minimize their harmful effects?

We turn to the news media for the accurate reporting of facts. This is a basic function of the press – to provide the public with the facts so that, in a democracy, the public can decide what is right and what ought to be done. But the results of the 2016 UK vote to leave the European Union (Brexit) and the US presidential election have raised serious questions about the influence of fake news in online sources and so-called social-media 'echo chambers', where misinformation and lies are spread. As Allcott and Gentzkow write (2017: 211), as early as the late 1990s and early 2000s, the growth of online news had triggered a new set of fears and dilemmas regarding access to a diversity of viewpoints. Some critics of the internet pointed out that the saturation of information would actually make it easier for like-minded citizens to form 'echo chambers' or 'filter bubbles', where they would be insulated from any contrary perspectives. That would lead towards isolation and even an unwillingness to be exposed to different opinions.

Twenty years on, scholars now study social media such as Facebook and Twitter, which have a radically different structure from previous media technologies. Content can be shared and spread among users with no significant third-party filtering, fact-checking or editorial and expert judgement. An individual user with no track record or reputation can in some cases reach as many readers as prestigious media companies such as the BBC, ZDF, *The Guardian*, *Democracy Now!* or the *New York Times*. In particular, following the US 2016 presidential election there has been much concern about the effect of false stories – fake news – circulated on different social media globally. A recent study by Allcott and Gentzkow (2017) shows that: (1) 62 per cent of US adults get news on social media; (2) the most popular fake news stories were more widely shared on Facebook than the most popular mainstream news stories; (3) many people who see fake news stories say that they believe them; and (4) the most discussed fake news stories tended to favour Republican candidate Donald Trump over Democratic candidate Hillary Clinton. Many agree that Donald Trump's victory has been a strong demonstration of how the internet can be used to achieve election to the US presidency. Some commentators felt that Trump used Twitter less as a communication device than as a weapon of 'information warfare', as well

CASE STUDY

SOCIAL MEDIA AND FAKE NEWS

as disseminating fake news, rallying his supporters and attacking his opponents with 140-character barrages. 'I wouldn't be here without Twitter', Trump claimed on *Fox News* (Chen, 2017). The internet did not just give him a megaphone, it also helped him to dominate media sources. Throughout the US presidential campaign, fake news stories, conspiracy theories and other forms of propaganda were reported to be flooding social networks. The stories were overwhelmingly pro-Trump (Chen, 2017).

Although the term 'fake news' has been popularized only recently, this and other related topics, such as media lies, propaganda and communication ethics, have been extensively studied by academic literature in media studies, journalism studies, communication studies, economics, psychology, political science and computer science. Allcott and Gentzkow (2017) define 'fake news' as news articles that are intentionally and verifiably false, and misinform and mislead readers. They point out how social media are well suited for fake news dissemination. But social media's use has risen sharply, they argue: in 2016, active Facebook users per month reached 1.8 billion and Twitter users approached 400 million. Who produces fake news? Prevailing versions of fake news articles originate on online sites that are created entirely to print intentionally fabricated and misleading articles. The names of these sites are often chosen to resemble those of legitimate news media organizations.

Allcott and Gentzkow (2017) point out that there are two dominant motivations for providing fake news: financial and ideological. First, news articles that go viral on social media can draw large advertising revenue when users click to the original site. This appears to have been the main motivation for most of the 'fake' producers whose identities have been revealed. The teenagers in Veles, Macedonia, for example, produced stories favouring both Trump and Clinton that earned them thousands of dollars. Second, many who create these sites strongly believe in a particular political idea, or a candidate, and they are willing to spend their time and resources on spreading lies.

This was, of course, not the first campaign to be dominated by misinformation and lies. In the 1930s in Europe, authoritarian leaders were being swept to power with the help of radio. For example, in Germany, the Nazi Ministry for Public Enlightenment and Propaganda deployed a force called *the Funkwarte*, or Radio Guard, who went around the city block by block to ensure that citizens tuned in to Hitler's major broadcast speeches (Chen, 2017). And in all parts of former Yugoslavia alike, the majority of mainstream print outlets and broadcasters turned to national(istic) histories, myths and culture during the 1990s. Slobodan

Milosevic, for example, in Serbia, created parallel realities for Serbs, while heavily controlling and manipulating the media, thus spreading lies. There was a growing inability, even unwillingness, to separate truth from lies. Milosevic himself was shameless in lying about obvious truths, such as that there was no ethnic cleansing in Bosnia and Herzegovina at the time. According to him and the mainstream media, Bosnian Muslims left their homes voluntarily.

But the sheer speed of the claims being made, and believed, suggested to many that the internet had brought about a fundamental devaluing of the truth. The problem was not simply that people had been able to spread lies, but that the digital platforms were set up in ways that made them especially potent (Chen, 2017). The 'share' button sends lies flying around the Web faster than fact-checkers can debunk them. Chen further argues that these are not neutral platforms – they use personalized algorithms to spread information based on precise data models of one's preferences, trapping us in so-called 'filter bubbles' that limit critical thinking and increase polarization. Today, online misinformation is seen as the front line of a reactionary populist upsurge threatening liberal democracy.

REFERENCES FOR CASE STUDY

Allcott, Hunt and Gentzkow, Matthew (2017) 'Social media and fake news in the 2016 Election', *Journal of Economic Perspectives*, 31(2): 211–236.

Chen, Adrian (2017) 'The fake-news fallacy: Old fights about radio have lessons for new fights about the internet', *New Yorker*, 4 September. Accessed 12 September 2017 at: www.newyorker.com/magazine/2017/09/04/the-fake-news-fallacy

Gottfried, Jeffrey and Shearer, Elisa (2016) 'News use across social media platforms 2016', *Pew Research Center*, 26 May. Washington, DC: Pew Research Center. Available at: www.journalism.org/2016/05/26/news-use-acrosssocial-media-platforms-2016.

QUESTIONS FOR DISCUSSION

1. Do you think the issue of fake news is of growing importance? Why or why not?

2. What do you think are some of the possible impacts of fake news on voting patterns?

3. Political cynicism towards politicians indicates that citizens are dissatisfied with politicians and their governments. Do you think that fake news exposure helps to foster feelings of inefficacy, alienation and cynicism about government?

4. Fake news not only falsely informs, but also entertains and, importantly, shapes political perceptions. Do you agree with the proposition that fake news not only educates viewers about political candidates and current affairs, but also contributes to deeper attitudes regarding the political world? Why or why not?

5. What do you think can be done to respond to the emergence of fake news and so-called post-fact societies? Do you think serious fact-checking might be helpful? Would media literacy education be of use? Which types of the mass media seem most trustworthy to you, and why?

FURTHER READINGS

Andrejevic, Mark (2013) *Infoglut: How Too Much Information is Changing the World*. **London: Routledge.**

This book is an analysis and critique of new media interactivity. Andrejevic argues that the rhetoric of interactivity fails to reflect its reality. The reality is one of increasing surveillance and information gathering by corporations and the state via new media technologies. Most consumers and citizens are aware their information is being collected when using a cell phone, internet search engine or credit card, but are ignorant of what information is gathered, how it is used and by whom.

Clark, Schofield Lynn (2012) *The Parent App: Understanding Families in a Digital Age.* **Oxford: Oxford University Press.**

This book investigates how digital and mobile media are both changing and challenging parenting for all families. Based on a ten-year study of hundreds of parents and children, Clark provides practical advice for parents on what works for both parents and kids when it comes to social media and new technologies. The book tackles a host of issues, such as family communication, online predators, cyberbullying, sexting, gamer drop-outs, helicopter parenting and technological monitoring.

Khalil, Joe (2012) 'Youth-generated media: A case of blogging and Arab youth cultural politics', *Television & New Media*, **14(4): 338–350.**

This article is about contemporary Arab youth cultural politics and public life as demonstrated through 'youthgeneratedmedia', which became famous in connection with protests in Tunisia, Egypt and elsewhere in the Arab world.

These include but are not restricted to Facebook, Twitter, blogs, graffiti, videos, songs and other forms of communication developed and circulated by young people. Khalil examines the contemporary configuration of youth cultural politics through self-expressive artefacts, probing in the process the changing mediascape in the Arab world.

Lewis, Tania (2016) 'Adventures in love, risk and romance: Navigating post-traditional social relations on Indian dating shows', *European Journal of Cultural Studies*, **20(1): 56–71.**

This paper examines a range of dating formats and argues that such television shows offer rich insights into the ways in which contemporary Indian media culture is negotiating and promoting models of gendered individualism and 'enterprising' modes of selfhood. Drawing upon qualitative and quantitative data, the analysis focuses on the complex relationship between the ideals of aspirational modernity and choice-based selfhood promoted by these shows and the realities of ongoing gendered social and economic inequities and the continued cultural potency of religious and familial notions of duty.

Penney, Joel (2017) 'Social media and citizen participation in "official" and unofficial" electoral promotion', *Journal of Communication*, **67(3): 402–423.**

This article reports a study on the impact of social media on elections. Data were collected from interviews with leaders of the effort to promote Bernie Sanders' campaign for the 2016 US presidential election on social media. The research contrasts the structure and content of various organizational networks to map the hybrid ecosystem of the contemporary digital campaign. The findings indicate structural differences in oversight and moderation that suggest varying levels of creative autonomy for citizens and reputational risk for the associated campaigns.

SAGE VIDEO SOURCES

In this video, digital media scholar Alfred Hermida discusses how we interact with the media, and how social media affect journalism and news. The video will help you to achieve the learning objective of understanding how social media change the way we communicate. Watch it to learn what it means to be a digital native, and much more about digital communication.

This video is available at http://study.sagepub.com/liu3e

We may have different religions, different languages, different colored skin, but we all belong to one human race.

Kofi Annan, 7th UN Secretary-General, 2001 Nobel Peace Prize Winner, 1938–2018

13

EFFECTIVE INTERCULTURAL COMMUNICATION IN A GLOBAL SOCIETY

LEARNING OBJECTIVES

At the end of this chapter, you should be able to:

- Explain the dialectics of the homogenization and fragmentation of cultures.

- Understand cultural diffusion, convergence, hegemony and colonization.

- Describe the localization of cultural products and cultural hybridization.

- Develop strategies to build intercultural communication competence.

INTRODUCTION

One of the challenges facing intercultural scholars is a shifting understanding of cultural boundaries in societies characterized by emerging forms of economic and cultural globalization. The 'global village' described by McLuhan in the 1960s represents only a partial social reality of the world we inhabit today. Globalization is making the world truly round, because of the compelling force of integration and interdependence at the political, economic, cultural, social, technological, and even personal levels. In addition, in the internet era, media content, once subject to limits imposed by both legal regimes and transport technology, now circulates around the globe at the speed of light. Global media such as ABC News (a national broadcaster with international reach, based in Australia) and CNN (an international broadcaster based in the United States) have generated passionate global debates about politics, international wars, religious conflicts, same-sex marriage, climate change, women's emancipation, refugees, humanitarian obligations and cultural integration. The same is true with local media products, such as Latin American *telenovelas*, Egyptian melodramas, Nigerian cinema, Arab reality TV and televised Hindu epics. Yet as Skalli (2006) points out, all these interconnections are embedded in a system of inherent differences. At one end of the economic scale, cosmopolitan elites work and study in several different countries, mastering multiple languages and moving seamlessly between cultural contexts. At the other end of the scale, ethnic minorities and Indigenous communities are trying to find ways to preserve their own cultural traditions and practices. Global trends of homogenization and local processes of fragmentation suggest multiple ways in which the global and local cultural realms are connected. Thus, globalization does not mean that cultural differences are being eradicated and that the whole world is being subsumed into one global culture. It does mean that cultures circulate in new and different ways, and that people are likely to reflect more and more about the impact of globalization on their local cultures at both the collective and individual levels. This is a time when intercultural communication is not only increasingly imperative, but also more complicated.

This chapter discusses how we deal with the various challenges we face in an increasingly globalized society through effective intercultural communication. In the global society, the dynamic forces of cultural homogenization and fragmentation intersect, the impact of cultural diffusion, convergence, hegemony and colonization is felt by the society, and intercultural competence becomes increasingly important. We first explain the dialectics of the homogenization and fragmentation of cultures and the effects of these processes on communities and individuals. Next, we introduce the concepts and theories of cultural diffusion, convergence, hegemony and colonization, along with examples to show their application in diverse cultural contexts. The chapter then presents how local cultures challenge, negotiate and adjust to globalization, including cultural hybridization. Finally, the chapter identifies strategies for developing intercultural communication competence. This concluding chapter picks up the themes in Chapter 1, where the challenges of living in a global society were identified; but this chapter goes further, to explain how to deal with those challenges as an effective intercultural communicator, by applying the knowledge and skills learned throughout the book.

DIALECTICS OF HOMOGENIZATION AND FRAGMENTATION

There are two countervailing tendencies associated with globalization: the overcoming of cultural or economic differences, known as *homogenization*, and new forms of cultural *fragmentation* and innovation. This dialectical process is reflected in communication between people of diverse cultural backgrounds.

Homogenization and fragmentation of culture

Globalization generally refers to an accelerated interconnectivity in the economic, social, political, cultural and even personal aspects of life. However, the suggestion that the spread of Western globalization means we need to be less attuned to cultural differences is misleading. On the one hand, the forms of isolation and insulation that once nurtured cultural uniqueness are being eroded, thanks to increasing economic and political interdependence and the spread of transport and communication technologies that shrink space and transmit culture. On the other hand, these same tendencies generate unique and culturally distinctive responses and enhanced opportunities for the expression and circulation of culture-specific products. Satellite television, for example, enables people around the world to remain in instantaneous contact, so that viewers in one hemisphere can watch real-time events unfolding in the other. At the same time, new information and communication technologies (ICTs) make it possible for Indigenous cultures to create their own media outlets and products, to circulate them widely, and to create connections with other Indigenous peoples. These same ICTs also make it possible for diasporic communities to maintain close ties with their countries of origin, even if they are living at the heart of their new cultures.

The dialectic of homogenization and fragmentation can be described as engagement versus isolationism or globalism versus nationalism (Lustig and Koestger, 2013). Economic interdependence sustains engagement and globalism. For example, in almost every country we can find signs of McDonald's, KFC, Pizza Hut, Starbucks, Nestlé, and Coca-Cola, which all contribute to globalism and the homogenization of cultures. Nevertheless, the desire to preserve cultural uniqueness promotes isolationism and nationalism. Nations take measures to protect their local economies from foreign products. One method that countries use to protect their trade is to enact tariffs, which are taxes levied on imported goods. This immediately raises the price of the imported goods, making them less competitive when compared to locally produced goods. For example, in early 2018, President Trump imposed tariffs on imported steel and aluminum – the aim was to favour US industries over their foreign competitors and to rebalance the US trade deficit. This may work well for a country that imports many consumer products, such as the United States, Australia and Singapore do. However, in the long run it can make the country, and the industries it is trying to protect, less competitive in the global market.

Nations may also protect their people from the perceived impact of beliefs, values, norms and social practices coming from exposure to 'foreign' cultural products. An example of this type of isolationism is illustrated by concerns over the celebration of 'foreign' religious and cultural festivals in China. Some scholars in China are concerned about the growing popularity among younger Chinese of celebrations of Western festivals, not just Christmas, but also St Valentine's Day, Halloween, Thanksgiving and more (Ye, 2010). The popularity of Western festivals in China reflects the fading significance of traditional Chinese festivals, such as the Mid-Autumn festival (celebrating the full moon and family reunion), Qing-Ming (remembrance of the deceased family members), and even the lunar new year (celebrating the lunar new year and family reunion). According to Ye (2010: 157), cultural protection should be in place in the era of globalization to 'counter such kind of cultural colonization in avoidance of the dissolution of our 5000-year Chinese tradition'. Interestingly, both small (objectively threatened) and large (dominant) cultures perceive threats coming from outside, and there are strong movements for the protection of culture and language even in countries like China and the United States, where outsiders may not perceive any external threat.

Concerns about the impact of foreign products is pervasive. There is a worry in many countries that American media products in particular, including Hollywood movies, will erode local cultures and local languages. For example, in Iran, some argue that the Islamic society is being 'corrupted' by values and ideas that they see as part of what they call the West's long-standing 'soft war' against Iran. Despite efforts to regulate the influence of foreign ideas and images, the growing exposure of Iranians to Western popular culture in their daily lives is undeniable. Millions of Iranians use illegal satellite dishes that give them access to channels from all over the world.

Beyond this, most of the world remains bilingual or multilingual, and new online translation devices (like Google translate) may ultimately encourage people to operate and publish more in their native languages. Furthermore, there is little evidence that the American accent is creeping into other native English dialects, in spite of the great concern outside the United States about this. There is some evidence of the internationalization of the English vocabulary, including American words entering other dialects and vice versa, but accents seem much more resistant. In an interesting example of this phenomenon, many people in England are worried that the Australian accent will creep into their language because of the popularity of Australian soap operas, yet there is very little evidence of this in a country which is now highly multicultural, and where all native English accents are routinely heard. Once again, even large and very dominant cultures are not immune to these concerns; in the United States, in spite of the great dominance of English throughout the world, there are thriving English-only movements that aim to preserve the status of English within that country.

Music provides another example of cultural resistance and cultural adaptation. Culturally rooted music styles become a tool for demarcating national and cultural identity – Samba for Brazilians, Klezmer for Jews, Punta for Garifuna people, and Cantopop for people in Hong Kong (Harwood, 2017). On the other hand, as a commercial product, music is adapted, modulated and transformed as it travels around the world. For example, rap music, which started in African-American neighbourhoods in the United States, has been adopted in a variety of countries, such as Japan, Germany, France and South Africa, with each culture adding its own innovations to the original style. Thus, globalization works dialectically: on the one hand, there is a growing interconnectedness between cultures; on the other hand, there are growing and deep-seated nationalistic sentiments to promote the distinctiveness of local cultures.

DO IT!

Architecture reveals and enhances the unique meaning, value and character of the physical and cultural forms of a community and gives a community a sense of place. At the same time, globalization and population growth in the major cities across the world result in the need for urban development, which can result in a standardized, functional architecture. Interview someone who knows about urban planning in your city (e.g., someone who works in urban planning, or who studies it, or who has a strong interest in it). Ask him or her what the local government needs to consider in urban planning in order to articulate the historic and cultural heritage of the community. Then present a summary of the discussion to the class.

Homogenization and fragmentation of people

We find ourselves living in a world of increasing cultural mobility. Modern means of transport and technology make travel faster and easier. As Edwards and Usher (2008: 16) note, 'What in the past would have taken months to move around the globe now takes hours or even seconds'. Moreover, thanks to the internet, people find themselves moving among different cultures without leaving home, or staying immersed in their home cultures even after they have geographically

PHOTO 13.1   The Changing of the Guard is one of London's most famous spectacles, going back thousands of years.

Copyright © Shuang Liu. Used with permission.

located elsewhere. At the same time, the uneven spread and access to technology and the uneven characteristics of Western globalization may create new forms of social and cultural stratification between those who participate in an increasingly transnational economy and those who still live and work in less developed regions or countries. Mutual cultural exposure does not necessarily imply mutual benefits or acceptance. Cultural exposure can highlight and exacerbate differences between groups or nations. Just as those living in traditional communities may feel shocked and threatened by the products of contemporary consumer culture, those living in the capitals of consumerism may find their own values and practices challenged by more traditional cultures. These issues make the global and local nexus more complex.

Scholarly discussions about global versus local, or about the homogenization and fragmentation of cultures, are gradually shifting away from a black-and-white view, as people recognize that 'cultural experience is both unified beyond localities and fragmented within them' (Skalli, 2006: 20). Despite the presence of a global economy and mass cultural products, people still interpret what they see or have by drawing upon their local beliefs, values and norms. Thus, at the same time that we recognize the far-reaching effects of technological, societal and economic forces, we need to recognize that all messages that we experience are interpreted through the meaning systems of our own culture (Lustig and Koester, 2013). While focusing on the cultural dimensions of homogenization–fragmentation dialectics, we cannot dissociate the economic and political aspects from the rest of the cultural realm. Rather, we view them through the lenses of culture and maintain their importance in the cultural prism.

DO IT!

Many internationally successful TV shows add local interest to standard formulas by recruiting cast members from the countries in which they are broadcast. As an example of this type of 'glocalization', the TV show *Temptation Island* was filmed on the same island in shifts – each shift was devoted to a different country and its associated cast members. Furthermore, many aspects of everyday life, particularly food, stay linked to local traditions. Select a TV show that runs in different countries, for example *The Bachelor* or *X Factor*. Watch a few episodes with a classmate and discuss with him or her how the programme reflects the media's simultaneous involvement in both globalization and localization.

DIFFUSION, CONVERGENCE, HEGEMONY AND COLONIZATION

With each contact between cultures, people leave some trace of their 'village' culture behind and add some new traits to it from other cultures. Albeit slowly, cultures are changing, and to some extent merging into one another. It is crucial to understand the dynamic interplay between cultural diffusion, convergence, hegemony and colonization.

Cultural diffusion and convergence

Through interaction between cultures, one culture may learn and adopt certain practices of another. *Cultural diffusion* happens when a culture learns or adopts a new idea or practice from another culture or cultures. Products can carry cultural values; many products represent a particular national identity and hence become cultural icons. An icon is a symbol that is idolized in a culture or is employed to represent it. For example, McDonald's represents the value placed on standardization, efficiency and control in American culture; Japanese gardens reflect the value of harmony in Japanese culture; koalas and kangaroos represent Australia to many as a friendly, carefree and relaxed country. It is believed that the receiving culture can unconsciously or uncritically absorb the values being transmitted via iconic products. For example, fast food has become an integral part of life for people in China since it opened up to the world in the 1980s. Signs of McDonald's, KFC and Pizza Hut can be seen in almost every city or town, as they can in the rest of the world. The concepts of efficiency, standardization and quantification which are valued in Western cultures are infusing into the Chinese food culture, where harmony, balance and perfection used to be valued in traditional Chinese cooking.

The increased sharing of information and agreement on mixing West with East leads to cultural convergence. Convergence is defined by Kincaid (2009: 189) as 'movement toward one point, toward another communicator, toward a common interest, and toward greater uniformity, never quite reaching that point'. Kincaid's convergence model was originally meant to address shortcomings of the transmission model of communication, advancing the view that no two people can ever reach the same meaning for information; it is just a matter of a greater or lesser degree of similarity. Over the years, the term 'convergence' has been expanded to cover the economy, media and culture. The concept of *cultural convergence* is more like the salad bowl metaphor (a larger culture made up of different cultures, with each maintaining its own characteristics), rather than the melting-pot metaphor (separate cultures all blended together into one larger culture). While the diffusion model focuses on what one culture does to another, the convergence model focuses on the relationship between individuals or groups of people who share information and converge over time towards a greater degree of mutual agreement (Jandt, 2016). 'McDonaldization' is often used as an example of cultural convergence because it exemplifies the idea of efficiency, predictability and control in mass production. Along with this, the McDonald's culture assumes that consumers will engage in the same set of behaviours in consuming food, regardless of the cultural context in which a McDonald's outlet is located.

THEORY CORNER

DIFFUSION OF INNOVATIONS

Diffusion of innovations is a theory that explains how, why and at what rate new ideas and technology are adopted. Everett Rogers, a professor of communication studies, popularized the theory in his book *Diffusion of Innovations*, first published in 1962 and subsequently in 1983. According to Rogers (1983), diffusion is the process by which an innovation is spread over time among people in a social system. An innovation is not adopted by all individuals in a social system at the same speed. Hence, adopters can be categorized as innovators, early adopters, early majority, late majority and laggards, based on how long it takes for them to begin using the new idea (Rogers, 1983). According to Rogers and Shoemaker (1971), innovators are eager to try new ideas, to the point where their adventurousness becomes an obsession. Early adopters tend to be more integrated into the local social system than innovators, and are usually opinion leaders in their social systems. People in the early majority category adopt new ideas just before the average member of a social system, but often do not hold leadership positions. The late majority, on the other hand, adopt new ideas just after the average member of a social system. They are sceptical about innovations and are reluctant to adopt until most others in their social system do so first. Laggards, the last to adopt an innovation, are likely to be suspicious not only of innovations, but of innovators and change agents as well. In fact, there is some evidence that acceptance of innovations is linked to a number of other factors, including social identity and the extent to which one is affected by the innovation. Thus, someone who is eager to adopt an ICT innovation, such as a new smartphone, early may be more of a laggard for another type of innovation.

The adoption of new ideas takes place through communication networks. Two key concepts in the diffusion process are homophily and heterophily. Homophily is the degree to which pairs of individuals who interact are similar in certain attributes, such as beliefs, education, social status, and the like, and heterophily refers to the opposite (Rogers and Shoemaker, 1971). Homophilous individuals engage in more effective communication, because their similarities lead to a greater similarity in knowledge, attitudes and behaviour. However, diffusion also requires a certain degree of heterophily to introduce new ideas. If two individuals are identical, no diffusion occurs, because there is no new information to exchange. Therefore, an ideal situation needs a balance between homophily and heterophily. Take the example of promoting healthy behaviour. People who engage in unhealthy behaviours, like smoking and eating junk food, may also be less likely to access information about a healthy diet. Developing heterophilous ties to unhealthy communities by early adopters of healthy diets can increase the effectiveness of the diffusion of healthy eating habits. Once someone from the unhealthy network adopts the behaviour or innovation, the other members of that group are more likely to adopt it. This is particularly true as there is increasing evidence from research in the UK and Australia that the idea that 'everyone is doing it' is a more powerful motivator for change than a message that the new behaviour is 'better' (Plows et al., 2017). Of course, many factors contribute to an individual's decision to adopt a new idea. Diffusion theories can never account for all variables, and the one-way information flow of the theory alone is insufficient to capture the multidirectional information flow in the communication network.

REFERENCES

Plows, Stefanie E., Smith, Francine D., Smith, Joanne R., Chapman, Cassandra M., La Macchia, Stephen T. and Louis, Winnifred R. (2017) 'Healthy eating: A beneficial role for perceived norm conflict?', *Journal of Applied Social Psychology*, 47(6): 295–304.

Rogers, Everett M. (1983) *Diffusion of Innovations* (3rd edn). New York: Free Press.

Rogers, Everett M. and Shoemaker, Floyd F. (1971) *Communication of Innovations: A Cross-Cultural Approach*. New York: Free Press.

Cultural hegemony and colonization

Along with the spread of cultural products from the West to the rest of the world, some nations perceive the increasing popularity of global iconic products, particularly those from the United States, as a form of *cultural hegemony*, defined as the structurally enabled predominant influence of one culture over another (Ritzer, 2010). Historically, resistance to cultural hegemony is documented not just in developing countries. For example, the French resistance to the linguistic influence of English (decreasing in recent times) is well documented in the literature, as are Japan's resistance to American movies and India's resistance to Coca-Cola. When products travel from one culture to another, they transmit cultural values to the receiving culture and change people's lives. Private ownership of cars was not popular in China in the 1980s. However, since the 1990s, a car has become more and more of a 'necessity' for business people, government officials and families – as a status symbol rather than a means of transport. The ownership of foreign cars, in particular, shows the status of the owner: Audi, Mercedes-Benz and BMW are among the popular foreign models. In this, the Chinese are doing what Western people have done for many years: showing their high status through their material possessions.

Contact between cultures may also lead to *cultural colonization*, which accompanies economic colonization (Lee, 2016). The term is sometimes used synonymously with *cultural imperialism* and includes more particular forms of cultural domination, including media, educational, academic, intellectual, scientific and linguistic colonialization. At the core of cultural colonialization is the concept of 'othering', which is predominantly used to refer to stereotypical images of non-white populations (Jandt, 2016). Cultural colonialization has a long history. When European seafarers discovered and colonized the Hawai'ian Islands, they labelled the Hawai'ians as 'the other' on the basis of their not being civilized by European standards. Similarly, in Australia, the Aboriginal people were labelled by Anglo-Saxon Australians as being not evolved or civilized. Along with the global spread of American products, Americanization is taken as a form of cultural colonization.

PHOTO 13.2   Cola Turka – the Turkish version of Coca-Cola – standing in a public square in Istanbul.

Copyright © Zala Volčič. Used with permission.

Ritzer (2010) pointed out that in the realm of politics, political campaigns in European elections have become increasingly like those in America. However, he did caution that economics, politics and culture are often separate facets of globalization, and to equate globalization with Americanization on different fronts is an oversimplification. While the diffusion of cultural products and identities occurs at the global level, such diffusion works hand in hand with local cultures.

Cultural hybridization

Local customs and traditions do not just fade away when global cultural products flow across borders. The transmission of cultural values and the transformation of the lives of people via cultural products depends on how well the global products are received by the local cultures. *Cultural hybridization* refers to a new cultural form that combines elements of other cultures. Cultural hybridization is often regarded as a common characteristic of globalization. For years, business people and corporations have devoted huge amounts of resources to adapt global products to local needs. The hybridized product, like hybridized culture, combines elements of two or more original cultures. Elements of those original cultures often appear in an adapted form in the hybridized new product or culture, rather than in their original state or form.

For example, in France, McDonald's Quarter Pounder is called a Royal, and it is not just the name that is different. French visitors and locals can also order Le P'tit Moutarde, a smaller-size burger with mustard sauce, and they can pair it with a banana caramel shake. In the Netherlands, McDonald's serves a McKroket (a fried beef croquette on a bun). In Germany, it offers shrimp with cocktail sauce. The 280 Gr. is an Italy-only burger, which a person can order with real Parmigiano-Reggiano cheese. There is a burger on pita bread for the Greek market (the Greek Mac), and a McKebab is offered in Israel. In Russia, in order to enhance the local food preferences, McDonald's Russia introduced potato wedges, cabbage pie and cherry pie. These examples illustrate that hybridized products are formed as global products become localized to gain acceptance and sustainability in local cultural contexts.

In addition, new products can themselves be hybridized. For example, the popularity of pizza-kebab shops in the UK shows how two migrant cultures can be combined in a local context. Britain, in particular, has a long history of acceptance of foreign food, as the popularity of Indian food attests; now the British are taking the process one step further. In this sense, contact from one culture to another does not necessarily displace another culture, but may lead to hybridized cultural products that maintain local cultural traditions. A further example of this process is a skyscraper, which is an icon universally recognized to represent participation in global economy (Lee, 2016). However, the Petronas Twin

PHOTO 13.3   This artwork at Beijing International Airport symbolizes local Chinese cultural tradition in the international space.

Copyright © Shuang Liu. Used with permission.

Towers in Kuala Lumpur, which were designed to put Kuala Lumpur on the world map, were localized to represent Islamic design and Malaysian mosque architecture (King, 2008). Similarly, the design of the Taipei 101 building in Taiwan is reminiscent of bamboo in Chinese culture. In Russia, Moscow's skyline is defined by the seven towering skyscrapers nicknamed 'The Seven Sisters', or 'Stalinskie Vysotki', that are one of the architectural legacies of the Stalinist period. Stalin was afraid that Westerners would look down on Moscow as lacking modern, capitalist buildings, so he asked top architects to erect eight ornate, monumental skyscrapers (the last one was built in 1957, after Stalin's death), which have since become synonymous with Russian architecture under the communist leader.

Similarly, Starbucks has adjusted its architectural and spatial designs around the world. Mexicans see Starbucks as a sort of 'bar', where group conversations and get-togethers take place. For that reason, Starbucks changed its look to emulate a local bar on the streets of Mexico. Even in different Disney theme parks around the world, Disney has made adjustments to appeal, for example, to French customers – in that context, Disney lifted an alcohol ban and renamed Disney characters based on French originals with their original French names. Thus, the castle of Sleeping Beauty is known as Le Chateau de la Belle au Bois Dormant. In the Asian region, Changi Airport in Singapore seems to conform to other international airports as far as global travellers are concerned. However, it distinguishes itself from other international airports through a re-familiarization that is designed to be understood by and appeal to local Singaporeans, with sculptures like satay chicken and chilli crabs.

DO IT!

Foreign ideas, foods and cultural products are assimilated into local cultures, resulting in practices that mix local and globalized practices into something new and hybrid. Locate an example of a hybrid cultural product in your country (e.g., a piece of architecture, or a food or a television programme) and analyse how the local and the global elements are mixed together to project cultural hybridization.

THEORY CORNER

CULTURAL SCHEMA THEORY

Cultural schema theory has been applied to the study of intercultural communication and cross-cultural adaptation (Nishida, 2005). *Cultural schemas* refer to generalized knowledge of past experiences that have been organized into related categories and are used to guide people's behaviours in familiar situations. When entering into a communication act, each of us brings a stock of knowledge about appropriate behaviours in a particular context in our own culture. This pre-acquainted knowledge is referred to as cultural schemas. Cultural schemas are therefore conceptual structures that enable an individual to store perceptual and conceptual information about his or her culture and interpret cultural experiences and expressions. As an individual encounters more similar situations, the cultural schemas become more organized, abstract, compact and usable. Our communication becomes much easier through the application of cultural schemas.

However, when sojourners enter into a new culture, they experience cognitive uncertainty and anxiety because of their lack of cultural schemas for the new situation. They usually go through two processes to adapt to the unfamiliar cultural context: self-regulation and self-direction. In the self-regulation stage, sojourners try to resolve ambiguities of information by drawing upon their familiar home culture schemas to understand the new cultural context. In the self-direction stage, they try to reorganize their home culture schemas or to develop new culture schemas in order to adapt to the new environment. Cultural schemas play a crucial role in the meaning-making process. For example, kinship is the pillar of existence, and the extended family is the essence of Aboriginal Australian identity. Close family ties among Aboriginal Australians are clearly marked in the systems of kin terms in Aboriginal languages. Malcolm and Sharifian (2010) noted that many features of Aboriginal languages instantiate Aboriginal cultural schemas and categories of family. Thus, the word 'walk' stimulated ideas of extended family and kinship among speakers of Aboriginal English, whereas in European Australian English the word 'walk' signifies exercise or transport only. If a non-Aboriginal Australian interacts with an Aboriginal person, his or her old cultural schema governing the use of language will need to be adjusted to account for these features of oral discourse in Aboriginal English.

REFERENCES

Malcolm, Ian G. and Sharifian, Farzad (2010) 'Aspects of Aboriginal English oral discourse: An application of cultural schema theory', *Discourse Studies*, 4(2): 169–181.

Nishida, Hiroko (2005) 'Cultural schema theory', in W. B. Gudykunst (ed.), *Theorizing about Intercultural Communication*. Thousand Oaks, CA: Sage. pp. 401–418.

DEVELOPING INTERCULTURAL COMMUNICATION COMPETENCE

Along with the changes brought about by globalization comes the need to redefine personal and cultural identities. At the same time as people see themselves as 'global citizens', they also identify themselves by a nation or a local community. The balance between global and local, when we view it through a cultural prism, occurs along a continuum rather than as an all-or-none phenomenon. Therefore, it is important to build intercultural communication competence in order to function effectively in both global and local contexts.

Components of intercultural communication competence

Scholarly debates on defining *intercultural communication competence* have gone on for more than five decades, yet no consensus has been reached. The term has been variously defined as the ability to accomplish interpersonal tasks and relate to others (Weinstein, 1969). The extent to which individuals manifest aspects of their culture in the communication process is what makes an interaction intercultural. Factoring in the concept of culture, Spitzberg and Changnon (2009: 7) define intercultural communication competence as 'the appropriate and effective management of interaction between people who, to some degree or another, represent different or divergent affective, cognitive and behavioural orientations to the world'. At the core of all the conceptualizations of intercultural competence is the notion of effectiveness and appropriateness. Effectiveness refers to an individual's ability to achieve the intended goal through interaction with the other communicator(s) or environment(s). Appropriateness refers to an individual's ability to act and speak in a way that leads to positive communication outcomes (or avoid negative outcomes). However, what is 'appropriate' and 'effective' is context-bound. The same behaviour may be perceived as competent in one context (e.g., direct confrontation in conflict situations in an individualistic culture) but not in another (e.g., indirect and high-context communication in a collectivistic culture). Intercultural communication competence is contextual. Judgements of intercultural communication competence depend on cultural expectations about the appropriate behaviours for a particular situational and relational context (Lustig and Koester, 2013).

Various perspectives on defining intercultural competence mean that the choice of indicators of competence and the relations among them are complex. LaFromboise and colleagues (1993) identified six components of bicultural competence: cultural knowledge, positive attitudes, bicultural efficacy, communication ability, role repertoire and a sense of being grounded. These components are reflected in the facework-based model of intercultural competence formulated by Ting-Toomey and Kurogi (1998). The facework-based model consists of cognitive (knowledge and mindfulness) and behavioural (interaction skills and facework competence) dimensions of intercultural communication competence, grouped into four categories (see Figure 13.1).

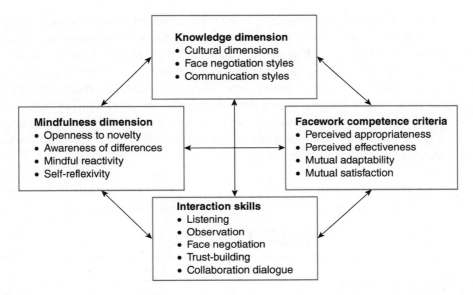

FIGURE 13.1 Facework-based model of intercultural competence

Source: Adapted from Spitzberg, Brian H. and Changnon, Gabrielle (2009) *The SAGE Handbook of Intercultural Competence*. Thousand Oaks, CA: Sage.

Note: Spitzberg and Changnon adapted this model from Ting-Toomey and Kurogi's work: Ting-Toomey, Stella and Kurogi, Atsuko (1998) 'Facework competence in intercultural conflict: An updated face-negotiation theory', *International Journal of Intercultural Relations*, 22: 187–225.

The knowledge dimension refers to a communicator's understanding of differences in cultures, such as individualism versus collectivism and power distance, and facework negotiating styles. Applied in intercultural interactions, the primary skills include listening, observation, trust building, dialogic collaboration and face negotiation. The mindfulness dimension represents abilities such as taking multiple perspectives, being aware of one's own and others' positions, being open to novelty, and empathy. Here is an example from an experience of working with people in an Indigenous community in Australia. An academic from a university, David, developed a good working relationship with the Indigenous people in the community while working with them on his research project. As he was about to leave the community upon completion of the project, an older person who worked with them asked David for $200 as a 'gift'. Unfamiliar with such practice, David feared he might be accused of 'bribery' if he did so; he thus told the old Indigenous person that he did not have the money. Having heard the reply, this Indigenous person immediately took out $500 from his pocket and gave it to David, saying that he regarded David as his grandson and a grandfather should help his grandson if he is in need of money. The misunderstanding occurred because both were acting in accordance with their own cultural norms. In some Indigenous cultures, giving money to a friend as a gift represents maintaining the friendship in the future, not necessarily helping someone who needs money. Of course, such a practice might not be generalizable to other Indigenous cultural groups. The point here is that communicating with culturally different others suggests experiencing novel practices, and familiar cultural cues may not be adequate to interpret messages. Thus, an effective intercultural communicator should always be mindful of differences and be open to unfamiliar and novel practices when engaging in intercultural communication.

THEORY CORNER

TRANSCULTURATION THEORY

The concept of *transculturation* was proposed by Cuban anthropologist Fernando Ortiz (1995) in his book *Cuban Counterpoint: Tobacco and Sugar*. It refers to the converging and merging of cultures. Within the dominant framework of acculturation research in the twentieth century, acculturation was viewed as a linear process of transformation from one culture to another, resulting from cultural contact. Ortiz introduced the concept of transculturation in 1947 to recognize the mutually influential relationships between cultures, and the diverse, nonlinear and multidirectional processes of cultural identity formation. The term encompasses acquiring or adapting elements of home and host cultures, as well as the subsequent creation of new cultural elements. Ortiz (1995: 98) explained that transculturation is a more appropriate and less ethnocentric term to use to describe the multifaceted cultural change in Cuba, occurring in the economic, institutional, legal, ethical, religious, artistic, linguistic, psychological, sexual and other aspects of life in the creation of Cuban culture: 'The real history of Cuba is the history of its intermeshed transculturations'.

Ortiz's theory of transculturation continues to be broadly applicable in the globalized society where interactions between people, objects, meanings and cultural practices are constantly negotiated. Kath (2016) applied Ortiz's theory of transculturation to explain many of the common ways in which Latin American dances have been transmuted in the Australian context. She related her personal experience of having a Cuban-born dancer who lived in Melbourne talk to her class of university students about Cuban dance and give a short dance demonstration to them. She observed that, although the Cuban person danced to the sounds of traditional Batá drums, the dance and music were tailored for an audience of Australian students, most of whom had little experience of Latin American dance and music forms. Kath (2016) states that the concept of transculturation here challenges some of the commonly held notions of 'cultural authenticity' as a static commodity that can be transported and reproduced in the Australian context. While the idea of authenticity is important, 'no cultural practice can ever be transported across time and space without being transformed through that passage' (Kath, 2016: 29). The process through which Latin American music and dance co-constructs Latin American identity in Australia is locally embedded. Kath (2016) concludes that the Latin American people who migrated to Australia create new cultural elements and incorporate them into their traditional cultural products and practices, as they influence and are influenced by both home and host cultures.

REFERENCES

Kath, Elizabeth (2016) 'On transculturation: Re-enacting and remaking Latin American dance and music in foreign lands', in J. C. Lee (ed.), *Narratives of Globalization*. London: Rowman & Littlefield International. pp. 21–35.

Ortiz, Fernando (1995) *Cuban Counterpoint: Tobacco and Sugar*, translated by Harried de Onis. Durham, NC: Duke University Press.

Building empathy in intercultural communication

Intercultural awareness is one of the foundations of communication. It involves two qualities: one is the awareness of one's own culture; the other is the awareness of another culture. Intercultural awareness means the ability to stand back from one's own point of view and to become aware of the cultural values, beliefs and perceptions of other cultures. However, the mere realization of cultural awareness is not enough. Many scholars claim that we also need to create a sense of empathy. As a word from the Greek '*empatheia*', empathy means understanding others by entering their world, or standing in somebody else's shoes. Empathy is associated with many important aspects of communication behaviour, for example formulating communicative intentions and goals, devising strategies to accomplish communicative purposes, and constructing messages consistent with communicative strategies. These and other communication behaviours are usually seen as being influenced by communicators' attempts to consider the perspective of the other person (Broome, 1991). As Broome writes, 'an empathic encounter results in more than each individual developing a deeper understanding of the other – it leads to the creation of a unique whole that reflects a merging of each individual's construction of the other' (Broome, 1991: 245).

Strategies to develop intercultural communication competence

Increased intercultural contact provides opportunities for understanding between people as well as the potential for misunderstanding. We propose three strategies to ensure more success than failure when communicating with culturally different others.

Seek commonalities. In intercultural encounters, the first thing we tend to perceive is difference: differences in appearance, dress, language, diet, religion, customs, and even political orientation. If we adopt self-focused conversation strategies or use only our own cultural norms to guide us, intercultural communication is unlikely to be successful. To overcome the barrier of difference, we need to build mutual understanding with the other person. One way to achieve this is to focus on similarities rather than differences. As we gain more knowledge about each other, we may find that despite the visible differences, we share many similarities. As Morris (1994: 6) describes, 'We may wear different hats but we all show the same smile; we may speak different languages but they are all rooted in the same basic grammar; we may have different marriage customs but we all fall in love'. Perceived similarities reduce uncertainty and hence facilitate intercultural communication.

Overcome stereotyping and prejudice. One of the most important barriers to intercultural competence is ethnocentrism, the degree to which other cultures are judged as inferior to one's own. Ethnocentrism is usually based on stereotyping and prejudice about outgroup members compared to the ingroup. Stereotyping and prejudice prevent us from seeing evidence that does not confirm our presumptions. In order for people to become more competent intercultural communicators, it is important to decrease ethnocentrism and avoid prejudiced attitudes. One way to achieve this goal is to practise cultural relativism, which encourages us to understand the behaviour of others from their own cultural perspectives (i.e., to practise empathy). We can try to give the other person, and their group, the benefit of the doubt, and to make the starting assumption that they are behaving appropriately in terms of their own cultural values and norms. However, we acknowledge that cultural relativism has its own limitations.

Develop flexibility and openness. Universally, communication is rule-governed behaviour, but rules vary from culture to culture. Cultural rules govern the distance that is perceived as appropriate between speakers, the loudness at which a person should speak during an interaction, the appropriate amount of gestures, and the appropriate information to be shared between speakers based on their relationship, along with nearly everything else. When we enter an intercultural interaction, we may not know all the rules governing appropriate behaviour in the other culture. We must keep an open mind and be aware that what we practise in our culture may neither be the only correct way nor the best way of doing things, and be flexible in adapting our communication as the situation requires. Our knowledge of cultural dimensions and values will go a long way to help us adapt to new situations.

It is important to remember that communication across cultures takes place in a context. For every encounter there is an intergroup history, and that history can contain sources of tension, hostility and prejudice, as well as (or instead of) more positive elements. There is also an interpersonal history – the individuals may know and like each other, be total strangers, or dislike each other. There are circumstances where intercultural communication requires enormous skill, patience and luck – communication competence is not enough. Fortunately, in many situations we can make use of the skills and strategies described here to help prevent misunderstandings and to achieve positive interactions.

SUMMARY

- The flow of many global cultural products has not only transmitted cultural values from one country to another, but has also transformed people's way of living.
- Cultural homogenization and fragmentation work dialectically. The homogenization of cultures generates opportunities for the expression and circulation of culturally specific products.
- Cultural diffusion, convergence, hegemony, colonization and hybridization are processes of contact between cultures. Globalization suggests multiple ways in which the global and the local cultural realms are articulated.
- In order to develop intercultural communication competence, we need specifically to focus on seeking commonalities, overcoming stereotyping and prejudice, and developing flexibility and openness.

JOIN THE DEBATE

WILL OUR ATTITUDES AND TASTES BECOME MORE 'PROVINCIAL' IN THE GLOBAL ECONOMY?

Global media, the internet and travel have increased our exposure to cultural practices that are different from our own. One of the most prominent forms of response or resistance towards global dominance is when local brands present alternatives to global brands. An interesting example involves the many local and regional versions of the symbol of American global colonization and hegemony: Coca-Cola. In addition to the traditional colas that continue to be popular, such as the Italian drink chinotto, there are several examples of local colas that have been created either to imitate or resist the original one. For example, Mecca Cola, which targets Muslim markets, was introduced as an ethical alternative to resist the American hegemony. Cola Turka, the Turkish equivalent of the popular soft drink, is another such example. The promotion of local and national colas illustrates how our attitudes and tastes can become more provincial. It may be that national and local touches will be employed in order to emphasize diversity in the global context. While some scholars argue that diversity makes our thinking and being more global, others claim that diversity evokes new forms of ethnic and religious chauvinism – the more we inhabit a global world, the more we cling to our 'uniqueness', whether it is in our language, music, food or festivals. Could our attitudes and tastes become more provincial in the global economy?

CASE STUDY

CHINATOWN AS A TRANSNATIONAL SPACE

For over two centuries, Chinatowns have been recognized as some of the most visible symbols of overseas Chinese communities across the world. From Asia to the Americas, Europe, Africa and Oceania, there is always a Chinatown. Established in the 1840s, the Chinatown in San Francisco, for example, is the largest and oldest Chinatown in North America and also the largest Chinatown outside Asia. For early Chinese immigrants, from the 1850s to the 1900s San Francisco served as a port of entry to the United States. Some of the Chinese immigrants found jobs working for large companies seeking labourers; others worked as transcontinental railroad workers or miners, hoping to become rich during the 1849 Gold Rush (Wong, 2011). Chinatown in Vancouver, which was established in the 1890s, is the largest Chinatown in Canada, with the Millennium Gate as its trademark. Due to the size of the ethnic Chinese population in Vancouver, especially immigrants from Hong Kong, Vancouver is nicknamed 'Hongcouver'. In Latin America, Barrio Chino was established in the 1850s in Lima and is South America's oldest Chinatown. In Europe, Chinese seamen set up one of the earliest Chinatowns around the docks in Liverpool in the nineteenth century. Subsequently, the Chinatown in London came into being at the turn of the twentieth century. In the 1920s, the Chinatown in Paris, Quartier Chinois de Paris, became the largest Chinatown in Europe. The largest Chinatown in Africa was established in the 1900s in Johannesburg, South Africa. By far the oldest Chinatown in the world, established in 1594, is Binodo Chinatown in Manila, in the Philippines. Singapore's Chinatown, which was built in the 1820s, is known as 'bull cart water' because in the nineteenth century Chinatown's water supply was primarily transported by animal-driven carts. Turning to Oceania, the oldest Chinatown was established in the 1850s in Melbourne, Australia. The Chinatown in Broome, Western Australia, has never had many Chinese residents (most of its people were Japanese pearlers or merchants from Southeast Asia), but it took the name because Chinatowns were already an iconic part of Australian towns and cities. These are just a small number of the thousands of Chinatowns across the world.

Chinatowns are residential and commercial areas in some parts of the world; in others, they are not residential communities but shops selling Chinese products serving the ethnic communities (Wong, 2011). Typical features of Chinatowns across the world are the colourful and ornamental archways, often called the dragon gates, that mark the entry to the Chinese space. Similar gates appear in Chinese architecture – in palaces or places of historical interest. Archways mark entries to a specific territory and mark boundaries. Physical walls mark borders between countries, such as the Israeli West Bank barrier or the US–Mexican border fence. In the town of Michalovce in Slovakia, residents built a cement barrier to separate themselves from the town's majority Roma population. Interestingly, unlike the ancient fortresses in China, the archways in Chinatowns are simply 'gates', with no physical walls surrounding them. Often the entry and the exit are not clearly marked, that is, people can go in and out on different streets or return to where they entered. Nevertheless, 'gate without walls' does not suggest that Chinatowns do not have borders. The 'walls' are cultural; they are built by the Chinese language (the distinctive Chinese characters found on businesses or street signs) and indicate a world that stands apart from the rest of the city, whether it is in multicultural New York, Johannesburg, London, Paris or Melbourne.

Chinatowns originated due to segregation by majority groups and colonial governments as much as to the desire of Chinese migrants to maintain their cultural links to the homeland (Inglis, 2011). Chinatowns became more visible and distinctive with the migration of Chinese in the nineteenth century as labourers or sailors to port cities and other places of opportunity worldwide. The early Chinatowns, such as the one in San Francisco, were the result of opportunities such as the California Gold Rush and the Transcontinental Railroad. Residents in ethnic-concentrated areas like Chinatowns had access to ethnic, social and support networks, economic opportunities and the presence of community associations, which acted as an intermediary between them and the larger cultural society. From Canada to Peru, South Africa to Australia, in the UK and elsewhere in Europe, the Chinese grouped themselves together for mutual support, and Chinatowns represented an emblematic space for community solidarity and communication (Inglis, 2011). The symbolic and physical space was seen to create a pathway for Chinese migrants, particularly early Chinese migrants, as a link to their home culture and at the same time as a route to assimilation into the larger host society (Zhou and Lin, 2005).

Modern-day Chinatowns, although still a place of representation, are more like cultural icons, images in stories, literature, movies or television than a place of cultural identification for modern Chinese migrants and transmigrants. Around the world, cities point to Chinatowns as markers of globalization and diversity and as tourist attractions for Chinese migrants, local residents and travellers alike (McDonogh and Wong, 2012). They are also a site of transnational space where Chinese immigrants, non-Chinese, their hybrid descendants and other citizens interact and intersect. These changes to the original meaning and purpose of Chinatowns occurred over time as our societies became more global and the Chinese diasporic population became more diverse in terms of education and occupation. More importantly, the expectations and attitudes to immigrants in host countries have changed from assimilation to integration. Chinatowns are now tourist attractions as well as places where people shop for Asian food and enjoy Chinese cuisines. The links to the home culture for the Chinese diaspora can also be achieved through the celebration of traditional cultural festivals in Chinatowns. Such events not only bind the Chinese diaspora together, but also extend Chinese culture into the larger society. For example, during the celebration of the Mid-Autumn festival in Philadelphia, the varied pan-Asian performances underscore Chinese-American relations to other ethnic/political groups, including Asian immigrants from Vietnam, Korea, Singapore and Japan (Wong and McDonogh, 2013). Old images of Chinatowns, which encapsulate the characteristics of a ghetto and a stepping stone to assimilation, are gradually being replaced by Chinatowns that are simply sites of cultural diversity in a multicultural society and unique cultural symbols standing in a predominantly non-Chinese cultural environment.

REFERENCES FOR CASE STUDY

Inglis, Christine (2011) 'Chinatown Sydney: A window on the Chinese community', *Journal of Chinese Overseas*, 7: 45–68.

McDonogh, Gary W. and Wong, Cindy H. (2012) 'Beside downtowns: Global Chinatowns', in M. Peterson and G. W. McDonogh (eds.), *Global Downtowns*. Philadelphia, PA: University of Pennsylvania Press. pp. 274–296.

Wong, Bernard (2011) 'Chinatowns: Persistence and change', *Journal of Chinese Overseas*, 7: 1–5.

Wong, Cindy H. and McDonogh, Gary W. (2013) 'Negotiating global Chinatowns: Difference, diversity and connection', *Anno III*, 6: 41–54.

Zhou, Min and Lin Mingang (2005) 'Community transformation and the formation of ethnic capital: Immigrant Chinese communities in the United States', *Journal of Chininese Overseas*, 1(2): 260–284.

1. What are the symbolic meanings of Chinatowns and how have they changed over time?

2. In what ways can a transnational space like a Chinatown facilitate immigrants' cultural transitions? In what ways can attachment to such a space limit their cross-cultural adjustment?

3. In what ways can the immigration policies of a host country influence how an ethnic community will relate to the larger society?

4. What can immigrants and transmigrants do to build a sense of cultural identity, belonging and home which transcends geographic borders?

5. Do you know any other 'towns' like Chinatowns? What are they, and do they have similar social and cultural functions as Chinatowns?

Imre, Aniko (2009) *Identity Games: Globalization and Transformations in the New Europe*. Cambridge: MIT Press.

This book examines the corporate transformation of the post-communist media landscape in Eastern Europe. Avoiding both uncritical techno-euphoria and nostalgic projections of a simpler, better media world under communism, Imre argues that the demise of Soviet-style regimes and the transition of post-communist nation-states to transnational capitalism has crucial implications for understanding the relationships among nationalism, media globalization and identity.

Krajewski, Sabine (2011) 'Developing intercultural competence in multilingual and multicultural student groups', *Journal of Research in International Education*, 10(2): 137–153.

This article offers a case study with a focus on building intercultural competence through an assignment that invites experiential, self-directed learning. Students' previous intercultural experiences as well as their personal attitudes, it is argued, have a strong influence on what they learn during their studies. The assignment presented in the case study draws upon the expertise that individual students already have when they enter the classroom, and aims at further developing their intercultural skills. The results of the survey show that students rated this particular assignment more useful in comparison with more traditional assessed tasks,.

Magu, Stephen (2015) 'Reconceptualizing cultural globalization: Connecting the "cultural global" and the "cultural local"', *Social Sciences*, 4: 630–645.

This article argues that culture is a dynamic, adaptive concept and practice which 'borrows' liberally from the ideological and technological innovations of other cultures and integrates these borrowed aspects into the construction and modification of culture across spatial and geographical divides to ensure a particular culture's survival. The research shows that cultures actively adopt and integrate globalization's technological artefacts.

Moon, Sangkil, Mishra, Arul, Mishra, Himanshu and Kang, Moon Y. (2016) 'Cultural and economic impacts on global cultural products: Evidence from US movies', *Journal of International Marketing*, 24(3): 78–97.

This article examines the economic and cultural factors that influence consumers' acceptance of new global cultural products across countries. Its empirical context is the box office performances of 846 US movies in 48 national markets. The findings identified a U-shaped impact of inter-country cultural distance in the presence of cultural compatibility and a decreasing linear impact of cultural distance in the absence of cultural compatibility.

Morley, Michael and Cerdin, Jean-Luc (2010) 'Intercultural competence in the international business arena', *Journal of Managerial Psychology*, 25(8): 805–809.

This article identifies four major threads in the international business literature dealing with cross-cultural competence. They are related to a lack of agreement on what constitutes intercultural competence, an almost total absence of studies of cross-cultural competence in international business, a tendency to ignore the larger environments in which expatriate managers operate, and too broad coverage of the topic in the workplace diversity. The article draws attention to the importance of intercultural competence in workplaces.

In this video Professor Toby Miller examines how film and television exports from the U.S. and former colonial powers influence culture around the world. The video will help you to achieve the learning objective of understanding cultural diffusion, convergence, hegemony, and colonization. Watch it to learn more about global popular culture.

This video is available at http://study.sagepub.com/liu3e

SAGE VIDEO SOURCES

GLOSSARY

Accommodating A conflict management strategy which refers to behaviours that conceal or play down differences by emphasizing common interests.

Acculturation The changes that cultural groups undergo when different cultures come into continuous first-hand contact, with subsequent changes in the original culture of either or both groups.

Activity orientation The value orientation which refers to the use of time for self-expression and play, self-improvement and work.

Affection Sharing emotions, showing love to and being loved by others.

Affective/instrumental communication style A verbal communication style dimension, which is concerned with the extent to which communication is receiver-focused or sender-oriented, process-oriented or outcome-oriented.

Agenda-setting The theory sees mass media as focusing attention on certain aspects of life and, in doing so, sets the agenda for the public.

Anxiety/uncertainty management theory This theory posits that effective interpersonal and intercultural communication is a function of how individuals manage the anxiety and uncertainty they experience when communicating with others.

Assimilation A type of acculturation strategy which means giving up one's heritage culture in order to gain acceptance into the host culture.

Attribution theory This theory assumes that a person seeking to understand why another person acted in a certain way may attribute internal or external causes to the behaviour.

Autonomy versus embeddedness One of the three dimensions of Schwartz's cultural taxonomies; cultures valuing autonomy view an individual as more independent whereas cultures valuing embeddedness view the person as an entity embedded in the collectivity.

Avoiding A conflict management strategy which refers to behaviours of physical withdrawal or refusal to discuss the conflict.

Belief People's understanding of what is true in reality as viewed through their culture.

Bicultural identity integration The degree to which a bicultural individual perceives his/her bicultural identity as compatible or conflictual.

Categorization The process of ordering the environment by grouping persons, objects and events based on their similarities.

Channel The means by which a message moves from one person to another. The channel can be sound, words, letters, telephone, the internet, fax and so on.

Chronemics A type of nonverbal behaviour which is concerned with the use of time.

Collaborating A conflict management strategy which refers to facing a conflict directly and examining possible solutions with the intention of achieving a win-win solution.

Collectivism One of Hofstede's cultural dimensions, collectivistic cultures emphasize primary groups in which people see themselves as interdependent with others and individual goals are secondary to those of the group.

Communication The process by which people use shared verbal or nonverbal codes, systems and media to exchange information in a particular cultural context.

Communication accommodation theory This theory explains conditions under which communicators negotiate and accommodate each other's communicative behaviour through linguistic and non-linguistic moves.

Communication style How language is used to communicate meaning.

Communicative ethical approach This approach recognizes that humans are socialized into a particular set of cultural norms but are capable of critically reflecting upon and changing them.

Competing A conflict management strategy which refers to the use of power in satisfying one's position, even though it means ignoring the needs of the opponent.

Compromising A conflict management strategy which refers to behaviours that aim at finding a midpoint between the opposing viewpoints to achieve a mutually acceptable solution.

Conflict Arising from the interaction of interdependent people who perceive opposition of goals, aims and values, and who see the other party as potentially interfering with the realization of these goals.

Confucian work dynamism Also known as long-term or short-term orientation, it refers to the work practices and outcomes of dedicated, motivated, responsible and educated individuals with a sense of commitment and organizational identity and loyalty.

Connotation The cultural meanings that become attached to a word or an object.

Constructivist Constructivists argue that language acquisition involves unveiling the patterns of language and requires interaction with a structured environment.

Contextual/personal communication style A dimension of verbal communication style which is concerned with the extent to which the speaker emphasizes the self as opposed to his/her role.

Control The ability to influence others, the environment and ourselves, along with the desire to be influenced by others (or not).

Coordinated management of meaning theory This theory sees communication as idiosyncratic and social at the same time.

Creole A new language developed from the prolonged contact of two or more languages; a full, linguistically complex language in its own right with its own grammar, morphology, lexicon, phonetics and phonology.

Critical media theory This theory examines the relationship between media, power relationships and society.

Cross-cultural adaptation The process of increasing one's level of fitness in a new cultural environment.

Cultivation theory This theory claims that exposure to vast amounts of violence on TV conditions viewers to view the world as an unkind and frightening place.

Cultural colonization Particular forms of cultural domination, including media, educational, academic, intellectual, scientific and linguistic colonialization; sometimes used synonymously with the term cultural imperialism.

Cultural convergence The process through which cultures move towards one another based on commonality.

Cultural diffusion The process through which one culture learns or adopts a new idea or practice from another culture or cultures.

Cultural hegemony The structurally enabled predominant influence of one culture over another.

Cultural hybridization The process by which different cultures mix to form a new, third culture.

Cultural identity A type of social identity derived from a person's identification with and perceived acceptance into a cultural group.

Cultural relativism The degree to which an individual judges another culture by its context.

Cultural schemas Generalized knowledge of past experiences organized into related categories and used to guide one's behaviour in familiar situations.

Culture The particular way of life of a group of people, comprising the deposit of knowledge, experience, beliefs, values, traditions, religion, notions of time, roles, spatial relations, worldviews, material objects and geographic territory.

Culture shock The feeling of disorientation and anxiety that a sojourner experiences when entering a new culture.

Decoding The process by which a receiver converts a message encoded in verbal or nonverbal codes back into meaning.

Denotation The descriptive, literal meaning of a word or an object.

Developmental model of intercultural sensitivity (DMIS) A model created by Milton Bennett as a framework to explain people's reactions to cultural differences.

Diaspora People who settle away from their ancestral homeland.

Diffusion of innovations The theory explains how, why and at what rate new ideas and technology are adopted; sometimes known as technology diffusion.

Direct/indirect communication style A dimension of verbal communication style which refers to the extent to which the speaker's intentions, wants and desires are communicated in the interaction.

Discourse Ways of thinking and producing meaning, either in written or spoken form.

Discrimination The prejudicial treatment and disadvantaging of an individual based on their actual or perceived differences.

Elaborate/succinct communication style A dimension of verbal communication style which refers to the quantity of talk a culture values.

Emic approach Viewing each culture as a unique entity that can only be studied from inside the culture. See also Etic approach.

Empathy Understanding others by entering their world or standing in someone else's shoes.

Encoding The internal process by which thoughts, feelings and concepts are converted into a message by using shared verbal or nonverbal codes.

Ethical relativism This approach denies the existence of a single universal set of values and norms and instead conceives them as being relative to particular individuals or groups.

Ethical universalism This approach proposes the existence of universal ethical principles that guide behaviour across all societies at any time – what is wrong in one place will be wrong elsewhere.

Ethics The moral standards and rules that guide the behaviour of members of a society regarding what is right or wrong, good or bad.

Ethnic identity Identity derived from a sense of belonging to or an identification with an ethnic group.

Ethnocentrism Seeing one's own culture as the point of reference and seeing other cultures as insignificant or even inferior.

Ethnography A method used mainly by anthropologists to study culture in its natural setting.

Ethnolinguistic vitality The degree of prestige, acceptability and importance attached to a group's language.

Etic approach The approach assumes that culture can be examined with predetermined categories that can be applied to all cultures in the search for cultural universals.

Expectancy violation theory The theory assumes that humans anticipate certain behaviour from the people with whom they interact; the violation of expectations can result in communication difficulties.

Feedback Information generated by the receiver and made available to the source that allows the source to make qualitative judgements about the communication event.

Femininity One of Hofstede's cultural dimensions; feminine cultures permit more overlapping social roles for the sexes and place high value on feminine traits such as quality of life, interpersonal relationships and concern for the weak.

Fragmentation The process through which different cultures maintain their own individual place rather than merging with other cultures.

Gender identity A person's self and social identity; the term 'gender' entails social roles established for the sexes.

Gender-neutral language Language use that discourages the generic use of masculine pronouns in referring to persons of either sex.

Generative universal grammar The idea that any language's rule structure allows speakers to generate sentences that have never before been spoken; from a finite set of sounds and rules, speakers of any language can create an infinite number of sentences, many of which have never before been uttered.

Global village Marshall McLuhan's description of a world in which communication technology brings news and information to the most remote parts of the world.

Globalist Viewing globalization as an inevitable development that cannot be resisted or significantly influenced by human intervention through traditional political institutions, such as nation-states.

Globalization The process of increasing interconnectedness between societies such that events in one place of the world are having more and deeper effects on people and societies far away.

Guanxi A special type of Chinese relationship which contains trust, favour, dependence and adaptation.

Halo effect The tendency to presume that someone who has one good trait is likely to have other good traits.

Haptics Nonverbal behaviour which is concerned with the use of touch.

Hierarchy versus egalitarianism One of the three dimensions of Schwartz's cultural taxonomies; cultures that value hierarchy view the unequal distribution of power as legitimate and desirable, whereas cultures that value egalitarianism encourage people to recognize one another as moral equals.

High-context culture Cultures typically gathering information from the physical, social and psychological context rather than relying on verbal codes.

Homogenization The transformation of different cultural practices into one blended, uniform cultural practice.

Human nature orientation The value orientation which addresses the innate nature of humans; good versus evil.

Identity A person's subjective experience of himself or herself in relation to the world.

Identity negotiation theory This theory claims that there are particular influential identity domains that individuals acquire and that they further develop their identities through interaction with others.

Ideological asymmetry hypothesis This hypothesis suggests that hierarchy-attenuating ideologies appeal more to low-status groups than to high-status groups.

Implicit personality theory This theory suggests that people organize their perceptions into clusters; individual personality traits are related to other traits, and when we identify an individual trait in someone, we assume they also possess other traits in the cluster.

Inclusion A sense of belonging or of being involved with others, as well as of including others in our activities.

Indirect/direct communication style A verbal communication style dimension, which refers to the extent to which the speaker's intentions, wants and desires are directly communicated in the interaction.

Individualism One of Hofstede's cultural dimensions; individualistic cultures emphasize individuals' goals over group goals.

Ingroup A special membership group characterized by internal cohesiveness among its members, often with a shared culture, worldview or interest, i.e., 'us'.

Instrumental/affective communication style A verbal communication style dimension which is concerned with the extent to which communication is receiver-focused or sender-oriented, process-oriented or outcome-oriented.

Integrated threat theory This theory identifies four domains of threat: realistic, symbolic and negative stereotypes and intergroup anxiety, which can lead to prejudice towards outgroups.

Integration A type of acculturation strategy which means maintaining heritage cultural traditions and practices while attempting to gain acceptance into the host culture.

Interactive model This model views communication as a process of creating and sharing meaning upon which context, experience and perception exert influence.

Intercultural communication Communication between individuals from different cultural or ethnic backgrounds or between people from subculture groups.

Intercultural communication competence The ability to communicate effectively and appropriately with people of other cultures.

Intercultural conflict Conflict arising when there is a perceived or actual incompatibility of goals, interests, resources, values, expectations, processes or outcomes between two or more interdependent parties from different cultures.

Intergroup conflict Conflict arising when two cultural or social groups perceive disagreements over resources, stereotypes, territory, policies, religion or identities.

International conflict Conflict arising when there are disputes and disagreements between nation-states.

Interorganizational conflict Conflict arising from disputes and disagreements between two or more organizations.

Interpellation The process by which people ascribe identity to other people.

Interpersonal conflict Conflict arising at the level of individuals when they are competing for scarce resources or having disagreements.

Interpretation The process of verbally expressing what is said in another language; it can be either simultaneous or consecutive to the original speaker.

Kinesics Nonverbal behaviour which is concerned with body movement, including gestures, hand and arm movements, leg movements, facial expressions, eye contact and posture.

Linear model This model views communication as a linear process whereby information 'packages' are transmitted from source to receiver, as if along a pipeline; also known as the transmission model.

Long-term orientation An aspect of Hofstede's long-term and short-term orientation which encourages thrift, savings, perseverance towards results and a willingness to subordinate oneself for a purpose.

Low-context culture Low-context cultures gather information predominantly from explicit verbal codes.

Man–nature orientation The value orientation which refers to the relationship between humans and nature; it can be subjugated to, in harmony with, or mastery over nature.

Marginalization A type of acculturation strategy which refers to individuals devaluing their cultural heritage but not having significant contact with the host society either.

Masculinity One of Hofstede's cultural dimensions; masculine cultures strive for a maximal distinction between male and female roles and the attributes ascribed to them.

Mastery versus harmony One of the three dimenions of Schwartz's cultural taxonomy; mastery cultures encourage people to actively control and change the world, whereas cultures that value harmony encourage acceptance and fitting harmoniously into the environment.

Message The verbal and/or nonverbal form of ideas, thoughts or feelings that one person wishes to communicate to another person or group within a specific context.

Monochronic time orientation People of monochronic time orientations view time as linear, progressive and being able to be compartmentalized.

Morphology The combination of basic units of meaning – morphemes – to create words.

Multiculturalism Multiculturalism can be used to characterize a society with diverse cultures and can refer to a society's tolerance towards diversity and acceptance of equal societal participation.

National identity Identity characterized by one's individual self-perception as a member of a nation.

Nativist Nativists argue that language acquisition involves triggering pre-programmed models in the human mind, e.g., Noam Chomsky.

Noise Psychological, semantic or physical elements that interfere with the communication of the message.

Nominalists Those who argue that our perception of external reality is shaped not by language but by material reality.

Nonverbal codes Any means, other than verbal codes, that are used to communicate meaning.

Nonverbal communication The use of non-spoken symbols to communicate a message.

Olfactics Nonverbal behaviour referring to humans' perception and use of smell, scent and odour.

Orientalism Developed by Edward Said as a discourse for understanding the relationship between the East and the West, Orientalism is based on European cultural power dominating political and economic interests.

Outgroup The group whose attributes are dissimilar from those of the ingroup, i.e., 'them'.

Outgroup homogeneity effect The tendency to see members of outgroups as 'all alike', without recognizing the individual differences.

Paralanguage The vocal qualities that accompany speech. Paralanguage can be divided into two broad categories: voice qualities and vocalizations.

Perception An active process in which humans use sensory organs to selectively identify the existence of stimuli and then subject them to evaluation and interpretation.

Personal/contextual communication style A dimension of verbal communication style which is concerned with the extent to which the speaker emphasizes the self as opposed to his/her role.

Phonology The rules of a language which determine how sounds are combined to form words.

Pidgin A make-shift language used to communicate when two people who do not share a common language come into contact.

Polychronic time orientation People of polychronic time orientation conceive time as cyclical and attempt to perform multiple tasks simultaneously.

Power distance One of Hofstede's cultural dimensions, this refers to the extent to which a culture tolerates inequality in power distribution.

Pragmatics The use of language in a social context.

Prejudice A negative attitude towards individuals resulting from negative stereotypes.

Proxemics Nonverbal behaviour which refers to the use of space, including territory, that an individual claims permanently or temporarily.

Racism The belief that one racial group is superior and that other racial groups are necessarily inferior.

Receiver The intended target of a message.

Referent What a word or phrase denotes or stands for, although there is no natural relationship between a word and its referent.

Relational orientation The value orientation which addresses the modality of a person's relationship to other people.

Relativists Relativists believe that the language one speaks determines the person's ideas, thought patterns and perceptions of reality.

Religious identity The sense of belonging based on membership of a religious group.

Reverse culture shock The culture shock experienced by some when they return to the home country after an extended period of stay in a foreign culture.

Sapir-Whorf hypothesis This theory proposes that language and thought are inextricably tied together, so that a person's language determines the categories of thought open to the person.

Self-disclosure The process of revealing personal information that another person would be unlikely to discover through third sources.

Self-fulfilling prophecy A statement that causes itself to become true by directly or indirectly altering actions.

Semantics The study of the meaning of words and the relationship between words and their referents.

Separation A type of acculturation strategy which means adhering to one's heritage culture only and not participating in the host culture.

Short-term orientation One aspect of Hofstede's long-term and short-term orientation cultural dimension, this is consistent with spending to keep up with social pressure and represents a preference for immediacy.

Signified In structural linguistics, the signified refers to the mental pictures, concepts, ideas or objects which are attributed meaning by the signifier.

Signifier In structural linguistics, the signifier refers to the spoken or written words in a language system.

Similarity attraction paradigm The paradigm is based on the assumption that if we perceive our attitudes as similar to some people, we are attracted to them, because the similarity in attitudes validates our view of the world.

Social exchange theory This theory explains how individuals establish and continue social relations on the basis of their expectations that such relations will be mutually beneficial.

Social identity An individual's self-concept that derives from his or her membership in a group together with the value and emotional significance attached to the membership.

Social media Networked interactive digital platforms that enable the formation of social groups connected by patterns of two-way communication either one-to-one or one-to-many.

Social penetration theory This theory states that, as an interpersonal relationship develops, the interpersonal exchange of information moves from superficial and impersonal to intimate and personal.

Socialization The process of learning a culture's rules, rituals and procedures, including proper and improved behaviour and communication within the confines of these cultural rules.

Source The sender, or origin, of the message being sent.

Stereotype Preconceived beliefs about the characteristics of a certain group based on physical attributes or social status that may not be generalizable to all members of the group.

Structural linguistics The theory that views language as a coherent system whereby every item acquires meaning in relation to other items in the system.

Subculture The smaller, coherent collective groups which exist within the larger dominant culture and which are often distinctive because of race, social class, gender, etc. (also referred to as co-culture or microculture).

Succinct/elaborate communication style A dimension of verbal communication style which is concerned with the quantity of talk a culture values.

Symbol An arbitrarily selected and learned stimulus that represents something else.

Syntax The study of grammatical and structural rules of language which we use to combine words into sentences in order to communicate meaning.

Time orientation The value orientation which refers to the temporal focus of human life, i.e., past, present or future.

Traditionalist Traditionalists believe that most economic and social activity is regional rather than global, and they still see a significant role of nation-states.

Transactional model The model posits communication as the process of continuous change and transformation, where people, their environments and the medium used are changing at multiple levels.

Transculturation The converging and merging of cultures.

Transformationalist Transformationalists believe that globalization represents a significant shift, but they question the inevitability of its impacts.

Transitional justice A range of approaches to deal with the legacies of widespread or systematic human rights abuse, as they move from a period of violent conflict or oppression towards peace.

Translation The process of converting a source text, either spoken or written, into a different language.

Transmission model See Linear model.

Transnationalism The process by which migrants forge and sustain multi-stranded social relations that link together their societies of origin and settlement.

Uncertainty avoidance One of Hofstede's cultural dimensions, this refers to a culture's tolerance of ambiguity and acceptance of risk and uncertainty.

Value orientation theory This theory claims that cultures develop unique positions in five value orientations: man–nature orientation, activity orientation, time orientation, human nature orientation and relational orientation.

Values Concepts of ultimate significance and of long-term importance which inform the cultural group members on how to judge good or bad, right or wrong, and what is appropriate or not appropriate.

Verbal code Spoken or written language; it comprises a set of rules governing the use of words in creating a message.

Worldview The philosophical outlook a culture has about the nature of the universe, the nature of humankind, and the relationship between humanity and the universe.

REFERENCES

Adler, Peter S. (1975) 'The transitional experience: An alternative view of culture shock', *Journal of Humanistic Psychology*, 15: 13–23.

Alba, Richard D. (1990) *Ethnic Identity: The Transformation of White America*. New Haven, CT: Yale University Press.

Allport, Gordon (1954) *The Nature of Prejudice*. New York: Macmillan.

Altman, Irwin and Taylor, Dalmas (1973) *Social Penetration: The Development of Interpersonal Relationship*. New York: Holt, Rinehart & Winston.

American Society for Aesthetic Plastic Surgery (2017) *ASAPS 2016 statistics*. Accessed 1 January 2018 at: www.surgery.org/sites/default/files/ASAPS-Stats2016.pdf

Anderson, Benedict (1983) *Imagined Communities: Reflections on the Origin and Spread of Nationalism*. London: Verso.

Ang, Ien (2000) 'Transforming Chinese identities in Australia: Between assimilation, multiculturalism, and diaspora', in T. A. See (ed.), *Intercultural Relations, Cultural Transformation, and Identity*. Manila: Kaisa Para Sa Kaunlaran. pp. 248–258.

Anti-Semitism Worldwide Report (2016) *Anti-Semitism Worldwide Report*. Accessed 15 March 2018 at: https://english.tau.ac.il/sites/default/files/media_server/ENGLISH/Shoah_2016.pdf.

Ardizzoni, Michela (2007) *North/South, East/West: Mapping Italianness on Television*. Boulder, CO: Lexington Books.

Argent, Hedi (2003) *Models of Adoption Support: What Works and What Doesn't*. London: British Association of Adoption and Fostering.

Arweck, Elisabeth and Nesbitt, Eleanor (2010) 'Young people's identity formation in mixed-faith families: Continuity or discontinuity of religious traditions?', *Journal of Contemporary Religion*, 25(1): 67–87.

Asrul Hadi, Abdullah S. (2011) Foreign Worker Levy Hike in 2011. *The Malaysian Insider*. Accessed 2 January 2014 at: www.themalaysianinsider.com/malaysia/article/foreign-worker-levy-hike-in-2011/

Augsburger, David (1992) *Conflict Mediation across Cultures*. Louisville, KY: Westminster/John Knox Press.

Australian Bureau of Statistics (ABS) (2005) *Year Book Australia 2005* [online]. Accessed 2 October 2006 at: www.abs.gov.au/AUSSTATS/abs@nsf/Lookup/6A5AABD7621230ADCA256F7200832F77.

Banks, Ingrid (2000) *Hair Matters: Beauty, Power and Black Women's Consciousness*. New York: New York University Press.

Barbour, Stephen (2002) 'Nationalism, language, Europe', in S. Barbour and C. Carmichael (eds.), *Language and Nationalism in Europe*. Oxford: Oxford University Press. pp. 1–17.

Barker, Valerie, Giles, Howard, Noels, Kimberly, Duck, July, Hecht, Michael and Clement, Richarde (2001) 'The English-only movement: A communication analysis of changing perceptions of language vitality', *Journal of Communication*, 51(1): 3–37.

Barnlund, Dean C. (1970) 'A transactional model of communication', in J. Akin, A. Goldberg and G. Myers (eds.), *Language Behavior: A Book of Readings in Communication*. The Hague: Mouton & Co. pp. 43–61.

Basch, Linda, Schiller, Nina G. and Blanc, Cristina S. (1994) *Nations Unbound: Transnational Projects, Postcolonial Predicaments, and Deterritorialized Nation-States*. Langhorne: Gordon and Breach Publishers.

Baxter, Leslie (1988) 'A dialectical perspective on communication strategies in relationship development', in S. W. Duck (ed.), *Handbook of Personal Relationships: Theory, Research, and Interventions*. New York: Wiley. pp. 257–273.

BBC (2017) North Korean Media. *BBC News*. Accessible at www.bbc.com/news/world-asia-pacific-15259016.

Beamer, Linda and Varner, Iris (2008) *Intercultural Communication in the Global Workplace* (4th edn). Boston, MA: McGraw-Hill/Irwin.

Bennett, Milton J. (1986) 'A developmental approach to training for intercultural Sensitivity', *International Journal of Intercultural Relations*, 10(2): 179–195.

Bennett, Milton J. (1993) 'Towards ethnorelativism: A developmental model of intercultural sensitivity', in M. Paige (ed.), *Education for the Intercultural Experience*. Yarmouth, ME: Intercultural Press. pp. 343–354.

Berelson, Bernard R., Lazarsfeld, Paul F. and McPhee, William N. (1954) *Voting: A Study of Opinion Formation in a Presidential Campaign*. Chicago, IL: University of Chicago Press.

Berger, Charles R. and Calabrese, Richard J. (1975) 'Some explorations in initial interaction and beyond: Toward a developmental theory of interpersonal communication', *Human Communication Theory*, 1: 99–112.

Berlo, David (1960) *The Process of Communication*. New York: Holt, Rinehart & Winston.

Berry, John W. (1980) 'Acculturation as varieties of adaptation', in A. M. Padilla (ed.), *Acculturation: Theory, Models and Some New Findings*. Washington, DC: Westview Press. pp. 9–25.

Berry, John W. (2001) 'A psychology of immigration', *Journal of Social Issues*, 57: 615–631.

Berry, John W. (2005) 'Acculturation: Living successfully in two cultures', *International Journal of Intercultural Relations*, 29: 697–712.

Berry, John W. and Kalin, Rudolf (1995) 'Multicultural and ethnic attitudes in Canada: Overview of the 1991 survey', *Canadian Journal of Behavioral Science*, 27: 301–320.

Blake, Robert R. and Mouton, Jane S. (1964) *The Managerial Grid*. Houston, MA: Gulf.

Blank, Thomas, Schmidt, Peter and Westle, Bettina (2001) '*Patriotism – A contradiction, a possibility, or an empirical reality?*', paper presented at the ECPR Workshop 26, National Identity in Europe, Grenoble, France.

Bogardus, Emory S. (1933) 'A social distance scale', *Sociology and Social Research*, 17: 265–271.

Bonvillain, Nancy (2014) *Language, Culture and Communication: The Meaning of Messages* (7th edn). Upper Saddle River, NJ: Pearson/Prentice-Hall.

Bourhis, Richard Y., El-Geledi, Shaha and Sachdev, Itesh (2007) 'Language, ethnicity, and intergroup relations', in A. Weatherall, C. Gallois and B. M. Watson (eds.), *Language, Discourse, and Social Psychology*. Basingstoke: Palgrave Macmillan. pp. 15–50.

Bourhis, Richard Y., Moïse, Lena C., Perreault, Stephane and Senécal, Sacha (1997) 'Towards an interactive acculturation model: A social psychological approach', *International Journal of Psychology*, 32(6): 369–386.

Boussouar, Brice and Mailliet, Anne (2008) *German Nudists versus Polish Puritans* [online]. Accessed 22 November 2013 at: www.france24.com/en/20080803-usedom-island-baltic-sea-border-germany-nudists-poland-puritans.

Bratich, Jack (2015) 'Transnational flashpublics: Social media and affective contagions from Egypt to Occupy Wall Street', in M. Vujnovic and V. Mele (eds.), *Globalizing Cultures: Theories and Paradigms*. London: Brill Publications. pp. 174–195.

Brislin, Richard W. (1981) *Cross-Cultural Encounters*. Elmsford, NY: Pergamon.

Broome, Benjamin J. (1991) 'Building shared meaning: Implications of a relational approach to empathy for teaching intercultural communication', *Communication Education*, 40(1): 235–249.

Brown, Wendy (2011) *Walled States, Waning Sovereignty*. New York: Zoned Books.

Brubaker, Roger (2001) 'The return of assimilation? Changing perspectives on immigration and its sequels in France, Germany, and the United States', *Ethnic and Racial Studies*, 24(4): 531–548.

Buber, Martin (2000) *I and Thou*. New York: Simon & Schuster.

Buruma, Ian (2007) *Murder in Amsterdam: Liberal Europe, Islam, and the Limits of Tolerance*. London: Powell Books.

Bygnes, Susanne (2013) 'Ambivalent multiculturalism', *Sociology*, 47(1): 126–141.

Cantle, T. (2014) 'National identity, plurality and interculturalism', *Political Quarterly*, 85(3): 312–319.

Carbaugh, Donal, Berry, Michael and Nurmikari-Berry, Marjatta (2006) 'Coding personhood through cultural terms and practices: Silence and quietude as a Finnish "natural way of being"', *Journal of Language and Social Psychology*, 25: 203–220.

Carey, James (1977) 'Mass communication research and cultural studies: An American view', in J. Curran, M. Gurevitch and J. Woolacott (eds.), *Mass Communication and Society*. London: Sage. pp. 409–425.

Castells, Manuel (1997) *The Power of Identity*. Oxford: Blackwell Publishers.

Castles, Stephen (2000) *Ethnicity and Globalisation*. London: Sage.

Charon, Joel M. (2007) *Ten Questions: A Sociological Perspective* (6th edn). Belmont, CA: Wadsworth.

Chen, Guo-Ming (2017) 'The Yin and Yang of conflict management and resolution: A Chinese perspective', in X. Dai and G.-M. Chen (eds.), *Conflict Management and Intercultural Communication*. Abingdon and New York: Routledge. pp. 144–154.

Chen, Guo-ming and Starosta, William J. (2005) *Foundations of Intercultural Communication.* Lanham, MD: American University Press.

Chiang, Nora Lan-Hung (2011) 'Return migration: The case of the 1.5 generation of Taiwanese in Canada and New Zealand', *China Review*, 11(2): 91–123.

Chin, Christine B. N. (2003). 'Visible bodies, invisible work: State practices toward migrant women domestic workers in Malaysia', *Asian and Pacific Migration Journal*, 12(1/2): 49–74.

Chomsky, Noam (1975) *Reflections on Language.* New York: Pantheon.

Chomsky, Noam (1980) *Rules and Representations.* Oxford: Basil Blackwell.

Clark, Anna E. and Kashima, Yoshihisa (2007) 'Stereotypes help people connect with others in the community: A situated functional analysis of stereotype consistency bias in communication', *Journal of Personality and Social Psychology*, 93(6): 1028–1039.

Clifford, James (1997) 'Diasporas', in M. Guibenau and J. Rex (eds.), *The Ethnicity Reader: Nationalism, Multiculturalism and Migration.* Cambridge: Polity Press. pp. 283–290.

Coleman, Peter T. (2000) 'Power and conflict', in M. Deutsch and P. T. Coleman (eds.), *The Handbook of Conflict Resolution.* New York: New York Press. pp. 115–123.

Colovic, Ivan (2002) *Politics of Identity in Serbia.* New York: New York University Press.

Condon, John C. (1977) *Interpersonal Communication.* New York: Macmillan.

Condon, John C. and Yousef, Fathi S. (1975) *An Introduction to Intercultural Communication.* Indianapolis, IN: Bobbs-Merrill.

Cooper, Pamela J., Calloway-Thomas, Carolyn and Simonds, Cheri J. (2007) *Intercultural Communication: A Text with Readings.* Boston, MA: Pearson.

Craig, Robert T. (1999) 'Communication theory as a field', *Communication Theory*, 9(2): 119–161.

Dance, Frank E. X. (1970) 'The "concept" of communication', *Journal of Communication*, 20: 201–210.

de Saussure, Ferdinand (1983) *Course in General Linguistics.* Edited by C. Bally and A. Sechehaye, translated and annotated by Roy Harris. London: Duckworth.

Deetz, Stanley A. (1994) 'Future of the discipline: The challenges, the research and the social contribution', in S. A. Deetz (ed.), *Communication Yearbook 17.* Thousand Oaks, CA: Sage. pp. 565–600.

Democrazy on Deadline (2017) 'Media ownership'. Accessed 14 December 2017 at: www.pbs.org/independentlens/democracyondeadline/mediaownership.html.

Department of Education and Training (Australia) (2017) https://internationaleducation.gov.au/research/International-Student-Data/Pages/InternationalStudentData2017.aspx.

Dion, Karen K. and Dion, Kenneth L. (1993) 'Individualistic and collectivistic perspectives on gender and the cultural context of love and intimacy', *Journal of Social Issues*, 49: 53–69.

Dobbs, Richard, Manyika, James and Woetzel, Jonathan (2015) *No Ordinary Disruption: The Four Global Forces Breaking All the Trends.* New York: PublicAffairs.

Dodd, Carley H. (1998) *Dynamics of Intercultural Communication* (5th edn). Boston, MA: McGraw-Hill.

Dumitrascu, Sorin (2017) *Fundamentals of Cross Cultural Communication*. Independently published.

Edwards, Richard and Usher, Robin (2008) *Globalisation and Pedagogy: Space, Place and Identity* (2nd edn). Abingdon and New York: Routledge.

Ehrenreich, Barbara and Russell-Hochschild, Arlie (eds.) (2002) *Global Women; Nannies, Maids and Sex Workers in the New Economy*. New York: Henry Holt and Co.

Ekman, Paul and Friesen, Wallace V. (1969) 'The repertoire of nonverbal behavior: Categories, origins, usage, and coding', *Semiotica*, 1: 49–98.

Ekman, Paul and Friesen, Wallace V. (1971) 'Constants across cultures in the face and emotion', *Journal of Personality and Social Psychology*, 17: 124–129.

Elliott, Anthony (2001) *Concepts of the Self*. London: Polity Press.

Elliott, Deni (1997) 'The Great Hanshim earthquake and the ethics of intervention', in F. L. Casmir (ed.), *Ethics in Intercultural and International Communication*. Mahwah, NJ: Lawrence Erlbaum. pp. 43–58.

Evanoff, Richard (2004) 'Universalist, relativist, and constructivist approaches to intercultural ethics', *International Journal of Intercultural Relations*, 28: 439–458.

Everett, Daniel (2002) 'From threatened languages to threatened lives' [online]. Accessed 12 April 2009 at: http://yourdictionary.com/elr/everett.html.

Fisher-Yoshida, Beth (2005) 'Reframing conflict: Intercultural conflict as potential transformation', *The Journal of Intercultural Communication*, 8: 1–16.

Fiske, John (1982) *Introduction to Communication Studies*. London: Methuen.

Fitzpatrick, Frank (2017) 'Taking the "culture" out of "culture shock" – a critical review of literature on cross-cultural adjustment in international relocation', *Critical Perspectives on International Business*, 13(4): 278–296.

Flew, Terry (2014) *New Media* (4th edn). Melbourne: Oxford University Press.

Furnham, Adrian and Bochner, Stephen (1982) 'Social difficulty in a foreign culture: An empirical analysis of culture shock', in S. Bochner (ed.), *Culture in Contact: Studies in Cross-Cultural Interaction*. New York: Pergamon. pp. 161–198.

Gauntlett, David (2002) *Media, Gender and Identity*. New York: Routledge.

Geertz, Clifford (1973) *The Interpretation of Cultures*. New York: Basic Books.

Gershon, Ilana (2010) *The Break-Up 2.0: Disconnecting over New Media*. Ithaca, NY: Cornell University Press.

Gessen, Masha (2017) *The Future Is History: How Totalitarianism Reclaimed Russia*. New York: Riverhead Books.

Gitlin, Todd (1978) 'Media sociology: The dominant paradigm', *Theory and Society*, 6(2): 205–253.

Glaser, Linda B. (2016) 'Migration, immigration and refugees today'. Accessed 10 January 2018 at: http://as.cornell.edu/mes/migration-immigration-and-refugees-today.

Godin, Marie-Noelle (2006) 'Urban youth language in multicultural Sweden', *Scandinavian-Canadian Studies*, 16(2): 126–141.

Goffman, Erving (1969) *The Presentation of Self in Everyday Life*. London: Penguin Books.

Goss, Blaine (1995) *The Psychology of Human Communication* (2nd edn). Prospect Heights, IL: Waveland Press.

Gramsci, Antonio (2000) *The Antonio Gramsci Reader. Selected Writings: 1916–1935.* New York: New York University Press.

Greelis, Jim (2007) 'Pigeons in military history' [online]. Accessed 7 October 2013 at www.theamericanpigeonmuseum.org/military.html.

Gudykunst, William B. (2004) *Bridging Differences: Effective Intergroup Communication* (4th edn). Thousand Oaks, CA: Sage.

Gudykunst, William B. and Kim, Young Y. (1984) *Communicating with Strangers: An Approach to Intercultural Communication.* New York: McGraw-Hill.

Gudykunst, William B. and Ting-Toomey, Stella (1988) 'Verbal communication styles', in W. B. Gudykunst and S. Ting-Toomey (eds.), *Culture and Interpersonal Communication.* Newbury Park, CA: Sage. pp. 99–115.

Guirdham, Maureen and Guirdham, Oliver (2017) *Communicating across Cultures at Work* (4th edn). London: Palgrave.

Gullahorn, John T. and Gullahorn, Jeanne E. (1963) 'An extension of the U-curve hypothesis', *Journal of Social Issues*, 19: 33–47.

Gupta, Nilanjana (1998) *Switching Channels: Ideologies of Television in India.* New Delhi: Oxford University Press.

Hall, Bradford J. (2005) *Among Cultures: The Challenge of Communication* (2nd edn). Belmont, CA: Thomson Wadsworth.

Hall, Edward T. (1959) *The Silent Language.* New York: Doubleday.

Hall, Edward, T. (1966) *The Hidden Dimension.* New York: Doubleday.

Hall, Edward T. (1976) *Beyond Culture.* New York: Doubleday.

Hall, Edward, T. (1977) *Beyond Culture.* Garden City, NY: Doubleday.

Hall, Edward T. and Hall, Mildred R. (1990) *Understanding Cultural Differences: Germans, French, and Americans.* Yarmouth, ME: Intercultural Press.

Hall, Stuart (2001) 'Negotiating Caribbean identities', in B. Meeks and F. Lindahl (eds.), *New Caribbean Thought: A Reader.* Jamaica, Barbados, Trinidad and Tobago: The University of the West Indies Press. pp. 122–145.

Hall, Stuart (2014) 'The whites of their eyes', in G. Dines and J. M. Humez (eds.), *Gender, Race, and Class in Media: A Critical Reader* (4th edn). London: Sage. pp. 81–85.

Hardiman, Rita (2001) 'Reflections on white identity development theory', in C. L. Wijeyesinghe and J. B. Bailey (eds.), *New Perspectives on Racial Identity Development: A Theoretical and Practical Anthology.* New York: New York University Press. pp. 12–34.

Harwood, Jake (2017) 'Music and relations: Exacerbating conflict and building harmony through music', in G. P. De Marchis (ed.), *Review of Communication Research.* Published online: January 2017. DOI:10.12840/issn.2255-4165.2017.05.01.012.

Haviland, William A., Prins, Harald E. L., McBride, Bunny and Walrath, Dana (2011) *Cultural Anthrology: The Human Challenge* (13th edn). Belmont, CA: Wadsworth Cengage Learning.

Hecht, Michael, Warren, Jennifer R., Jung, Eura and Krieger, Janice L. (2005) 'The communication theory of identity', in W. B. Gudykunst (ed.), *Theorizing about Intercultural Communication*. Thousand Oaks, CA: Sage. pp. 257–278.

Heidelberg Institute for International Conflict Research (HIICR) (2016) *Conflict Barometer, 2016*. Accessible at www.hiik.de/en/konfliktbarometer/pdf/ConflictBarometer_2016.pdf.

Hendrix, Katherine G. (2017) 'Home as respite for the working-class academic', in A. González and Y.-W. Chen (eds.), *Our Voices* (6th edn). New York: Oxford University Press. pp. 260–266.

Hestroni, Amir (2000) 'Relationship between values and appeals in Israeli advertising: A smallest space analysis', *Journal of Advertising*, 29(3): 55–68.

Hiew, D., Halford, K., van de Vijver, F. R. and Liu, S. (2016) 'Communication and relationship satisfaction in Chinese, Western and intercultural Chinese-Western couples', *Journal of Family Psychology*, 30(2): 193–202.

Hirchman, Charles (2004) 'The role of religion in the origins and adaptations of immigrant groups in the United States', *International Migration Review*, 38(3): 1206–1233.

Hilton, James L. and von Hippel, William (1996) 'Stereotypes', *Annual Review of Psychology*, 47: 237–271.

Hockett, Charles F. (1960) 'The origin of speech', *Scientific American*, 203: 89–97.

Hoersting, Raquel C. and Jenkins, Sharon R. (2011) 'No place to call home: Cultural homelessness, self-esteem and cross-cultural identities', *International Journal of Intercultural Relations*, 35: 17–30.

Hoff, Erika (2001) *Language Development* (2nd edn). New York: Brooks/Cole.

Hofstede, Geert (1980) *Culture's Consequences: International Differences in Work-Related Values*. Beverly Hills, CA: Sage.

Hofstede, Geert (1991) *Cultures and Organizations: Software of the Mind*. New York: McGraw-Hill.

Hofstede, Geert (2001) *Culture's Consequences: Comparing Values, Behaviors, Institutions and Organizations across Nations* (2nd edn). Thousand Oaks, CA: Sage.

Hofstede, Geert and Bond, Michael H. (1988) 'The Confucius connection: From cultural roots to economic growth', *Organizational Dynamics*, 16: 5–21.

Hogg, Michael (2003) 'Intergroup relations', in J. Delamater (ed.), *Handbook of Social Psychology*. New York: Kluwer Academic/Plenum Publishers. pp. 479–501.

Hogg, Michael A. and Abrams, Dominic (1988) *Social Identifications: A Social Psychology of Intergroup Relations and Group Processes*. London: Routledge.

Hogg, Michael A. and Terry, Deborah J. (2000) 'Social identity and self-categorization processes in organizational contexts', *The Academy of Management Review*, 25(1): 121–140.

Houkamaua, Carla A. (2010) 'Identity construction and reconstruction: The role of socio-historical contexts in shaping Maori women's identity', *Social Identities*, 16(2): 179–196.

House, Robert J., Hanges, Paul J., Javidan, Mansour J., Dorfman, Peter W. and Gupta, Vipin (eds.) (2004) *Culture, Leadership and Organizations: The GLOBE Study of 62 Societies*. Thousand Oaks, CA: Sage.

Hübinette, Tobias and Lundström, Catrin (2011) 'Sweden after the recent election', *NORA: Nordic Journal of Feminist and Gender Research*, 19(1): 42–52.

Hui, C. Harry and Triandis, Harry C. (1986) 'Individualism-collectivism: A study of cross-cultural researchers', *Journal of Cross-Cultural Psychology*, 17(2): 225–248.

Hutchinson, John (1987) *The Dynamics of Cultural Nationalism: The Gaelic Revival and the Creation of the Irish Nation State*. London: Allen and Unwin.

Hwang, Hyisung and Matsumoto, David (2017) 'Emotion display and expression', in L. Chen (ed.), *Intercultural Communication*. Boston, MA and Berlin: De Gruyter. pp. 219–238.

Institute of International Education (IIE) (2017) 'IIE releases Open Doors 2017 data' [online]. Accessed 26 June 2017 at: www.iie.org/Why-IIE/Announcements/2017-11-13-Open-Doors-Data.

International Organization for Migration (IOM) (2006) *World Migration* [online]. Accessed 24 July 2009 at: www.iom.int/iomwebsite/Publication/ServletSearchPublication?event=detail&id=4171.

Internet Society (2012) 'Global Internet User Survey 2012'. Accessed 12 September 2017 at: http://wayback.archiveit.org/9367/20170911022514/www.internetsociety.org/internet/global-internet-user-survey-2012.

Jandt, Fred (2016) *An Introduction to Intercultural Communication: Identities in a Global Society* (8th edn). Thousand Oaks, CA: Sage.

Jeong Jae-Seon, Seul-Hi Lee and Sang-Gil Lee (2017) 'Korean Wave – when Indonesians routinely consume Korean pop culture', *International Journal of Communication*, 11(2): 2288–2307.

Jitpiromsri, Srisompob (2008) '4.5 years of the southern fire: The failure of policy in Red Zone', *DWS's Research Database* [online]. Accessed 18 September 2008 at: www.deepsouthwatch.org/index.php?l=content&id=265.

Jones, Gavin and Shen, Hsiu-hua (2008) 'International marriage in East and Southeast Asia: Trends and research emphasis', *Citizenship Studies*, 12: 9–25.

Katzenbach, Jon R. and Smith, Douglas K. (2003) *The Wisdom of Teams: Creating the High-Performance Organization*. New York: Harper Business.

Keblusek, Lauren, Giles, Howard and Maass, Anne (2017) 'Communication and group life: How language and symbols shape intergroup relations', *Group Processes & Intergroup Relations*, 20(5): 632–643.

Khan, Anber Y. and Kamal, Anila (2010) 'Exploring reactions to invasion of personal space in university students', *Journal of Behavioural Sciences*, 20(2): 80–99.

Kim, Young Y. (1988) *Cross-Cultural Adaptation: Current Approaches*. Newbury Park, CA: Sage.

Kim, Young Y. (2008) 'Intercultural personhood: Globalization and a way of being', *International Journal of Intercultural Relations*, 32: 359–368.

Kim, Young Y. (2015) 'From culture to interculture: Communication, adaptation, and identity transformation in the globalizing world', in L. A. Samovar, R. E. Porter, E. R. McDaniel and C. S. Roy (eds.), *Intercultural Communication: A Reader*. Boston, MA: Cengage Learning. pp. 430–437.

Kimball, Charles (2002) *When Religion Becomes Evil*. New York: Harper Collins.

Kincaid, D. Lawrence (2009) 'Convergence theory', in S. W. Littlejohn and K. A. Foss (eds.), *Encyclopedia of Communication Theory*. Thousand Oaks, CA: Sage. pp. 189–192.

King, Ross (2008) *Kuala Lumpur and Putrajaya: Negotiating Urban Space in Malaysia*. Singapore: National University of Singapore Press.

Klopf, Donald W. (1995) *Intercultural Encounters: The Fundamentals of Intercultural Communication*. Englewood, CO: Morton.

Kluckhohn, Florence and Strodtbeck, Frederick (1961) *Variations in Value Orientations*. Evanston, IL: Row, Peterson.

Knapp, Mark L. and Hall, Judith A. (1997) *Nonverbal Communication in Human Interaction* (4th edn). Philadelphia, PA: Harcourt, Brace, Jovanovich.

Kolar-Panov, Dona (1997) *Video, War and the Diasporic Imagination*. New York: Routledge.

Kosic, Ankica, Mannetti, Lucia and Sam, David L. (2005) 'The role of majority attitudes towards out-group in the perception of the acculturation strategies of immigrants', *International Journal of Intercultural Relations*, 29: 273–288.

Kraidy, Marwan (2005) *Hybridity, or the Cultural Logic of Globalization*. Philadelphia, PA: Temple University Press.

Kraimer, Maria, Bolino, Mark and Mead, Brandon (2016) 'Themes in expatriate and repatriate research over four decades: What do we know and what do we still need to learn?', *Annual Review of Organizational Psychology and Organizational Behaviour*, 3(1): 83–109.

LaFromboise, Teresa, Coleman, Hardin L. K. and Gerton, Jennifer (1993) 'Psychological Impact of biculturalism: Evidence and theory', *Psychological Bulletin*, 114: 395–412.

Lakoff, Robin (1975) *Language and Woman's Place*. New York: Harper & Row.

Lasswell, Harold (1948) 'The structure and function of communication in society', in L. Boyson (ed.), *The Communication of Ideas*. New York: Harper. pp. 32–51.

Lee, Julian C. H. (2016) 'Reflections on the global condition', in J. Lee (ed.), *Narratives of Globalization*. London: Rowman & Littlefield. pp. 1–6.

Lee, Kang (2000) *Childhood Cognitive Development: The Essential Readings*. Oxford: Blackwell.

Lesko, Alexandra C. and Corpus, Jennifer H. (2006) 'Discounting the difficult: How high-math-identified women respond to stereotype threat', *Sex Roles*, 54: 113–125.

Lewicki, Roy J., Saunders, David M., Barry, Bruce and Minton, John (2003) *Essentials of Negotiation* (3rd edn). Boston, MA: McGraw-Hill/Irwin.

Liebkind, Karmela and Jasinskaja-Lahti, Inga (2000) 'The influence of experiences of discrimination on psychological stress: A comparison of seven immigrant groups', *Journal of Community & Applied Social Psychology*, 10(1): 1–16.

Lindell, Martin and Arvonen, Jouko (1996) 'The Nordic management style in a European context', *International Studies of Management and Organization*, 26(3): 73–93.

Lippmann, Walter (1922) *Public Opinion*. New York: Macmillan.

Littlejohn, Stephen W. (1996) *Theories of Human Communication* (5th edn). Belmont, CA: Wadsworth.

Liu, Shuang (2007) 'Living with others: Mapping the routes to acculturation in a multicultural society', *International Journal of Intercultural Relations*, 31(6): 761–778.

Liu, Shuang (2015) *Identity, Hybridity and Cultural Home*. London: Rowman & Littlefield International.

Looney, Rob (2004) 'Saudization and sound economic reforms: Are the two compatible?', *Strategic Insights*, 3(2): 1–9.

Louw, Eric (2004a) 'Political power, national identity, and language: The case of Afrikaans', *International Language of Social Languages*, 170(1): 43–58.

Louw, Eric (2004b) *The Rise, Fall, and Legacy of Apartheid*. Westport, CT: Praeger.

Lowenstein, Ralph L. and Merrill, John C. (1990) *Macromedia: Mission, Message, and Morality*. New York: Longman.

Lustig, Myron W. and Koester, Jolene (2013) *Intercultural Competence: Interpersonal Communication across Cultures* (7th edn). Boston, MA: Pearson.

Lysgaard, Sverre (1955) 'Adjustment in a foreign society: Norwegian Fullbright grantees visiting the United States', *International Social Science Bulletin*, 7: 45–51.

Mankekar, Purnima (2015) *Unsettling India: Affect, Temporality, Transnationality*. Durham, NC: Duke University Press.

Marden, Peter and Mercer, David (1998) 'Locating strangers: Multiculturalism, citizenship and nationhood in Australia', *Political Geography*, 17(8): 939–958.

Markus, Hazel R. and Kitayama, Shinobu (1991) 'Culture and the self: Implications for cognition, emotion, and motivation', *Psychological Review*, 98: 224–253.

Marsella, Anthony J. (2017) 'Assessing fractionation: Principles for arbitrating the "common good"'. Accessible at: www.transcend.org/tms/2017/05/addressing-fractionation-principles-for-artibrating-the-common-good.

Martin, Judith E. and Nakayama, Thomas K. (2001) *Experiencing Intercultural Communication: An Introduction*. Mountain View, CA: Mayfield Publishing Company.

Massey, Douglas and Taylor, Edward J. (eds.) (2004) *International Migration: Prospects and Policies*. Oxford: Oxford University Press.

Mastro, Dana E. and Greenberg, Bradley S. (2000) 'The portrayal of racial minorities on prime time television', *Journal of Broadcasting and Electronic Media*, 44(4): 690–703.

McCombs, Maxwell and Shaw, Donald (1972) 'The agenda-setting function of the mass media', *Public Opinion Quarterly*, 36: 176–187.

McCowan, Clint (2003) 'Imagining the Zapatistas: Rebellion, representation and popular culture', *International Third World Studies Journal and Review*, XIV: 29–34.

McDaniel, Edwin R. and Samovar, Larry A. (2015) 'Understanding and applying intercultural communication in the global community: The fundamentals', in L. A. Samovar, R. E. Porter, E. R. McDaniel and C. S. Roy (eds.), *Intercultural Communication: A Reader*. Boston, MA: Cengage Learning. pp. 5–16.

McLuhan, Marshall (1964) *Understanding Media: The Extension of Man*. New York: McGraw-Hill.

McSweeney, Brendan (2002) 'Hofstede's model of national cultural differences and their consequences: A triumph of faith – a failure of analysis', *Human Relations*, 55: 89–118.

Mehrabian, Albert (1982) *Silent Messages: Implicit Communication of Emotion and Attitudes* (2nd edn). Belmont, CA: Wadsworth.

Merry, Sally E. (1989) 'Mediation in cross-cultural perspective', in K. Kressell and D. Pruitt (eds.), *The Mediation of Disputes: Empirical Studies in the Resolution of Social Conflict*. San Francisco, CA: Jossey-Bass. pp. 75–103.

Miller, Daniel (2011) *Tales from Facebook*. Cambridge: Polity Press.

Minkov, Michael and Hofstede, Geert (2012) 'Hofstede's fifth dimenions: New evidence from the World Values Survey', *Journal of Cross-Cultural Psychology*, 43(1): 3–14.

Mohanty, Chandra Talpade (2003) *Feminism without Borders: Decolonizing Theory, Practicing Solidarity*. Durham, NC: Duke University Press.

Moreton-Robinson, Aileen (2015) *The White Possessive: Property, Power and Indigenous Sovereignty*. Minneapolis, MN: University of Minnesota Press.

Morley, David (2000) *Home Territories: Media, Mobility and Identity*. London and New York: Routledge.

Morley, David (2017) *Communications and Mobility*. London: Wiley-Blackwell.

Morley, David and Robins, Kevin (1995) *Spaces of Identity: Global Media, Electronic Landscapes and Cultural Boundaries*. London: Routledge.

Morris, Desmond (1994) *The Human Animal: A Personal View of the Human Species*. New York: Crown Publishers.

Mortensen, C. David (1972) *Communication: The Study of Human Interaction*. New York: McGraw-Hill.

Motley, Michael (1990) 'On whether one can(not) communicate: An examination via traditional communication postulates', *Western Journal of Speech Communication*, 54(1): 1–20.

Mulder, Niels (1996) *Inside Thai Society: Interpretations of Everyday Life*. Amsterdam: Pepin Press.

Mullen, Brian and Hu, Li-Tze (1989) 'Perceptions of ingroup and outgroup variability: A meta-analytic integration', *Basic and Applied Social Psychology*, 10: 233–252.

Navitski, Rielle (2017) *Public Spectacles of Violence*. Durham, NC: Duke University Press.

Neuliep, James (2017) *Intercultural Communication: A Contextual Approach* (7th edn). New York: Sage.

Newbold, Chris (1995) 'The media effects tradition', in O. Boyd-Barrett and C. Newbold (eds.), *Approaches to Media: A Reader*. London: Hodder Arnold. pp. 118–123.

Nguyen, Angela-Minh Tu D. and Benet-Martínez, Verónica (2013) 'Biculturalism and adjustment: A meta-analysis', *Journal of Cross-Cultural Psychology*, 44: 122–159.

Nguyen, Han (2017) 'Indonesia is fastest growing country for internet use'. Accessible at: www.rappler.com/world/regions/asia-pacific/indonesia/bahasa/englishedition/159593-internet-social-media-statistics.

Niehoff, Arthur (1964) 'Theravada Buddhism: A vehicle for technical change', *Human Organization*, 23: 108–112.

Nisbett, Richard E. and Miyamoto, Yuri (2005) 'The influence of culture: Holistic versus analytic perception', *Trends in Cognitive Sciences*, 9(10): 467–473.

Oberg, Kalervo (1960) 'Culture shock: Adjustment to new cultural environments', *Practical Anthropology*, 7(4): 177–182.

Office for Democratic Institutions and Human Rights (ODIHR) (2008) *Anti-Semitism Worldwide Report* [online]. Accessed 18 April 2008 at: www1.yadvashem.org/about_holocaust/holocaust_antisemitism/media_holocaust.html#FAQS.

Ogden, Denise T., Ogden, James R. and Schau, Hope J. (2004) 'Exploring the impact of culture and acculturation on consumer purchase decisions: Toward a microcultural perspective', *Academy of Marketing Science Review*, 3 [online]. Available at: www.amsreview.org/articles/ogden03_2004.pdf.

Ota, Hiroshi, McCann, Robert M. and Honeycutt, James M. (2012) 'Inter-Asian variability in intergenerational communication', *Human Communication Research*, 38(2): 172–198.

Pacanowsky, Michael E. and O'Donnell-Trujillo, Nick (1983) 'Organizational communication as cultural performance', *Communication Monographs*, 50: 126–147.

Park, Hyun-Sun and Rubin, Allen (2012) 'The mediating role of acculturative stress in the relationship between acculturation level and depression among Korean immigrants in the U.S.', *International Journal of Intercultural Relations*, 36(5): 611–623.

Park, Robert E. (1924) 'The concept of social distance', *Journal of Applied Sociology*, 33(6): 881–893.

Pearce, Barnett W. (2005) 'The coordinated management of meaning (CMM)', in W. B. Gudykunst (ed.), *Theorizing about Intercultural Communication*. Thousand Oaks, CA: Sage. pp. 35–54.

Pettigrew, Thomas F. (1997) 'Generalized intergroup contact effects on prejudice', *Personality and Social Psychology Bulletin*, 23: 173–185.

Pew Internet (2017) *Themes for 2017*. Accessed 3 January 2018 at: www.pewresearch.org/.

Pew Research Center (2016) *Key facts about the world's refugees*. Accessed 10 January 2018 at: www.pewresearch.org/fact-tank/2016/10/05/key-facts-about-the-worlds-refugees.

Phinney, Jean S. (1990) 'Ethnic identity in adolescents and adults: A review of research', *Psychological Bulletin*, 108: 499–514.

Piaget, Jean (1977) *The Development of Thought: Equilibration and Cognitive Structures*. New York: Viking Press.

Pondy, Louis R. (1967) 'Organizational conflict: Concepts and models', *Administrative Science Quarterly*, 12: 296–320.

Putnam, Linda L. and Poole, Marshall S. (1987) 'Conflict and negotiation', in F. Jablin, L. Putnam, K. Roberts and L. Porter (eds.), *Handbook of Organizational Communication*. Newbury Park, CA: Sage. pp. 549–599.

Redfield, Robert, Linton, Ralph and Herskovits, Melville J. (1936) 'Memorandum for the study of acculturation', *American Anthropologist*, 38: 149–152.

Reid, Scott A. and Giles, Howard (2010) 'Ethnolinguistic vitality', in J. M. Levine and M. A. Hogg (eds.), *Encyclopedia of Group Process and Intergroup Relations*. Thousand Oaks, CA: Sage. pp. 252–255.

Ritzer, George (2010) *Globalization: A Basic Text*. Oxford: Wiley-Blackwell.

Robinson, Peter W. (1996) *Deceit, Delusion, and Detection*. Thousand Oaks, CA: Sage.

Robinson, Piers (1999) 'The CNN effect: Can the news media drive foreign policy?', *Review of International Studies*, 25: 301–309.

Rogers, Everett M. (1995) *Diffusion of Innovations* (4th edn). New York: Free Press.

Rogers, Everett M. (1999) 'Georg Simmel's concept of the stranger and intercultural communication research', *Communication Theory*, 9(1): 1–25.

Rogers, Everett M. and Steinfatt, Thomas M. (1999) *Intercultural Communication*. Prospect Heights, IL: Waveland Press.

Rohmann, Anette, Florack, Arnd and Piontkowski, Ursula (2006) 'The role of discordant acculturation attitudes in perceived threat: An analysis of host and immigrant attitudes in Germany', *International Journal of Intercultural Relations*, 30: 683–702.

Rooney, David, Paulsen, Neil, Callan, Victor J., Brabant, Madeleine, Gallois, Cindy and Jones, Elizabeth (2010) 'A new role for place identity in managing organizational change', *Management Communication Quarterly*, 24(1): 44–73.

Sachdev, Itesh and Bhatia, Tej (2013) 'Language attitudes in South Asia', in H. Giles and B. M. Watson (eds.), *The Social Meanings of Languages, Dialects, and Accents: International Perspectives on Speech Styles*. New York: Peter Lang. pp. 141–156.

Samovar, Larry A., Porter, Richard E., McDaniel, Edwin R. and Roy, Carolyn S. (eds.) (2013) *Communication between Cultures* (8th edn). Boston, MA: Wadsworth.

Savani, Krishna, Morris, Michael W. and Naidu, N. V. R. (2012) 'Deference in Indians' decision making: Introjected goals or injunctive norms?', *Journal of Personality and Social Psychology*, 102(4): 685–699.

Sax, David (2018) 'Toronto suddenly has a new craving: Syrian food'. Accessed 24 January 2018 at: www.nytimes.com/2018/01/12/dining/toronto-syrian-food.html.

Sayegh, Liliane and Lasry, Jean-Claude (1993) 'Immigrants' adaptation in Canada: Assimilation, acculturation, and orthogonal cultural identification', *Canadian Psychology*, 34(1): 98–109.

Schramm, Wilbur (1954) 'How communication works', in W. Schramm (ed.), *The Process and Effects of Communication*. Urbana, IL: University of Illinois Press. pp. 3–26.

Schutz, William (1966) *The Interpersonal Underworld*. Palo, Alto, CA: Science and Behavior Books.

Schwartz, Shalom H. (1994) 'Beyond individualism/collectivism: New cultural dimensions of values', in U. Kim, H. C. Triandis, C. Kagitcibasi, S. C. Choi and G. Yoon (eds.), *Individualism and Collectivism: Theory, Method, and Applications*. Thousand Oaks, CA: Sage. pp. 85–119.

Schwartz, Shalom H. (1999) 'A theory of cultural values and some implications for work', *Applied Psychology: An International Review*, 48(1): 23–47.

Seib, Philip (1997) *Headline Diplomacy: How News Coverage Affects Foreign Policy*. London: Praeger.

Seton-Watson, Harry (1977) *Nations and States: An Enquiry into the Origins of Nations and the Politics of Nationalism*. Boulder, CO: Westview Press.

Shannon, Claude and Weaver, Warren (1949) *The Mathematical Theory of Communication*. Urbana, IL: University of Illinois Press.

Shepherd, Gregory J. (1993) 'Building a discipline of communication', *Journal of Communication*, 43(3): 83–91.

Sidanius, Jim and Pratto, Felicia (1999) *Social Dominance: An Intergroup Theory of Social Hierarchy and Oppression*. Cambridge: Cambridge University Press.

Siddique Haroon and Laughland, Oliver (2017) 'Charlottesville: United Nations warns US over "alarming" racism', *The Guardian*, 23 August. Accessed 15 January 2018 at: www.theguardian.com/world/2017/aug/23/charlottesville-un-committee-warns-us-over-rise-of-racism.

Siegman, Aron W. and Feldstein, S. (eds.) (2014) *Multichannel Integrations of Nonverbal Behavior*. New York: Psychology Press.

Simič, Olivera (2010) 'Breathing sense into women's lives shattered by war: DAH Theatre Belgrade', *Law Text Culture*, 2(1): 117–133.

Simmel, Georg (1950) *The Sociology of Georg Simmel*. Translated by Kurt H. Wolff. New York: Free Press.

Singer, Marshall (1987) *Intercultural Communication: A Perceptual Approach*. Englewood Cliffs, NJ: Prentice-Hall.

Skalli, Loubna H. (2006) *Through a Local Prism*. Lanham, MD: Lexington Books.

Slobin, Dan I. (2000) 'Verbalized events: A dynamic approach to linguistic relativity and determinism', in S. Niemeier and R. Dirven (eds.), *Evidence for Linguistic Relativity*. Amsterdam/Philadelphia, PA: John Benjamins. pp. 107–138.

Smith, Anthony D. (2007) 'Nations in decline? The erosion and persistence of modern national identities', in M. Young, E. Zuelow and A. Sturm (eds.), *Nationalism in a Global Era*. London: Routledge. pp. 16–30.

Snikars, Peller and Vonderau, Patrick (eds.) (2009) *The YouTube Reader*. Stockholm: National Library of Sweden.

Soysal, Yasemin N. (1994) *Limits of Citizenship: Migrants and Postnational Membership in Europe*. Chicago, IL: University of Chicago Press.

Spitzberg, Brian H. and Changnon, Gabrielle (2009) 'Conceptualizing intercultural competence', in D. K. Deardorff (ed.), *The SAGE Handbook of Intercultural Competence*. Thousand Oaks, CA: Sage. pp. 2–51.

Sveningsson, Elm (2007) 'Young people's presentations of relationships in a Swedish internet community', *Young*, 15(2): 145–156.

Synnott, Anthony (1996) 'Sociology of smell', *Canadian Review of Sociology and Anthropology*, 28(4): 437–460.

Tajfel, Henri (1978) 'Social categorisation, social identity and social comparison', in H. Tajfel (ed.), *Differentiation between Social Groups: Studies in the Social Psychology of Intergroup Relations*. London: Academic Press. pp. 61–76.

Tannen, Deborah (1990) *You Just Don't Understand: Women and Men in Conversation*. New York: William Morrow/Ballantine.

Tannen, Deborah (1994) *Talking from 9 to 5: How Women's and Men's Conversational Styles Affect Who Gets Heard, Who Gets Credit, and What Gets Done at Work*. New York: Oxford University Press.

Tanti, Chris, Stukas, Arthur A., Halloran, Michael J. and Foddy, Margaret (2011) 'Social identity change: Shifts in social identity during adolescence', *Journal of Adolescence*, 34(3): 555–567.

Tardif-Williams, Christine Y. and Fisher, Lianne (2009) 'Clarifying the link between acculturation experiences and parent–child relationships among families in cultural transition: The promise of contemporary critiques of acculturation psychology', *International Journal of Intercultural Relations*, 33: 150–161.

The Telegraph (2017) 'Who owns Facebook and when was it created?' Accessible at: www.telegraph. co.uk/technology/0/owns-facebook-created/.

Ting-Toomey, Stella (1994) 'Managing intercultural conflicts effectively', in L. Samovar and R. Porter (eds.), *Intercultural Communication: A Reader* (7th edn). Belmont, CA: Wadsworth. pp. 360–372.

Ting-Toomey, Stella (2005a) 'Identity negotiation theory: Crossing cultural boundaries', in W. B. Gudykunst (ed.), *Theorizing about Intercultural Communication*. Thousand Oaks, CA: Sage. pp. 211–233.

Ting-Toomey, Stella (2005b) 'The matrix of face: Updated face-negotiation theory', in W. B. Gudykunst (ed.), *Theorizing about Intercultural Communication*. Thousand Oaks, CA: Sage. pp. 71–92.

Ting-Toomey, Stella and Chung, Leeva C. (2005) *Understanding Intercultural Communication*. Los Angeles, CA: Roxbury Publishing Company.

Ting-Toomey, Stella and Kurogi, Atsuko (1998) 'Facework competence in intercultural conflict: An updated face-negotiation theory', *International Journal of Intercultural Relations*, 22: 187–225.

Trammell, Key, Tarkowski, Alek, Hofmokl, Justyna and Sapp, Amanda (2006) 'Examining Polish bloggers through content analysis', *Journal of Computer-Mediated Communication*, 11: 702–722.

Triandis, Harry C. (1977) *Interpersonal Behavior*. Monterey, CA: Brooks/Cole.

Triandis, Harry C. (1984) 'A theoretical framework for the more efficient construction of culture assimilators', *International Journal of Intercultural Relations*, 8: 301–330.

Tuchman, Gaye (1978) *Making News: A Study in the Construction of Reality*. New York: Free Press.

Turner, Graeme (1994) *Understanding Celebrity*. London: Sage.

United Nations Department of Economic and Social Affairs, Population Division (2016) *International Migration Report 2015: Highlights* (ST/ESA/SER.A/375). . New York: United Nations. Accessed 10 January 2018 at: www.un.org/development/desa/en/news/population/world-population-prospects-2017.html.

United Nations, Department of Economics and Social Affairs, Population Division (2017) World Population Prospects: The 2017 Revision. Accessed 15 January 2018 at: https://esa.un.org/unpd/wpp/publications/Files/WPP2017_KeyFindings.pdf

United Nations High Commissioner for Refugees (UNHCR) (2018) 'Figures at a glance'. United Nations High Commissioner for Refugees. Accessed 10 January 2018 at: www.unhcr.org/en-au/figures-at-a-glance.html.

Van Dijk, Teun A. (2004) *Ideology and Discourse: A Multidisciplinary Introduction*. Barcelona: PFU.

Volčič, Zala (2005) 'The notion of "The West" in the Serbian national imaginary', *European Journal of Cultural Studies*, 8(2): 155–175.

Volčič, Zala and Simič, Olivera (2016) 'Geographies of crime and justice', in A. Björkdahl and S. Buckley-Zistel (eds.), *Spatializing Peace and Conflict: Mapping the Production of Places, Sites and Scales of Violence.* Basingstoke: Palgrave Macmillan, pp. 286–295.

Vukeljic, Marijana (2008) *Vpliv medijev na oblikovanje identitete druge generacije Srbov v Sloveniji* [*The Effects of Media on Forming Identities of the Serbian Second Generation in Slovenia*]. Maribor: Univerza Maribor Press.

Ward, Colleen (2008) 'Thinking outside the Berry Boxes: New perspectives on identity, acculturation and intergroup relations', *International Journal of Intercultural Relations*, 32: 114–123.

Ward, Colleen, Okura, Yutaka, Kennedy, Antony and Kojima, Takahiro (1998) 'The U-curve on trial: A longitudinal study of psychological and sociocultural adjustment during cross-cultural transition', *International Journal of Intercultural Relations*, 22(3): 277–291.

Wasko, Janet (2001) *Understanding Disney: The Manufacture of Fantasy.* Cambridge: Polity Press.

Watzlawick, Paul, Bavelas, Janet B. and Jackson, Don D. (1967) *Pragmatics of Human Communication.* New York: W. W. Norton & Company.

Weber, Elke U. and Hsee, Christopher (1998) 'Cross-cultural differences in risk perception, but cross-cultural similarities in attitudes towards perceived risk', *Management Sciences*, 44: 1205–1217.

Weinstein, Eugene A. (1969) 'The development of interpersonal competence', in D. A. Goslin (ed.), *Handbook of Socialization and Research.* Chicago, IL: Rand McNally. pp. 753–775.

Whorf, Benjamin L. (1956) *Language, Thought and Reality: Selected Writings.* Edited by J. B. Carroll. Cambridge, MA: MIT Press.

Williams, Raymond (1989) *Resources of Hope: Culture, Democracy, Socialism.* London: Verso.

Wittgenstein, Ludwig (1922/2001) *Tractatus Logico-Philosophicus.* London: Routledge.

Woodrow, Lindy (2006) 'Anxiety and speaking English as a second language', *RELC Journal*, 37: 308–327.

Xi, Changsheng (1994) 'Individualism and collectivism in American and Chinese societies', in A. Gonzalez, M. Houston and V. Chen (eds.), *Our Voices: Essays in Culture, Ethnicity, and Communication.* Los Angeles, CA: Roxbury Publishing Company. pp. 125–167.

Ye, Xiang (2010) 'Cultural invasion and cultural protection: Should Chinese celebrate Christmas?', *Asian Social Science*, 6(1): 157–160.

Yum, June O. (1988) 'The impact of Confucianism on interpersonal relationships and communication patterns in East Asia', *Communication Monographs*, 55: 374–388.

Zagefka, Hanna and Brown, Rupert (2002) 'The relationship between acculturation strategies, relative fit and intergroup relations: Immigrant–majority relations in Germany', *European Journal of Social Psychology*, 32(2): 171–188.

Zebrowitz, L. A. and Montepare, J. M. (2008) 'Social psychological face perception: Why appearance matters', *Social and Personality Psychology Compass*, 2(3): 1497–1517.

Zhang, Shuangyue and Kline, Susan L. (2009) 'Can I make my own decision? A cross-cultural study of perceived social network influence in mate selection', *Journal of Cross-Cultural Psychology*, 40: 3–23.

Zheng, Lili (2017) 'Does online perceived risk depend on culture? Individualistic versus collectivistic culture', *Journal of Decision Systems*, *26*(3): 256–274.

Zhou, Lianxi and Hui, Michael K. (2003) 'Symbolic value of foreign products in the People's Republic of China', *Journal of International Marketing*, *11*: 36–43.

Zhou, Min (2014) 'Segmented assimilation and socio-economic integration of Chinese immigrant children in the USA', *Ethnic and Racial Studies*, *37*: 1172–1183.

Zubrzycki, Jerzy (1997) 'Australian multiculturalism for a new century: Towards inclusiveness', *Immigration Policies and Australia's Population*. Canberra: Australian Ethnic Affairs Council.

INDEX